P9-EEL-238

WITH THE ARMIES
OF THE TSAR

Florence Farmborough at the Russian Front, 1915

WITH THE ARMIES OF THE TSAR

A Nurse at the Russian Front in War and Revolution, 1914-1918

Florence Farmborough

Cooper Square Press

First Cooper Square Press edition 2000

This Cooper Square Press paperback edition of *With the Armies of the Tsar* is an unabridged republication of the edition first published in Briarcliff Manor, New York in 1974.

Copyright © 1974 by Florence Farmborough

All rights reserved.
No part of this book may be reproduced in any form or by any electronic or mechanical means, including information storage and retrieval systems, without written permission from the publisher, except by a reviewer who may quote passages in a review.

Published by Cooper Square Press
An Imprint of the Rowman & Littlefield Publishing Group
150 Fifth Avenue, Suite 911
New York, New York 10011

Distributed by National Book Network

Library of Congress Cataloging-in-Publication Data

Farmborough, Florence.
    [Nurse at the Russian Front]
    With the armies of the Tsar : a nurse at the Russian Front in war and revolution,
    1914–1918 / Florence Farmborough.
        p. cm.
    Originally published: Nurse at the Russian Front. New York : Stein and Day, 1974.
    Includes bibliographical references and index
    ISBN 0-8154-1090-5 (pbk. : alk. paper)
        1. Farmborough, Florence. 2. World War, 1914–1918— Personal narratives, British. 3.
    Nurses— Great Britain— Biography. 4. World War, 1914–1918— War work— Red Cross. 5.
    World War, 1914–1918— Russia. I. Title.

    D640 .F287 2000
    940.4'7547— dc21
                                                                          00-058998

⊖™ The paper used in this publication meets the minimum requirements of
American National Standard for Information Sciences— Permanence of
Paper for Printed Library Materials, ANSI/NISO Z39.48–1992.
Manufactured in the United States of America.

Dedicated in gratitude
to the memory of my eldest sister, Margaret,
who preserved my diary and photographs
during my many travelling years.

CONTENTS

ILLUSTRATIONS

End of a journey: Vladivostok, 1918

Florence Farmborough taking a photograph

Maps

The maps were devised by Kate Grimond
and drawn by Patrick Leeson

PUBLISHER'S NOTE

Florence Farmborough's diary, which was never intended for publication, ran originally to some 400,000 words, which for obvious, practical reasons has had to be cut down to less than half that length. As a result many interesting sidelights, events and descriptions have had to be sacrificed, as well as many of Miss Farmborough's own comments upon situations as she saw them at that time.

A further difficulty arose in the form in which the diary was written. During the most hectic periods from 1914 to 1918, particularly during the great Russian retreat of 1915 and the tumultuous time of the Russian Revolution, the 'diary' consisted of odd scraps of paper on which were hastily written a few disjointed words – sometimes only one word – from which at a later date Miss Farmborough was able to bring a whole episode vividly to mind and write it down. This explains the occasional abrupt change of tense.

For ease of reading, modern transliterations of Russian spelling have been adopted. Dates throughout are in the Russian style, that is, thirteen days behind those of the western world.

Despite the cuts, what remains is an immediate and exciting eye-witness account of some of the most important events of the twentieth century.

PREFACE

'Strong and content,
I travel the Open Road.'
Walt Whitman

I always knew that I should have to travel. The longing was strong within me from my earliest years. As the fourth of a family of six children, there were few obstacles in my way when, still in my teens, I expressed the wish to go abroad. My feet were restless with the urge to wander and my eyes strained after the veiled ways ahead, eager to behold all that the wide, wonderful world held in store for me. . . . When I am asked: 'Which land did you love most?' unhesitatingly, I answer: 'Russia; because she taught me the meaning of the word "suffering".'

The open road is narrowing now; my feet have grown weary and lost the will to wander. But the wonder of the world remains with me, its beauty undimmed. The last lap of my journey is at hand. My greatest wish is to be able to echo the words of a great Christian whose physical strength was slowly failing: 'My bags are packed. I am ready to go.'

F.F.

January 1974

PART ONE

1914, The Beginnings

I was 21 when I first went to live in Russia in 1908, and after two years in Kiyev moved to Moscow, where I stayed with the family of Doctor Pavel Sergeyevich Usov, a famous heart surgeon, teaching English to his two daughters, Asya, who was 19, and Nadya three years younger. Now, in 1914, after a holiday in England, I was spending a carefree summer with this happy, generous family, who treated me just as one of themselves. We were staying in their dacha *(or country house) not far from Moscow.*

At the beginning of August Germany declared war on Russia. The news that filtered through to our woodland home was vague, and in any case both Germany and war seemed remote. But the next few days brought worse news: Germany and England were on the brink of war. Germany had already declared war on France and Belgium. Our anxiety mounted. Then at last came the news that England, France, Belgium and Russia had met the challenge and were already at war with Germany and Austria.

A few days later we returned to Moscow buoyed up with youthful enthusiasm.

Later that month, Nicholas II, Tsar of all the Russias, for the first time since his coronation, came to visit Moscow.

August, Moscow

The city was astir at an early hour and the streets were packed with excited crowds. The Emperor's reception by the people would be very sincere and warm, for he ranged side by side with God in the affection and estimation of the peasant masses. What *Batyushka* [Little Father] Tsar could not do for them, *Batyushka* God would bring about, and what *Batyushka* God would not do, *Batyushka* Tsar could bring to pass. In almost every peasant home

in the land, an icon or sacred picture hung on the wall, alongside
a print of the beloved Tsar. . . . Small wonder, then, that the
people were eager to express their love and reverence for such an
august figure and to pay homage to the Heaven-chosen representative of their Church and country.

We managed to enter the Kremlin early, through the Spasski
Gate, and to take up our stand at a vantage point from which we
could command a clear view of the raised platform along which
the Imperial family would make their way from the Great Palace
to the Cathedral of the Assumption. There, a solemn Service and
Mass were to be held and there the Tsar Nicholas would humbly
kneel and pray to God that the Imperial Army might issue invincible from a victorious stand against the onslaughts of a ruthless
enemy.

The waiting seemed endless and the atmosphere had become
tense with expectancy when, in the distance, a group appeared.
As they drew nearer, figures and faces became recognisable. The
Tsar and Tsarina walked in front: he, a slim, refined figure in full
uniform with many decorations; she, tall and elegant, moved
slowly in step with him at his side. The four young Grand Duchesses
followed, walking slowly two by two: Olga and Tatiana, Anastasia
with Maria. They were lovely girls and exquisitely dressed in long
frilled frocks and large picture hats. They walked easily, but with
dignity. Another impressive figure was advancing – a tall, massive,
broad-shouldered Cossack, in full Cossack uniform, bearing in his
strong arms the childish figure of the Grand Duke Alexis, only son
and youngest child of the Emperor and heir-apparent by divine
right to the sovereign power of the Great Russian Empire. The
small boy was of delicate frame and sickly constitution; not
allowed to walk far, lest he should overtire himself, his stalwart
Cossack nurse was always in attendance. The Imperial party
bowed and smiled, acknowledging the vociferous acclamations of
the crowds, moving towards the ancient cathedral, where the
highest ecclesiastics were gathered. There, with the Patriarch
at their head, they would be received and welcomed with all the
ceremonial solemnity and glittering splendour of the Orthodox
Church.

With earnest scrutiny, intent on noting every single detail of
that remarkable royal spectacle, our eyes followed those elegant
figures slowly disappearing from view. Between the high platform

and the crowd of spectators, there was a well-defined space of some twelve to fifteen feet. Into that empty space the figure of an old man of the peasant class suddenly stumbled headlong forward. In his hand he held a roll of paper which he stretched towards the Tsar with a beseeching flourish. Then he was on his knees, the paper still held aloft, and then, there were men alongside him, obliterating his crouching figure from view. Then the space was empty again. Not a sound had been heard, no cry, no scuffle, for we were out of earshot, but soon around us an undertone of voices was heard; it rose to a murmur of inaudible words, for each was whispering to each and the keyword of the whispers was 'petition'. The people around us were now speaking clearly though softly. Those who had seen were telling those who had not, and the facts – real or imagined – were being vehemently discussed. Ah! they sighed, the usual thing: an attempt by a peasant to hand the Tsar a petition, but his effort had – again the usual thing – been frustrated. 'Wretched man,' they told each other in hushed voices, 'that means prison for him, perhaps even hard labour, or banishment.' It had happened so quickly, so quietly, the majority of people had not seen, but the Emperor had undoubtedly seen, though he'd made no sign. Calmly, with undeviating step, he had continued on his way.

As soon as war had been declared we all began to consider in what way we could help Russia and had come to the unanimous conclusion that it would be through Red Cross work. A hospital for wounded soldiers was opening in Moscow under the patronage of Princess Golitsin. Pavel Sergeyevich had already been appointed a member of the medical staff, and he managed to persuade the Princess to accept Asya, Nadya and myself as Voluntary Aids at the hospital or lazaret *as it was called.*

We are elated beyond words. We too, in our small way are to help the country's cause. But in my mind another deeper, more lively impulse is stirring: perhaps at the end of my training, I might be found worthy to be accepted as a nurse in a Red Cross Front Line unit! This thought has been in my mind all day. It has become more than a wish, it has grown into a longing which I know has to be gratified. . . .

But when in an unguarded moment I alluded surreptitiously to
that longing, I was surprised to learn that it met with emphatic
disapproval. 'You would not be able to stand it for more than a
month or two.' My protest was drowned by an authoritative voice:
'They never take inexperienced nurses to the Front; there are
already thousands of experienced women waiting to be called up.
Only a *krestovaya sestra* [Red Cross Sister] is allowed to join a
Front Line unit.' 'Then I shall become a Sister of the Red Cross,'
I said defiantly.

*The wounded began to arrive in twos and threes, and Princess
Golitsin's hospital was the first in Moscow to receive them. Our
training started without delay, and we threw ourselves heart and
soul into our work; no task was too menial for us, nor too heavy.
But there were difficulties to overcome.*

We are very raw recruits, and it's not surprising that we sometimes
wince, even shrink into the background, when an unusually ugly
wound is bared for dressing, or when a man's cry of anguish
follows an awkward attempt to alleviate an excruciating pain.
It is, however, astonishing how quickly even a raw recruit can
grow accustomed, though never hardened, to the sight and sound
of constant suffering. It is a special and merciful dispensation of
God that, in time of great stress, both mental and physical, extra
strength is given, with the ability *to do* and *to bear*.

Our days are hectically active, since the number of wounded
grow daily, and there is always work and to spare for willing
hands. The wounded first pass through first aid stations and are
then sent on to us with a brief account of their wounds, together
with name, age, home address, regiment, etc. Walking cases do
their best to be of assistance to both nurse and comrade. There is
always a remarkable camaraderie among them: White Russian
mingles in most friendly fashion with Ukranian; Caucasians with
soldiers from the Urals; Tatars with Cossacks. They are mostly
patient, long-suffering men, grateful for what care and attention
they receive; seldom, if ever, does a grumble pass their lips. Quite
a few are already well on the way to recovery; in due course, they
will be found 'fighting fit' and sent back to their regiment and the
Front Line. There are some men who seem to find the period of
convalescence both trying and boring and voice their longing to

be back in the trenches. These are real heroes and more than once
we have gone out of our way to see that they receive some special
comfort. But there are others, more severely injured, whose
wounds refuse to heal; they worry us, and they worry the doctors
and surgeons. . . .

This morning it was found that a soldier's leg wound had become unusually inflamed and that a strange red rash was spreading
around it. The doctor shook his head and, with a pencil, drew a
blue line just above the border of the rash. When he came again
this afternoon, the rash had spread well beyond the line. He called
other doctors to the patient, and they have diagnosed the rash as
erysipelas, loosing a storm of medical invective over our heads.
Someone has been grossly careless; someone has been shockingly
negligent. Could it have been I? The chastening thought takes
my breath away.

We Farmboroughs are such a robust family at home in England
– born, bred and brought up in such a healthy country district of
Buckinghamshire – that, until I came to Russia, I had never even
seen a sick adult in bed! Now, in this hospital, there are rows and
rows of them, sick with dreadful flesh wounds, with crushed and
broken bones; yet, somehow, we believed that with constant care
they would recover. We all felt that the healing art was practised
at its highest level in our hospital, so that all wounded soldiers
treated within its walls should recover, if not their amputated
limbs, at least a very sound state of health. It was, therefore, a
matter of great concern when it was found that one or two men
were deteriorating rather than progressing; that their bodies had
been so enfeebled by the shock of battle, so impaired by the
physical injury inflicted upon them that, despite constant nursing
and medical attention, they were losing strength and dying. We
took this decline greatly to heart. Surely, with all our experienced
doctors and surgeons, with all the new and wonderful medicines
and drugs, surely some remedy could be found?

I had just reached the hospital for the day's work, when in the
hall, I met one of the night nurses. She looked tired and tense.
'Vasiliy died early this morning,' she said in an undertone as she
passed. 'They have taken him into the mortuary.'

Vasiliy has died – that frail, little fair-haired man, who has not
even been a real fighting soldier, but only a cavalry officer's groom.
And his gaping stomach wound was inflicted, not by the enemy,

but by the iron hoof of a restive, frightened horse. He was operated on, but only to discover an incurable tumour. So Vasiliy is the first to go; his the first death in our hospital. For only three weeks, he lay quietly in his bed, unable to eat, but constantly thirsting for water. And as quietly he has passed away, uttering no lament, and without the comfort of a familiar face, or the touch of an affectionate hand.

I wanted to see him; I wanted to see Death. I opened the door quietly and shut it behind me. This was my first meeting with Death. It was not so frightening as I had thought it would be; only the silence awed me. He was lying wrapped in a sheet on a stretcher, so small and thin and wizened that he looked more like a child than a grown man. His set face was grey-white, never had I seen that strange colour on a face before, and his cheeks had sunken into two hollows. On each closed eyelid was – I looked more closely – yes, a lump of sugar! The stillness in the room, the immobility of the statuelike figure began to disturb me. Death is so terribly still, so silent, so remote. I breathed a short prayer for Vasiliy and went away shaken and troubled. Later I asked about the sugar and was told that it had been placed there to prevent the opening of the eyelids.

The weeks passed quickly. Christmas came and went, but the holiday season brought little respite. The war continued with unabated violence; the news from the Western Front was not good and our Allies seemed to be making little progress. Several of the soldiers had left the hospital, some to return to the Front, others to their villages and families for an extra period of convalescence. We received letters from several of them, expressing gratitude for our comfort and care. I, too, had my share of these thank-you letters, often so ungrammatical, but expressing such simple beauty of mind and thought as to make them very precious.

PART TWO

1915, The Long Road

The Russian Front Lines in
January 1915 and July 1917

——————— January 1915
— — — — July   1917

0   20   100
|————|—|—|—|—|—| miles

BALTIC
SEA

● Riga

EAST
PRUSSIA

Molodechno
● Grodno   Rakov
Skidel   ● Minsk

Neman

● Belostok

Bobrysk●   Bryansk
● Warsaw   ●
P O L A N D   Zhlobin●
● Brest Litovsk   R U S S I A
Bug   Kalinkovichi
Vistula   Vlodava●   Mozyr●   Khutor Mikhaylovsk
● Lyublin   ●
Holm●
                          ● Ovruch
                          ● Koresten   ● Konotop
● Rzheshchuv
● Yaroslav   ● Novograd Volynskiy
E. GALICIA   Lemberg/Lvov ●   Shepetovka●   ● Kiyev
Tarnopol●
Podgaytsy● Skalat● Volochisk● Starokonstantinov●
CARPATHIANS Buchach●   ● Kopchintse Vinnitsa● ● Kazatin
Stanislav/   Chortkov●
Ivano-Frankovsk●   U K R A I N E
                 ● Zhmerinka   Dnepr
AUSTRIA—   ● Chernovits
                 Dnestr
HUNGARY   Seret●
           ● Dorogoy
Suchava● ● Botushany
                 ● Pashchany Prut
                 Yassy● ● Kishinev
                                     Dnepr
                        Odessa●
                                          CRIMEA
R O U M A N I A   B L A C K   ● Simferopol
                          S E A
                               Sevastopol● ● Yalta

By the end of October 1914, the Russians had advanced in Poland, Bukovina, East Prussia and Galicia. Heavy fighting went on throughout November and December, and the Russians were forced to give ground, but by the end of December they had once more driven the Austro-Germans into retreat in Poland and Galicia, and were making raids into Hungary.

New Year came. We finished our six months' training in Princess Golitsin's hospital, and the time arrived when the Voluntary Aid Detachment (VADS) were to be examined for their diploma from the Red Cross Society. Besides the practical experience I had gained in both the medical and surgical sections of the hospital, my knowledge of Russian had rapidly improved at the hospital, since the soldiers enjoyed a chat and we had only to express a wish to hear about their family and home to open a floodgate of eloquence.

They can obviously tell from my accent that I am not quite Russian! 'From which part of Russia do you come, *Sestritsa* [Little Sister]?' someone asks. And another: 'Are you from Siberia, *Sestritsa*?' I explain that I am an English woman from 'Anglia', an ally of their mother-country. Some have heard of England, others have not, but their geographical knowledge, or lack of it, matters little, because they all accept me. I am as truly a *Sestritsa* to them as any of the others.

But the theoretical language was a different matter. All those long unpronounceable words defeated me. In desperation, I learnt whole chapters parrot-fashion, opening my book on anatomy on every tram ride, and attending Red Cross lectures for three hours every evening. However, when the exams came, Asya, Nadya and I all passed. We

were elated. A special church service was held to mark the promotion
from VAD *to qualified Red Cross nurse.*

Before each jewelled icon the *lampada* glowed with a ruby light.
On the altar the high brass candlesticks held steadily-shining
candles; near them stood a silver chalice containing holy water,
with the Book of Books alongside; a silver plate, heaped with red
crosses, had been placed in the centre of the Holy Table. In front
of the congregation, standing side by side, were sixteen young
women, the first draft of nurses from a class of nearly two hundred.
They were wearing the light grey dress, white apron and long white
head-veil of the hospital nurse. A priest, in full canonicals, entered
and slowly made his way towards the altar. Soon his rich, resonant
voice was heard reciting the beautiful Slavonic prayers of the Greek
Orthodox liturgy. Heads were reverently bowed; a murmur of
voices rose and fell. The censer was swung lightly to and fro,
emitting trembling breaths of fine grey, fragrant smoke.

Finally there was silence. The golden-robed priest rose from
his knees and faced the congregation, crucifix in hand. At a sign
from him, the nurses moved slowly, in relays, to kneel at the altar.
The priest then pronounced God's blessing on the red crosses and
on their recipients and, taking the crosses in his hand, moved
towards the kneeling nurses. Bending down, he asked each one her
name; the answers came, softly but distinctly: 'Vera', 'Tatiana',
'Nadezhda'. . . . Over each he intoned a prayer, placed the red
cross on her white apron and held his crucifix to her lips. Asya
was kneeling at my side. 'Your name?' 'Anna,' she replied. He
handed her the red cross and she pressed her lips to the crucifix.

Now he was standing before me. 'Your name?' 'Florence,' I
answered. The priest paused and whispered to his deacon-acolyte.
A book was brought and consulted, then he consulted me: 'Of the
pravoslavny [Orthodox] Church?' 'No,' I whispered, 'of the Church
of England.' Again the whispered consultation, again the book
was referred to. I felt myself growing cold with fear. But he was
back again and resumed the prescribed ritual, his tongue slightly
twisting at the pronunciation of the foreign name: 'To thee,
Floronz, child of God, servant of the Most High, is given this token
of faith, of home, of charity. With faith shalt thou follow Christ
the Master, with hope shalt thou look towards Christ for thy
salvation, with charity shalt thou fulfil thy duties. Thou shalt tend

the sick, the wounded, the needy: with words of comfort shalt thou cheer them.' I held the red cross to my breast and pressed my lips to the crucifix with a heart full of gratitude to God, for He had accepted me.

One by one, we moved back to our appointed places. On our breasts the Red Cross gleamed. I looked at my Russian sisters. We exchanged happy, congratulatory smiles. As for me, I stood there with a great contentment in mind and spirit. A dream had been fulfilled: I was now an official member of the great Sisterhood of the Red Cross. What the future held in store I could not say, but, please God, my work must lie among those of our suffering brothers who most needed medical aid and human sympathy – among those who were dying for their country on the battlefields of war-stricken Russia.

Asya and Nadya continued to work in Princess Golitsin's hospital. Their parents were adamant: Asya was too delicate to risk her health in any hazardous service on the Front; Nadya was too young. Then we heard of a Front Line Surgical Unit about to recruit its personnel in Moscow. Once again, Pavel Sergeyevich came to the rescue. He contacted the Upolnomochenniy [plenipotentiary] of the Unit, Ugrimov, who arranged an interview for me and, shortly afterwards, I received notice of my enrolment as a surgical nurse in the 10th Otryad *of the All-Russian Zemski [Provincial] Soyuz.*

January 30th

Preparations for my departure are well under way. I am breath-lessly impatient to be off, but there is much to be done and the Unit itself is not yet fully organised. My nurse's dresses, aprons and veils have been made already, and I have bought a flannel-lined, black leather jacket. An accessory to this jacket is a thick sheepskin waistcoat, for winter wear, whose Russian name, *dushegreychka*, means 'soul-warmer'. I hear that our Unit will be stationed for a time on the Russo-Austrian Front in the Carpathian Mountains and that we will have to ride horseback, as direct communication can be established there only by riding; so high boots and black leather breeches have been added to my wardrobe.

The Red Cross Unit to which I was assigned was the 10th Field
Surgical Otryad of the Zemstvo of all the Russias. It was divided into
three parts: the 1st Letuchka, (Flying Column) which being mobile,
could be called at any moment to attend any section of the Front re-
quiring first aid workers. It was staffed with four surgical sisters, one
housekeeping sister, two doctors, a feldscher *(hospital assistant),*
four male nurses, about 30 sanitars (ambulance orderlies) and an
officer, with an assistant, in charge of the stores and feeding arrange-
ments. The 2nd Letuchka consisted of the same personnel in number
and rank. To each Letuchka were attached two dozen light, two-
wheeled carts with canvas hoods, on which a large Red Cross was
painted, the same number of horses, their grooms and drivers. Our
transport also included two motor-cars and several large drays (drawn
by two horses), which were stationed at No. 3, the Base, where several
supply officers and their assistants looked after the stores of food and
Red Cross material required by the Letuchkas, and provided head-
quarters for the Unit's Army visitors.

But before I joined my Unit there was one more ceremony in which
I was to take part. . . .

At the moment of my departure, Anna Ivanovna, my Russian
'mother', bade me kneel before her. Taking from her pocket a little
chain, she fastened it round my neck. Then she blessed me,
kissed me three times, 'In the name of the Father, of the Son and
of the Holy Spirit', and wished me 'God speed'. I, too, was a
soldier, going to war, for thus did all Russian mothers to their
soldier sons. The little chain, with a small icon and cross attached
to it, has already been blessed by a priest.

Wednesday, 11th March
At 5 o'clock in the afternoon we, the members of the newly organised
Red Cross Unit, met on the military platform of the Aleksandrovski
Station in Moscow.

Our seats found, our luggage arranged, we walked up and down the
platform for nearly two hours, trying to pass the intervening time
more quickly. At last we steamed off to the Aleksandrovski passenger station. There, all was bustle and excitement; the platforms and waiting-rooms were packed with an eager and animated

crowd. The entraining of a Red Cross Unit, bound for the Front, was not a daily occurrence and Moscow did not believe in doing things by half. One of the waiting-rooms served as a reception room, where our friends and relatives had gathered to wish us farewell. Among them walked our Head in his new military coat with a large fur collar. He gave a cheery word here, a smile there, but, when not engaged in conversation, his face took on a grim, half-sad expression of determination.

On one of the walls of the waiting-room a large icon had been hung; under it, on a slightly raised base, was an Altar – the whole presenting the appearance of a shrine, not an unusual sight in waiting-rooms of Russian stations. Here we met our Chaplain for the first time: a quiet, thin, hairy-faced man. He stood on the Altar steps, admonishing us solemnly to fulfil all our duties manfully, no matter what the cost. The benediction followed and we filed past the Altar one by one and kissed the crucifix held out to us.

When we went out on to the platform the noise had increased a hundred-fold; everyone was trying to speak. I stood with a group of my friends near my carriage, for the long train, composed of heated passenger-carriages, vans and trucks, was already waiting. My Russian mother and sisters and several friends, came to see me off. They loaded me with boxes of sweets and flowers, such beautiful flowers: tulips, carnations, even roses. It was difficult to safeguard them from pressure, so many people were thronging around me with their good wishes. Outwardly, I was calm and self-possessed; inwardly, a wild exhilaration swept like fire through my veins; we were off, off to the Front! My very gladness left me speechless. 'You are tired already,' a friend said pityingly. I protested – never had I been less tired! '*Posmotrite! posmotrite! Vot anglichanka!* [Look! look! There is the English woman!] I turned at the words and saw a group of onlookers. 'Yes,' I nodded, with a smile, 'I am the English woman!' Immediately, a shower of smiles and 'good luck' wafted across to me. How kind everybody was and how supremely happy I was!

Somewhere a clock struck nine. A voice from the far side of the station began to sing the Russian National Anthem; from the vans – the quarters of the Red Cross orderlies – came echoing voices – then the sound of cheers. A close embrace, a firm pressure of the hand, a chorus of good wishes and, with my arms full of flowers, I stumbled into the carriage. The train gave a convulsive

jerk forward and slowly we glided out of the station. The cheers
grew fainter. The engine puffed and snorted, gathering speed with
every inch of ground it covered. Soon Moscow city and its outskirts
were left behind and we were off, skimming over the land in the
darkness, bound for a mysterious, unknown destination.

South-West Front, East Galicia
Saturday, 11th April, Gorlitse
We travelled a long way since we left our train and reached
Grodzisko on 16th March. Our itinerary has taken us through
Przhevorsk, Lantsut, Rzheshchuv, Shchani, Ropchytse, Dembitsa,
Yaslo, Krosno to Gorlitse, where we arrived today, exactly a
month after leaving Moscow. Gorlitse is a poor, tormented town,
under constant fire from the Austrian guns. For over five months,
its inhabitants have been obliged to lead the existence of night
birds. Their days are spent in the cellars, for the slightest movement in the streets could bring a shower of bullets. After dusk,
they come creeping out, begging sympathy and food from each
other and from the soldiers – the Russian soldiers; for Gorlitse
and all of the above-mentioned towns were captured from
the Austrians during the early months of warfare in the autumn
of 1914. The people are half-starving and that is what takes up
most of our time. Every evening, the mobile kitchens of the Red
Cross Unit are sent into the town and daily provide no fewer than
300 portions of food. We are hoping, in due course, to send 500
portions, for the misery among these unfortunate Austrian subjects
is quite appalling.

Sunday, 12th April
The Sisters and personnel of our *Otryad*'s 2nd Flying Detachment
have left us today to drive to the place destined for their future
work. We have already chosen our hospital; it is a well built
house, with several nice, airy rooms. Everything is being scrubbed,
painted and white-washed; the operating-room will be a splendid
sight when finished; our *apteka* [pharmacy] is already full of
medicinal and surgical material and there are rows of labelled
bottles on the shelves. We have no idea how long we shall be here;
it might be six months – or six hours! The site is very beautiful for
we are practically surrounded by the lovely, undulating ranges of

the Carpathians. I love watching them at night, when the mountains lie mysteriously quiet and passive, outlined clearly against the night sky and overswept by the moon's luminous radiance.

Wednesday, 15th April

We have had a busy day; some 50 wounded men have been sent to us. We dressed their wounds and sent them on to Yaslo, where they will be sorted out and despatched to various parts of Russia. The booming of cannon is often heard, but spasmodically, and sometimes at long intervals. The soldiers tell us that they are well looked after and well fed in the trenches, but they all voice their dismay that German troops and heavy guns have been sent to this section of the Front. 'We are not afraid of the Austrians,' they explain, 'but the German soldiers are quite different.' We had heard that the Germans had transferred both man-power and guns to the Austrian Front; a sure sign that they consider the fortifications of their Allies to be inadequate. A sure sign, too, that an enemy offensive is imminent. We can do nothing but wait and watch.

Friday, 17th April

There is definitely something stirring on the Front. It was about 6 o'clock last night when the guns first began to roar and they roared all night long until this afternoon when, just after 4 p.m., they suddenly ceased, as though their giant strength were exhausted and they were seeking rest. Our transport vans picked up as many wounded as they could find, for under that hail of shells some of the injured men preferred to remain in the trenches, rather than venture out into an open, unprotected place. We are shocked to find so many seriously wounded, but our doctors insist on sending them to Yaslo with the least possible delay. After midnight, we Sisters went to our room, but did not undress, for we expected to be called at any minute.

Wednesday, 22nd April, Frishtak

So much has happened. I am dreadfully tired. We are *retreating!* In that one word lies all the agony of the last few days. We were called from our beds before dawn on Saturday 18th. The Germans had launched their offensive! Explosion after explosion rent the air; shells and shrapnel fell in and around Gorlitse. The roar of

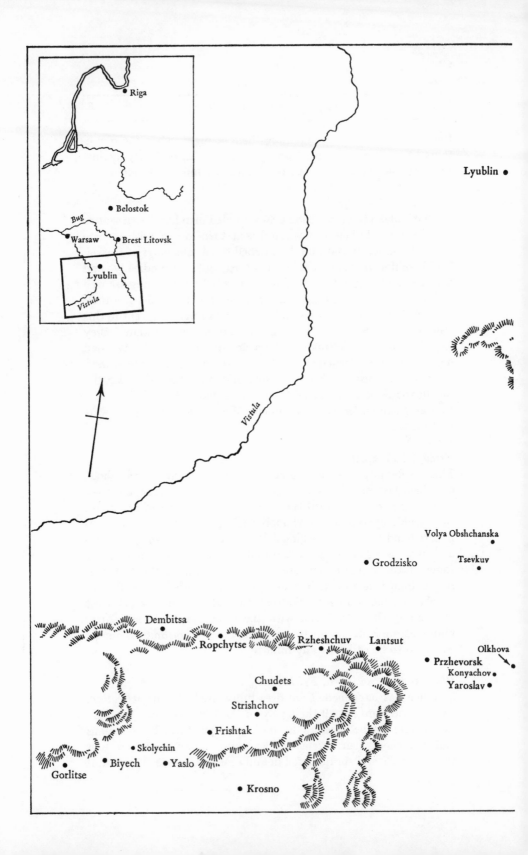

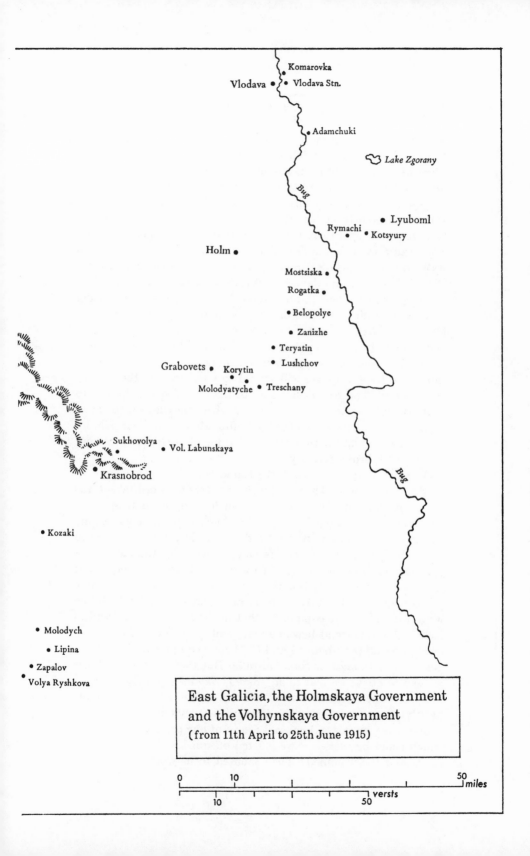

Komarovka
Vlodava • • Vlodava Stn.

Adamchuki

꙳ Lake Zgorany

Вид

Lyuboml •
Rymachi • • Kotsyury

Holm •

Mostsiska •
Rogatka •
• Belopolye
• Zanizhe
• Teryatin
Grabovets • • Korytin • Lushchov
Molodyatyche • • Treschany

Sukhovolya
• • Vol. Labunskaya
Krasnobrod •

• Kozaki

Bug

• Molodych
• Lipina
• Zapalov
Volya Ryshkova

East Galicia, the Holmskaya Government
and the Volhynskaya Government
(from 11th April to 25th June 1915)

0   10   50 ⌐ miles
                                        ⌐
         10   50
                              versts

the rival cannons grew increasingly intense. Rockets and pro-
jectors were at work. Patches of lurid, red light glowed here and
there where fires had been kindled by shells. Our house shook to
its very foundations, its windows rattling and quivering in their
hinges. Death was very busy, his hands full of victims. Then the
wounded began to arrive. We started work in acute earnest. At
first we could cope; then, we were overwhelmed by their numbers.
They came in their hundreds, from all directions; some able to
walk, others crawling, dragging themselves along the ground.
We worked night and day. And still they came! And the thunder
of the guns never ceased. Soon their deadly shells were exploding
around our Unit; for hours on end, the horror and confusion continued. We had no rest and were worn out with the intensity
and immensity of the work. The stream of wounded was endless.
Those who could walk were sent on immediately without attention. 'The Base hospitals will attend to you,' we told them; 'Go!
go! quickly!' The groans and cries of the wounded were pitiful to
hear. We dressed their severe wounds where they lay on the open
ground; one by one we tended them, first alleviating their pain by
injections. And all the time the bombardment of Gorlitse was continuing with brutal ferocity.

On Sunday, the violence of the thunderous detonations grew in
length and strength. Then, suddenly, the terrible word *retreat* was
heard. At first in a whisper; then, in loud, forceful tone: 'The
Russians are retreating!' And the first-line troops came into sight:
a long procession of dirt-bespattered, weary, desperate men – in full
retreat! We had received no marching-orders. The thunder of the
guns came nearer and nearer. We were frightened and perplexed;
they had forgotten us! But they came at last – urgent, decisive
orders: we were to start without delay, leaving behind all the
wounded and all the equipment that might hinder us. A dreadful
feeling of dismay and bewilderment took possession of us; to go
away, leaving the wounded and the Unit's equipment! It was impossible; there *must* be some mistake! But there was no mistake,
we had to obey; we had to go. '*Skoro! Skoro!*' [Quickly] shouted
familiar voices. '*Skoro! Skoro!*' echoed unfamiliar ones from the
hastily passing infantry. 'The Germans are outside the town!'

Snatching up coats, knapsacks, any of our personal belongings
which could be carried – we started off quickly down the rough
road. And the wounded? They shouted to us when they saw us

leaving; called out to us in piteous language to stop – to take them with us; not to forsake them, for the love of God; not to leave them – our brothers – to the enemy. Those who could walk, got up and followed us; running, hopping, limping, by our sides. The badly crippled crawled after us; all begging, beseeching us not to abandon them in their need. And, on the road, there were others, many others; some of them lying down in the dust, exhausted. They, too, called after us. They held on to us; praying us to stop with them. We had to wrench our skirts from their clinging hands. Then their prayers were intermingled with curses; and, far behind them, we could hear the curses repeated by those of our brothers whom we had left to their fate. The gathering darkness accentuated the panic and misery. To the accompaniment of the thunder of exploding shells, and of the curses and prayers of the wounded men around and behind us, we hurried on into the night.

We had hoped to stop in Biyech, if only for an hour or two, but it was quite impossible. Infantry, cavalry, artillery were pressing forward. This was no place, or time, to think of rest or food. The enemy was close behind; his shells were falling ever nearer and nearer, claiming many victims. We reached Yaslo on Monday morning, but there, too, were confusion and chaos; and with that huge wave of retreating men and vehicles we were swept forwards, ever eastwards. There was no alternative . . . *Retreat* had us in its grip.

We came to a place called Skolychin and, miraculously, an empty house was found to be available. We were ordered to halt and open a dressing-station immediately. I don't know where the food came from, but even while we were unpacking some of the bales which contained first aid equipment, a cup of hot tea and a slice of black bread and cheese were put in our hands. Mechanically, we ate and drank; then, refreshed, we prepared to receive our wounded. They were already at our door, clamouring for help and food. Many there were who could no longer walk, and could scarcely speak, their bodies sorely wounded and their minds numbed by the severity of those wounds, yet their strength of will had been such as had enabled them to traverse many painful versts* in those first tragic hours of retreat. It is only today that we have heard that the bombardment of Gorlitse was quite unequalled as yet in the present War's history. But our men have suffered enormous

*One verst = 3,500 feet, that is, slightly more than one kilometre.

casualties; it is said that our 3rd Army has been cruelly decimated and that the 61st Division, to which we are attached, has lost many thousands of its men.

Monday, 20th April, Skolychin
Weary and dustladen we looked at each other, conscious of the calamity at our Front. There was no time for questions, or for explanations; the sullen and continuous tramping of retreating feet on the roads told its own tale. What is happening there? What will soon happen here? The stricken faces and frightened eyes of the wounded told us. They were exhausted beyond words, too exhausted to groan as their wounds were dressed. Gun-carriages, batteries, motor-lorries lumbered in and out of the streams of marching soldiers. Dust hung about the road in a thick grey mist; the sun beat down mercilessly. Now and then ambulance vans would pull up in front of our house and the orderlies would hastily drag the occupants out and deposit them on the ground near the entrance. Cries and groans accompanied this performance, but we were too busy to leave our posts and, beyond a much-needed admonition to the orderlies to use their hands more gently, the newcomers and their sufferings had, for the time-being, to be ignored. The wounds were dreadful: bodies and limbs were torn and lacerated beyond repair. Those in a hopeless condition were set apart and not sent on with the more promising cases to the Base. All those who could still walk, unless obviously in need of treatment, were dismissed at once without examination. But there were few of these, for the 'walkers' preferred to walk on. Not even a mug of tea could tempt some of them to turn off from the road for a few minutes' rest. This was no time for resting, with the enemy at one's heels.

Into our 'dressing-room' hurried the tall figure of Alexander Mikhaylovich one of the Divisional surgeons. A few whispered words and he was gone. Alexander Mikhaylovich's usually care-worn face had taken on a more serious expression, but he was silent and we went on working. After a few minutes, he looked up and said: 'In half an hour's time, I want two sisters to be ready to return to Biyech. There are many wounded there and we must open a dressing-station at once.' Then came eager voices: 'May I go?' 'May I go?' We were all so anxious to be the chosen ones. My anxiety to be one of the two was so intense that I was speechless and could do nothing but clasp and unclasp my hands. 'Vera Vasiliyevna is on duty and must, therefore, remain here; Olga Ivanovna, as dispenser, will take my place here in my absence. Sister Florence and Sister Anna will be ready to leave at 6.30 p.m., that is in half an hour.' I could scarcely refrain from crying aloud my thanks to him. Anna seized me and together we rushed off to the wagon on which our stores of material for dressings were packed. Hastily collecting several large drum-shaped, air-tight boxes, which held our sterilised dressings, we placed them, with bundles of wadding, bandages and the like, on two large sheets and tied them all together. We packed, too, the most necessary liquids, instruments, candles, gloves, splints. Our equipment complete, we donned our leather coats and clambered into a huge, dirty-looking lorry which was waiting for us. It was a divisional vehicle and the chauffeur, a stranger, offered no information.

Anna and I were both feeling the same excitement at unknown dangers. She was squatting down in her corner, with hands tightly folded on her lap and eyes bright with excitement, staring across the open country. Alexander Mikhaylovich came out of the house. His first glance told him that we and our equipment were ready; he nodded approval and carefully, but with some difficulty, because of his stoutness, climbed up and took his seat. The divisional officer suddenly appeared and jumped in, followed by two orderlies. During the journey there was no conversation, only a few instructions given by the divisional surgeon to the chauffeur in an undertone. We were far from comfortable; the straw upon which we were sitting was coarse and scanty. Alexander Mikhaylovich, too, was not happy; every time the car bumped and jolted, which was often, he was tossed up and down like a rubber ball. The evening was growing cool and a keen east wind was rising. We saw innumerable soldiers; their faces all turned in one direction and wearing grim, dogged expressions. Some were hurrying, others stumbling. Many of them looked at us in amazement, wondering what was impelling us to return to the scene of disaster. Small bands of wounded, with blood-stained bandages round head or arm, met us. There were those, too, who were limping painfully, who, noticing the *kosinka* [head-veil] of a Sister, would stop, and with inarticulate sounds point beseechingly to their wounded limbs. But we could not stop and explanations in that continuous din were of no avail; we could but point towards

the road we had traversed, trying to make it clear to them that
help was at hand if they would only continue their journey.
Saddest of all sights was to see wounded men exhausted, lying by
the side of the road – unable to drag themselves any further. We
saw, too, how more than one soldier would stop to speak, to try
to assist them to rise; then, finding that it was useless, would look
awhile, sorrowing, and pass on.

Nearing Biyech, we met a hooded van containing wounded
and our car drew up for a moment while the divisional doctor
interrogated the driver. It seemed that all was quiet in the town
save for an occasional shell from the enemy; the inhabitants were
sheltering in their cellars, but many badly wounded men were
there, unable to leave owing to lack of Red Cross assistance and
transport.

At last we pulled up at the gate of a large white monastery.
Alexander Mikhaylovich, considerably shaken after his rough ride,
hastily got down from the lorry and, passing down the small front
garden, disappeared through the white doorway. After a few
minutes he beckoned us to follow him. In the doorway stood a
black-robed priest; his face was stern and very pale, but so calm
and passive was his manner, it was evident that this was not the
first time that he had encountered a uniformed contingent. We
followed him from room to room as he explained, in broken
Russian, that we were at liberty to make what use we pleased of
the monastery with its scanty supply of furniture. We told him
that only water and basins were necessary and he at once brought
in a bucket of water and three small tin pans. The large room,
chosen for the dressing-room, was devoid of furniture, but some
benches dragged in from an adjoining one were easily transformed
into a table, on which we arranged our equipment. All this was
done in feverish haste, Alexander Mikhaylovich having impressed
upon us the fact that we might have to leave at any minute, and
therefore, could not afford to waste a single moment.

Before we had had time to put on our white *khalati* [overalls],
the wounded were in the room – all stretcher cases, all in a terrible
state of suffering and exhaustion. To enquire as to when and how
the wounds had been inflicted was impossible; in the midst of that
great wave of suffering, the acuteness of which was plainly visible
and audible, we could but set our teeth and work . . . and work.
The orderlies would carry them in on improvised stretchers, would

lift them on to the floor and would return for others. Where they found them, God only knows – but there was no dearth of them – and they carried them in, one after another until our room and the adjoining ones were full of them; and the stench of the wounds and the unsanitary conditions of many of the sufferers filled the place with a heavy, oppressive atmosphere. By this time, several ambulance vans of our Transport, together with some half-dozen from the divisional vehicle-column, had arrived and, with the help of a few divisional orderlies, we packed many of the wounded into them and sent them off to the Base. Now and then there was a shrapnel scare, but it caused little or no confusion. As the day drew on, however, the bombardment became more severe and, after 9 in the evening, heavy shells began to fall.

In the next two hours we worked blindly and feverishly, knowing that many lives depended on the swiftness and accuracy of our handiwork. 'Water,' gasped parched lips, but we dared not break away until the bandaging of the wound was complete. Hearing, yet as with deafness, we listened to the entreaties of those agonised souls. 'Give me something to ease my pain; for the love of God, give me something, *Sestritsa*.' With cheering words we strove to comfort them, but pain is a hard master; and the wounds were such as to set one's heart beating with wonder that a man could be so mutilated in body and yet live, speak and understand.

The priest gave us what little help he could: supplying us with fresh water, carrying off receptacles of blood-stained clothes and bandages. In and out among the wounded he walked; placing more straw under one man's head, raising a leg into a more comfortable position, holding, now and then, a cup of water to thirsty lips. His lips were compressed, his face drawn, but only once did I notice that he was affected by the sights around him. A soldier was lying in a corner, breathing heavily, but otherwise quiet. It was his turn now; I went and knelt down on the straw at his side. His left leg and side were saturated with blood. I began to rip up the trouser-leg, clotted blood and filth flowing over my gloved hands. He turned dull, uncomprehending eyes towards me and I went on ripping the cloth up to the waist. I pushed the clothes back and saw a pulp, a mere mass of smashed body from the ribs downwards; the stomach and abdomen were completely crushed and his left leg was hanging to the pulped body by only a few shreds of flesh. I heard a stifled groan at my side and, glancing round, I saw

the priest with his hand across his eyes turn and walk heavily
across the room towards the door. The soldier's dull eyes were still
looking at me and his lips moved, but no words came. What it
cost me to turn away without aiding him, I cannot describe, but
we could not waste time and material on hopeless cases, and there
were so many others . . . waiting . . . waiting. . . .

From one room to the other we went always bandaging and,
when darkness fell, bandaging by the flickering light of candles.
Those whose wounds were dressed were carried off immediately
to the Transport vans or cars awaiting them, and orders were
given to the drivers to make their way as quickly as possible to the
Divisional Base *lazarets*, and to send back any other vans or cars
available without delay. Shrapnel was falling thickly now, but the
monastery did not alarm us overmuch. If only the wounded could
be sent away to a place of safety in time, that was the problem
which worried us.

I think that, by now, some curious change had come over both
Anna and me. Anna's face was stony, quite expressionless, and
while she worked, the same words came from her lips every few
moments. '*Nichevo! nichevo! golubchik. Skoro, skoro!*' [It's nothing!
It's nothing! my dear. Quickly, quickly!] Suddenly, with a shock
I realise that I, too, have been repeating similar words, repeating
them at intervals when the groans and cries of my patient have
been too heart-rending. I caught a glimpse of my white overall,
covered with blood-stains and dirt, but this was no place to
probe my feelings, or to ask myself what were my impressions,
my sympathies. It was as though I had become blunt to the fact
that this was *war*, that these were *wounded*. Mechanically my
fingers worked: ripping, cleaning, dressing, binding. Now this one
was finished, another one begun; my heart seemed empty of
emotion, my mind dull, and all the time my lips comforted:
'*Skoro, golubchik, skoro!*'

I was bandaging a young soldier, shot through the lung, when
the first heavy shell fell. He was sitting up sideways against the
wall, a wound the size of a small coin on his right breast and a
wound big enough to put my hand into in his back. His right
lung had been cruelly rent and his breath was coming out of the
large back-wound in gurgling, bubbling sobs. The wounds had
been quickly cleaned; the larger one filled with long swabs, a pad
tightly bound over it, when an angry hiss was heard, grew louder

and louder and then the explosion! The roar was deafening, the room shook and there were frightening noises of splintering, slicing masonry and of glass breaking and falling. A great silence followed, but the room continued to shake and tremble; or was it, perhaps, our own limbs? The soldier in front of me was shaking as with ague. '*Chemodan!* [heavy shell]' he whispered hoarsely. I turned towards the table for a new roll of bandage. When I returned my patient had disappeared. In his half-bandaged condition he had run off, not caring for aught else and possessed with the one wild desire to escape to a safer place. Strangely enough, the rooms had emptied themselves of several of their wounded occupants; many of those whom we had thought too weak to move had, under this violent shock, been imbued with supernatural strength, as it were, had arisen and crawled away out into the night.

After this, the work seemed to slacken. The remaining wounded were in a terrible, nervous state; the new ones brought in begged only to be sent on: no need for bandaging now, they urged. Almost every five minutes the explosion would be repeated, sometimes more distant, sometimes very near, so near as to seem on our very roof-top.

The divisional surgeon had taken his leave and had retired with his men. Alexander Mikhaylovich told us to prepare to leave in about a quarter of an hour; one of our light cars had been detained for us. The last vans had left; all the wounded had been safely despatched, with the exception of those who were nearing death's door. Our stained overalls off and folded up, we stood by the door, waiting for orders. Outside the night was dark.

The priest came round the corner of the house. 'There are three craters in the back garden,' he said in a muffled voice, 'and the outhouses have been destroyed.' 'Shall you stay here?' I enquired. 'Mademoiselle,' he answered slowly, 'I am in charge of the monastery. I cannot leave my post. And why should I leave when my flock remains?' 'Are there many people here?' 'There are many,' he replied, 'old men and many women and children.' He was silent and, in the half light, I saw that his eyes wandered towards the monastery windows, as if hoping to see some signs of life. I realised then that the house was a refuge for numberless poor people sheltering from the violent storms outside; and there might have been others in those 'outhouses' so lately destroyed.

'Pardon me,' the priest was saying, 'but Mademoiselle is not
Russian?' 'No,' I answered, 'I am English.' 'Ah! English!' his
voice took on a more animated tone. 'I knew that Mademoiselle
was not Russian, for you have the look of the Western world.
I, too, have been in France.' He broke off suddenly, the familiar
hiss was in our ears and, once again, earth and air seemed convulsed with hideous noise in a world which swayed and rocked.

There were faint cries from within the monastery. I turned from
the doorway and stepped inside over the littered floor and paused
by that row of silent figures stretched out on their straw beds.
Two were already dead, one with eyes wide open as though looking
attentively at something – or someone; I closed them and laid
his hands on his breast. To his left a man was lying; great convulsions ran every now and then down his long frame and a queer
gurgling noise was audible in his throat; Death had taken his hand,
too. And he – in the corner – was lying as before, with strangely
contracted limb and eyes still dull and glazed, but his lips had
ceased to move.

There were unaccountable noises outside – a sudden rush of
sound, the buzz of many voices hushed and subdued, the tramp
of many hurrying feet, and then Alexander Mikhaylovich's voice
– loudly, peremptorily. I turned to go, but, before I went, I
moved towards the corner and laid my hand on the clammy
forehead and seemed to hear once again his inarticulate entreaty.
'*Skoro, golubchik, skoro,*' I whispered.

'Florence! Florence!' Anna called. I stumbled down the steps
into the garden and followed her hurrying figure. There was
tumult in the air and tumult in my heart. 'I will do what I can for
them,' I heard the priest's voice say and then, to me: 'Adieu!
Mademoiselle.' Shrapnel was crackling in the air every now and
again with a fierce, metallic menace. We huddled together, Anna
and I, in the car.

Outside the gate, we found our own car and two large Red Cross
lorries. The lorries were packed with wounded. The drivers and
Alexander Mikhaylovich were doing their best to send off those
soldiers who, at the last moment, sought to climb on to them:
'*Nelzya! Nelzya!*' [Keep off!] The men, desperate to get away,
began tugging at the lorries, shouting and climbing over each
other to obtain a firmer grip. Then another shell boomed out its
savage warning from behind the monastery. It helped us in that

critical moment more than anything else could have done. In the hush that followed the explosion, one heard only the clatter of feet hurrying and stumbling away; running figures were faintly seen in the distance. '*Sestritsa!*' the wounded called to us again, '*Sestritsa!* Take us with you; we can't walk.' But the authoritative voice of Alexander Mikhaylovich came to our ears: 'To your car at once!'

The driver was in a dreadful state of excitement; but he drove well, though at a higher speed than usual. We huddled close to each other in the car and Anna whispered in my ear: 'They say that the Germans are entering Biyech at the other end.' The roadsides were strewn with wounded and exhausted men; they called to us as we rocked past, but we could not heed them. We could not have saved them *all*; there was other important work waiting for us to do. We drove on, but my heart seemed turned to stone and the weight of it was almost unbearable. Alexander Mikhaylovich had pulled his military cap far down over his eyes; Anna's face was hidden by her veil; and still we drove on. For all of us the evening's work had ended with nightmare-like horror. The remembrance of those dreadful curses thrown at us by desperate, pain-racked men could never be obliterated or forgotten.

Long after midnight Anna and I arrived back at our headquarters at Skolychin, too tired to eat or speak. At 8 a.m. we were back on duty attending to newly arrived wounded.

Biyech was now in German hands. Our Letuchka *had lost contact with the General Staff of our Division and were at a loss to know what to do. News came that the Germans were still advancing rapidly, and we were told to move on within the next two hours. After a hasty meal and packing the wounded into the last few vans, we moved to Przhiseki where we halted and set up a dressing-station.*

Tuesday, 21st April, Przhiseki

It was pitiful to see so many youngsters among the wounded; some looking scarcely a day older than fourteen although they must have been at least nineteen to be drafted. For the most part, these *novobrantsy* [recruits] were a sorry lot; sullen and cowed they sat there, holding out their dirty limbs for cleansing and bandaging. We had a number of wounded hands and fingers during

the morning; the number had surprised even me. So sullen were
some of these young lads that they refused to answer when a
question was put to them. At first, I ascribed this to weariness or
pain and told them compassionately that they should have food
and rest before they need attempt to take to the road again.
One boyish hand had a fearful wound on the back of it; jagged
and notched was the flesh and the knuckles were splintered and
rent. On the palm the wound was but a small hole, but, around
it, the skin was covered with a thick coating of blackened flesh,
resembling a heavy contusion. To my surprise, this black coating
came partially away when washing it with *perekis* [peroxide].
I called to one of the divisional doctors to ask his advice. He
looked at the hand and then suddenly turned on the soldier.
'Coward!' he cried. 'Coward and fool!' The young soldier hid his
face with his other arm and began to sob. I was aghast! What
had I done? The doctor seeing my miserable face, reassured me:
'It's nothing, *Sestritsa*; just another example of our gallant
samostreltsy [men with self-inflicted wounds], but he has done
his job a little too well, for the hand is finished.'

Before 8.30 p.m. we had left for Yaslo. It was high time, for
shrapnel had fallen and scattered around the edge of the garden.
Before leaving an orderly counted the number of wounded who
had passed through our hands during the four hours spent in
Przhiseki; there were just over 350. The vans being full, we, the
four Sisters and Mamasha, were packed into a car belonging to
the divisional doctors. It was with difficulty that we could make
even slight progress in the heavy traffic and several times we only
just escaped collision. Munition carriages of the artillery swept
along, taking up nearly all the road-space; and from in front and
behind, from either side came the shouts and oaths of exasperated
men, the unceasing tramp . . . tramp of feet, the hoarse interchange of question and answer; men's figures hastening, shoving,
pushing. . . . Confusion and commotion were everywhere, but
lights were out of the question, lest the enemy detect our escape-
route.

Far off, to the left and to the right, a tangle of disorderly voices,
a rumble of disorganised vehicles, told us that the wide fields too,
had their masses of human fleeing traffic. The night air teemed with
discordant clang and clatter; a crash here, as a gun-carriage fell
into a ditch or hole, followed by angry cries of men brought

unwillingly to a standstill; fierce retorts through clenched teeth and the sudden hush of fear.

Tuesday–Wednesday, 21st–22nd April. Yaslo

We reached Yaslo at midnight and occupied the first empty building which we could find. A horsehair sofa and a couple of chairs made a good makeshift bed; Anna and I lay down, wearied to an unutterable degree, and slept. . . . But our rest was short. At 3 a.m. a vigorous shaking woke us, a brother nurse told us that we must leave immediately, for the Germans were already very close to Yaslo. For some minutes I sat on our rough bed feeling, seeing nothing. A great distress enveloped me, and the violence of my longing to sleep left me giddy and sick. Annushka slid on to the floor and swayed as she walked across the room. Then Mamasha's voice was heard, coming ever nearer; she entered the room. '*Chto eto takoy?*' 'What is this? Aren't you ready yet? Is it possible that you don't understand that we have to leave Yaslo immediately? Hurry up at once! At once, I tell you!' To my muddled brain, as she stood there in the dim candlelight, she was the very embodiment of fury. We tied black veils over our white ones and followed her out into the street.

The retreat was, beyond all doubt, exceedingly serious. Before I was able to understand what was happening, three of us Sisters were pushed on to a wagon and found ourselves seated among oil-cans and pneumatic tyres. It was cold and windy, but the keen air helped to revive us as we moved slowly down the crowded streets; and not the air only, for the continual shaking and jolting were such as to guarantee a swift return to normal alertness.

Not a sound of a gun was heard; not once did the light of a rocket or exploding shell pierce the darkness. It was uncanny – this wild, frantic flight from an unseen enemy; an enemy so quiet he might almost be sleeping, while we, sorely pressed and desperately weary, rushed headlong through the black night. Dawn had come and in its pale half-light we pulled up in the village of Frishtak. We stumbled up to a hut and, peering through the windows, saw that the rooms were empty. But our knocking received no answer; only when a voice was raised threateningly, did the owner appear. She was a middle-aged woman of untidy appearance. Standing at a window, she refused to let us enter her home, until Alexander Mikhaylovich changed his tactics and

warned her that unless the door were opened it would be smashed
in. Thinking to frighten us, she said that the hut had been used
as a domicile for smallpox patients. Alexander Mikhaylovich
persisted, until finally, as a last poor subterfuge, she declared that
the door-key had been lost. At this an orderly was called to
break open the door. Upon his arrival, the woman instantly
produced the key – hidden in the bodice of her dress – and the
door was flung open. On the long flat table, on the whitewashed
stove surface, on the narrow wooden bench running the round of
the small room, we lay down . . . and slept . . . and slept.

Next morning, we learnt that great numbers of wounded men
were gathered round the railway station, hoping for a possible
means of escaping to a safer region. There was no one in attendance,
despite the fact that many of the men were suffering from severe
wounds. Hastily collecting the necessary material from our
wagon, we followed our guide to the station. The rough, wooden
structures which served as platforms were literally covered with
wounded soldiers, some sitting in groups, others lying prone on
the wooden planks. But there *was* someone in attendance! At a
corner of the main platform, two soldiers, wearing the badge of
the Red Cross on their sleeves, had opened a small dressing-station.
Around them they had gathered the most severely wounded and,
with iodine and *individualni* first-aid packets, were busily dressing
man after man. Who were they? From where had they come?
We had no time to ask. They were glad to receive us and their
eyes brightened when they saw the cases of dressing material
which we had brought with us. Every now and then a long line
of *dvukolki* [two-wheeled hospital vans] would be seen descending
the hill; they drove straight towards the station and deposited
their occupants outside the partially destroyed buildings; then
turned about and made their way up the hill again, westwards,
towards the defence positions.

Amid the dirt and grime, we worked feverishly. An hour went
by, two hours passed, and still no sign of a train. In and out among
the men we walked, examining the wounds, dressing the most
severe and administering injections to those whose injuries we
were powerless to soothe. Mamasha was flying about, flurried
and over-heated, with buckets of tea which she had prepared.
Mugs were handed round; it looked a muddy, weak sort of liquid
and railway smuts and dust were floating thickly on it, but never

was tea more appreciated. The bread, too, was carefully apportioned and soon demolished. But many there were in that large
host who could neither eat nor drink, and these lay motionless
with eyes filled with the agony of pain. In a small waiting-room
we placed the dead, lining them up one by one against the wall;
when there was no space left we took over an adjoining room.

Just before noon, six hours after the last one had left, the train
came in. We were overjoyed to hear the approaching rumble – the
wounded even more so. Before the carriages had ranged up
alongside the platform, waves of soldiers rushed to meet them,
straining every muscle to gain entrance. The confusion which
followed was indescribable. Our doctors and brothers threw
themselves into the fray. They succeeded in taking over about
half-a-dozen carriages and stoutly rebuffed every attempt to
enter. In authoritative voice, they shouted that there were
comrades who were unable to walk – that they must be carried into
the train, that places must be left for them.

When at last the train steamed out of the station, our hearts
grew somewhat lighter, but still the wounded came. They came in
groups, singly, on stretchers, in vans, battered and mutilated. We
cared for them as best we could; God knows that our hearts were
in our work, for we felt their agony, endured their despair and
shared their misery.

A second train drew in empty and steamed out filled to capacity
with hundreds of brown-clad figures, most of them pain-racked
and exhausted. Then we waited for the last train. God grant that
room might be found for all! But, down the hillside, we saw the
wounded coming, still coming.

The last train, the third, had come and gone. All the heavily
wounded had been evacuated; the few remaining soldiers were
able to continue the journey on foot. On leaving the station we
were surprised to find our car awaiting us; Alexander Mikhaylovich quietly told us that there was no time to return to the hut,
that it was essential to leave without delay. The two Red Cross
orderlies were offered seats in another car, but they quietly refused,
saying that they would walk without difficulty. We did not enquire
which was their route, we knew that there was only one, and we
left the two trudging along the dusty road in the heat of the
afternoon, their knapsacks strapped on their backs.

For a long time I could not, dared not, turn my head and look

behind, for I knew that the hill was still visible and I was afraid
to see small helpless figures dragging themselves over its summit.
We were soon entangled in a disorderly medley of horsemen,
wheels and legs and it was long before we could extricate ourselves. At last, we turned off the highway and sped down a quiet
road, coming, at length, to the little town of Strishchov. The dust
was thick on our faces and garments; we were dead tired and
ravenously hungry and, on entering the small apartment found
for us, our first desire was to eat, our second to sleep and then,
perhaps to wash! However, water making its appearance first,
in a couple of pails with accompanying basins, our wishes were
fulfilled in a more civilised manner. First we had a good wash,
then Mamasha opened her basket of provisions, which proved
to consist of black bread and hard-boiled eggs. A fire was lit in the
grate and we soon had tea brewing. There was no furniture in
the room, but a square of oil-cloth on the floor made an excellent
table. We ate, drank and were as merry as possible in the trying
circumstances, and then all of us, about ten or twelve persons,
laid ourselves down, just as we were, on the wooden floor, and slept
the sleep of the weary. All night we slept, not once were we disturbed, and in the morning we rose greatly refreshed in body and
soul.

Thursday, 23rd April, Strishchov
During breakfast, welcome news was brought to us by our 'rough-
rider' orderly, that the whereabouts of our Divisional Staff had
been ascertained and that the steady advance of the enemy had
been checked near Yaslo. It was then decided that we should
return to Frishtak, and without more delay we started off. The
morning air was fresh and pleasant, and the mere fact that we
were now returning towards the Front gave us renewed confidence.
From several people the news had come that, although the
Germans would be allowed to enter Yaslo, outside the town they
would meet with strong resistance, for our reinforcements were
increasing hourly. The advance will be definitely checked outside
Yaslo, we were told.

An isolated, four-roomed house, situated on a small branch road,
about three minutes' walk from the highway, was chosen as a
dressing-station. We had been bandaging peacefully for about
an hour; a dozen *dvukolki* were lined up in the open field near the

house; our three motors were ranged near them, the drivers resting on the grass, while groups of wounded men lay along the sides of the branch road, when the first bomb fell. The sudden explosion brought us out into the open air; for a few moments we were under the impression that a *chemodan* from the enemy had paid us a surprise visit; then a second bomb exploded and a faint whirr of engines was heard above us. Two small, white aeroplanes flew in circles around our little house, evidently taking in every detail possible. Then a third, fourth, fifth, sixth, seventh and eighth bomb fell, the last three simultaneously. The soldiers and wounded men panicked. Many of them rushed into the house for shelter and, feeling no certain safety under a roof, rushed out again to throw themselves flat on to the ground to escape any splinters which might be flying around. One of the chauffeurs, a boy of nineteen, seemed to lose his head for a time and ran round and round in wide circles, until he almost ran with open arms into a bomb, which gave him such an unpleasant surprise that, turning swiftly, he dropped into a trench by the roadside – from which he emerged in about half-an-hour's time looking very crestfallen and dejected. Not all were so lucky: two poor fellows who, five minutes previously, had been sitting quietly chatting, awaiting their turn to be called to the dressing-room, were brought in with fresh ugly wounds gaping in their bodies and succumbed in a very short time.

That afternoon all was quiet. News reached us that the 2nd Letuchka *had left Yaslo only a few minutes before us and with the medical staff of our Division were now stationed some 20 versts (about 13 miles) south of Frishtak.*

Late in that bitterly cold night, we retired to bed, using the roof straw from a broken-down shed as our bedding. Next morning the Germans dropped a further eight bombs around the house. There were no victims, but a sinister atmosphere remained. As it was obvious that our site was badly chosen, we were told to move on to Chudets, a small town about 10 versts south of Strishchov.

Saturday, 25th April. To Chudets

We had been so sure that all was going well on the Front, and then these sudden orders to leave at once for a destination many miles distant, in an easterly direction, caused us all great disquietude.

Two of the chauffeurs were helping a hospital orderly to dig a
grave for a young soldier who had died an hour or so earlier.
They dug a hole, none too deep for time was precious, and laid
him in it, just as he was – in his high boots covered with mud,
and covered him with his long military coat. No service was held,
for *Batyushka* [as the Chaplain was called] had been absent from
our *Letuchka* since the retreat from Yaslo, but one of the chauffeurs
dropped to his knees and sang the beautiful old Russian funeral
chant *Vechnaya Pamyat* (Eternal Memory). Two pieces of wood,
roughly nailed together in the shape of a cross, were stuck into
the ground at his head. Anna placed some twigs of fir upon the
freshly-turned sod, and on the open plain we left him, the simple
cross marking his resting-place. There were so many of these
lonely graves. We passed through Strishchov in haste. In Chudets
we found accommodation in a large, handsome house standing in
its own grounds, the property, we were told, of a wealthy Pole
who it was rumoured was fighting with the Austrian Army.

The weather had changed; dull, lowering clouds were creeping
up from the west and darkened the whole sky. Rain fell in miserable,
tireless rhythm, but we remembered the unwholesome dust of the
highroad and never a grumble was uttered. In the afternoon
we were sent to the assistance of a small Red Cross Unit which
was working on the railway station.

It was almost dark when we left it, and a fine rain was still
coming down.

Sunday, 26th April
It is now only a week since our departure from Gorlitse, but it
seems an age. The retreat is still at its height and who can say
when and where it might be arrested? The rumour that Yaslo
is to be the last town to be given up to the enemy has proved
false. This morning we were told that we might be ordered to leave
at any moment. Chudets already shows those familiar signs of
excitement which always mark a new stage in the retreat. On the
station, our friends too are working in a state of suppressed expectancy, they have heard bad news, but, impatient as we are to
know the worst, we can waste no time in questioning them.

*We received our orders the following evening. Throughout the day
we had seen the long, rolling clouds of dust along the road, heard the*

rumour of distant voices and countless wheels. Shrapnel was crackling once again and the ominous boom of large guns grew nearer and nearer. Jolting once more along the road, we heard a sudden tremendous explosion and saw a gigantic cloud of smoke rise – another bridge had been blown up by the Russians. We slept that night in the carts.

Once I remember waking abruptly because my head came violently into contact with something hard and sharp; an unusually acute jerk had flung me on to the bar at the van-edge. A second time a loud shout brought me swiftly to my senses and Machmet, our driver, nearly toppled backwards on top of us, as his horse was thrown on its haunches. In the confusion which followed, we were able to gather that a horse had fallen and, in falling, had blocked the road and two of the three streams of traffic which occupied it. When we were at last able to resume our journey, Machmet informed us that the poor animal – wounded, sick or merely exhausted – had had its traces cut, been dragged to the roadside and thrown into the ditch to die.

At dawn we reached the outskirts of Lantsut and halted for a few hours near the estate of Graf Pototski; we were too weary to look about us or attempt to recognise the countryside over which we had travelled only five weeks before and, having eaten a plate of cold, black kasha and a slice of bread, we lay back on the straw and went to sleep.

Feeling too sick and tired that evening to eat any dinner, I made some excuse and, finding a quiet shady corner near our baggage van, rolled myself up in some tenting material and fell fast asleep. Anna awoke me, calling me to supper. The sun was beginning to sink and I was amazed to find that I had slept for so many hours. The sleep had done little to improve my headache and the thought of more jolting and jarring during the long night hours helped to spoil both temper and appetite.

27th April

Yaroslav is well behind us and much of the horror which has beset us seems to have died away, leaving an unexpected composure in its place. . . .

Anna and Ekaterina were sleeping. The roads were smoother; the retreating soldiers less numerous; we were jogging along easily, collectedly. A wheel must have caught in a neighbouring wheel, for our van slid suddenly round to the side and remained locked, bringing all the vans in the rear to a standstill. The driver of the neighbouring cart shouted, trying to back his horse; our driver – a young man of twenty and almost stone deaf – made no movement. 'Rupertsov', I called. 'Turn the horse round.' He gave no answer, so I knelt up on the straw and nudged him; then I saw that he had been sleeping. I felt sorry for the boy, he was thoroughly tired, probably had had no sleep for two or three days, so I climbed up on to the front plank, and took the reins into my own hands. Rupertsov understood my motive, for he pulled his cap down over his eyes, crossed his arms, heaved a deep sigh of content and fell asleep. When was it that we last experienced a whole night's rest? It grew very chilly and the air smelt of damp marsh-land.

30th April. Olkhova

Near the small village of Olkhova we turned aside into a pine forest. With what joy we tumbled our aching bodies from our vans on to the green mossy ground! Camp-fires were alight in a very few minutes – and never had tea such a delicious flavour. The men were ravenous and the bread supply soon ran out, but we knew that before long our baggage train would reappear with fresh provisions. We were by no means the only occupants of the forest; through the trees we could see gleams of numerous camp-fires and now and again a buzz of conversation was borne across to us on the breeze. The world had suddenly become very tranquil, motionless and blissful.

Dawn came, the sun was rising high in the heavens – and still we slept on. An aeroplane did its best to disturb our peace, but to little avail. It was our own soldiers who finally drove all thoughts of further sleep out of our minds, for a company had descended upon the forest and encamped just in front of us, their vociferous chatter incessant and disturbing. The baggage train made its welcome appearance and ranged up alongside the ambulance vans. Many of the men were engaged in repairing the vehicles entrusted to their care; the horses were lying about on the ground, utterly exhausted. Much needed rest had come, at long last, to us all.

A group of orderlies was lolling in the shade; to the accompaniment of an accordion, they lazily sang verse after verse of the old folk-songs. On the chaussée, an artillery-train was rumbling by towards the assault position, with the guns still in their *chekhol* [dust-covers]; hearing the singing, the gunners took up the refrain and the pleasing melody of *Stenka Razin* swept through the pine trees and far down the dust-clouded highway. No marching orders were received that evening, so a tent was set up and, for the first time since we had abandoned Krosno, camp-beds were taken from the baggage-wagon and lined up in rows. The following day brought no fresh news, and we sat and rested, rejoicing in our surroundings and thankful for the unexpected respite. The bombardment sounded nearer and more frequent, but in our forest we were in another world; as we rambled here and there among its soft greenery, delighting in the play of the sun's rays in and out of the trees, we almost forgot that a fierce war was being waged outside our woodland bivouac. From the foliage above our heads came the twittering of birds, the soft cooing of wood-pigeons and, at intervals, the full-throated call of the cuckoo. Our hands were soon filled with spring's first floral offerings and, when we returned to our tent, we were as happy and gay as children and the terrors of the past days had faded from our memory.

The news that Red Cross Sisters were in the neighbourhood must have spread to the village, for on our return we found a peasant-woman standing by our tent with a boy of some ten years. She came towards us, seized Ekaterina's hand, kissed it and in tearful voice besought her to find some medicine for her son. From all appearances the child was consumptive, undersized and of a sickly sallowness; he had no appetite, she complained, and his life seemed to be daily ebbing from him. Ekaterina at once turned to ask advice from Alexander Mikhaylovich, but before she had had time to return with him, three other Ruthenian women had joined us, also asking for medicine. There and then, Alexander Mikhaylovich decided to open a small medical station and it was astonishing the number of peasant-patients who visited our improvised consulting-room that afternoon.

At 6 o'clock the following evening a despatch-rider appeared from Alexander Mikhaylovich who had gone ahead, asking us to set off immediately with a fresh supply of dressing material and provisions for Konyachov. At Konyachov, a nondescript hamlet, the majority

of the wounded had been bandaged and fed by midnight, but just as
we were beginning to relax new orders arrived: we were to leave
without delay. Two neighbouring huts were still filled with wounded,
our ambulance-vans had not yet returned for them. But our medical
chief was firm in his decision. Ten minutes later we had joined the
retreating soldiers on the highroad.

Along the Yaroslav horizon, fires were burning at many points and
the blazing town which we had noticed on the previous evening was
still shedding a red light on the sky around. 'Over there,' said
the soldier on my left, pointing towards Yaroslav, 'over there is
hell. For three days we held our ground against him without
shells or cartridges, then we could hold him back no longer. Ours
have fought like devils, with clubs and rifle butts – even with
fists when all else failed and we came face to face.' 'But now,'
groaned the soldier on my right, 'now, we cannot stop him.'
Some of the misery which was afflicting the old soldier must have
crept into my heart, for I, too, felt the utter hopelessness of defeat.

Then I lifted my head and looked around. What an extraordinary
world I was in! What a distorted side of life was teeming about me!
What a monstrous scene enveloped me! Could it be I who, barely
a year ago, was loitering along the tranquil, leafy lanes of the
English countryside? But here, indeed, I was; walking in the
darkness, at dead of night, down an unending, dusty road, trying
to keep pace with the muffled tread of innumerable exhausted
and footsore men, while behind us the cannon boomed and
shrapnel crackled and exploded in the keen night air. From the
great stretches of plain on either hand came the hoarse cry of
some night-bird. The inflamed heavens told their pitiful story.
One could sense the complete desolation of those burning towns
and villages. I saw them all and felt their weight.

On and on we walked through the chilly hours of early morning,
my feet stepping out proudly in the military rhythm of the marching men. Once a shrapnel, borne on whistling wings, exploded
almost over our heads; involuntarily, I started and shrank up
against my neighbour. '*Vy yeshchyo ne privykli, Sestritsa?* [You
have not yet grown accustomed, little Sister?]' he asked feelingly.

It was nearly 6 o'clock when we spied our encampment outside
Olkhova. A heavy dew lay on the grass; figures were lying huddled
up against each other beneath and beside the baggage-wagons;

one or two men with buckets were to be seen moving about among the horses. In the tent all were sleeping quietly; we flung ourselves down on to our camp-beds and shut our eyes. '*Bozhe moy!* [My God!]' cried somebody, 'there it is again.' Outside the tent, the place was in an uproar: loud shouting and the stamp of running feet. Inside, we stared at each other in consternation; several beds were emptied of their occupants before we had had time to ask questions or to comment on the sudden commotion. I was still half-asleep and sitting up in bed, but a very loud explosion startled me and brought me to my feet. About one hundred yards away, above the ragged outline of the forest a small cloud of darkish-coloured smoke was slowly expanding and melting into the blue background of the sky. Boom! a second appeared, almost in the same place. Shrapnel, voice of the enemy! 'He is here! Close at hand!' came the cry. '*Proryv! Proryv!* [A break-through!]' Frightened out of their wits and expecting an ambuscade to appear from the wood at any moment, the men rushed to their horses and, without waiting for orders, began harnessing them with all speed. General panic would certainly have ensued had not our Transport Chief kept his head and started calling the men everything but endearing names. 'Harness the horses and await orders,' he commanded and 'Every man to his place.' Meanwhile, the orderlies were taking down the tent; in their excitement and haste, they went to work with such a will that some of us had not yet succeeded in fixing our camp-beds before the heavy mackintosh cloth-sides fell in upon us. It was a rather ludicrous and un-dignified picture to see the submerged members crawling out on all fours from the tent débris, and a vehement rating was the outcome, dispelled only by the sight of a mounted Cossack in our midst. We knew what his presence implied. Alexander Mik-haylovich read the paper in silence. 'We start in ten minutes,' he said briefly.

Enemy aeroplanes hovered over us repeatedly during the day and the journey was terribly rough and sorely trying for limbs and nerves. That night, sleep came to few of us. The open field chosen for our bivouac was swept by cold night winds and our discomfort was intense. However, Zapalov, as this halting-place was known, proved to be more amenable in the daylight and an early visit to the small number of huts which composed the village was crowned with success. Not only did we find the peasant women

ready to sell eggs and poultry, but they willingly enough agreed
to wash our laundry. The real necessity of this latter can be well
understood, for since leaving Gorlitse (some two weeks ago)
our limited supply of garments had been continuously on the move
and the dirt accumulated from dusty roads and grimy quarters
was unspeakable, not to mention that other ever-present, never-
failing soldiers' friend: the louse, which, although small enough
in all good faith, was, perhaps, for us, the greatest source of worry
and annoyance during all our experiences at the Front. As the
luck of war had it, our garments had to be fetched before half
of them were dry, but they had been washed and we were grateful
for that main mercy.

4th May
*We left Zapalov in the afternoon for Volya Ryshkova, a village
ten versts away, where we were to await further orders from the
Headquarters of the 62nd Division to which we had just been transferred, the 61st Division having been ordered farther south.*

From Volya Ryshkova Olga and I were chosen to drive to the
field dressing-station of our new division, with Dr Markovich.
We found the doctors drinking tea in a pleasant, shady little
garden. When we told them that we had come to help them in
their work, they laughed heartily and said that they had been
sitting, twiddling their thumbs for three days and that the only
work in which we could assist was that of tea-drinking. The
frivolous manner in which they spoke of their work surprised
and shocked us, but, being so obviously of the 'new broom' species,
we imagined this jocular mood had been partly assumed for our
benefit; we were afterwards to learn by painful experience that
these were valiant men, with compassionate hearts, who could
always smile in the face of misfortune. And so we met for the
first time these members of the 62nd Division. Here, too, we
met Vaska, the division's mascot – a shaggy goat, famed for his
unique precocity and thieving ability.

    How little had we imagined the evening could have ended so
disastrously! A hurried conversation went on for a minute or two
between our Doctor and a tall, bearded newcomer: the official
message was read aloud: 'Instant retreat!' We could scarcely
believe our ears; it was but a few hours before that we had been

seated in a sunny garden, drinking tea and caressing a tiny brown rabbit! Swiftly we helped to place the wounded into the vans; many of those whose condition demanded a seat were denied one – if they could walk, walk they must, for the sake of their legless brothers. The light *furgon* [cart], in which we had driven from Volya Ryshkova, was filled with poor bruised bodies, and once again we set out in the darkness on foot along the highroad.

Is there anything so hopeless, so dreadful, as a retreat at night? The earth lies cold and forgotten, multitudinous human beings struggle onwards towards an unknown destination. How and when will it all end? All this I felt and more when I could think and analyse my feelings, but ever and again that strange, unaccountable wave of exultation would sweep over me. It was difficult to define, yet I knew well that, had I been offered an alternative I would have cried without a moment's hesitation: 'Hardships, a legion of them, and all else besides, but only to remain on active service.' I knew too, that once I had crossed the frontier and regained the land of ease and safety, it would be easy to lose touch with the intensity of life, to cease to feel the urge to grapple with destiny, or to pit one's strength against a thousand ills.

At Volya Ryshkova our Unit was up and doing. They had heard the news and were prepared for the worst. A score or so of ambulance-vans were drawn up outside our camp, their silhouettes clearly outlined against the grey dawn-sky; they had brought us over eighty heavily wounded men – some of them who were too weak to be moved we bandaged as they lay in the vans, the orderlies lighting the scene for us with candles.

My back was aching madly, I could scarcely drag my legs from the ground. My inanely stupid face must have expressed my feelings, for Alexander Mikhaylovich ordered me to go and lie down in our tent. I told him that I could not go, because I was *dezhurnaya* [on duty]; he looked at his watch and made no answer. At 9 o'clock I was relieved by the day-sister; I went to our tent and sleep came to my rescue. At noon I was roused, dinner was ready and we were to leave in an hour's time. Still half asleep, I ate and drank, listening in silence to the buzz of conversation going on around me; my head felt heavy and unnatural, my feet seemed to walk on air. 'Pull yourself together,' I told myself sharply. 'Remember where you are and what is expected of you.'

We took our places in the small cart and van allotted to us and started off along a branch road for the village of Lipina. Once a *sotnya* [hundred] of Cossacks met us, riding towards the *pozitsiya*; they came at a quick trot, enshrouded in dust, lances fixed and figures straight and singing a song, gay and free, of their combative race. A strong baritone sang each verse; the refrain came as a burst of triumph from all throats and, at the end of each chorus, a boyish voice, high and piercing, pealed out a light stanza in wild fantastic notes.

9th May
Two uneventful days were spent at Lipina, and then we were again on the road.

Although we commenced the journey driving in a van or small wagon, we had scarcely covered a half-mile before we were obliged to descend and continue the trek on foot – for the sake of the horses. The road was thick with sand, a most peculiar and unexpected hindrance, but we were soon to ascertain that the roads throughout the entire district were in a similar condition, for our 'rough-riders', sent out to spy the land, all returned with the same tale. We pedestrians were only slightly troubled by the difficulties of the route, but the horses suffered exceedingly. In some parts where the road widened, the track became invisible and the horses found themselves floundering about in sand above their knees. The lighter vehicles pulled through with comparative ease, but the baggage-wagons stuck repeatedly and it was a pitiful sight to see the poor animals straining their muscles to the utmost of their strength and struggling to obtain a firm footing in that sea of shifting sand, the while their drivers were loudly shouting encouragement and lashing their knouts threateningly. The fifteen odd versts which we traversed that day occupied no fewer than seven hours.

9th–30th May. Molodych
The village of Molodych was selected by the Medical Staff of our new Division as a temporary halt for our Red Cross Unit because of its closeness to the main body of the division stationed up the Line. Three

whole weeks were spent there. The wounded arrived sporadically with time for us to rest between. Several times news came that the Russians were sweeping the enemy back at different points along the Front Line and, once, in the late evening, hearing an unusual commotion outside on the road, we saw, in the light of the full moon, innumerable grey-clad figures with the tell-tale 'pickelhaube' on their heads, marching along between their Cossack escorts. Some six hundred Austrian and German prisoners passed.

All the next night the firing continued. Early morning came and it had not ceased. Before the morning had fully lightened, the wounded arrived. An endless stream of them flowed in until well after midday. We heard the latest news: with incredible stubbornness the enemy had made attack after attack, only to be beaten back and to suffer appalling losses. Our men had fought like demons and it was said that at one point a complete division of Germans had been surrounded and forced to surrender. But victory is bought at a price and we had but to look around at those mutilated, pain-racked men to realise how dearly they had paid. Many of them were laid to rest before the sun had set; wrapped in sheets, they were lowered one by one into a common grave and a wooden cross was raised at their feet, bearing an inscription that all may read the names of those heroes who fell that memorable night of May outside the village of Molodych.

A day or two later the head surgeon of our Army Corps paid us an official visit and thanked the members of our Unit for the valuable assistance which they had administered during the last critical weeks. There was a special word of praise for the hospital orderlies and transport drivers, who, in the face of countless dangers, had worked steadily and silently, seldom if ever receiving recognition of their services. *'Spasibo, brattsy!* [Thank you, brothers]' he called out once more when leaving them. *'Rad staratsya, Vashe Prevoskhoditelstvo!* [Glad to be of service, Your Excellency]' came the ready reply.

Day after day we watched over the wounded men in our tents; this is a new kind of service, not the hideous, spasmodic rush and bustle of recent weeks. Here we can note progress: which wounds respond to treatment, which men are now strong enough to be transferred to the Base. But there is one tent which cannot readily

be cleared; in it lie those who are the weakest, the mortally
wounded, those who are not far from death. Some of them rebel:
'Why am I not sent away?' 'If I must die, I want to die in Russia.'
And another, in agony cries: 'God! is it possible that they have left
me behind to die?' Day after day we watch, too, those other men,
the healthy ones, swinging along in the dust of the highroad.
Regiment after regiment tramp by, for reinforcements are plentiful: infantry, cavalry, artillery, with one objective only – to stem
the flood of the enemy advance.

The Grand Duke Nikolay Nikolayevich was now known to be on
our South Western Front and it was reported that he had ordered
our men 'not to move a step' from the River San. Night after night
the ceaseless cannonade was heard and daily the news was brought
of the magnificent stand of our men. A squadron of them, we were
told, swam across the San one night and the Germans, terrified at
finding the Russians in their midst so unexpectedly, broke away
and fled in all directions, and our dare-devils – a mere handful of
them – chased the enemy to right and left, as boys would scatter
a flock of sheep, until, weary of the game, they turned and plunged
once more into the river, followed by a rain of bullets.

Several of our divisions suffered severe losses about this time.
The 48th Division, which had sustained heavy casualties in the
defence of Gorlitse was by now almost a complete wreck, and for
a time was obliged to retire into the background in order to undergo reconstruction.

When off duty, we live the simple life of gypsies – strolling
through the woods, washing our linen on the river's bank, bargaining for eggs and milk with the peasant-women in the village.
Our Second *Letuchka* has recently encamped at a short distance
from Molodych, and often we meet, walk the woods together and
gather armfuls of the beautiful wild flowers which abound. The
yellow broom is in full flower and golden banks of it are massed
here and there among the tree-trunks; lilies-of-the-valley are there
in abundance and their sweet perfume brings nostalgic memories
of my home-garden in far-off Buckinghamshire.

Sometimes during the moonlit evenings we stroll towards the
woods to search for that most exquisite of perfumed night-flowers –
the wild *fialka*. I knew and loved this small flower when, in those
happy days before the war, I roamed, in the company of my

'Russian sisters', the woodlands of pine and silver birch which surrounded their *dacha*. There, it was called *Nochnaya krasavitsa* [Beauty of the night]; nor is it difficult to find, for the air around it is diffused with its sweet fragrance.

I remember well our first visit to a *nablyudatelny punkt* [observation point]. After riding for some time through thick, rough woods, we came to crossroads where two of the roads branched off from the wood into the open plain. Here we dismounted and left our horses with the orderlies. Half a dozen steps brought us out into the open, and, at a word from our guide, we all fell flat on to the ground, for in broad daylight no man might walk that road without inviting considerable risk to his personal safety. A broad stretch of undulating plain lay in front of us; dark furrows were traced in crooked confusion across its surface and, in the heart of this no man's land, lay a shining line of silver – the River San. Not a sign of life was seen, yet one knew that, at a given time, at a whispered word the men, hidden away so adroitly in burrow and hole, would spring into sight and action.

We turned sharply away from the Front Line and followed a trench which led up on to a slight incline. Another wall barred our way. At first, we were all rather disappointed to find that this empty trench, with a small *blindage* [armoured sheeting] at its extremity, comprised the observation post. We had expected something quite unique.

The officer on duty was busily scanning the landscape through a periscope and a couple of soldiers, sitting under cover near the blindage, were in charge of the telephone. We took turns at the periscope and were amazed to see the landscape spread out before us with such clarity. Now and again, shrapnel from the enemy came whistling over our heads and burst far back in the rear; we retorted immediately with a similar gift. Once only did we see a sign of life in the enemy camp and that only with the aid of the periscope or field-binoculars. A group of tiny figures had appeared and, by the movement of their arms, were engaged in some defensive work. 'That we won't allow in broad daylight,' said the officer, and gave instructions to the telephonists, who, in their turn, passed them on to the battery. We waited breathlessly. *'Gotovo! Ogon!* [Ready! Fire!]' An instant of time only and over our heads sped the shell and, in the vicinity of the workers, a sudden cloud

of thick smoke rose from the ground, followed by the dull boom of
the explosion. The range had been determined with astonishing
accuracy. The binoculars showed us that the group had dispersed,
but how great was our surprise when, after a lapse of some ten
minutes, other figures appeared. We could not make up our minds
whether 'impudent' or 'plucky' would be the more fitting epithet
to apply to those stubborn workers; but the officer in charge
applied the former without hesitation and a second *bomba* went
speeding in their direction.

That decided them; they worked no more that afternoon. I
wasted at least half-a-dozen plates trying to photograph the post
and the landscape in front of it, but with little success, and the
one or two negatives which were good enough to permit printing
were placed, while still wet, with a few others, against our tent-
wall to dry overnight. An unkindly fate intervened in the shape of
a rollicking early-morning wind which dislodged them from their
perch and threw them face-downwards on to the sandy ground.

One day our *Letuchka* met in full force to pay honour to the member who was celebrating his Name Day. Flowers, chocolates and
other goodies were plentiful, and I had been deploring to myself the
fact that such festive occasions were not recognised at home in
England. One of my Russian sisters and I had once searched the
long list of Russian women-saints to see if we could find the name
'Florence', but without success. Suddenly, one of our guests turned
to me: 'When is your Name Day, Sister Florence?' What spirit of
mischief propelled me, I'll never know, but in a flash I had given a
date, and a not far-distant one! The incident passed without
further comment and in a few minutes I'd forgotten it entirely.

About ten days later, I opened my eyes early one morning to see
our orderly standing by my bedside, a large bunch of lilac in his
hands; he placed it on the ground and left the tent. Who could have
sent me flowers? And why at this unearthly hour? I looked around;
the Sisters were sleeping. I stretched out my hand and drew the
flowers toward me. Among the purple blossom I spied a card: 'To
Sister Florence, with hearty congratulations on her Name Day,
from the Transport fellow-workers.' Goodness gracious! My Name
Day! Yes, this was the date which I had given in haphazard
fashion. I remembered it well – the 24th May – for it was my
Mother's birthday, also that of one of the greatest sovereigns –

Queen Victoria – and, of course, Empire Day! And so they had not forgotten! I laid back on my pillow and thought it over. It was too late to disclose the fact that it had all been a joke, for the flowers and greetings were at my side; so come what may, I must see the game through and, for one day at least, I should have a patron-saint all to myself!

Mamasha was the first to awake and must have caught sight of the flowers, for, from between my closed eyelids, I saw her stoop and take a small parcel from out of her *portpled* [hold-all]. My eyes shut tightly. She came towards me and I felt her place something against my pillow. My cheeks grew hot. What a hypocrite I was! Would it be possible to disclose the false role even at this eleventh hour? But it was already too late, for Annushka came rushing across to me with outstretched arms. Then came Vera Vasilyevna, Mariya Ivanovna and Ekaterina; they kissed me, congratulated me and wished me a long life. Flowers, chocolates, cakes, I had a store of them all before we sat down to breakfast, and there were two cards and a letter lying on my plate. It was really exciting, ten times better than a birthday! I began to hold up my hypo-critical head and, indeed, felt something akin to heroism when our head, Alexander Ivanovich, appeared on the scene and clasped my hand and wished me 'Good luck!'

But the crowning triumph was still to come. It came, wildly rebellious, carried tightly in the arms of a stalwart staff *pomosh-chnik* [assistant]. It was of a delicate whiteness, with tiny bunches of light purple lilac over each ear to harmonise with the pale pink eyes; round the fat little body, white satin ribbon was wound and tied in an elegant bow on the back; an inscription in gold letters was fastened to the bow. I could scarcely believe my eyes, for it was – a piglet! A real, little, live, lucky piglet! He squealed out his congratulations in a most ungallant manner and then upset by the strange noises around him, made a dash for safety. He was soon captured and a long cord, attached to a pole in our tent, was tied round one of his little hind legs; all day long he lay, blissfully content, in a cosy burrow which he had routed out for himself in the soft earth.

Dinner-time came and with it several enticing 'extras', not least of them being preserved peaches, served in a soup-tureen. The Doctors of the Divisional First Aid Unit joined us for tea and, once again, a congratulatory ceremony was enacted with all the well-established formality. By that time, it was not so difficult to play the role required of me; in fact, I had become fully persuaded that it was my Name Day.

In the early afternoon, after listening to the stirring music of a military band, several members of our 2nd *Letuchka* arrived, in reply to an official invitation. We had listened to the band with great satisfaction, for it was for the first time that the Italian National Anthem had been played and it did not surprise us to note that the drums got an extra tough beating and the cornets an extra vigorous blowing. It had been heartening to hear that Italy had entered into alliance with the Triple Entente. So we had a new Ally and the success of our military operations seemed even more assured.

Our friends of the 2nd *Letuchka* surprised us by calling an 'assembly' of our available personnel. We duly presented ourselves and they, with many a theatrical gesture, arranged us in a circle around a central figure who held a document in his hand. When all voices had been hushed, the portly doctor chosen to read the document, began: 'To Sister Florence, on the occasion of her Name Day!' I gasped and for a moment felt that I could not go on with the deception; if I could only confess now! The stentorian voice continued, but – I could not understand a word! The address was couched in the old Slavonic language! This address, which is beautifully printed and illuminated, by hand, in the decorative style of Old Russia, and signed by each member of the 2nd *Letuchka,* was presented to me.

Later in the evening, we made up a party and rode to the camp of the 2nd *Letuchka,* where we found a most cordial welcome awaiting us, and the moon was high in the sky when we finally reined in our horses in front of our own encampment. I had been wondering whether it would be wiser to acknowledge my duplicity to the Sisters before retiring to rest, but, I reflected, that would spoil the day for everybody concerned; the morrow would almost certainly present a favourable opportunity. But long before the morrow, good cause was given us to regret at least one dénouement resulting from my mock Name Day. The 'goodluck' piglet roused himself from slumber at the crack of dawn and, overcome by cold or loneliness, sent forth the most heart-rending, terrified squeals which, in the night air, must have been heard by everybody within the camp. I stared into the darkness and listened in dismay, hearing how the Sisters one by one, turned about restlessly, giving vent to their indignation in uncomplimentary language and wearied, disapproving sighs. The curious sounds emanating from that small animal were in no way proportional with its size and seemed to increase in volume as time went on; the strain on the pole, too, was intense, as the spasmodic, violent flapping of the tent-walls bore witness. A tirade of abuse came suddenly from the far corner of the tent where some of our hospital male staff were sleeping – had he had any option in the matter that damned pig would have been hung, drawn and quartered long before nightfall and not permitted to disturb the much-needed rest of the over-tired workers. I stopped my ears with my finger-tips and tried to sleep. Muffled squeaks were audible for some time; a series of distant grunting followed and then . . . all was quiet. In the morning I looked round the tent, the piglet had disappeared; the rope had been severed.

I suspected foul play, but my enquiries resulted in nothing definite, and investigations in the village proved fruitless. The lost animal was finally discovered in a neighbouring wood, scuttling serenely among the undergrowth. A length of cord was still attached to a hind leg and it had the sorry, bedraggled air of an abandoned creature, with all its festive finery tattered and besmirched. That night it was given shelter in the yard of a friendly peasant. I was rather perturbed to learn that Artimosov, our cook, had been billeted in the peasant's hut, but he assured me that he had great knowledge of such animals and promised to keep an eye on it.

Three or four days passed and then, one day, when we sat down for our midday meal we found a small roast pig, with brown rye kasha on the dining-table. 'How delicious!' someone cried. 'A porkling!' Mamasha, I noticed, had a very red face; she seemed flurried and avoided meeting my eyes. Cold meat was on the table too; I chose some; how could I eat my lucky piglet? After dinner, I determined to make an inspection. Walking through the yard, I saw Artimosov sitting in the hut. I knocked and, after a minute or so, the peasant opened the door. I went in; only the old man and his wife were there. Artimosov had disappeared – through the window! I made some excuse to the peasant and went away. I had found out all that I wished to know.

I took the whole matter very quietly. Too many protestations

on my part might have been unwise for the confession was still to
be made. It was made after a prolonged and satisfying dinner,
even the choice of time was an act of diplomacy. Contrary to my
expectations, it was received in a most congenial and friendly
spirit; surprise was certainly expressed, but one and all laughed
heartily, some even applauding the fraud and congratulating me
that I carried it through so successfully. It was unanimously
agreed that, while living in Russia, it was my bounden duty to
follow Russian customs, and they reminded me of their old proverb:
'*S volkami zhit, po volchi vuyt!* [If you live with wolves, you
must howl as a wolf.]' Mamasha added the final words which drew
down the curtain on my celebrations: 'I always knew,' she declared,
'that the lucky pig would be a white elephant!'

As the days wore on, discontent made itself felt in our Unit. The
severe strain of the past month was beginning to tell on us, and
times without number heated discussions gave way to open quarrels
and the general mood of the company was not of the gayest. There
was little work to speak of. . . .

Infectious cases now made their first appearance in our Surgical
Unit. Typhus and cholera prevailed. It was the latter which helped
to stir up the mutiny among our Sisters. A batch of six cholera
patients was the first to arrive. They were in dreadful pain;
sometimes the cramp would draw them up into hideous contortions
and they would writhe and twist in agony. An orderly fanned them
constantly to keep the persistent flies away and to cool them, but
apart from medicinal drinks and massaging their legs to relax the
distorted muscles, we were helpless to assist them. It seemed
strange to think of cholera now in May; even the doctors eyed the
patients disconsolately; its early presence could be a prediction of
an epidemic to come. The ambulance vans, set aside for such
infectious diseases, were ready and the men were picked up and
deposited carefully on the bed of straw. I stood by to see that all
went according to plan. A young man, one of the three in his van,
turned his head towards the neighbour at his side, 'Vasiliy!' he
gasped, '*Ty zdes?*' '*Zdes,*' came the hoarse reply. They had recognised each other. Even in their dire distress, it must have been
comforting for each to have found a friend. No sooner were the
premises clear than the straw and offal of the cholera victims were

burnt and the sheds which had housed them sprayed with a strong disinfectant.

It was in the evening that we Sisters talked it over and our words fanned the spark of mutiny smouldering within us into a flame. We agreed that our present work was not satisfactory, that such a large number of medical personnel was quite unnecessary and that, rather than continue to work in such a desultory manner, we would apply for a temporary transfer to the nearest cholera hospital. Only two of the five Sisters were against the proposition. Mamasha, of course, was one of them. '*Chepukha!* [Nonsense!]' she cried. 'So you imagine that, because you have been without work for about ten days, your service with the wounded has come to an end! How can you be sure that tomorrow will not see great battles on the *pozitsiya*? And, who knows, we may have to leave at a moment's notice.' 'Besides,' she added abruptly, 'we belong to the *Zemstvo* and we are bound to abide by its rulings. I have no patience with such grumblers.'

Our head however advised us to wait for a few days, for it was thought that the division might be transferred to the Caucasian Front, in which case we might go with them, or join the 8th Army positioned at Lemberg.

I was sitting near my tent; I had been on duty since 9 a.m. and it was now 3 o'clock in the afternoon. My patients had included about twelve soldiers, only slightly wounded, and a few peasants – mostly small children carried in their mothers' arms. On the roof of the nearby peasant's hut, two storks were chatting to each other with the funny, rattling noise peculiar to those remarkable birds. They had built a fine new nest on the thatch-top and were obviously pleased with the result. The peasant owners, too, must have been highly content, for a storks' nest on their roof is inevitably regarded as a prophetic sign of coming good luck. Across an adjoining field, some orderlies were carrying two stretchers, on each was lying a figure draped in white; the men were making their way towards the little cemetery in the corner of the field. We knew that cemetery well; we had watched it grow almost daily. One hundred wooden crosses measured our three-week stay here.

A hospital orderly from the 2nd *Letuchka* approached my tent and handed me a letter; it was addressed to the doctor on duty.

I told the man where to find him and asked him casually how things were going in their camp. He answered with suppressed excitement that shrapnel had fallen near them all morning and that their personnel had begun to pack, for rumours had reached them that the enemy had crossed the River San and were steadily advancing. 'The wounded say so,' he affirmed, 'and the wounded would never lie.'

I sent him about his business and then sat down again and tried to work out just what would happen if those rumours proved to be true. Perhaps this very night we would have to leave Molodych, its peaceful woodlands, its flowers, its friendly peasants. A vision of those treacherous roads of shifting sand behind and before us came to my mind – veritable death traps they would be for our artillery and heavy convoys; if only they could by-pass them on their way to Molodych! The orderlies were returning to the camp, carrying the empty stretchers easily in their hands. The storks were rattling and clacking on the thatched roof.

When one of the Brothers came to relieve me for his turn on duty I questioned him anxiously, but he knew next to nothing. The 2nd *Letuchka* had already left for a distant destination; our Plenipotentiary was still at headquarters and, so far, no orders had been sent through to us. Supper was waiting for me; the others had finished and had left. The few faces which I saw were perplexed and their owners offered no information. I could hear the booming of heavy guns again in the distance.

My supper finished, I went outside our tent and looked around; Anna was not far away. I called to her and she came instantly; we entered the tent together and sat down on one of the low beds. 'Annushka, tell me, I beg of you; what has happened?' 'At present there is little to tell,' she answered dully. 'We may leave at any moment. The enemy has crossed the San after all. It is said that they are pouring over in masses and nothing can stop them. We have the men, but we haven't the means. Whole regiments are said to be without a cartridge, and only a certain number of batteries can continue the shelling.'

'What will be the result?' I asked, stupefied. 'The result,' she cried, 'the result will be that our armies will be butchered, and it is but a day's march into Russia.' 'Surely,' I persisted to comfort her, for I had never seen her so moved, 'the frontier fortifications will hold their own and stop the advance; the enemy will have to think twice before he steps over on to Russian territory.' She shook her head vehemently. 'I see it all so clearly,' she exclaimed passionately. 'The San was thought to be invulnerable, but, when he was *ready*, he crossed it easily enough; and now he will sweep us all before him like sheep and his hordes will swallow up our land. And what will happen to our towns and villages? What will happen to the women and children? My God! My God! What will happen?'

She looked at me with unseeing eyes; she looked through me into her devastated homeland. *'Eto budet uzhasno!* [It will be terrible]' she whispered. 'What will become of Russia when *they* are there?' And flinging herself downwards on to the bed, Annushka covered her face with her arms and sobbed. 'Annushka,' I said, 'stop; this is not worthy of your nature.' She turned her head and looked at me; her face was drawn with grief and her eyes were inflamed with tears. 'Nature!' she flashed, 'What is this talk of nature? What talk of nature *can* there be? Is it *their* nature to kill?' pointing in the direction of the Western Front. 'Is it God's nature to allow this wholesale destruction? Not only does one lose one's nature among all this carnage, but one's soul dies too!' She covered her face again with her arms and her shoulders quivered and shook. I did not attempt to comfort her; I could find no comfort to give.

We were told to be in readiness to leave at a moment's notice and we began to collect and pack all our own and the camp's belongings with the greatest speed. Then an urgent message reached us: 'Wounded arrived.' We left the goods half-packed and hurried off to the dressing-tents. When we saw them we knew that the worst had happened; they were dazed and their faces were lined with an anxiety which dominated the keenness of their pain and there was that something in their eyes which checked all questioning. We cut away their clothing, cleansed and dressed their wounds while they lay prostrate on the ground. Anna was there, her serenity and activity restored; she had forgotten herself, forgotten everything save the bleeding bodies around her. The night was singularly clear; the light of a myriad stars relieved the darkness. The guns had ceased firing; all was very still. With a heavy, weary lumbering, a battery was drawn down the road and turned off on to the field adjoining our camp. The guns were immediately lined up into position, their nozzles, pointing westwards, gleamed as the starlight caught them. In the background the forest line cut

darkly against the sky and a glimmer of grey shadows in a far
corner marked the 'brothers' resting-place'.

Our tents were being hastily dismantled; we were to leave when
all were packed. As we hurried back to our sleeping-tent to pick
up our last remaining belongings, the recently trafficless road and
side-tracks were all astir; groups of horsemen seemed suddenly
to have appeared from nowhere. A peasant lad slipped past us and,
with head bent low, ran swiftly across the misty field towards the
wooded shelter beyond. In a peasant's yard a party of Cossacks
had dismounted and were searching for pigs and poultry. A scuffle
and loud shouting behind us – then a woman's shrill scream; in the
grey light we saw some Cossacks struggling with a slim, boyish
figure; in a moment it was down and a gruff voice was heard
calling for *veryovka* [rope]. The hut door was open and the sobs of
the woman were borne into the night. A little farther on, other
Cossacks were guarding a number of cows and pigs. Whether they
had received orders, or were acting on their own initiative, it was
difficult to tell, but hut after hut was turned upside down and
inside out; all livestock suitable for food was confiscated and men
and boys of military age were handcuffed and marched away
towards Russia as prisoners. The distress of their wives and mothers
followed us down the road, through the forest glades and its echoes
rang in our ears for many a long hour.

Those of us who were on duty were called apart to open a dressing-
station in the forest without delay. The last wagon of our Unit's
baggage-train had disappeared round a winding of the road, but
still the endless procession of ambulances, carts, wagons and other
vehicles rumbled down the uneven route. All through the chill
hours of early morning, our work never flagged. Ambulance vans
repeatedly drew up before our tent, to which a large Red Cross
placard was affixed.

The 49th Divisional Transport train passed near us, its vans
carrying numerous wounded; we could not allow them to go
by without attention – so pitiful were they to behold; so into the
vans we climbed and administered first aid to the most needy.
In one van a man had just died; his body was still warm, but his
face was the most colourless thing that I had ever seen in a human
being; even his fair hair seemed to have paled after death; his
lower jaw was hanging, disclosing his white teeth in a white gum.

Under him, the straw was saturated with scarlet and, from the wooden slats of the van floor, a thin stream of blood was still dripping into the brown dust of the road. But there was no time to dig graves and the ambulance vans swung on down the road, carrying their freight of living and dead.

We were ready to leave the improvised station at 5 a.m.; everything was packed and our doctor had taken his seat in the cart allotted to us when an under-officer, with a Red Cross badge on his sleeve, galloped up to our assembled group. He besought us to give first aid assistance to a large number of wounded who, he pointed out, were already in our vicinity, and indeed, far off up the road we saw the small procession of peasant-carts and wagons slowly winding their way in our direction. Once again, we opened up all the material which might be necessary, using a tarpaulin-sheet as a table. We found the men in a dreadful condition, many of them without so much as a rag to cover the wound to shield it from the dust and glaring sun. We expended as much care as we could over those gaping wounds, but time and material were fast giving out and of the 130 wounded who passed through our hands during the next five hours, we could provide only 10 with transport.

It was just after 11 o'clock when another note was brought, ordering us to start without delay. Thirty pain-racked forms still lay side by side in the shade of the pines. What could we do? It would be hours before our transport-vans would return. Doctor Markovich went towards the road. Soldiers were retreating in a steady stream on either side of a line of vehicles, packed with baggage and war-equipment. Our doctor forced his way in among the foot-soldiers and faced an oncoming wagon. '*Stoy!* I command you. *Stoy!*' he shouted. The astonished driver reined in his horse and stopped. The situation was explained to him, whereupon the man readily agreed to rearrange his goods so that room might be found for two or three of the wounded in his wagon. Little by little, places were found for them all, but more than one soldier-driver proved refractory to an irritating degree and valuable minutes were wasted in useless argument before they could be persuaded to give their wounded comrades a lift to safety. With infinite relief and thankful hearts we saw the last man driven off to the Base.

Monday, 1st June. Tsevkuv
In the village of Tsevkuv, our Red Cross Detachment was waiting
for us; it was all packed and corded and in 'marching order'.
Alexander Mikhaylovich was much upset at our long delay, but
our explanation quickly mollified him and plans were instantly
discussed for the despatch of personnel to another point where a
dressing-station was urgently needed. For three hours we sat in
an open field; it drizzled a little and we put on our mackintoshes.
I dozed at intervals, my head on my raised knees. Finally, our
Plenipotentiary arrived from the Military Staff of our new division
with instructions. We were to bivouac in the village for the night
and the members on duty were to leave instantly for a destination
some ten versts distant. The rain was then falling in real earnest
and when the news went round that a hut had been found to
accommodate us, we were truly thankful.

Tuesday, 2nd June
In the early morning we were driven to Lebedya, where we found
the field dressing post of our Division already stationed. A tent
had been set up for us, the ground around it swept and cleansed.
A few wounded came and went; a spasmodic cannonade was
heard at intervals, but, in general, a remarkable and quite unexpected peace reigned. But then: 'Pack and leave immediately!'
The orders were shouted out to us; our startled senses could scarcely take them in. Mechanically, our camp-beds, only just taken
from our bags, were folded and re-packed. Through the main
street of Lebedya galloped squadron after squadron of the 3rd
Caucasian Corps. Again the frantic bustle and whirl of retreat.

Groups of peasants stood here and there along the roadsides,
watching us with sullen indifference. Many of the women were
weeping and remembering the tragic scenes in Molodych, we could
guess the reason for their tears.

2nd June. The Russian Frontier, Holmskaya Government
That evening, we crossed the frontier and set foot on Russian
territory once again. The night was passed in the district of
Volya Obshchanska, in the Holmskaya *Guberniya* [Government],
on a small estate belonging to a Polish nobleman who was fighting
in the Russian Army. The garden, although in a bad state of
neglect, was very beautiful; as we wandered among the beds of

roses and irises, we wondered how long we would sojourn in that pleasant corner and we breathed many an ardent prayer that it might at least be possible, now that we were on Russian soil, to stem the threatened invasion of the powerful enemy.

But, again, all too soon, came orders: 'Continue Retreat!' Like dumb creatures, we collected our belongings and started re-packing, speaking no word of regret, scarcely daring to look into each other's eyes. Lebedya had fallen, that quiet little spot which had housed us for a few hours only yesterday was now in the hands of the enemy. In the garden, soldiers and orderlies were gathering armfuls of lettuces, spring onions and other green vegetables. We carried bunches of roses.

We were on the road again. Herds of cattle were being driven hurriedly over the plain; sheep and pigs were huddled together in droves. In the yard of the estate which we had just left, a thick mass of rolling smoke rose skywards – the ricks of hay and straw had been fired by our men. We looked across the miles of level ground in front and behind us as we moved along in monotonous rhythm over the sandy tracks; no trenches or fortifications of any description met our eyes – only the wide expanse of smooth earth, broken here and there by large patches of potato or corn land.

The sky had darkened over us and the after-glow of sunset had faded slowly away into the evening mists as we turned into a pine forest to seek shelter for the night. The ground was covered with a thick layer of dry, brown refuse from the pines; on this we spread our rugs and were astonished to find what a soft mattress had been provided for us by Nature. A single torch lighted us during our evening meal and, despite all efforts to appear hopeful and cheery, nobody seemed sorry when the half-eaten repast had been cleared away and we were at liberty to turn aside and rest. Two of our Sisters were far from well; they appeared to be suffering from a severe chill, but I think that the general anxiety was telling on them. Annushka produced some quinine tablets and insisted on each of them taking one. She was cheerful enough herself; she had her feelings well under control. We covered the ailing Sisters up in their rugs and made them as comfortable as circumstances would permit; then we lay down by them to rest and sleep. Long into the night, I heard the Sister at my side crying quietly to herself.

3rd June, Kozaki

In the early morning we transferred our camp to Kozaki, exactly
one verst away from our night's bivouac and there we instantly
began preliminary preparations for opening a First Aid Station.
The first tent had been unrolled and was about to be raised, when
the familiar figure of the Divisional despatch-rider came riding
down the forest path. In an hour's time we were once more jolting
along a dusty road.

Weary and discontented at the continuous buffeting from pillar
to post, we sat silent for most of the journey; a halt was at last
called and it was over an evening cup of tea that the drooping
spirits of our personnel revived. A doctor from the First Aid Unit
of our division, stationed about a stone's throw away from our
own, walked over to see us. He was a pleasant man, helpful and
kindly. Taking a cup of tea, he sat down and regarded us with a
pleasing smile, despite the stolid, blank faces which surrounded
him. 'Well,' he began, 'I have some good news for you. The
Germans are not yet in Russia; what is more, we have heard that
they do not intend to cross the frontier. So our present encampment may be for an indefinite period in this forest. Meantime, our
soldiers are getting ready for the fray; reinforcements in bulk are
available all along the line. Who knows, we may soon retrace our
steps!' We cheered him loudly; the riotous sounds brought other
of the medical staff across to us. We were happy again; the strain
had been considerably lifted.

4–15th June, Chistaya Smuga

Our district is called Chistaya Smuga, which literally translated
means 'clear stream'. The forest is large, majestic, and the pines
are old, high and stately. The clear stream runs alongside the
forest; in some places it is quite narrow and can be easily forded.
Here we bring our linen and, standing on the flat stones, dip,
scrub and rinse in true washer-woman style.

Our next-door neighbours are constantly contriving some kind of
amusement to while away the time until work shall engulf us once
again. Once a birthday party in their Surgical Unit claimed our
presence, with the popular Caucasian dish *shashlyk* as a special
feature of the birthday dinner. Our soldier-cook, although a
Muscovite, imparted to us the culinary secret on which its success
depends. Portions of raw mutton are chopped into pieces about the

size of a large walnut; these are placed in an earthenware pot and onion strewn over them; when the pot is filled with alternate layers of meat and onion, slightly peppered and salted, it is tightly covered and suspended in the open air at a suitable height from the ground for three days. The heat of the sun is not calculated to harm the meat, but rather to enhance its flavour. On the fourth day, the jar is opened and the meat, by this time very tender, is, with the onion, roasted on skewers over the red-hot ashes of a charcoal fire and served while hot.

Up and down the neighbouring highroad munition-wagons rumble at intervals, foot-soldiers straggle by and cavalry contingents speed now east – now westwards at a gallop. Our Red Cross Detachments are practically invisible from the road, save for the two large flags which bear the Red Cross and the number, name and origin of each Unit. A company of horsemen passed; we recognised them without difficulty as belonging to the 3rd Caucasian Corps. Our Divisional medical staff knew them well; how many times had these intrepid men flung themselves and their horses as a living wall in between the advancing enemy and the retreating infantry? Somebody of our division hailed the riders and one of the officers turned from the road and came riding towards us. In and out of the stately pines he rode. In his long dark-red, tightly-fitting coat, with its buckles and cartridge-cases of Caucasian silver; the long, curved silver scimitar at his side; the black felt *burka* [cloak] hanging loosely over his shoulders; the red *bashlyk* [hood] twisted round his neck and falling down on to the *burka*; the high furry *papakha* [fur cap] on his head, he presented a very attractive picture; and were it not that a certain reticence held me back, I should have run off to fetch my camera and immortalise him on the spot. He would not dismount and join our festive gathering, but he eagerly accepted the gift of a skewer of smoking-hot *shashlyk* and, with a graceful, deferential salute, and a gleam of strong, white teeth, he had reined his horse round and galloped off down a glade in pursuit of his men, waving the meat-studded skewer aloft as a medieval knight would brandish his sword in an attack.

Sometimes groups of Cossacks come riding among the trees. They eye us with curiosity and pass remarks to each other in undertones. It seems to me that they are not pleased to see Sisters among so many officers and more than once I have felt a curious

sense of relief when a company has ridden by without looking our
way. Of wounded there are few; our section of the Front seems
exceptionally quiet. It is said that the Germans have not succeeded
in bringing up their heavy guns into position on account of the
bad roads. Our artillery, we hear, has fared badly during the recent
retreat and several guns have been lost in the sand-beds near
Molodych. On the left flank however, an intense cannonade is
often repeated, nor are we very surprised to learn that, in several
places in a southerly direction, the Russian troops are rapidly
retreating.

The evacuation of Lemberg has caused general dismay, but now
we have learnt that Lemberg has actually fallen and the enemy
has succeeded in crossing the Russian frontier and is in possession of Volya Obshchanska, the last trace of optimism has faded
from our midst. We can do nothing but harden our hearts to
meet the dread challenge, and wait. . . .

In our forest, we learnt to build woodland houses, and so skilled
did we become in the art that we grew to despise tent-life. Our
dining-sitting-room was a picturesque three-walled arbour, composed entirely of pine-branches; it was much frequented and
admired until the day when rain fell in violent, swollen drops
from early morning to early evening. We then betook ourselves
to the tents, feeling thankful that we had something over our
heads which could withstand wet and windy weather. Often we
grumbled that work was scarce, that we were frittering away the
time in meaningless manner while the world around us groaned
with pain and misery. To comfort us, we were officially informed
that our Unit, during its short existence at the Front, had proved
that it was well able to cope with every hardship. The statistics
for April and May had shown a most satisfactory result of the
work performed and, our doctor added, many of the other Units
had had no opportunity to do half the strenuous work that had
come our way. With this we had to be content.

Among other wooden structures erected was one the completion
of which was hailed with delight by the members of both Units:
it was a *banya*, or bathing-house. This plain log cabin, with roof
of branches, contained two rooms: the bath and dressing rooms;
the former actually boasted of a wooden floor and a brick stove.
Our appreciation of the plentiful supply of hot and cold water was

sincere and in true Russian style the steam was concentrated in the tiny room and the temperature kept at such a height that we would emerge from the cabin with scarlet faces and an urgent longing for a cool drink.

One day I visited the Mariupolski Regiment which lay in reserve about a verst's distance away in a neighbouring forest. It was sometime previously that I had promised to take photographs of their encampment and, armed accordingly with my camera, tripod and a goodly number of plates, I set out in the afternoon, accompanied by a Brother as guide. Neither of us knew what the conditions were like at the Front and the peaceful life of the last eight days had caused the rules and regulations of our Unit to relax, so that an outing was regarded with lenient eyes. Our path took us through many lovely glades of pine and silver birch woods; the mysterious scents and sounds of the forest would surround us closely and the sweet warmth of tiny, compact plant-life emanated from the earth. Farther on, we discovered that the ground was thickly covered with small dark-green bushes, with blue-purple berries abundant on the miniature branches. They were the first *klyukvi* [cranberries] of the season. We seized the berries with delight and ate to our hearts' content. My dark-stained fingers caught my eye, and with not a little apprehension I realised that cranberry juice dyed unmercifully. Our lips and teeth were of a dark purple hue and, water and soap not being forthcoming, we were obliged to assume as brave a face as possible; so we marched into the encampment with the telltale-stains painfully visible. We were expected; two officers were waiting for us to escort us past the sentries. To our great satisfaction, both officers bore signs of having eaten the same kind of fruit. I questioned them tactfully; they laughed, 'We have been living on them since we entered the wood,' they said. We passed groups of soldiers, sitting or lying about at their ease; they sprang to their feet at our approach and saluted. Behind me I heard a whisper: *'Sestra anglichanka prishla!* [The English Sister has come!]' The news of our visit soon spread and a number of officers collected around us; they seemed genuinely pleased to see us and had we been royal guests we could not have had a warmer or more sincere welcome.

I entered the dug-outs and was shown a photograph here, a book there; and I peeped inside the leafy huts and saw wonderfully contrived seats and benches. The kitchens were smoking and, although the hour was still early, the whistle sounded and the soldiers came from all sides and ranged themselves in a double queue, their mess-tins clanking merrily the while. I fancy that the unusually early supper by no means came amiss to them. I was invited to sample the soup and found it so exceptionally savoury that, much to the amusement of the soldiers (who probably thought that I would 'graciously accept' only a spoonful) I finished the portion to the very last drop.

My camera received a great welcome. The officers were quickly snapped, but not so the soldiers. They all insisted on being photographed at once, dreading lest the second and third turn which I had promised them would prove but myths; and much laughter and fun attended the posing. One man held his violin to his shoulder, another brought his hand-harmonium, a third his beloved balalaika; then a little black mascot-kitten *must* be displayed; one young soldier pretended to be engrossed in reading a letter while his boyish companion held up the picture of a young girl. I spoke with many of them; they answered with charming simplicity, pulling out much-worn pocket-books and showing me photographs of wives or children; more than one letter was placed in my hand for my perusal.

One man spoke to me of his brother, who had served with him in the same regiment and had been wounded outside Molodych; he had been sent to our *Letuchka* in a most precarious condition. Did I perhaps see him? the man asked. Did I perhaps remember him? He mentioned his name: Yevgeniy Gromov. Yes! I *did* remember him, incredible as it might seem! It was his name that had imprinted itself on my memory, for he was our first soldier with that name. His skull had been pierced by a shrapnel splinter and *trepanatsiya* [trepanning] had been performed with success. He had lain for four days in our tent and had then been despatched to the Base. The soldier was quite overcome at this news of his brother and his face lit up with the look of a man who had suddenly received an overwhelming joy.

One of the officers, a good English scholar, showed me a collection of books which he had unpacked to read while in reserve. Among them were novels by W. J. Locke, also Oscar Wilde's *De Profundis* and the *The Picture of Dorian Gray*. I was not surprised to see these latter, knowing well what a keen appreciation of Wilde's works existed throughout Russia. The officer, a student of Moscow University, had been twice in England and spoke highly of the country and its people. 'Would to God that our unhappy country would follow their example, but autocracy has us by the throat and we are gradually being strangled.' He broke off, as though afraid to say too much, and then added: 'But the day will come when the people will come into their own and may I live to see that glorious day.' 'Did you take any part in the revolution of 1905?' I asked. 'No,' he answered. 'I was too young to be of any use, but my father worked hard for the Cause and gave his all. He died in prison of a broken heart; a comrade betrayed him.' 'Sestritsa,' said a voice at my elbow, 'we must not allow Dmitri Sergeyevich to monopolise you entirely. Besides, he is a red hot revolutionary and will come to a bad end one of these days.'

We turned to make our adieux and depart, but the officers insisted that we join them at supper; already a meal had been prepared and the table was spread. But what a mess-room! What a table! The former consisted of a simple, narrow trench, approximately two feet in depth which ran around a square of flat, grassy ground; the square served as a table, the trench as a receptacle for the feet of the diners who were seated on the ground. A post stood at each corner of the trench; to the four posts lanterns were fixed and a tarpaulin sheet was stretched from post to post. A slightly raised seat marked the customary place of the Colonel; this seat was promptly allotted to me. The meal was simple, but when the tea was handed around, chocolates and candied fruits appeared in surprising quantities.

Gradually it grew dim; the lanterns were lighted and small camp-fires crackled merrily in our rear as a guard against the mosquitoes and vampire-flies which haunted the forest after dark. From my dais I scanned the faces around me; they were mostly young, eager and buoyant. Like a queen I sat there and they – my gallant courtiers – told gay tales and sang merry songs to please me! An officer, Roumanian by birth, brought out a guitar and with magic fingers picked out strange, plaintive folk-music of his country, droning, now and then, some unknown words in a soft, far-away voice, quite forgetful of our presence.

Then, of a sudden, someone called out, 'Vanya! Where is Vanya?' And even as his name was uttered, a figure jumped up from the table and disappeared among the trees. But Vanya was quickly found, brought back to his seat and, sensing that there was none to help him and that obey he must, he began to sing.

I had seen him already and yet scarcely noticed him, so insignificant had he seemed: small in stature, fair-haired, with narrow, drooping shoulders, a weakling beside the stalwart figures of the majority of officers then present. 'Vanya,' said someone with pride in his voice, 'Vanya is our *prima voce*, our nightingale; to listen to Vanya is to forget all else.' And at the first note it was evident that here was no ordinary voice, here was something genuine and unaffected – a tenor voice of beautiful quality, pure and mellow, softly clear. In a moment all conversation was hushed. I placed my cup of tea on the grass-table and laid the unfinished sweetmeat at its side.

Vanya sat in a corner, with his head slightly tilted, leaning against a post; the light from the lantern just eluded him and his face was in semi-shadow. There was no applause as the song ended and no one moved; we waited and soon the voice sounded again. To enumerate the songs he sang would be impossible. They were all in Russian, some describing the life of the peasant; others declaring his steadfast, honest faith in God and Nature; not a few were full of the pathos, stoicism and divine endurance of a sorely-tried people. . . .

We had said goodbye, thanked them and turned away down the woodland path, accompanied by two officers who were anxious to show us a short-cut to our camp. A soldier stepped forward and, saluting, placed a large tin of ripe *klyukvi* in my hand. I recognised him as the brother of the wounded soldier Yevgeniy, who had passed through our Dressing Station. 'These are for you, *Sestritsa*,' he said hurriedly; 'If you see my brother again, tell him, please, that his brother, Anton Ivanovich Gromov, greets him.' Before I had time to reply, he had disappeared. I set off again, the tin of purple berries in my hand and a great peace in my heart.

We had walked but a short distance when we caught sight of our lights glimmering through the trees. I made straight for the Sisters' tent; it was nearly ten o'clock and they would be retiring to rest. As I passed the dining-tent, I noticed that the sheeting which covered the plank-table (a serviceable side-board during meals) had gone; the planks had also disappeared. 'Hm!' I thought, 'they are evidently going to make a new side-board tomorrow.' I lifted

the flap of the tent and entered silently for fear of disturbing a
possible sleeper.

But no one was sleeping. They were – *packing*! 'Mamasha!' I
said, for she was just before me. 'Why are you packing?' *'Pochemu?
Potomu chto nuzhno!* [Why? Because it is necessary!]' she answered
sharply. Then, turning a red, flurried and wrathful face towards
me, she cried accusingly: 'And I would advise you to do the same.
You seem to imagine that the war is at a standstill for your benefit, and that there is nothing for you to do beside taking walks and
paying visits.' 'Mamasha,' I gasped. *'Chto vy govorite?* [What are
you saying?]' 'Has there been some work in my absence?' Anna
moved towards me, her face expressing compassion. 'There have
been only two wounded since you left,' she said, 'but we have been
told that the men in our section of the Front have been forced to
retreat and we have had orders to be ready to leave at any
moment.'

It was 9 a.m. when the orders came, we were ready to the last
man; the tents had been dismantled and were packed, together
with other equipment, on our baggage-wagons. We started on
our way, directly behind the long *oboz* carrying the movable equipment of the Divisional Red Cross Detachment. Twice we followed
a false track and twice the command was passed to us to retrace
our steps and to traverse a side-road. The roads, no matter which
we took, were sand-bound and considerably impeded progress.
All day long we jolted along the plains, or through woodlands, and
wherever we looked we could see the moving figures of homeless
people. It was said that the Cossacks had received orders to force
all inhabitants of villages and hamlets to leave their homes, lest
they be made to act as spies and, in order that the enemy should
encounter widespread devastation in his progress, the homesteads
were set on fire and crops destroyed.

Thus a new word was added to our daily vocabulary – that of
refugee, and from that day onward for many weeks to come the
life of our Unit was closely interwoven with that of the refugees.
Their plight was heart-rending. They took what they could with
them: their horses, cows, pigs, poultry and the household goods on
a cart. The peasantry of the Holmskaya Province seemed to have
been fairly well-to-do to judge from the cattle and other animals
which they drove before them, but, little by little, on that long

trek, the animals' strength gave out and we would see panting, dying creatures by the roadside: cows, calves, goats, unable to go any farther. Sometimes a cart had broken down and the family, bewildered and frightened, would choose to remain near their precious possessions, so loath to part with them were they, until they too were driven onwards by the threatening knout of the Cossack, or the more terrifying prospect of the proximity of the enemy.

All night long this great tireless movement continued on plain and road. The sullen thud of numerous feet intermixed with the creaking of the over-laden peasant-carts never ceased; sometimes the angry shout of a harassed man, a guttural encouragement to a lagging horse, or the long, plaintive lamentation of a sick or hungry child would rise high above the widespread undercurrent of confused noise and disorder. I listened to that dull and heavy tread, trudging, plodding ever onwards, and prayed that these hours of dread apprehension might soon pass. Fiery red patches were dotted about the western horizon; there was that in the air which smelt of destruction.

We drove all night, and the next day halted at an old white house on an estate belonging to country gentry who had fled. It was a very old house, said to have stood there for over five hundred years, and its rooms were permeated with that musty smell which so persistently clings to all things pertaining to bygone days. Much of the lighter furniture had already been removed, but the beautiful, dark-oak dining-suite had doubtless proved too cumbersome for transportation and had been left intact.

Monday, 15th June
Krasnobrod, as the district around was known, boasted of an attempt at fortifications; as we moved into it in the early morning, we had seen many lines of wire-entanglements about the wide, adjoining plain and, in the forest, a long, yellow-red streak of sand-trenches ran in and out among the pines. The walls of these trenches were boarded up to prevent their collapse, and the sunlight, catching the sand in golden patches, made a colourful display against the pine background.

Our stay was a brief one. Soon after midday we were back on another stage of our endless journey. We noticed at once that a change had come over the plain for the sand had all but disappeared, and, in its stead, large boulders blocked our way as we trundled over the track, and the hard, stony surface proved almost as trying to the horses as the sandy dunes had done. Stone trenches ran away from us to right and left; they were remarkably well-made and their hewing out must have necessitated much forethought and immense labour.

Last night we halted in a potato field outside the village of Sukhovolya. Refugees were camping in the same field; they instantly besieged us, imploring us to tell them where they were to go. We were at a loss as to how best to advise them and could only point along the eastward-winding road. '*Bozhe moy, chto budet s nami?* [My God, what will become of us?]', they moaned, as they turned away. We echoed the same words as we followed them into the dark night an hour or two later.

At 7 a.m. we stopped to rest and feed the horses, but German shrapnel found us and forced us to take to the road again. One by one in a wild tumult of shouting we followed and clattered down the chaussée. The retreat was at its height. We were almost submerged in the flood of humanity which swept down that dusty road.

A man was down! He was under the wheels of a gun-carriage! A flash of a white face – a cry above the confusion – that was all; we still clattered along and the gun-carriage pressed forward without heed. Here, indeed, was the law of the primitive world – the survival of the fittest! To fall was to be crushed, abandoned, and to die, while the swollen tide of wheels and feet swept on and on in fitful, passionate fury, engulfing horse or human which impeded its passage. And ever the lazy, threatening drone of enemy planes sounded in our ears silenced only by the quick, sharp bark of enemy shells at our heels.

A wild plain opened before us like a green oasis in the wilderness of our despair. The carts and wagons scrambled across the ditch. Here, at last, were both space and liberty and our tired animals, gathering together their remaining strength, made off across the stubbly ground with unexpected energy. We were called to a halt at the large wine factory of Grabovets and were at once promised a night's shelter in the proprietor's roomy home.

16th June. Grabovets

A jumble of confused sounds and voices woke me suddenly. I
jumped to my feet and saw that the other occupants of the room
were astir. It was still dark, but the whole house was in a turmoil.
The jumble of voices which I had heard in my sleep was deepening
into a roar: a stamping of heavy feet in the room above; shouting
and rushing outside in the yard. No need to ask the reason; it was
plain to one and all. We seized our blankets and water-flasks and
pushed our way down the passage. Two Polish girls whom we had
seen the previous evening were standing, already dressed, near the
doorway. *'Prosze pania! Prosze pania!'* they cried as we approached. 'Take us with you. We have nowhere to go. Take us
with you; for the love of God and the Blessed Virgin take us with
you.' They followed us, crying with short, frightened gasps, as we
went out into the yard which was separated from the road by a
wooden fence. In the dim light, we saw that the fence had gone.

The movement on the road was indescribable; the noise terrifying. All the world was retreating! Refugees intermixed with the
infantry and artillery; gun-carriages and baggage-wagons rocked
side by side; Cossacks galloped madly by. A medley of wild cries
mingled with the shouts and imprecations of the soldiers: women's
voices beseeching, pleading, cursing; the cackle of frightened
geese; the barking of startled dogs; the clamour of harassed domestic animals and, now and again, above the babel, a child's shrill
sobbing. We were led, pushed, towards a *dvukolka* and ordered to
climb in. The Polish girls had disappeared; there was no time to
look for them. We lay at full length on the straw, with our blankets
as pillows.

Once I looked out, but the scene was so dreadful that I could
look no more. I covered my head with my blanket and pressed my
fingers into my ears. The utter impotence of our situation! The
fierce outcry of men tested beyond endurance! The plaintive wail
of frail human-beings! The tumult ceased by degrees. Far behind
us I could still hear faint sounds of discordant voices dying away,
until I fell asleep.

17th June

I awoke as our vans lined up among the trees in the wood of
Korytin. The horses were covered with sweat and dust; they
panted with long, harsh breaths of exhaustion, heaving sides and

dilated nostrils telling their own story. The drivers too were coated with dust which lay in ridges on their faces, giving them the appearance of wrinkled old men. Their eyes were heavy and dull for they had not yet had a chance to rest. They had driven throughout that long, turbulent night, while I had slept.

The heat was great and the comfort and shade afforded by the leafy trees were more than welcome. All round, men and horses were resting after the night's exhausting march. The infantry were massed together, lying close to each other in strange, unnatural positions; their rifles were stacked near them in groups, looking like sheaves of dark corn, with the fixed bayonets pointing skywards. To our left, the artillery park of our division was stationed; the men were busy over their fires; the whinnying of the tired, hungry horses resounded plaintively through the glades. Refugees were still streaming down the road. One old man hobbled by leaning on a stick, driving three heifers before him; a number of *telezhki* [small truck-carts], drawn by small puny-looking horses, or 'cats' as the soldiers called them, rumbled along; they were packed tightly with boxes, barrels and household furniture; the heads of the children and very old men and women were often to be seen protruding from the midst of these loads. Women and children walked by in large parties, all carrying bundles of varying dimensions. One woman, with a sleeping infant in her arms, was bowed almost double by a large wicker-basket containing poultry, which was strapped on her back.

As the afternoon approached, many of the sleepers rose, greatly refreshed. With Anna and Ekaterina I went deeper into the wood in search of strawberries, the fragrance of which had already been noticed in the air. In one corner we found a carpet of them and quickly filled the tin which had been handed to us by Mamasha; retracing our steps, we met two soldiers whose messtins were full of similar ripe berries. They offered them to us and would not hear of a refusal, nor would they agree to any payments; so my black apron was lined with large green leaves and the messtins were emptied into it; with great triumph we returned to our camp and presented our booty to Mamasha.

While we were still enjoying the fruit, instructions were brought to Alexander Mikhaylovich that we were to leave without delay for the village of Molodyatyche. Zamostay had fallen to the enemy who was closing in rapidly on our section of the Front.

Our Head Doctor's first thought was for the horses – would they stand another long journey? For three full days we had been on the road – day and night; the rare hour or two of respite had surely not been enough for the exhausted animals. We Sisters, too, were over-tired and sick at heart that, although surrounded by suffering, we were not allowed to minister to those who most urgently needed our help.

Night was falling as we drew up in a cornfield of Molodyatyche; tired and frustrated, we lay down to sleep, still dressed in our travelling uniform. The following morning a First Aid Post was opened by the roadside, where the Sister-on-duty took up her position. We were only two and a half versts from the Front Line and liaison was promptly established with our Regiments. Only a few wounded were brought to us during the day; we watched over them with zealous care, strong in the belief that, after many days of enforced idleness, we were about to recommence the work which we had undertaken to do. Here it was that the 20th Division of the 5th Caucasian Infantry Corps took up its position on one of our flanks; our 62nd Division was now attached to this Corps, the losses of which, we heard, had been terrible. Out of 25,000 *shtykov* [men with bayonets] only 2,000 were left.

The air was hot and sultry; the growling of the guns became less distinct. Because of the heat, we opened our tent-flaps and fastened them to the side; thus we could view from our camp-beds a large stretch of landscape. The horizon was an unbroken line of conflagrations. Far up into the sky their ruby reflections spread. Many villages were on fire; large forage stores were being destroyed; friend and foe seemed to have one and the same intent, the destruction of the countryside.

From one of the numerous groups of soldiers bivouacking in that cornfield, a violin was suddenly heard. I don't think that the violinist possessed any great talent, nor was his instrument of any special worth, but the melody which was drawn from its strings was sweet and restful and full of the beauty and magnetism of visionary happiness. I recalled Vanya's clear, lovely voice among the pine trees at Chistaya Smuga. I heard Mamasha lift herself up in bed – the better to listen – and I heard from the camp-bed at my side Anna's long-drawn sighs of blissful contentment.

19th June

Just after 1 o'clock of that same night we were once again ordered to take to the road. But at Lushchov, our next halting-place, we remained for three and a half days, for the good news had reached us that the Germans had suffered a considerable reverse at the hands of the men of the 49th Division, who, it was rumoured, had re-taken six versts of captured territory. But the success was short-lived, lack of ammunition forced our men to retreat once again.

22nd June. Treschany

From Lushchov we journeyed to Treschany and encamped on a plain by a river. All night long rain fell and a thick mist rose from the river and enveloped us in its icy embrace. We were sleeping in the open-air and shivered continually, for the damp stood out on our blankets like beads of perspiration. Next morning, two of our Sisters had developed high temperatures; a third, the eldest of our party, a quiet woman with soft grey hair, had reached such a pitch of nervous tension owing to the lack of sleep and incessant buffeting of the last weeks that she felt her health was giving way. She conferred with our doctors, who regretfully accepted her resignation and she left for Moscow on the following day.

Because of the incessant rain and mist, we transferred our camp to an apple-orchard standing on higher ground, and our dressing-tent was set up exactly opposite us on the other side of the road. After we had settled in there, the weather changed and we found our tent-home delightfully cool during the sultry noonday hours. Outside the orchard a large corn-patch was gradually turning golden; poppies and cornflowers grew abundantly among its waving, slender stems; a little farther away a field of poppies all colours, from pink to dark mauve, made a lovely splash of brightness.

Scarcely a day passed that did not bring some of our Divisional doctors or officers from the surrounding villages. They had many tales to tell and one and all were loud in their praise of the 3rd Caucasian Cavalry Corps, who, they affirmed, fought like 'devils and not men'. Our own 62nd Division was not far behind; at Yaroslav, as everybody knew, it had more than distinguished itself. With a scanty supply of ammunition, it had been ordered to hold the enemy at bay for 36 hours; it had resisted for three days, the soldiers using the butts of their rifles as clubs when the cartridges gave out.

The first sign that the Germans had succeeded in bringing up their heavy artillery on to our Front was received by us during one moonlit night when, quite suddenly, shells came sweeping over our heads to explode with much violence at a distance of about two miles eastwards. Next morning we were told that the house in which the divisional staff was stationed had been destroyed, some of the men and officers had been wounded and many horses killed. The commotion caused by this unexpected event was, naturally, very great. In the first place, no one had realised that heavy artillery could have been brought up on to our Front because of the treacherous roads; then, too, the extraordinary accuracy of the German aim was ascribed to the treachery of the village and town inhabitants, some of whom, it was discovered, had been in touch with the enemy and had supplied him with the vital information. During the day one or two of us were given the opportunity to view the ruined mansion. It was certainly a neat piece of work: ten shells had been expended in all – three or four of them falling directly on to the house and smashing in both roof and walls; the remainder exploding in the garden, where large *voronki* [craters], broken trees and about fifty dead horses bore silent witness to the devastating power of the missiles which had descended upon them in the night. This episode and several other instances of treachery in the surrounding districts probably helped the Military Authorities to come to their harsh decision which demanded the expulsion of the peasantry from all those villages which had to be evacuated by our retreating soldiers.

How we felt for them – these homeless wanderers. We heard their muffled voices early in the morning hours, long before the birds began to stir and twitter, and we heard their footsteps in the late hours when darkness had fallen and only the cannonade broke the peace of evening. Sometimes they came to us for bread, begging us to exchange a few loaves for poultry or a small pig. Once a distraught peasant came lumbering from a neighbouring wood to beg food for his two children. His wife had died the previous day giving birth to a baby. In barely coherent language, he told us how he had buried her there among the trees – the living baby on her breast, for he could not feed the infant, and he dared not watch it die.

And when we told him that we had but little to give him – how far would a couple of loaves go with hungry children? – he turned without a word, and with bowed head went back into the wood. His speechless grief communicated itself to us, for our hearts were heavy for many days, and in quiet moments my thoughts would often turn towards the mother and baby, the dead and the living who had found a grave together.

There was no doubt that the Germans were advancing. By now, the cannonade was ceaseless; sometimes it sounded far distant, sometimes it seemed thundering on the very threshold of Treschany. Wounded men were sent to us daily, not in large numbers and not so much wounded in body as in dire distress of soul. There was one of them who cried: 'I saw them, saw plainly; they set fire to the thatch . . . and when he . . . came out . . . such an old one . . . like my old grand-dad . . . they were on to him with a pitch-fork . . . and he so old and not at fault. . . . Not far away is my little home. . . . My grand-dad is sitting there . . . he is waiting for me . . . what will be with him when they come? . . . Oh! Merciful God! . . . what will be with him?'

After leaving Chistaya Smuga, their reserve period ended, the Mariupolski Regiment had been sent again to the Front Line. The 2nd Company had almost been wiped out under a terrific barrage of the enemy, who emptied some 25,000 shells on to their section of the Front. The Company's officers were all killed; one of the two officers who had escorted us back to our *Letuchka* in the evening was among the victims.

One afternoon in Treschany as I was sitting near the dressing-tent, a peasant-cart driven by two soldiers and containing a coffin drew up on the road before me. Somewhat surprised at the sight of such a well-made coffin at a time when coffins were impossible to get, and thinking that the men had brought a dead soldier for burial in the brothers' cemetery, I directed them towards the hut where I knew Batyushka had found a billet. 'No, Sestritsa,' said one of them. 'There is no dead man here. We have come to fetch the body of an officer,' and, producing a paper from his pocket, he handed it to me. They had come for the body of the student-officer with the pale, serious face, who had spoken English with me.

'Is he really here?' I questioned. *'Tak tochno, Sestritsa* [Exactly so],' was the answer. 'We buried him here two days ago.'

I walked across the road and up the hill. The crosses stood
starkly silhouetted against the sky. I went towards the newest
graves and one after the other read the names inscribed on the
crosses. Here was the one I had been searching for – *'Umer ot
ran* . . . [Died from wounds]'.

The wooden cross was drawn out. 'Don't destroy it, the name
can be erased and it will do for someone else,' said Smirnov our
head hospital-orderly. Carefully they dug away the earth. He was
in his long military coat and his hands were crossed on his breast.
So this was my 'red-hot revolutionary', who had loved his country
over much and was ready to die for his countrymen! Was this the
'bad end' which had been playfully prophesied for him? I watched
them drive down the hill, passing the golden cornfield and the
field of dancing poppies on their way.

The day before we left Treschany held both glad and sad hours
for us. We knew that we must leave very soon, our armies were
retreating and we could find no rest because of the raging of the
rifles and guns. Lately, ammunition had been sent in large quantities to our Front, but little of it had been of any use. Out of one
consignment of 30,000 shells, fewer than 200 were found to be
serviceable. Cartridges were sent in their hundreds of thousands
and distributed amongst the men in the trenches, but they were
of a foreign cast and would not fit the Russian rifle. Large stores
of Japanese rifles had been despatched to neighbouring divisions,
but the Russian cartridge failed to fit them. Later, we learnt that
Japanese cartridges had been supplied to our Armies on other
Fronts, with the same disastrous results. So once again our Russian
soldiers raised the butt of their rifles against the advancing
enemy, many of them hewed themselves clubs from the forest.

So we knew quite well that today or tomorrow we had to go. In
the morning I had been collecting letters from the soldiers stationed
in our village to send to Moscow with a member of our *Letuchka*
who was leaving that same evening. One soldier presented me with
a handkerchief, bearing the flags of the Allies in colours. It had
been given to him, while in hospital in St Petersburg, by the
Empress Alexandra, but, he declared, it had always proved a source
of discomfort and worry, as he was in constant fear of soiling or
losing it. 'It will bring you luck, *Sestritsa*,' he added, 'and I shall
be content knowing that it is in safe hands'.

And, indeed, joy and luck were to attend my footsteps that day!

Alexander Ivanovich, our Plenipotentiary, arrived an hour or two later, bringing with him a batch of long-awaited letters for me, which he had collected from my 'Russian family' in Moscow. There were fifteen letters in all – twelve from England! Those from my Mother – which were instantly recognisable because of her beautiful writing – I put on one side, they were to be read after the others; a literary 'bonne bouche' as it were, for they were the choicest and most precious letters of them all.

That day, some of our members were presented with the little silver medal of St George, the 4th degree, and a modest banquet was arranged to celebrate the occasion. The award was for the faithful carrying out of arduous duties in the face of great danger on the Russian Front and was awarded to the Surgical Personnel of the 1st *Letuchka* of the 10th Red Cross Detachment of the *Zemstvo*, etc., etc., in recognition of their services during the incessant bombardment of the months April to July, etc., etc. When we were alone together in our tent, Anna and I looked with pride at the medals, with their black and gold striped ribbon.

Shrapnel was falling thickly in and around Treschany as we hurriedly made our exit during the evening of the following day. The road was scarcely distinguishable in the darkness, but we followed the preceding vehicle and moved slowly over the invisible track. Rain began to fall, at first slowly and then in large, angry drops. I was aware that my black veil was soaked through and that something cold was trickling down my neck under the leather collar.

6th July

Day dawned and brought with it a decided sense of relief. I was at last able to extract my legs from their cramped position among sundry sacks, barrels and boxes and find a seat on the narrow, wooden bench next to the driver. He was in an unfriendly mood and no wonder, for, despite his thick coat and the sacking over his head, he was drenched to the skin. Once when I drew his attention to some fine fortifications in front of a village which I was later to learn was named Teryatin, he nodded his head and turned and looked at me; after that he seemed to ease his sullen mood and became more amiable. I attributed the change to my miserable, dishevelled appearance.

We journeyed on for a mile or so to Zanizhe, where we found

that our *Letuchka* and its baggage-train had halted. Turn where one would in Zanizhe – flies and mud were sure to follow. For the first night we were forced to sleep among the cabbages in a garden plot, with our camp-beds sunk a foot into the oozy mire. A regiment bivouacking in the same village left the next morning for the Defence Position and we came into possession of a two-roomed hut. Alas! our joy was shortlived; one glimpse of the hut's interior made us deeply regret that we had parted with our tent. The flies came out in flocks to greet us, and so warm was their reception that within minutes coats, aprons, any available garments, were cutting the air with a savage swishing and swirling sound. But the flies seemed to enjoy it and regard it as a game and grew quite as excited as we did over it. After we had succeeded in opening the windows which had been sealed hermetically against the winter frosts, we swept the rooms of their accumulation of mud.

For five days we stayed in Zanizhe, and for five days we waded about in mud a foot deep and were infested by multitudinous flies and other highly obnoxious insects. We killed them in their thousands and in their thousands they resuscitated. We discovered them in our tea, in our soup; the Egyptians of old could not have been more plagued with locusts than we were by our flies. And although they worried us incessantly by day, by night we had another crafty adversary – the bedbug. Our blankets, sleeping-bags and rugs became its happy hunting-ground; we tried all kinds of remedies and disinfectants, but, somehow, it seemed to be indestructible. Once I heard a voice in our hut in the middle of the night – it was counting slowly: '67 . . . 68 . . . 69. . . .' It was Mamasha, not engrossed in housekeeping accounts, as at first I had thought, but hunting in desperation for the 'livestock' which tormented her so persistently; as each minute vampire was caught, she burnt it in the flame of a flickering candle at her side, counting all the while!

About two hundred yards from our hut, three 6-inch guns were stationed; they were covered with leafy branches and, from a distance, their artificial shelter resembled a small coppice. They fired seldom, but when they did so the village vibrated with the powerful detonation. At each report our hut shook violently and the already-cracked ceiling would drop bits of mud-stucco into our tea and pepper the company with a fine soot-like dust. There was little work and those on duty were able to cope with the scanty numbers of wounded. It rained without ceasing and one and all began to suffer from irritability; even Alexander Mikhaylovich came under the influence of those trying days and, habitually silent, grew more and more taciturn and moody.

Annushka alone retained her cheerful, childlike spirits and with sprightly humour would endeavour to dispel the gloom and bring smiles to the most forlorn of faces, and little witch that she was she invariably succeeded. Who would not smile with Anna? I greatly admired this young Sister, she had so many high qualities, not least of which was the ability to control her feelings when her nerves were at breaking-point. More than once, when alone together, I had seen and sensed the depth of her despair.

When one of our party remarked that it would be a relief to receive marching-orders and to be rid of the mire and the vermin, Alexander Mikhaylovich, pessimistic for the first time aloud, murmured that this constant journeying in fits and starts was sorely telling on him, but, he added with a little hopeless gesture: 'I cannot expect to find rest here except it be under a wooden cross.' A shriek of derision from Anna – who saw the grotesque in everything – met this utterance. Over Alexander Mikhaylovich's venerable face a shade of pink mounted up to the roots of his hair; his usually mild eyes flashed fire, but he stroked his beard and laughed in a slightly embarrassed and half-apologetic fashion.

11th–17th July. Belopolye
A large brick-yard at Belopolye was our next halting-place and there we found our divisional *Otryad* already stationed. The houses and buildings around were all constructed of brick and we welcomed with delight their clean, salutary appearance. That night the men of the 62nd Division repulsed two fierce onslaughts of the enemy, but the price exacted for the resistance was heavy and extreme. At dawn, many of those who had paid were brought to us. Over the brick floor of a long low store-house, straw was thickly scattered and the wounded were placed there side by side. So numerous grew their number that our transport vans and those of the divisional *Otryad* were not sufficient to meet our needs, and it was a great relief when news came that a motor-ambulance column had promised to help transport the men. Twelve ambulance-cars and three lorries appeared that same evening. After we

had fed, clothed and bandaged them, we packed the men up
carefully in the comfortable ambulances.

One soldier the orderlies had considerable difficulty in raising
from the ground; he shook his head violently when told he was
to be sent to the Base, pointing repeatedly to his chest and picking
at his shirt with his weather-beaten hands. His lower jaw was
smashed and his tongue half-torn out. I noticed the little scrimmage
and heard the somewhat impatient assurance of the orderlies
that he was only to be sent to the Base hospital and that no
harm could come to him on the way. I approached the small
group; the soldier stretched out a beseeching arm towards me.
'Don't you want to be sent to the Base,' I enquired. He shook his
head, comprehension clear in his eyes, and pointed to shirt and chest.
In the pocket of my overall were pencil and paper; I held them
out and they were clutched eagerly. Laboriously for his neck
was very swollen, he bent his head while the blood trickled from
under the bulging upper-lip. The distorted handwriting was not
easy to decipher: '*Ikona . . . Rubashka* [Icon . . . shirt].'

Ah! I understood! 'Your icon was sewn on to your shirt?' He
looked up at me enraptured, breathing hard. 'Yes! Yes!' His eyes
assented. 'The shirt was taken off and thrown away. Was it taken
off here?' He nodded. 'Then we will look for it,' I assured him,
and, turning to the orderlies, I told them that in the meantime he
could remain in our care. He thanked me silently, and when a
moment's breathing-space came, I went to fulfil my promise. I
looked, searched, hunted; with an orderly's help I turned over a
heap of evil, smelly garments which had been stripped off the
wounded and thrown together in a pile for burning. It had come
to my notice before that some of the soldiers had their icons
sewn on to their shirts. But, earnestly as I tried to find it, I was
disappointed. Heaps of discarded clothes had already been burnt
that day; doubtless the man's shirt with the icon had been among
them. It was almost as bitter a disappointment to me as it would
be to him.

That night I avoided him; let him sleep if possible in the hope
that the morning would bring his treasure. If only it had been
found! Could I replace it with another? Impossible! It would never
be the same. So I broke the bad news to him and watched the light
of expectancy die in his eyes. He gave no gesture of distress, he
could not turn his head; he simply shut his eyes. Later, when the

orderlies came to transfer him to the Base, he offered no resistance, but, leaning on the men's arms, slowly dragged himself on to the stretcher at his side.

Cholera patients were numerous; some *dvukolki* were set apart to convey them to the nearest hospital for infectious diseases. Refugees were frequently among the patients. Their presence held for us a special significance. We dared not think what the result would be of a cholera epidemic among those throngs of destitute beings. Sickness was already prevalent in their midst; we were able to treat those in our vicinity and medicine was doled out in large quantities. Sometimes they would come to us on quite a different quest – a spade to dig a grave in the forest.

One morning Anna and I had been tidying up the wards after despatching all the wounded who were in fit condition to be moved. It was a hot, sultry day, despite the wind which blew small clouds of dust into our long brick building. Swarms of flies flew around our heads and hovered over the men whose wounds were too severe to permit transfer. Our hospital-orderlies were busy, waving long leafy branches in slow fan-like motion over the prostrate forms. '*Sestritsa*, a wounded man is here,' came the voice of our head-orderly. '*Seychas, Smirnov, seychas*,' I called and, to Anna, who was about to rise from her kneeling position beside a wounded man, 'I will go.'

Near the dressing-room, an officer was sitting; his arm was in a sling; his batman stood at his side. As I cut the stained bandage, I noticed that he was trembling violently and his face was ashen-grey. 'Nerves,' I inwardly commented, and had him placed on the table at once lest he should faint. Alexander Mikhaylovich looked in. 'Compound fracture,' he nodded, 'the usual splint and to the Base with him.' An ambulance-car was in the yard and a place was at once reserved for him. The dressing completed and splint applied, he sat up; '*Spasibo, Sestritsa*. You do not recognise me?' 'No, I don't,' I answered, looking at him with curiosity. He mentioned his name and added: 'I played the guitar at the Georgiyevski fête in your Unit; I told you that I should come to see you and I have kept my word.'

Then I remembered, but this man was older by many years, with haggard face and lines round his eyes, and more than a month's growth of dusky hair about his chin. That other, who had played and sung on that memorable day when St George's medal

had been presented to us, had been little more than a boy. Could
a few days have brought about such a great change? 'No wonder,'
he said with a painful laugh, 'no wonder that you don't recognise
me, for I am not the same person that I was. I am not even I!
The someone who was I has been rooted out for ever; I feel it, I
feel the immense void. I cannot recognise myself, so how can I
expect others to recognise me?' His voice broke. He was quite
unnerved, I could see, and very near a collapse. I pitied him with
all my heart. Gently I led him into the yard. 'No, Stepan Grigoriyevich,' I said. 'You must not despair; believe me, not one
of us but is changed by this violent, abnormal life; it could not
be otherwise. But behind it all, deep down within us, in perfect
safety, is our true self – which can never change.' Again he laughed,
a mirthless, empty laugh.

'All that wants thinking about,' he said, 'and there is no time
to think. Perhaps out there,' he pointed eastwards, 'there will be
an opportunity. Meanwhile, it is not agreeable to be a mere husk,
a walking shadow. When faith and hope vanish, what is a man's
life?' He stopped and looked at me; there were tears in his eyes
and he was not ashamed of them.

'That is a difficult question,' I answered hurriedly, for I was
afraid for him, 'but you will think it over and I am convinced
that you will find the right answer. At present, Stepan Grigoriyevich,
don't think, don't try to think. You are tired, you must rest, sleep.'

'Sleep,' he cried, 'I have forgotten how to sleep. Can one sleep
when the world around is in chaos?' The engine started, the car
glided out of the yard. I could not keep myself from thinking of
that young soldier who had presented such a strange figure as he
stood there with tears in his eyes; I had been at a loss as to how
to speak to him. He was so different: an Englishman would never
have stood in a yard full of people and, with tears in his eyes,
spoken with sorrow of the loss of his soul. The average Englishman,
even in normal times, would not wish to talk about his soul at all
and, to the best of my knowledge, the average Englishman when
brought to bay, with his shoulders well squared against the wall of
Stern Realities, would usually whistle a music-hall ditty, quote the
latest joke from *Punch* or voice a mighty voluminous swear-word.

I had thought to relate to Anna my encounter with our former
acquaintance, but I found her with an old peasant just inside the
door of our second 'ward'. On the straw-litter a child – a boy of

about six years – was lying; he was dead and his little face was shrunken to miniature proportions. 'Where has he come from?' was my first thought and then I saw the bowed figure of the peasant step forward, drop on to his knees by the child's side, kiss the sallow, sunken cheeks with passionate intensity, rise hastily, snatch at Anna's small brown hand, touch it with his lips . . . and disappear. At the same moment, two men came towards me, followed by Smirnov and three other orderlies. One of the strangers was wearing the uniform of a Russian 2nd lieutenant, the other was in semi-military uniform, minus epaulettes.

The former – the elder of the two – introduced himself and his friend and stated that they had received permission from our doctor to try to alleviate the sufferings of the wounded soldiers. So I accompanied the men to our long, main 'ward'; groans were heard throughout the building and one man, lying not far from the door, cried out continually in a hoarse, unnatural voice; his thigh was fractured and his whole body was heavily contused. The two strangers made their way towards him and the younger, a pale, clean-shaven man, knelt down beside him and looked him long and steadily in the face.

The soldier, scarcely conscious of their presence, continued his cries. I watched the trio with casual eyes until something in the face of the kneeling man arrested my attention. 'What is your name?' he asked. The answer came without hesitation: 'Pyotr.' 'Now, Pyotr, look at my hands.' The stranger raised his hands; they were thin, nervous, white hands and they were poised above the soldier's face; they trembled, as the wings of a hawk tremble when they hover over a heedless prey. Now those white hands dipped, then they swayed – this way and that; they wavered, now they were held in repose. The eyes of the soldier were fixed on them and he watched their movements as if fascinated . . . his cries were hushed, he had forgotten his pain.

I left them for a few moments and returned to the shed where I had left Anna. She had exchanged the dirty linen clothes of the dead child for a soldier's clean white shirt; the long sleeves had been turned back, leaving the tiny, folded hands exposed to view. She was still on her knees by the side of the baby-form; her face was a study, grief and misgivings were clearly stamped on it. She followed me back to the main 'ward' and, like myself, was startled to see the strange scene being enacted there.

The face of the kneeling stranger was set like marble and was
very white; now and then some muscular contraction seemed to
shake his whole frame. His hands had ceased to move, they were
holding tightly the wrists of the wounded soldier; his head was
bent and he was whispering words quite indistinguishable – they
rose and fell like an incantation. Then he was silent; the soldier
watched him in silence and we watched, scarcely daring to breathe,
because of the silence. The set, marble-like face relaxed ever so
slightly. 'Now, Pyotr,' said the stranger's voice, brusque but gay,
'tell me; you feel much better now, don't you?' '*Tak tochno!*
[Exactly so!]' came from the soldier in an almost natural voice.
A hush fell upon our little group; it seemed miraculous that the
pain had ceased to worry the wounded man. Smirnov whispered
in my ear that Alexander Mikhaylovich would never have permitted such a procedure had he known; the other orderlies were
looking on with amusement, not unmixed with awe; here and there,
a soldier lifted up head and shoulders from the crackling straw
and peered at the strangers.

Suddenly and for no apparent reason, the wounded man began to
weep; loud, hysterical weeping, and with the weeping the pain
returned. '*Bolit, oh! bolit* [It hurts],' he moaned. The face above
him tightened visibly and the eyes held those of the soldier as
if in a clamping-vice. Once again a battle of wills raged. 'I have no
will, I have only pain,' the prostrate figure seemed to reveal.
'My will is stronger than pain,' urged the set, white face. An uncanny atmosphere pervaded the building. In Anna's eyes I read
a feeling of strong revulsion. An orderly behind us gave a half-
smothered laugh. After that, things began to lose their significance
and it was evident that the soldier would and could pay no need
to aught else save his own pain; his cries continued as before,
as though nothing had intervened.

The kneeling man rose to his feet; he looked worn-out and immediately left the building, walking with tired, uneven steps,
and leaving a distinctly displeasing impression behind him. '*Chto
eto takoy? Chto eto takoy?* [What's it all about?]' resounded from
different directions. Disapproval was plainly stamped on many faces.
'*Eto ne po-nashemu!* [That is not our custom!]' exclaimed one old
soldier gruffly. It was difficult to explain to those simple-minded men
the power of hypnotism in connection with alleviation of pain, and
I did not attempt it. Besides, there was work waiting to be done.

That evening Anna and I sat together in the garden; our work for the time-being was over. I mentioned the meeting with Stepan Grigoriyevich and the change which had been so quickly wrought in him. She pondered for a while and then 'Poor lad,' she said. 'He was too highly strung, perhaps. And yet how many there are who don't seem to see the horrors.' 'Habit has something to do with it,' I asserted, 'he was fresh to the Front.' 'Somehow, I can't really be glad that habit has such an influence over us,' Anna said, 'but it has, one can't deny it. Do you know, Florence, I have often wondered what it was, and now I know that it *must* be habit – that strange, distant feeling I have when I am bandaging some dreadful wound, or hearing cries of pain. I realise that I see the wounds and hear the cries – and yet they scarcely seem to affect me.' 'Yes', I nodded, 'it has been so with me of late; one hears, one feels, but in a numb, apathetic sort of way – as though all the edge of reality had been smoothed away.'

'Oh yes! indeed it is so,' she cried eagerly, 'I am so glad that you, too, feel the same. It has worried me to think that I was beginning to be less sympathetic to their sufferings, when in reality, I feel so much! Why! a year or two ago, it would have killed me to look on such dreadful wounds.' 'A year or two ago, you were too young for such things,' I pointed out. 'No,' her voice was full of indignation, 'you are wrong. Youth is the bravest of all ages; Youth dares all! No, it was not that I was too young, but that suffering held something very fearful for me. I could never associate suffering with life. It seemed, somehow, to be something quite superfluous – which could be passed by, if one so willed; like a fungus growing on a tree-trunk, which, with a flick of the finger, could be dislodged. And now I realise that life is not all that is beautiful, healthy, strong and true, but that life is – and must be – composed of sorrow and bitterness and suffering, and it is only the manner in which we endure this suffering that can make life beautiful – or hideous.'

'But you, Annushka, you cannot have experienced much trouble?' I queried. 'No,' she replied softly, 'up till now, my life has held much happiness. I have not known the real joy of home-life, because I lost my father in infancy and my mother when I was in my teens, but Grandmother has filled their places so wonderfully that I have never really understood the magnitude of my loss.' She was silent, but I saw that her mind was working fever-

ishly. Then suddenly she said: 'I would never have believed that
I could grow indifferent to pain and grief. In another year's time,
if the war still continues, what shall we be feeling if we feel numb
now?'

'Perhaps it is more merciful so,' I murmured. 'Merciful,' she
cried, 'to be hardened against all compassionate feeling? I would
rather feel the most intense pain and writhe under sorrow as
under a sharp blade than that I should grow callous and indifferent
to human suffering. I shall always pray that I may never look on
the distress of the world with dulled or deadened senses.' I did not
answer, for she was voicing my own feelings.

Then she added in a quieter voice: 'Once, years ago in Smolensk,
my little cousin died. He was only five. My aunt was mad with
grief and I – I cried for days on end, although I was only very
young, but it was my first acquaintance with death, and to me it
seemed so wrong that death could break in and conquer life –
young life – which had only just begun. And this afternoon when
the peasant brought him – that poor little homeless one, for they
are refugees, you know, and haven't even a spade to dig a grave,
I looked at him and he reminded me of my cousin and – strange as
it may seem – I felt *nothing*. He had been ill for more than a week,
the old Father said; of course, it was due to exposure. I lifted
him up on to the stretcher when the orderlies came to bury him;
he was only a feather-weight, there was scarcely anything of him
left. And still I didn't feel anything . . . and I began to be afraid.'

Two armoured cars had been stationed for the last three days in a
corner of the brick-yard; '*Mikhaylovets*' was the name written in
white letters across the iron side of the larger car. The tall figure
of its young captain was often to be seen roaming around, carrying
a tiny black kitten, his mascot, with him; it would lie contentedly
for hours curled up – a black ball of fluff in the hollow of his hand.

It was during the night following the unsuccessful attempt at
hypnotism and my talk with Anna in the garden, that, hearing
some slight commotion outside, I peered through the small
window and saw the two cars quietly making their way across
the yard and turning down the high-road in the direction of the
defence-position.

Two hours later came the order to leave. By the time the
wounded had been despatched and the *Letuchka*'s equipment

packed, it was comparatively light. As our van jogged out of the
yard, a small black object sped suddenly across our path, narrowly
escaping a blow from our horse's hoof, and disappeared like a
streak of lightning into the garden; it was the Captain's little
black kitten! Perhaps he had forgotten it, or it may have strayed
away at the last moment. Simultaneously Anna and I jumped up
in the van and as simultaneously sat down again. It was out of
the question; we dared not cause a delay; our soldiers were withdrawing from their position and the enemy was accelerating his
progress over Russian soil.

*We bivouacked for the night at Golendry, eight versts away. And,
early the next morning, again took to the road, with the Germans
breaking through the Russian defences and swarming across the
country. We halted in Rogatka and opened a first aid station. But
by the middle of the night, we were on the move again.*

19th July. Rymachi

At a large *folvark* we stopped to snatch a hasty breakfast; the
journey was then resumed until we reached Rymachi, which,
we were told, would be our halting-place. Weary and irritable,
we sought refuge in sleep, and no sooner were the tents erected
than each retired to his or her allotted corner.

It was 11 p.m. when the first alarm came. Shouts and cries
broke our much-needed rest. Footsteps hurried past the tent, an
extraordinary light was over everything, the glow penetrated
into the darkest recesses of our tent. 'Fire! Fire!' shouted someone
in the distance, as if to confirm our misgivings. We opened the
tent-flap and in the midnight blackness, a vivid red illumination
could be seen, causing tree and dwelling to stand out in astonishing
relief. A crash of fallen timber and the light around us grew still
brighter; some huts were burning on the outskirts of the village.

'Thank Heaven, it is only a fire!' said one of our Sisters, 'I
thought the Germans had come.' We lay back on our camp-beds
and tried to compose ourselves for sleep. Smirnov's vehement
voice aroused us – his head and shoulders were in the tent; his
face betrayed agitation and alarm. '*Sestritsa, Yuliya Mikhaylovna,
vstavayte, radi Boga, vstavayte poskoreye!* Get up quickly. The whole
village is on fire. Alexander Mikhaylovich orders us to get up at
once and drive off.' The village was on fire in four different places;

there was no doubt that foul play was responsible for the outbreaks.

Alongside a large lake in Rymachi our *Letuchka* drew up and prepared to bivouac for the time-being. We could not completely
leave the village, for no orders had been received, nor could we
remain within its precincts as the burning huts made the roads
almost impassable. The village was larger than average and the
small one-storeyed huts – containing at best only two or three
rooms – were separated one from the other by a miniature garden
or yard. The straw-thatched roofs on these small homesteads
sped the wholesale destruction of the buildings.

From our new halting-place we could see the burning village in
its entirety. Once it had gained strength, the fire spread rapidly
from hut to hut, swallowing everything in its path. Soon the
village was burning on all sides. A strong wind, blowing from
across the lake, lifted up flaming portions of thatch and dropped
them on to neighbouring roofs. These, in their turn, would flare
up until, one by one, the little homes fell victim to the fire.

We stood in an orchard adjoining a heap of smouldering logs
which had once been a home and watched. Groups of mounted
Cossacks galloped up and down the streets at intervals; there
was something cynical in the manner in which they viewed the
holocaust. Our thoughts and prayers were with the homeless
peasantry who were mad with grief and fear. Who had done this?
Whose treacherous hand had destroyed their homes?

It was said that there were soldiers hard at work felling trees
and pulling down sheds in an attempt to prevent the fire from
spreading to the surrounding woodlands; but we did not see any
attempt being made to lessen the fury of the fire. A peasant woman,
old and wrinkled as a fairy-tale witch, stopped near us. Peering
into our faces, she told us with breathless, excited mutterings
that she had seen the villains who had lighted the fire; she had
seen them, she avowed, in the act of igniting a straw thatch.
'*Kazaki oni byli! Nashi ruskiye; svoi ruskiye!* [Cossacks they were!
Our Russians; our own Russians!]' and, she continued, 'What
could the poor and helpless do when their own people turned
against them?'

In the morning we could see the charred remnants of the village.
It was rumoured that two other villages had been burned at the

same time, but had not been utterly laid waste as was the case with
Rymachi. 'German spies!' denounced the soldiers; '*Kazaki!*'
moaned the peasants under their breath. In the fields around they
sat – these forlorn beings, looking towards the site on which
their homes had stood and which was now but a mass of smoking,
smouldering ashes. They sat in groups, surrounded by those
household goods which they had been able to save. We called
them to our Unit, to eat the soup which our mobile kitchens had
prepared for them. They followed us dejectedly, the spirit crushed
out of them, as emotionless as wooden figures. That same day,
many of them set off across the plain, with bundles slung over their
shoulders, driving before them the livestock which still remained
to them.

22nd–24th July
Our Letuchka *continued its journey through Kotsyury and Lyuboml,
where we made our way to the railway station. The 61st Division
were there waiting to entrain for an 'unknown' Front.*

Crowds packed the station premises. Polish gentry and peasantry
thronged the platforms hoping to be lucky enough to get a seat.
Young and old, strong and feeble – they were all there, sitting,
standing, lying. The peasant class predominated, but here and
there among the rough, white-linen tunics of the men and the
coloured head-scarves of the women were gathered small groups
of the gentry. They kept to themselves, their feelings well under
control. They were, I knew, a proud, noble people, whose lives
had been embittered and estates harassed for many a century by
pitiless, arrogant neighbours. They stood or sat on improvised
seats, melancholy little groups, all in dark clothes and many of
the women in hats and veils. Trunks, boxes, bundles, bags and
packages made formidable barricades along the platform.

Some of the peasants had spread out their sacks and were sitting
on, or leaning against them, trying to sleep, but for most sleep was
out of the question. We were told that many of them had been on
the station for three days already, and the appearance of a train
always renewed the hope that a seat might at last be found for
themselves and belongings. One passenger train had already been
that day, we were told, and another was expected before morning.

It might be the last . . . no one knew! And a disquieting rumour
had it that the station was soon to be closed to civilians.

On returning to the *Letuchka*, we received the news that Warsaw
had fallen to the enemy. We were told not to undress as our
journey would be resumed at 3 a.m. Forty-five versts were to be
traversed in *pokhodnym poryadke* [regular marching order] for
the roads were very uneven. Despite those bad roads and the
bumps and bruises which we sustained on their account in our
dvukolka, we, my two companions and I, managed to sleep away
the first few hours of our long journey, until we stopped for a
brief respite on the banks of the large and lovely Lake Zgorany.
Around and near the lake refugees were living. Children ran about
half-naked; camp-fires were burning; women sat crooning their
babies to sleep. 'Gypsies!' one would have commented with
conviction a few months previously. But now half the countryside
had become gypsies.

We halted for lunch at Polshchero, and then took to the road once
more until we reached our destination, Adamchuki. Before we
fell asleep that night, we unanimously agreed that nothing and
no one could force us to relinquish our night's rest. Feeling particularly obdurate, I heard myself insist more than once: 'As for
me, I will not stir from my bed this night, even if the Kaiser
himself enter our tent!' And Mamasha's drowsy voice admonished
me: 'It's quite nice, Florence, to hear that you have so much
spirit left in you; you sound most emphatic!'

24th–28th July
We stopped at Zaleze to eat the delicious cold cutlets which
Mamasha had prepared for us. We ate them sitting on the grass
in the sunshine, like children at a picnic, without thought for
propriety or manners, and we watched each other's cheeks redden
and tan under the sun's rays.

A fine iron bridge leading into Vlodava stretched across the
River Bug which sparkled and dimpled in the sunlight. In the
distance we could see the golden cupolas of the Russian Orthodox
church and the tapering spire of the Polish *Kosciol* rising above the
less important town-buildings. Up a steep, winding hill we climbed
and came into full view of the railway station; seen from this

height, it looked small and insignificant, but one glimpse was sufficient to prove that it was pulsating with life and movement.

Dotted about the surrounding plains were innumerable encampments – military and civilian – while directly alongside the station premises there were three clusters of large white tents. As we drew nearer we saw that the first group of tents was given over to bread-baking. A number of men were stacking newly baked loaves of black bread in piles on to *telezhki* which stood in a row by the tents. The bread was bundled just as it was into the dirty-looking conveyances, and lay there, without covering, exposed to the dust and scorching sun. When the carts were loaded, the driver jumped up on to the narrow, front plank which served as a seat, while a couple of soldiers clambered up behind and actually installed themselves, sitting or reclining, on the freshly baked loaves.

The second collection of tents belonged to the 1st Red Cross *Otryad* of the *Zemski Soyuz*, which, organised as a 'feeding station', was daily supplying food to hundreds of the poorest refugees encamped in its proximity. The remaining group of tents was in the hands of a Red Cross Unit which superintended the admission to – and transportation from – the station of the wounded soldiers. Several trains were standing in the station, and, conspicuous among them, one of the beautifully equipped hospital-trains of the Tsaritsa, Alexandra Feodorovna; each long white carriage bore the name of its august patroness, and the red cross shone in scarlet brilliance on wall and roof.

A bivouac for our *Letuchka* near the station was out of the question and we drove on. Finally, we were called to a halt in a wood near the village of Komarovka; two days were spent in that wood in perpetual expectation of an official call to entrain and, had it not been for a heavy rain which went on for twenty-four hours without stopping, we might even have been able to extract some enjoyment out of those idle, relaxed hours. Contradictory messages arrived at intervals from our Staff Headquarters, indicating a state of disordered opinions and decisions quite incredible. Little could be gleaned as to the progress of operations at the Front, but we knew that no good news was forthcoming. During the third night the rumble of heavy gun-fire broke ominously on our ears: nor were we greatly surprised when, a few hours later, the tidings reached us that, because of the rapid advance of the enemy

upon Vlodava, all idea of entraining our Unit from that station
would have to be abandoned. Brest-Litovsk was now to be the
chosen location for our departure to another Front.

The tents were taken down and packed away; we sat under the
trees and waited for the *dvukolki* to appear. In the usual military
marching-order we jogged down the highroad – a long line of
cars, vans, wagons, carts, all belonging to our 1st Flying Column of
the 10th Detachment of the *Zemstvo*. The road was already filling
fast with divers regiments and companies, followed by their individual baggage-trains, all making for the same destination – Brest.

After a tedious drive of some twenty-three versts, we stopped at
Leplyovka for supper. Only once were we obliged to halt en
route. An ambulance van broke down in our path and one of the
three cholera patients narrowly escaped being run over by one
of our baggage-wagons. The shock of finding himself suddenly
thrown out on to the hard road and directly under horses' hooves
caused him to faint and, to our anxious eyes, it looked as though
he had been killed, but, a little later, to our great relief he opened
his eyes. Some women who were mending the road came towards
us and helped the soldiers push aside the débris of the broken van,
and the three men were immediately consigned to other places
in the ambulance-train which proved to be composed only of
cholera patients. At the first mention of cholera, it was noticeable
how the soldiers who had, from curiosity, gathered round the fainting man, quickly drew back and disappeared. Not so the women:
their faces were alight with sympathy for the sufferers and they
sought to comfort them by placing armfuls of straw under their
heads and by tucking their military coats more securely around
their feet. This done, they shouldered their spades and pickaxes
and resumed their work with the large heaps of rock and stone at
the roadside. Strange specimens of womanhood they were, with
their square, squat figures, weather-beaten faces, thickset legs
and shapeless bare feet, but not one of us who had been an onlooker was untouched by those simple acts of homage towards
their suffering countrymen.

29th July, Brest-Litovsk–1st August, Belostok
Between sleeping and waking, between strange troubled dreams
and fitful periods of consciousness – ever accompanied by the

screeching of rolling wheels and the incessant hoot of passing motor-vehicles – the night of 28th July was passed on the straw mattress of our mobile bed. At length we peered through the flaps of our canvas hood and saw stretched before us in the near distance the ancient town of Brest-Litovsk – our destination! Despite the early hour, activity and commotion were visible on all sides. The roads, tracks, paths, all leading towards the town, were cluttered with moving forms and vehicles. Men, clad in the sombre brown-green of the Russian military uniform, were working here, there, in all directions, boring into the earth, digging with astonishing vigour, setting up strange, ponderous earthworks, excavating hollow underground shelters. Like so many mechanical manikins were these men, alert and agile, keenly alive to the fact that the fortifications which they were creating might prove the salvation of their historic town from a hostile enemy. Beyond these new lines of defence and dugout lay the capacious, formidable stronghold of the fortress which had come to the rescue of the old Slav town at many a critical stage in its past. The cannon were in position – their long, hollow nozzles turned towards the west.

We pulled up outside the town and breakfasted in the shady orchard of a Jewish house. Our intrusion gave cause for much noisy controversy amongst the members of the family and loud, querulous voices were heard from within, disputing and contending in a curious nasal jargon. Then figures appeared in the doorway; at first they studied us from a distance, evidently awe-struck by our numbers; then, gathering courage, they approached by degrees until we had a silent row of spectators within a dozen yards of our improvised breakfast table. Having satisfied their curiosity, the elders withdrew, but the youngsters stood as if glued to the spot, contemplating us in silence and only rarely exchanging a whispered remark among themselves. We slept for a while in the shade of the apple trees, under the mistrustful guard of the inquisitive children until Alexander Mikhaylovich appeared with the news that we were not leaving until that evening; in reply to our request, he permitted us to motor into Brest on a shopping expedition.

We hadn't seen such shops since leaving Moscow and the variety of goods was a delight. Well satisfied with our purchases we were 'homeward bound', motoring slowly in and out of the heavy traffic, for the streets were teeming with life and animation, when to our astonishment, we saw a long line of *dvukolki* and baggage-wagons belonging to our *Letuchka*. It slowly drew nearer and its mounted vanguard-supervisor reined in his horse to explain that the hour of entrainment had been altered and that we must make for the station with all possible speed. It was quite half-an-hour before the car could turn, and some time more before we finally reached the station and were packed safely on to the train. It was a goods-train and a single carriage had been apportioned to the surgical personnel. We stowed away our hand-luggage in the Sisters' coupé and sat down to await the signal for our departure. An hour passed, two, three hours; what were we waiting for? Surely the Unit's equipment had been securely loaded by now?

The unexpected appearance in our midst of Alexander Ivanovich, our Plenipotentiary, raised a volley of eager questioning and with dismay we learnt that our breathless bustle and rush had been in vain, for the train was not to leave before the early morning hours. Another important piece of news was that the destination now chosen for us was not the Caucasian Front, nor the North German Front, but Belostok, an old Polish town about 130 versts from Brest-Litovsk. The arrival of the 2nd *Letuchka* of our Red Cross Detachment, en masse, outside the station quickly dispelled our gloom and before many minutes had passed the compartments of our carriage were crowded with familiar faces and ringing with merry voices. It was a happy meeting; we had not seen each other for several weeks. I was especially glad to meet my countrywoman Elizabeth Hopper again, and to slip into an easy conversation in my mother-tongue.

When night came, the members of the 2nd *Letuchka* left us to install themselves on straw on the platform. For several hours we slept peacefully, but, about 6 a.m., our train awoke, gave a mighty lurch forward, and slowly steamed out of the station. One and all of us seemed to be conscious of the fact that we had at last started on our journey. '*Poyekhal!* [Started!]' murmured sleepy voices. '*Poyekhal!*' I repeated to myself, and sleep took on an added enchantment under the soothing influence of the rhythmical roll of the wheels.

Upon rising the next morning, we found that about 100 versts of our journey still remained to be covered. Our train dragged along at a painful pace, stopping at every station for long, intermediary halts. On one station we made the acquaintance of three Red Cross Sisters who had been in the Retreat from Warsaw. One of them was Japanese, but spoke fluent Russian and was serving in a Russian Red Cross Unit. The elder of her companions described some of their experiences and spoke with horror of the poisonous gas employed by the Germans. In one district near Warsaw, she said, there was a field the memory of which could never be erased. It was heaped with the bodies of soldiers who had been gassed and the terrible positions of the men in death added to the ghastly spectacle: she had heard that over 6,000 men had been forced to *vyyte iz stroya* [fall out of formation] that day from gas alone.

At 4 o'clock the next morning our train-journey came to an end, and within an hour or two after having been awakened from sleep we were on the road again. We camped that day at Batzechi where Dr Ivan Nikolayevich told us that he had news of much importance to discuss with us. . . . He told us that the Regiments of the 62nd Division were already in the trenches, *that* we knew, but what we did not know was that marching-orders had come for us to leave at 4 a.m. on the following day! The situation at the Front was critical, he explained, the whole length of the Russian Line was slowly giving way under the overwhelming pressure of enemy forces. Thousands of homeless people were at large about the countryside; food-supplies and prices were causing great concern, for stores were growing scanty and prices were becoming higher; the chief towns of Russia were seething with unrest; around St Petersburg, it was rumoured, new fortifications were in progress. The doctor paused for a few moments and then continued: in the south things were no better; General Ruski, who had been appointed in Radko Dmitriyev's place, as Commander-in-Chief of the Galician Front, had been heard to say that, if the worst came to the worst, 'we shall defend Kiyev'. Ammunition was plentiful – somewhere about the country – but at the Front it was lacking. Even means of transport were daily growing more limited.

1st August
It was raining a little as we started our journey at 4 a.m. We were glad to be going into the thick of it again; it was so seldom these days that we journeyed with our faces turned in the direction of the reddening skies and the barking guns. We were a long line

of swaying, white-hooded vans; the heavy baggage-wagons had been left behind at Batsechki for the time-being; on and on we drove, but no signs of our division. Enquiries were made here and there, but all to no purpose. Soldiers were often to be seen, some working, some resting, so we jolted onwards in quest of someone who could supply information respecting our regiments. Soon the uniformed men became fewer, only at intervals we came across Cossacks, stationed singly, as if on sentry duty. Finally, we drove into a wood and the wheels and horses' hooves sank lightly into the soft, marshy track. All was very still; the guns had ceased to speak, even the trees around us seemed strangely silent; not far away, the wood lightened and, in a couple of minutes, we should be in the open again. A figure blocked our path – a sentry,

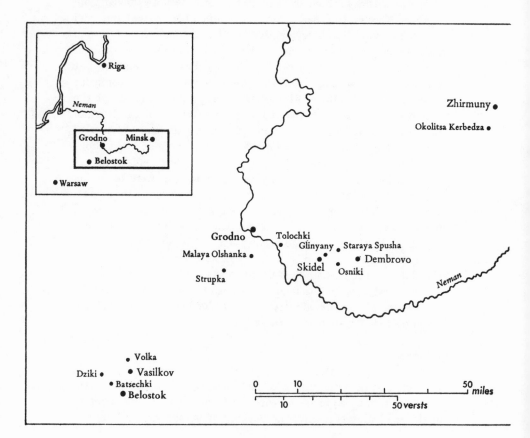

with upraised arm. In an undertone, he demanded the password; then began a heated dialogue, still in a whisper, with the Brother who, as vanguard, led our train of vehicles, on horseback. There was a flourish of pointing fingers and gesturing arms; then suddenly, in the twinkling of an eye, the foremost *dvukolka* turned and drove past us; our van followed and soon we were all hastening helter-skelter out of the wood: all unwittingly we had driven within one hundred yards of the Front Line. The driver and occupants of the first *dvukolka* professed they had even seen the trenches on the outskirts of the wood – and our soldiers in them! Over plates of hot soup, the maps were brought out and carefully studied – we had gone 24 versts out of our prescribed route.

Another interesting feature of that memorable drive was our

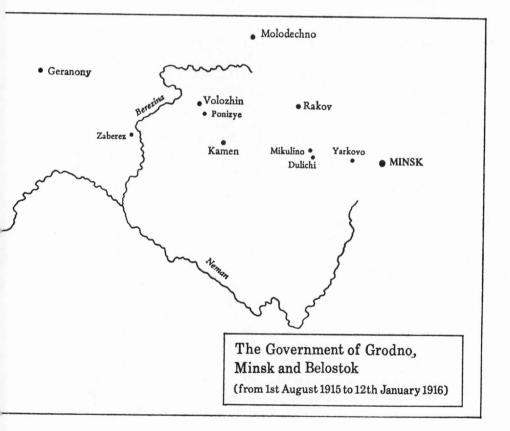

The Government of Grodno, Minsk and Belostok
(from 1st August 1915 to 12th January 1916)

discovery of an Austrian 'Lager', or prisoner-camp. With remarkable lack of military foresight, the Grodno Government
had been selected as a suitable locality for the internment-camp
of no fewer than 3,000 Austrians. The prisoners were employed
in repairing roads, digging trenches, setting up wire-entanglements,
etc., and although their comrades in arms were but a short distance
away and still advancing, the expedience of their removal to a
more distant camp had not even been considered. The Cossacks
who were in control of the camp seemed to think, however, that
there was little cause for alarm; the prisoners were friendly and
docile, they explained, and far from attempting to free themselves
from their captors, they learnt with considerable trepidation of
the gradual advance of their 'Allies', and were not at all anxious
for an encounter with them.

3rd–9th August. Dziki

At a further distance of three versts we stopped at the village of
Dziki, where we found our friends the doctors of the divisional
Otryad already installed and awaiting us. Dziki, a village of
considerable size, proved to be friendly towards us in every way
except one: every morning we rose and dressed to the sound of
falling rain and every evening we were lulled to sleep by the
weeping skies. So accustomed did we grow to the weather that
after a time we scarcely noticed the steady downpour of rain on
our heads; when a *kosinka* [head-veil] became too saturated with
rain, there was always a dry one at hand, and the wettest garment
dried – to a certain extent – overnight. Somebody told us that
Dziki was built on marshland and never experienced hot, dry
weather for any length of time. Marshland there certainly was in
plenty and innumerable ponds and rambling streams everywhere
in and around the village. Some of the ponds were the home of
water-lilies and large yellow flowers of the kingcup species.

One of our orderlies was particularly good at collecting the most
beautiful lilies from these ponds. He had never been taught to
swim, but felt at home in water, having been accustomed to it all
his life; he never dried his clothes what with the rain and pond-
wading – in which he indulged daily. The water-lilies made a
beautiful table-decoration and our dining-room, arranged under
apple-trees, was never without an abundance of them. Soon
after our arrival at Dziki, a small fawn had been given to us – a

lovely little creature and remarkably tame. Gazelle, as she was called, was discovered more than once nibbling at the white petals which adorned our table.

The rain and thick night-fogs took their toll of victims, nevertheless, and the number of sick among the soldiers billeted in the village rapidly increased. Apart from the Sister on duty, another Sister was appointed daily to help with the out-patients, among whom were three of our own orderlies and a hospital-Brother whose condition gave our doctors much cause for worry. There were few wounded, the enemy had apparently called a temporary halt in the offensive, while the shortage of ammunition gave our soldiers no choice in the matter of initiative.

The 33rd Siberian Regiment of the 9th Corps, which had been severely cut up, was now arriving back at the Front with renewed strength. They took over a section of the Line on the right flank of our Regiments and many tales were told of their daring. One or two of the Sibiryaks had even penetrated into the German trenches and brought back strange mementoes, but one of their chief delights was to irritate and badger the enemy into a bad humour. Effigies of German magnates were set up in prominent places on no-man's land; bells were hung on barbed-wire entanglements and pealed at intervals by means of string connected with the Russian trenches, and over and over 'Guerman' would fall prey to these devices, and volley after volley would come sweeping through the air, testifying to the condition of Teutonic nerves.

Our evenings were spent quietly with our divisional doctors and regimental officers who came to talk or play cards. One of the officers of the Mariupolski Regiment, Alexander Vasiliyevich, had a beautiful voice, and when he was there with his guitar we spent the whole time singing or listening to him perform.

Our goat Vaska was undergoing an operation. From the sound of those frantic bleatings it was as if an entire herd of goats were being tortured mercilessly. We hastened to the origin of the distressing sounds: there, within the tent, lay Vaska; held on the ground by two sturdy orderlies of the Divisional Unit, while the Head Surgeon bent over him with small surgical scissors in his hand. Besides him stood Petya, a young medical student who had just come from University in St Petersburg for a month or two of practical training, holding sterilised pieces of lint at the end of

long pincer-like tongs. There had been a slight accident and poor
Vaska had been run over; he had escaped great injury, but one
of his hind legs had been partially crushed. The operation completed, Pyotr Andreyevich rose; '*Gotovo!* [Finished],' he said, and
Vaska slipped from the hands of his tormentors and sped off as
best he could on three legs, his bandaged hoof held carefully away
from the ground.

Pyotr Andreyevich's handsome face was shining with pleasure.
'*Zaftra poyedu domoy* [Tomorrow I am going home],' he said,
answering our enquiring glances. 'I applied for leave some weeks
ago, and at last it has been arranged that the doctors shall take
it in turn. They say that I am to start the list. Naturally, I am
not against a month's holiday in the Crimea!' 'Wise man,' laughed
Mamasha, a little mocking note distinct in her voice. 'Perhaps
in a month's time we shall all be in the Crimea.' 'How is that?'
he answered quickly. 'Do you really think that the Retreat will
now soon continue?' and, in a more thoughtful voice: 'If I
imagined that *that* would be the case, I should not go away. But
it seems to me quite possible that, in a month's time, I shall come
back to you in Dziki!' 'Time will show!' Mamasha threw the
words back to him from over her shoulder, and walked briskly
away.

The following day Pyotr Andreyevich left for his home in the
Crimea; with him he took the fawn – a parting gift from Mamasha
(to whom, by the way, the fawn had not been given), who vowed
that 'Gazelle would be infinitely happier in the sunny south than
sharing in our hardships behind the fighting-line in the North'.
Of course, she was right; nevertheless, we who were very fond of,
and had a share in, the lovable little creature, were sorry to part
with it.

Two hours after the departure of Pyotr Andreyevich, a change took
place on the Front. The stuttering of machine-guns and the
plop-plop of musket fire raged throughout the evening. As night
fell the cannonade increased. 'The enemy is attacking,' we told
each other, and the Sister-on-duty stood outside the dressing-tent
watching intently the long, uneven road which led from the
pozitsiya.

Before we retired for the night, restlessness had descended upon
us all and the sure knowledge that a crisis was at hand weighed

heavily upon our minds. We stood under the apple trees in our orchard listening to the roar of the guns and conjuring up mental pictures of the ghastly scenes being enacted near our defence lines, and of the disastrous results which might befall our men and their homeland. An officer, followed by two mounted soldiers, came down the road; he pulled in slightly as he passed the orchard and dimly outlined among the tree-trunks we could see his silhouette. 'Goodbye, my Sisters; God be with you!' He was gone, but we recognised his voice. It was Alexander Vasiliyevich. He was on his way to the Front Line.

The next day the wounded came or were brought to us; we sorted them out, bandaged some, sent others to the Base; a few died in transit – for them a resting-place was made by our orderlies under the shady branches of an apple tree. Evening came and still the uncanny hush prevailed and then – at 1 o'clock of the new day – we were told! We had expected it, so there was no fuss; quietly and collectedly, we gathered together our belongings and took our seats in the *dvukolki* standing silently along the roadside; and off we trundled into the darkness.

9th August. Zdroya

An officer we knew from the Bakhchisaray Regiment, spoke of the pitiable plight of the men in the trenches. Their clothes were torn and filthy, many were without boots; water and food were scarce. He related an incident he'd seen: A party of wounded soldiers was walking along the highroad when a general in a car drew up and began a scathing interrogation. Most of the men were dreadful to look upon – dirty, unkempt, with blood on their hands and faces. '*Merzavets!* [Villain!]' he shouted at one man. 'Where are thy boots?' The soldier, with green, grey face and blood-stains on his shirt, made answer in a weak, scarcely audible voice; the general, suddenly enraged, rose from his seat and struck the man full in the face with his gloved fist. Not a sound from the soldiers. The car sped on and the tired feet, booted and bootless, trudged on their way.

He went on: 'Our soldiers are simply heroes. Look how they are fighting. The trenches are badly made – they're quite unworthy of the name of trench, for they are just burrows, some of them not even an *arshin** in depth. The sappers hadn't time to finish

*1 *arshin* = 28 inches.

them was the excuse and we have to pass on this abominable lie
to our men.'

That evening I was sent to a peasant's hut to buy fruit. The door
was open and a tall soldier – a Cossack – stood just inside. *'Zhal
tebya, papasha* [I pity you, little Papa],' he was saying. 'I very
much pity you, but an order is an order, and it would be worse
for you if *he* were to come here.' He turned about, saw me and
saluted, then left.

The peasant and his wife had not noticed my entrance, nor did
they seem aware of my presence. They were standing as if turned
to stone, looking through the doorway in the direction in which
the Cossack had gone. 'Janek,' I heard the woman murmur.
Janek was the name of her son, who, I had heard, was somewhere
on the Front. I could sense calamity in the air, but I had to give
my message, so I asked, quietly: 'Have you had news of Janek?'
Then they saw me; the woman turned away so that her face was
hidden; the old man lurched heavily backwards and dropped down
on to the wooden bench.

'Prosze, Panya [Please, lady!],' he said hoarsely, 'the Cossack
tells us that we shall have to go away from here . . . we must pack
. . . we must be ready to leave. Please, lady! What can we do?
Where can we go?' Then I understood. The man looked at me with
haggard face and burning eyes, the woman came towards me,
opened her arms beseechingly, but spoke no word. In the corner,
near the brick stove, the ancient mother was standing, with bowed
head, crying softly into her folded hands. Flies buzzed about me,
settling on to my face and hands; the smell of potatoes, boiled in
their skins, pervaded the room. Outside, a cart lumbered down the
road, the soldier-driver was singing snatches of a song. Suddenly
the old man rose from the bench; his bowed head was raised and
there was a wonderful composure in his face. I saw, too, that
there was that in his eyes which spoke plainly of the solving of a
grave problem. And this is what he said: 'One is born once and
one must die once. It is the Will of God. We are in God's Hands!'
That was all, but the whole scene changed. The woman looked
at her husband and her drawn face relaxed; she repeated his words,
crossed herself and bowed low before the icons on the wall. The
little old mother lifted up her head and, taking a wire skewer,
prodded the potatoes boiling over the fire. I slipped from the

hut and returned to the hay-shed; I could not find it in my heart to ask for pears or plums.

Late in the evening I heard them busy in their hut, the man appeared several times carrying boxes and pots and pans over to a barn near which a *telega* stood. I went over to them; could I help them? I asked. They thanked me, but no! they were nearly ready. The peasant and his wife had – to all appearances – become quite reconciled to the idea of departure; only the ancient mother moaned and drooped as if in pain. More than once she came and stood on the threshold of her home, looking out into the night and listening to the silence, broken only by an occasional explosion in the far distance. Once the sky lit up with a warm red glow; '*Chto eto?* [What is that?]' she asked in a frightened whisper. I told her that it was probably a fire somewhere on the *pozitsiya*. She leaned her head against the door-support and wept long and silently.

Four sharp attacks were made in the night by the enemy and were repulsed by our men. The ambulance-vans arrived early in the morning and, after depositing their load of wounded, made their way back to the Front. Some hundred or so walking cases had gathered outside our dressing-tent and were lying about on the ground, awaiting their turn, for, as usual, the stretcher-cases claimed our immediate attention. One man walked slowly up to me in the tent; I told him: 'You must go outside and await your turn.' He said nothing, but lifted up his blackened shirt and showed his left hand supporting a mass of his own intestines which had spilled out from a cruel gash in his abdomen. In that condition he had walked nearly three versts!

Among the severely wounded, head injuries were the most numerous. At one time I had thought it a most terrible thing to have a man's brains bespattering my hands and white overall; but, as the Retreat continued, I grew accustomed to it. No fewer than three instances of wounds caused by a *razryvnaya pulya* [dumdum bullet] came to our notice that day – for the first time in our Front-Line work. In two of three cases, several small particles of metal were extracted from the wounds; they proved without doubt that they had belonged to those barbaric explosive bullets. We had heard that other Red Cross Units had found similar cases among their wounded. Alexander Mikhaylovich gathered the new scraps of evidence together, for a protest was already being drawn up by the most prominent of Russia's surgical officers, and these fragments would add to the evidence which clearly indicated that the Germans were using these small but deadly projectiles.

By the evening, the number of wounded had decreased; soon the last walking-case had been bandaged and discharged. The peasant and the women had left their home in the morning; the hut was standing open and desolate. The icons, cooking utensils, bed quilts, stores of vegetables, fruit and grain, had all disappeared; only the empty bed, the stove, the wooden benches round the wall remained.

Shrapnel was crackling and flashing all evening on the outskirts of our village, but Ivan Nikolayevich, our acknowledged *nachalnik* [head] of prospective journeyings, had informed us that we should not be leaving Zdroya before 7 o'clock the following morning. Seizing the seemingly favourable opportunity, I determined to develop my several exposed photographic plates which had accumulated during the last few days and to refill the cases. One of the empty rooms in the peasant hut afforded excellent accommodation as a darkroom, for the tiny windows were easily draped and darkened. Three plates had been developed and were in their salt bath, the fourth was in the developer, when a loud tapping on the door was heard and Ivan Nikolayevich's voice called me to pack and leave my occupation without delay – we were to start within five minutes! It seemed incredible! I looked ruefully at the precious wet plates, but alas, war has never been an obliging field-day.

Through the grim, dark night we drove and in the village of Belusi we found accommodation for a few hours' rest; a peasant-woman, two small children and three little pigs shared the room with us. It was raining outside and the tents were not allowed to be unpacked otherwise we would willingly have slept in the open air; however, in spite of the discomforts which were legion, we were thankful to have a roof over our heads. The woman, very obligingly, took herself and the children off to the flat surface of the stove and invited us to share the wooden bed; we looked at the old sheepskin counterpane and shook our heads decisively. The narrow bench looked less disquieting and with a little care it would be possible to lodge on it in such a manner as to insure a few minutes' sleep. But sleep was out of the question – not even for a few minutes; we had scarcely settled down before the woman rose and commenced cleaning out the stove and preparing the fire to cook the potato-cakes for breakfast. The children fidgeted and cried; the pigs squeaked in chorus – so much for our night's rest.

With the new day, sunshine came into a world washed clean by the night's downpour; it aroused a better and more congenial spirit within us. But in a few hours we were again called to resume our journey. On and on we ambled until night again enveloped us, and still the long line of *dvukolki* and wagons swayed forward, though constantly impeded by the ever-increasing traffic.

The morning mists were showing grey and indistinct over the landscape as we stopped outside the large *Folvark Volka*; here, for a couple of hours at least we might rest. As the mist lifted the sun came out and lit up the fields of ripening corn. On some of the corn-plots, soldiers and peasants were actively engaged in cutting the corn and binding it together in sheaves; each assisting the other to garner the grain, lest the harvest fall into the hands of enemy reapers. In the orchard the fruit was ripening speedily; everywhere the harvest was at hand. How sad was the thought that this countryside was soon to be overrun by a hostile people!

The news was indeed bad. Osnovetz*, Kovno†, Novo Georgiyevski had been given up to the Germans; Belostok had just fallen and Vilna was said to be evacuating. If today brought us these lamentable reports what would tomorrow bring? As the German hordes swept over the land, they found large supplies of food and fodder everywhere awaiting them and their animals; the reaping of that vast harvest on Poland's fruitful ground had been given into their hands. What could be taken, or destroyed by our men and the peasantry at this eleventh hour, had been, but it was an insignificant trifle in comparison with the broad, fertile acres of grain, and of vegetables and fruit land, left to the foe. And when would the advance be checked? When would the retreat be ended? Those were the questions which we could read in each other's eyes, but no one answered, because no answer could be found. . . .

*Polish-Russian frontier fort.
†Kovno – Lithuanian fort.

Supper came – and with it orders to leave! 'Give us an hour or
two to sleep,' said discontented voices. As I climbed into the
dvukolka, a soldier, passing at that moment, held out something
towards me. 'Take it, *Sestritsa*,' he entreated. 'I found him, he
is ill.' He put a little rabbit into my hand; one of its paws was
swollen and the little creature was shivering with fright. I covered
it over with hay inside the van; it looked like a small brown mouse,
curled up in the corner; so then and there we christened it
Myshka.

The roads were in a terrible condition and in the darkness any
attempt to keep clear of the large stones which were littered
about was out of the question; we were knocked, bruised and
thrown in all directions. The groans and sighs emanating from
the vans preceding and following us proved that we were not the
only sufferers – but it is a noteworthy fact that Kouzmin, our driver,
slept at least three-quarters of the journey, despite the continuous
shaking and convulsive jerking of our small vehicle.

17th August. Strupka

The village of Strupka was pleasant to look upon, despite the
squalor of the poor huts, and its inhabitants were picturesque,
despite their poverty. They showed a spirited will of their own
in their determination to extract payment from those soldiers
who were intent on despoiling their small gardens of carefully
cultivated produce. Wrangling and loud arguments in peasant
vernacular constantly reached our ears, and the soldiers invariably
came out of the contest with downcast air and a sheepish look
on their faces. We were not sorry to see the peasants carry their
point to such a good result, for it had long been a topic of heated
discussion amongst the medical men of our Unit as to the most
emphatic way one could bring home to the soldier-orderlies that
the peasants – their own kith and kin – must not be robbed
wholesale in the outrageous manner which had, of late, been in
vogue. If the gardens had been abandoned, all well and good,
but – our doctors dictated – while the owners occupied their
premises, permission should at least be asked.

Whether the soldiers would not, or could not, understand, it
was difficult to say, but there was no doubt that the bad habits
acquired in the conquered territory in Galicia were still with them.
When approached on the subject, very few of them could explain

why they had found it possible to plunder the gardens of the Ruthenian peasantry, and why it was a thing unpardonable to strip the gardens of their fellow-countrymen. 'No,' was their stubborn reply. 'We are soldiers, and soldiers are allowed to do so.' And when they found that this absurdly stupid reasoning brought the house down over their heads, they resorted to yet another excuse: 'Why is it forbidden to us Russian soldiers?' they asked perversely. 'If we don't have them, the German soldiers will.'

Soon we were on the move again, this time to Grodno, one of Russia's most ancient strongholds.

By the time we arrived in the fortification-zone the moonlight was almost as bright as day. The massed rows of wire entanglements glittered. We passed line after line of trenches whose solid, well built look gave us confidence. Dugouts, with blindage sheeting, lined the roadside; lights shone in the apertures which served as windows; now and again the head of a soldier was to be seen, trying to catch a glimpse of our passing cortège; or a figure, sitting outside his earth-house, blissfully enjoying his *makhorka* and exhaling thin wreaths of smoke into the night air.

We drove slowly between two forts and eagerly craned our necks to see all that there was to be seen: strangely-shaped earthworks; long dark lines of iron-clad balustrades; mysterious passages winding in and out of streamlined trenches; a connected series of tier-like platforms ranged along cavernous holes on a hillside, looking for all the world like a series of well-formed rabbit burrows, or the front-doors to the underground homes of a community of troglodytes. Here and there were the dark silhouettes of cannon; the strange outlines of artillery parks; a group or two of soldiers; the alert figures of armed sentries.

But all around that great fortress a remarkable silence reigned. Something akin to disappointment came over us; this was not what we had been expecting to find. Where was the zealous energy? and where the strenuous effort and tireless labour? Daylight would surely present a different picture. We reminded ourselves of the gratifying rumour, circulated from Staff Head-quarters, that this sudden falling back of the Russian Front to the Grodno Line held great strategic importance. 'Invulnerable' was the epithet which had been freely applied to Grodno's famous fortress. . . .

However, despite Grodno's boasted invulnerability and its definite historic renown, news came that it was to be given up to the Germans without a struggle.

17th August
During the evening we were given permission to visit some of Grodno's forts. At Fort Seven we found that which we had unconsciously sought on the previous evening: a confused activity, excited energy, a thronging and a hurrying which plainly indicated that an operation of great consequence and pressure was being carried out. The guns had already been removed, their platforms stood bare and desolate. Cases of powerful explosives were stacked on one side; wires were being drawn around the concrete masonry which encircled the fort, while others were being threaded through the main subterranean passages; all in preparation for the coming destruction of the fortifications. One by one the forts were to be destroyed – by the same men who had built them.

The soldiers themselves felt to the full all that the task implied; some of them were quite heart-broken. One old soldier's voice shook with suppressed emotion and his eyes grew watery as he related how he had watched the growth and development of that same fort during the several years of its construction, and now, the space of one short minute would be enough to pull it down entirely. It was hard, he agreed, more than hard, but the High Command had sent urgent orders and who should know better than they what would be best for the Mother-Country?

We walked through a subterranean passage and mounted some iron steps leading to an iron-clad gallery. Looking through slits cut in the armoured sides of the wall, we could command a wide view of the countryside around. Below the parapets spread a broad, winding ribbon of wires interlaced and twisted in intricate fashion – they were electrified. Beyond them were trenches, connected with the fort by means of underground communication passages, then wire entanglements, and again trenches with other wire barricades. To the right, to the left, there were other forts. Away to our right, on the northern side, we could see the outline of forts Three and Four. Over these two, endless numbers of small shells were bursting; sometimes a cloud of thick, dark smoke would rise suddenly from within their walls and a dull thud would be heard. The Germans had their guns already within range; doubtless, before long, No. Seven would hear the low, hissing warning of approaching destruction.

We were startled from sleep in the early morning by a terrific explosion. Our first thoughts were for the Grodno forts, and we were not a little surprised to learn that only a bridge had been blown up. Later, a party of sappers tramped by, after a long night's work; they had had no bread since the previous morning and had been informed that their purveyance intendant was not now in a position to supply them with rations. Mamasha quickly settled the matter by sending for a dozen loaves of black bread from our kitchen-wagons.

It was a free morning and a fine morning and the temptation to take some photographs of the forts could not be resisted. Armed with camera, tripod and plates, with Anna as an interested and willing companion, I set out. Many houses, sheds, granaries and military buildings were being fired about the districts out-lying Grodno. A long row of barracks behind a fort was blazing fiercely, the strong wind fanning the flames to a white heat. Out-side one fort we were stopped by a sentry who refused us entrance on the ground that the fort had been deserted and was already wired for the explosion. At another we were allowed to enter, but were accompanied by an old veteran and told which paths might be considered safe. The fort was empty, only here and there a soldier stood as sentry; the low, winding breast-works looked sullen and resentful in their desertion. Shells were still falling thickly on the western and northern forts; there was no doubt that the enemy was determined to waste no time in gaining possession of the town and fortress.

When the summons came to us to withdraw, it came quickly and, as usual, during the hours of darkness. It was near midnight and we were sleeping when Ivan Nikolayevich called us to be 'up and away'. Ten minutes, he shouted, was the time-limit given us to prepare ourselves and our belongings for the journey. His voice was hoarse and excited; instinctively we knew that the news was bad, but he was gone and it would be useless to recall him.

A Brother, who came hurrying up to assist in carrying our

hand-luggage to the *dvukolki*, gave us some information. The
Germans were pressing in on Grodno with unexpected strength;
everything and everybody fell before them. At any moment the
worst might happen and our 1st Army be surrounded; it was
rumoured that in all probability it might be found necessary to
sacrifice the 38th Corps, to which our 62nd Division was attached.
In our vicinity, only one bridge over the Neman was left intact,
but it was to be destroyed before the night was over. Would we
reach it in time?

A cold high wind was blowing; with every gust of air which
blew through and around me, a fresh picture of warfare unfolded
itself. The hopelessness of the Russian military situation came
vividly to my mind. How dreadful it all was! This continual running away; the ever-present fear that the enemy would suddenly
spring up in our midst; the utter lack of resistance and the complex
futility of all resistance. What was wrong? And if there were
wrong, who could right it? In the background, the outline of the
doomed town showed darkly against the fire-reddened sky.

Our driver sat upright on his narrow plank like a figure carved
out of stone. '*Kak kholodno*, Anton!' I ejaculated, shivering violently. '*Tak tochno, Sestritsa*,' he answered, and I heard his teeth
chattering somewhere under his upturned collar. What will the
autumn bring us, I wondered, if an August night can be so cold
and unfriendly?

When we came to the Neman, the wind had hushed somewhat
and the bridge was whole. On all sides uniformed men were to
be seen. Some mounted soldiers, near the bridge entrance, were
directing the streams of vehicles across in a passably orderly
fashion. Spread about the plain, as far as the eye could see, were
long lines of baggage trains drawing ever nearer. Groups of civilians
were clustered together; companies of soldiers were marching
towards the river. All were converging towards the bridge which,
like a life-line, would carry them away from danger and lead
them to protection and safety. Our foremost vans were slowly
moving – it was our turn! With a creaking and a lumbering,
we lurched this way and that and finally gained a narrow position
on the bridge.

But our passage was obstructed; we could not move for, a
little ahead of us, a clash had occurred between two side-lines of
vehicles. Cossacks were stationed at intervals along the bridge,

inciting, with loud, angry voices and constant cracking of their
knouts, the packed lines of transport vans and wagons to move
ever more and more quickly. '*Vperyod! Skoreye! Zhivo!* [Forward!
Quicker! Look alive!].' Suddenly we swayed and moved forward.
A Cossack – a giant of a man – stood in the midst of that confused
commingling of man, horse and vehicle and tamed them all to
his will. With fierce, coarse oaths, he impelled forward movement,
bringing his knout down upon the horses' flanks with reckless
impatience; the startled animals, quivering with fright, swerved
restively from side to side, but so close, so compact was the line
that a step sideways or backwards was impossible. The river lay
below us; we could catch a glimpse of its gleaming waters and we
heard them gurgling and lapping against the high bank. A rumble
of moving wheels grew more distinct, the warning shout came
down the line to us and we once again moved forward. So the bridge
was at last traversed and it was with a feeling of infinite relief
that we turned off from the crowded highway on to a side-track
almost deserted.

*We pressed on, spending one night at the Polish village of Tolochki,
the next at Skidel – in the luxurious surroundings of the old manorial
home of the wealthy Polish Prince Chetvertinski who had already
fled. After dressing the wounded who were drenched to the skin,
exhausted, hungry, we prepared for bed.*

22nd August

We were all so sure that we should sleep well that night, for we
were to sleep on real bedsteads, on real mattresses! And we could
actually undress! We spread our sheets and blankets with careful
hands; how wonderful, how simply delicious, would be our sleep!
For supper we had roast chicken and fruit compote, served on a
large carved-oak table, surrounded by high-backed, carved-oak
chairs! We laughed from sheer light-heartedness. We were in a
world of make-believe, where strife and sorrow were unknown.

Darkness fell and we retired for the night. Three large bedrooms
had been set apart for the Sisters. My bed looked large and inviting;
from the adjoining room came shrill little cries of delight from
Anna as she nestled down for the night. She and Mamasha had
had the choice of rooms and, wishing to be together, had chosen
one containing the most gigantic four-poster we had ever seen;

four people could have slept on it, without the slightest inconvenience.

'Annushka!' I shouted. 'Isn't it glorious to be here?' '*Da! Da!*'
she called back, all laughter. '*Eto pryamo roskosh!* [It is simply
magnificent!]' and she went on: 'It is not every day that we can
sleep on a Princess's bed!' '*Da! Da!*' I answered. 'In spite of the
Germans we'll be princesses for once!' '*Nu*, children,' warned
Mamasha, 'make the most of it; don't chatter all night long.'
There was silence for a time, then Anna's voice again: 'How nice
it is to be a princess,' she laughed merrily. 'Oh! Mamasha, I have
forgotten to say the magic rhyme; you know that this is the right
moment for it, and don't tease me, little Mamasha, if I say it
now!' And slowly, emphatically, she recited: 'To sleep on a new
bed, is for the maiden to dream of a bridegroom! Now, there,'
she laughed delightedly, 'I've said it; now I shall dream of a handsome young prince.' 'Sleep! Sleep!' came Mamasha's tired but
amused voice.

They told us that it was at 2.30 a.m. that the first explosion
came. A second followed quickly. I was unaware of both. At the
third I awoke with a start. It was pitch dark and the windows
were still shaking from the shock. I knew that *something* had
happened. Frightened exclamations came from the adjoining
rooms where the Sisters were sleeping. It was comforting to
know that there were people in the vicinity who had also *heard.*

Anna and Mamasha were quiet; they, too, were listening.
And then, through the open windows, we heard it coming . . . nearer
. . . nearer . . . borne on whistling wings. Dear God, protect us!
It was here . . . over us! . . . I crouched, convulsively, pulling the
bed-clothes over my head, jamming them tightly over my ears.

When it was over, when the loud thunder of it had somewhat
diminished, I was aware that there was an uproar both within and
without the house. Mamasha's voice came through my open door:
'Get up, Florence, get up at once! They are shelling our *folvark*!'
And, simultaneously, there came a loud pounding on the doors and
excited voices were shouting to us to leave the house. In a couple
of minutes we were fully dressed and, in another two or three,
had dragged ourselves and our goods down the dark stairs into a
room below. Then came the fifth explosion. The noise was deafening; the house rocked as in an earthquake; a crash of timber
splitting, falling; a cascade of broken glass spilling from a height.

Above the tumult which prevailed Alexander Mikhaylovich's voice was heard: 'I think that the best thing is for us to remain here in this room. The walls are a protection to a certain extent,' the calm voice continued, 'and we must remember that so far *no* orders to leave this place have been received.' We rallied round him immediately; he was our leader, under his guidance all would be well. Conversation quietened and faces took on a more normal and hopeful expression. After the eighth shell had fallen and spent its fury, the bombardment ceased. For a long time we waited expecting every minute to hear the dread, warning signal, but none came. Then we were told that the house was to be locked up and that we were to await marching-orders on the verandah below.

For an hour and a half we stood outside in the chilly air of early morning. . . . Then: 'Well, if we must wait, at least let us wait in the warmth,' called out a cheery voice, and the soundness of the suggestion dispelled all grumbling. A door was soon re-opened and, dragging our bags inside, we sat down in a long corridor. The scene might have amused a casual onlooker, the piles of baggage, the woebegone faces and listless figures of the would-be travellers would give the impression of the waiting-room of a remote railway station.

A door in the corridor wall suddenly yielded to somebody's hand and that somebody cried out with astonishment: 'Ah! this is nice! Ladies and gentlemen! Come here; here it is warmer and more comfortable!' We pulled ourselves to our feet and made our way to the open door. The room was large and beautifully furnished in the Victorian boudoir style. A thick carpet of some pale colour covered the floor; elegant divans and slim, curved-legged chairs stood here and there. With sighs of relief we dropped on to the chairs and sofas, but they were too small and delicate to afford much comfort and, before long, we had rejected them and sought refuge on the carpeted floor. Once I opened my eyes; the sound of heavy breathing and rasping snores was in the air and somebody was groaning in their sleep; the light was fairly strong in the room and I saw Alexander Mikhaylovich's stout figure rise, shake itself and with an exasperated sigh lie down again, this time, crawling under the grand piano, hoping perchance that a closer proximity to a music-making instrument might soothe his slumbers.

We were standing about in groups, yawning, stretching, rubbing sleepy eyes. Mamasha had called out 'Breakfast!' and so versed were we in the Unit's disciplinarian routine that we had risen to our feet at once prepared to obey the call. Alexander Mikhaylovich had emerged from under the 'Flügel', he had crawled out on his hands and knees in his usual composed and natural manner. After we had eaten slices of bread and cheese and drunk mugs of tea, we made a tour of some of the rooms. The caretaker and two of his men were busily packing away the silver and ornaments in large wooden boxes. . . .

It was after midday before marching-orders came. The morning passed quietly enough; now and again a desultory explosion re-echoed from the village behind the mansion. No wounded came and the transport-vans were sent to a more distant post. A Red Cross orderly was carried in from the neighbouring village by two soldiers just before noon; his was a serious abdominal wound and he was dying. We were helpless to save him and, apart from the injection of morphia, there seemed nothing else to be done. As Sister-on-duty, I sat by his bed-stretcher and watched the long convulsions of pain seize him, watched the eyes narrow and shut, the teeth clench, the lips curl back in agony. As morphia took hold, he quietened and his groans grew less frequent. The hand which I held was growing cold and clammy; beads of perspiration were standing on his brow. My heart was sore for him. In the trenches, carrying the wounded away from under a rain of bullets, his life had been spared. For this? That one bright morning, in a quiet village-street, a treacherous shell should spring from the clear air and strike him?

The sick man stirred and moaned: 'I can see nothing, *Sestritsa*; it is growing very dark.' I sought to soothe him: 'The evening will soon be here.' 'No, it is not that,' he answered faintly. 'It is getting dark, because I am going to die.' They came to call me, to tell me that the vans were ready and waiting, but I could not, would not, leave him; the end was so near. Insistent calls fell on my ears; in stubborn distress, I refused to listen to them. Then Alexander Mikhaylovich appeared at the door and his irate voice sounded: '*Sestra*, we are waiting.' 'Alexander Mikhaylovich,' I urged, 'it will be very soon.' 'There is nothing for you to do here,' he replied roughly. 'Vasiliy will remain with him.' And still more roughly: 'Have the goodness to come *at once*.' His

words were final and he turned away. Mechanically I rose and
unclasped the clammy fingers. 'Don't go, don't go,' he gasped
piteously, 'don't leave me in the dark. *Sestritsa, Sestritsa,* give
me light, for God's sake!'

*We halted at Glinyany, a village a few versts away, and set up our
dressing-station.*

23rd August

Loud explosions rent the air repeatedly, but the frame of mind of
the soldiers proved more optimistic than was expected. The Germans had been beaten back on two sections of the Defence Lines;
the River Neman was proving a powerful resisting-force against
enemy invasion, while, near Vilna, the Germans had been obliged
to retreat several versts. Towards evening on 24th August, the
wounded became more numerous. The guns roared throughout
the long night and our wounded were nervy and troubled.

The Petrovski Regiment of a neighbouring Division had been
forced to withdraw from the Front Line and an opening had thus
been given to the Germans. We realised what this news implied
and prepared for possible departure. We were packed and in
readiness to leave, when an officer rode up to our Unit and presented a document from the Divisional Staff, which contained an
order to the effect that we were to remain in Glinyany and await
further developments. Another small document was handed to
me; it was a copy of a message from King George V to the Russian
troops; the Staff had remembered my nationality and thought
that the paper would interest me.

That night we realised the full importance of our present halting-
place. The wounded poured in from all sides; we worked hastily,
mechanically, with never a moment in which to rest or think.
'*Sestritsa*, I am so cold; I have been lying on the ground so long,'
cried a man, shot through the lungs, whose life-blood had already
almost ebbed away; a look at his marble face – that was all, for
there was no time to waste on hopeless cases.

Finger and hand cases came to the fore again; many of them
had walked in themselves, despite the fact that they had been
warned to apply for aid only at the divisional Unit, where the
medical staff had its own harsh methods of treatment for self-
inflicted wounds. One old soldier, with grey threads in his beard

and pathetic brown eyes, held out a trembling, blood-stained hand;
I washed it and, under the thick blood-coating, there was revealed
the dark tell-tale stain of a wound received at close quarters. I
looked at him and he knew that I *knew*, but nothing even akin to
cowardice could be read in that haggard face; I saw in it only
despair and a great exhaustion of mind and body. I painted the
wound quickly with iodine; the dark stain faded somewhat
under the yellow tincture. He was trembling all over now; I
bandaged him; the necessary details of name and regiment were
written down and he was despatched, together with other walking
cases to the Base. A man with a self-inflicted wound is a difficult
person to deal with; one could not hastily condemn him, for so
many conflicting influences would first have to be taken into
consideration and we became sensitive to the signs from which
we could detect those cases which were the outcome of cowardice.
On the other hand, it was not difficult to distinguish the soldiers
whose excitable nature and raw-edged nerves could induce them,
in a weak, desperate moment, to seek this outlet as a definite
means of deliverance from the scene of their physical suffering
and mental anguish.

*We were on the move again. The Germans had broken through the
Fighting Line and a mass advance was said to be imminent.*

26th August
A heavy shower came down as we set forth on the journey and
turned the already muddy roads into bog-land. We passed a batch
of German prisoners, escorted by mounted Cossacks; they marched
along sullenly and silently, with stolid, tired faces; as we drove
past them, I noticed that they were drenched to the skin and did
not even trouble to move aside to avoid the shower of muddy
liquid which sprayed upwards from the wheels of our *dvukolki*.

27th August
It was just after midnight when we arrived at the *folvark* of
Prince Sapega, near the village of Novaya Spusha, but it was
2 o'clock before we could at last retire to rest. At 7 a.m. I tumbled
out of bed, I was on duty from 7.30 onwards, and walked down-
stairs with heavy head and legs which felt that they would crumble
under me at every step. Ekaterina, whom I relieved, looked white

and drawn from sleeplessness; she was puffing away at a cigarette outside the dressing-room door. '*Slava Bogu!* [Thank God!]' she said brusquely. 'Now I can go and sleep', and she threw the end of her cigarette away. There had been no wounded to occupy her hands; I could well believe that the hours had hung heavily. Garbovski, the orderly-on-duty, was nodding in a corner of the room; I didn't wish to wake him, so walked quietly towards the house-door and looked out. Along the road which fringed the yard a few scattered pedestrians were visible; they were for the most part refugees. Women's voices reached me – high-pitched tones in an unintelligible jargon. Many of the women were bowed down with the weight of goods on their backs; most were bare-footed; their voices rasped on my ears, creating discord in the otherwise still morning-air. When I returned to the room, Garbovski's head was still hanging low over his chest; he had not noticed my entrance. I sat down and waited. It was all very quiet. I felt my head nodding.

A cart rumbled up into the yard; signs of life were heard in the corridor. I sprang up. 'Garbovski,' I called. '*Ranenyye priyekhali!* [Wounded have arrived!].' Four wounded men were in the van – three soldiers and an officer whom I recognised as an old acquaintance. While I was completing the last bandage, Mamasha called me to breakfast and, after seeing that the soldiers were provided with food and hot tea, I led the officer into the room where our members were breakfasting.

Over his tea, he told us sorry tales of Front Line happenings. Under a terrible barrage of enemy fire, a regiment on one of the flanks of our 62nd Division abandoned their trenches and receded well beyond the Defence Lines, only to be met with a volley of bullets from the reserves who were stationed behind them. Whether it were accident, or in obedience to a command, it had not yet been ascertained, but the fleeing men, stopped by their own comrades, turned again towards their trenches, this time to come face to face with the Germans who were pouring down upon them through the breach. Panic ensued and the regiment was almost wiped out.

We have been ordered to a new destination much nearer the Front. It was already dark when we left Prince Sapega's estate and most of the way lay through forest-land. Everyone seemed in high spirits. What a very little thing was necessary to change the humour and the outlook of the soldiers; the mere mention of the word 'advance' was sufficient to brighten their eyes, straighten their shoulders and give them the 'up and ready' look. And it was not surprising, for the last four months had taken high toll of their morale.

As usual the horses gave much trouble on the road. An opening of a verst or more in length lay between two forests and was entirely composed of marsh-land; in some places, the track was so uneven that pieces of wood and branches had to be thrown across it to serve as bridges. On one of these primitive constructions our wagon came to a standstill – a wheel had slipped into a hole and the wooden plank in front of it impeded all progress. The driver shouted, as only Russian drivers can shout, and cracked his whip, much to the discomfort of one of our two horses, which started kicking right and left, and almost upset our vehicle. To avoid a possible catastrophe, we slid down on to the miry ground, but the wagon gave an unexpected swerve and the horse's hoof shot out in my direction. Instinctively, I started backwards and found myself knee-deep in sticky, evil-smelling marsh water. It was a cold drive for the rest of the journey and my feet were like stone.

On arriving at the village of Osniki soon after midnight, I determined to thaw my frozen toes without delay, but there was work to be done and, donning my white overall, I hastened to fulfil my duties as Sister-on-duty. The night was dark, but the lighted window of a hut indicated the location of the wounded. There was only one young soldier and he was lying on a wide wooden bench, covered with a piece of white *kleyonka* [oilcloth]; the leg below the knee was shattered and, in the uncertain light of a lantern and a couple of candles, the foot and ankle looked blue and lifeless. At first sight it seemed that amputation was inevitable. With the pincettes in his steady hand, one of our doctors was extracting small scraps of bone from the torn flesh. When the wound had been cleaned, the tourniquet was slowly untied; as it loosened, we leaned forward ready to grapple with the expected rush of arterial blood, but – none came; with unspeakable relief we realised that the artery had not been damaged. There was no mistake, in half-an-hour's time – the foot was a little warmer; hidden away safely among the shattered bone and flesh, the

unharmed artery was already feeding the leg and restoring it to
life. The *shina* [splint] having been applied to the doctor's complete satisfaction, the patient was removed from the improvised
operating-table and placed on a mattress in a corner of the dressing-
room for the night, under the vigilant eye of the Brother-on-duty.

I returned to the hut where the Sisters were sleeping. Everything was quiet when I entered; a lighted candle had been placed
on the mud floor by the side of my bed. In its dull glow, the hut
looked cosy and inviting. The peasant woman and a young girl
were sleeping on a wooden bed near the stove; on the stove, two
small boys lay cuddled together – their long-drawn breaths telling
of the deep sleep so natural to healthy, carefree childhood. It
was, indeed, a homely cottage scene and the homely cottage
smell – not exactly to my liking – seemed acceptable as 'part of
the picture'. My boots and stockings were encased in mud; I
had quite forgotten that my feet were wet and cold; hot water at
that hour would be impossible to find. I threw all precautions to
the wind, curled up in bed and was soon fast asleep.

Mamasha had us out of bed at an early hour; grumbling was of
no avail, for the beds had to be packed away to make room for the
breakfast table; at 8.30 a.m. we were drinking tea and eating
kasha and black bread. Various messages reached us from the
divisional staff, but the all-important document instructed us
not to open a dressing-station as our Division was to be sent into
reserve for a few days and we might leave at any moment for the
Base. 'And our advance?' We looked at each other blankly;
'Where was our advance?' Yes, we were assured, there was an
advance *somewhere*. The Russians had gained a great victory
and taken many prisoners; nothing, however, had as yet been
confirmed. It was not even certain on which Front the victory
had taken place. We had seized the word 'advance' with such
avidity; we were so thirsty for victory. The disappointment was
almost unbearable.

*Instructions came to move on to Staraya Spusha, then to wait. We
waited . . . and waited. . . .*

From our position we had a view of the entire field. The evening
was very still and a golden haze lay like a dusty, iridescent sheen
over all; in the background, the ubiquitous pine forest stood out

darkly green against the delicately tinted sky. The transport vans
and goods' carriages were drawn up in military array; some of the
drivers were singing to the accompaniment of an accordion.
Hearty laughs resounded from the company whom we had left
over the tea-cups. . . . The question repeated itself in voiceless
vehemence: 'Can this be *war*? Can this be *war*?' My wishful
thinking churned the question this way and that. No, definitely,
this was not a warlike scene, here was no conflict of arms, no
hostile activity; this was but an outdoor, merry-making, picnic
party!

Despite our rugs, Ekaterina and I were shivering with the cold
and began to wonder whether we would ever enjoy warm feet
again. The divisional staff had probably forgotten our existence;
no instructions had been received and night was at hand. When
the darkness finally descended, it was arranged that the Sisters
should take refuge from the bleak air in the village. Accordingly,
in Staraya Spusha, a hut was found which contained only one
old woman and her young son – the rest of the family, they said,
had left the village and gone with other refugees to a neighbouring
wood. We slept in comparative comfort until 4 a.m. when the
long-awaited summons arrived; we returned to the field, seated
ourselves in the *furmanka* and jogged off down the highroad in
the direction of Novaya Spusha. Here, to our surprise and delight
we halted and were told that we were to take up our abode again
in the old *folvark*; and, before long, we found ourselves actually
installed in the very same room in which we had lodged only some
36 hours previously. So much for our 'advance'! It had been but
a myth!

The news of the Russian victory near Tarnopol in Galicia had
now been confirmed; some 10,000 prisoners had been taken. But
almost in the same breath came the news of a Russian reverse;
about 50 versts away a strong German force had broken through
our Defence Lines and our men, in danger of being surrounded,
had beaten a hasty retreat; they were now making for their next
line of fortifications near Dembrovo. Simultaneously, an order
reached us that we were to leave the *folvark* without delay.

30th August, Kuzmy
We spent the night, huddled together in a *khata* [small hut], for the
sky had clouded over and rain was falling heavily. Our *khata*,

minute though it was, served as a dressing-room the following morning and, as Sister-on-duty, I administered to the needs of the various patients. No wounded soldiers had arrived, but the refugees provided plenty of work for hands and mind. The tales of woe which were poured into my ears were heart-rending. At each fresh tale, our old host and hostess, who were sitting in a corner of their one-roomed home, nodded and groaned their sympathy. A woman-refugee came in with a badly poisoned hand; her two small children had been missing for several days; she had combed the forests and the countryside, but to no avail, and on returning to the encampment, she had found it empty – her husband with their eldest child had been sent away together with other refugee-neighbours. She was alone, without money, without food, but it was her children, her man, she wanted. . . . Surely the good God in His mercy would protect them and bring them to her again. . . .

A peasant entered to beg something for his eyes which were causing him great pain. While preparing the lotion, I asked him where he lived. He pointed to a forest in the distance. 'There,' he said, 'we live. There are perhaps two or three hundred of us in that forest alone.' 'And how do you live there?' I enquired. 'We live,' he answered laconically, 'there are berries, mushrooms; those who have potatoes and grain give to others. . . . We live.' 'When are you leaving?' He looked at me with vacant eyes. '*Kogda skazhut i kuda skazhut* [*When* they tell us and *where* they tell us]' he replied, and there was complete resignation in his voice.

Another peasant entered the room; the two men greeted each other and the man with the lotion left the hut. The newcomer came forward: '*Prosze Pania*, give some medicine for two weak children,' he said. 'Weak,' I interrogated, 'in what way weak? What illness have they?' 'Only weakness: they are not ill only nearly dead of weakness; one was buried yesterday, but two are very weak.' 'But I can't give medicine unless I see the children, or, at least, know what is the matter with them.' 'Only weakness, *prosze Pania*, no illness at all. This is what happened.' And he went on to explain how he with others from a far-off village had moved to a new encampment and had come across a small band of deserted children in a forest. A *baba* [countrywoman] who recognised them said that they had been purposely deserted by their parents, 'who had not had enough food to keep them alive'. 'And,' he threw out his arms with a tragic gesture, 'this may,

indeed, be so. I have known this summer more than one *baba*
who has thrown her infant away because she could not bear to
see it die before her eyes.' 'But these children might have strayed
away and lost themselves; perhaps their parents are searching
for them?' 'God only knows,' he said unsteadily, 'one we found
dead and we buried him yesterday; the two eldest have a lot of
life left in them, but the other two are overcome with weakness
and it would be better for them if they both died.'

'And where do you live?' His hand stretched out towards the
forest-line. 'Is there much distress there?' He waited a moment
before replying and then: 'Distress is immense.... Bitter is our lot,
but what to do? Over there,' pointing again towards the forest,
'is Vasiliy Platonovich, a good man – loves God. And what comes
to him? A week ago his wife dies ... only married a year. He loved
her like his own life. On the road a baby came – a little son;
always wanted a son did Vasiliy Platonovich, but the woman dies.
At night we bury her over there in the wood. I helped dig the hole
... and we put her in ... and he ... he goes and puts the little
one on to her cold breast. And I to him ... "Vasiliy Platonovich,
what are you doing?" And he on to me like a savage beast. And
he levelled the earth above them and pressed upon it with his
hands and feet. Then he stood upright. "*I tak*, Ivan Feodorovich,"
he says. 'And so, now my life has finished; it lies there, with them
... the three together. And now, night and day, like a shadow
he goes ... and he is a good man ... and loves God.'

I looked at him, but I could not speak. He took the parcel of
food which the orderly had brought for him and, bowing low,
he turned and went.

Someone touched my arm, I turned and saw our peasant host.
'*Prosze Pania*,' he said. 'What do you think? Is it better for us to
leave?' The defiant look was still upon his face; he was ready to
brave the elements, ready to risk health and life; the woman's
head had fallen forwards and she was sitting propped up against
the wall – asleep. She looked very tired and very old: her brown,
stumpy fingers were knotted and swollen with rheumatism.
'You must think of her,' I whispered, 'she would not be able to
stand the hardships for long. Perhaps it would be better to stay
here for her sake.' We were silent for a long time. The old woman
snored fitfully; the peasant sat with his head in his hands. Stepchenko, the orderly was leaning against the door-post, gazing

with dreamy eyes away into the distance; he had a wife and
children and his heart was sore for them. And I sat and thought.

'Yes! Here, in here!' Stepchenko's voice resounded from the
doorway; a minute or two later a man and woman entered the
hut. They were neatly dressed in black and at a glance one could
see that they belonged to the Polish middle-class. The man,
keeping hold of his wife's arm, came forward. 'I kiss your hand,
Pana,' he said, 'and I beg you of your mercy to assist my wife.'
'In what way can I be of assistance?' I asked. 'Her mind is sick;
great sorrow has caused her to lose her balance.'

The woman was suffering from the madness of despair. She
looked at me with vacant wandering eyes which were never still.
I tried to converse with her, but her voice was monotonous and
she murmured rather than spoke. Her husband explained that
she thought that she had committed a great sin which had bereft
her of body and soul and, although living, she believed herself
to be dead; she was constantly asking how she could go on living
when her body and soul were dead. She could not rest, but was
always anxious to go in search of them. As though to confirm the
truth of his words, the woman suddenly slipped off the bench
and, before one could stop her, had rushed out to the hut. . . .
Through the window I saw her running swiftly down the road, her
husband and Stepchenko in pursuit. . . . I turned away; the
peasant had resumed his old position, and, head in hands, sat
silently on a stool; the breathing of the sleeping woman and the
buzzing of numerous flies were the only sounds to be heard.

*News of a German breakthrough arrived and once more we were
on the move. This time to Koshatsy, 40 versts away. A night there and
we moved again. News had come through that our* Letuchka *was to
rejoin the 62nd Division which had been removed from the Front Line
and would remain in reserve until its ranks had been replenished. It
had suffered heavy losses and now numbered only 13,000 fighting
men. The Mariupolski Regiment had been reduced from 4,000 to
600, while the Berdyanski Regiment had but 150 men left.*

As we travelled by night a battery rumbled alongside for several
versts. Some of the men sitting on the guns and the gun-carriages
were sleeping and several of the mounted gunners were nodding in

their saddles – their well-trained horses leading them warily over the more intricate places. I recalled the first tragic days of the Retreat when the craving for sleep was so great that one could actually sleep while walking. I remembered, too, seeing more than once sleeping men on sleeping horses; sometimes, I was told, they would fall off and continue their sleep on the ground, and the sleeping horse would continue on its way.

2nd September

The village of Okolitsa Kerbedza was chosen as our first étape; we arrived there at 5 a.m., took refuge in a peasant hut and awaited further developments. To our utter consternation we learnt that the night's journey had been in vain, for the 62nd Division had, despite its decimated ranks, been ordered again to the Front Line and we, too, were to retrace our steps and follow our men towards the position.

3rd September

When dawn came we started off; the September fog hung over us like a curtain, clinging to and moistening everything it touched. In Zhirmuny we stopped awhile for dinner. Nearby, on the high-road, a continuous stream of infantry and artillery was passing – our men, our batteries, all retracing the ground which they had but yesterday traversed. The 69th Division followed ours; they at least could boast of new additions. A company of recruits was with them; the men marched along in perfect rhythm – head erect and arms swinging (for they as yet carried no rifles) to the music of their tramping feet.

On and on we went, the journey seemed unending. As a village came into sight, we would tell ourselves: 'Surely we shall stop here'; but no, we would pass through and emerge once again on the endless highway. We came to a compact group of houses nestling on the edge of a forest. 'Ah! at last; this must be the halting-place.' But, again, we were doomed to disappointment. When the light was fading and those inevitable red glows on the horizon in front of us had grown in intensity to a dull scarlet, we stopped to find a halting-place for the night. 'No huts available, all occupied by the Infantry.' Our faces fell; that meant a cold night in the open air.

But the wood in front of us drew us to it. Before us stretched a broad space of ground which had been cleared of its trees some years previously; many of the old gnarled roots were decayed to such an extent that they crumbled almost immediately under the pressure of strong hands. The tall trees on three sides stood like a strong wall between us and the high winds. A carpet of leaves covered the level ground; we gathered armfuls of the decaying wood and piled them up in its centre. The fire crackled merrily; the sparks flew around like fire-flies and the flames leapt up and danced gaily for our amusement.

The memory of those cheerless 45 versts just completed faded rapidly away; food and hot drink comforted and warmed us. We could hear the wind whistling and howling beyond our leafy fortifications, but scarcely a suggestion of its cold breath could penetrate into our sanctuary. . . .

A loud, rushing noise among the high trees which surrounded us, a persistent rattle on our tent roof and the rain came down in torrents. Within a few minutes we were all awake. 'My goodness! My bed is completely soaked!' 'Water is pouring on to my head!' Similar cries came from right and left. It seemed that an old tent had been set up for us that evening – a makeshift, for who could have dreamt of rain? The saturated canvas dripped on to us, at first in heavy drops and then, as the rain grew in volume, in an unceasing sprinkle like a fine spray. Groans of annoyance made themselves heard – mackintoshes were our only hope. I sat up and pulled out my mack from the bag under my bed and spread it quickly over my rug, but not quickly enough, for my pillow, meanwhile, had absorbed a goodly amount of water and my head fell back into a wet pool.

The rain continued the whole of the next day. Our mossy, leafy glade was now more like a swamp; the charred remains of our congenial camp-fires lay sodden on the oozy ground; the tree-stumps were hopelessly wet; it was long before a fire could be lighted to boil the kettles for our morning tea.

Under threatening rain clouds and to the angry whistling of a cold, east wind we finally left the forest as night was descending and started for the Front. It rained without a stop throughout our journey. We four Sisters sat in the open *furmanka*; Mamasha was in a small covered cart with piles of housekeeping equipment which had to be kept dry at any price. Our head-veils were soon drenched through and through – and our hair under them; now

and then a chilly stream of water would run down our backs and
the rugs round our knees and feet were heavy with wet. On and
on our long train of vehicles dragged through the long night;
but we had made only 20 versts when we halted in the village of
Ramutsy at 4 a.m.

There a hut was found, inhabited by a peasant, his wife and five
small children. The room was stuffy and heated to suffocation –
just what we wanted – what we had longed for more than anything
else. Our leather coats discarded, we took off our veils and skirts
and hung them up in the hot air to dry. We had no beds, no luggage
of any description; everything had remained packed on the *oboz*
stationed on the other side of the village; we sat on the wooden
bench, rested our heads on the table, or leaned against the wall
and tried to sleep.

*In the evening a sudden and violent explosion was heard as Russian
soldiers blew up the railway station. This could only mean retreat.
Smirnov arrived with further news:*

'Yuliya Mikhaylovna! *Sestritsa!*'

We caught only snatches of what Smirnov was telling Mamasha.
. . . 'Most serious situation! . . . regiments ringed around . . . our
division surrounded on three sides . . . German cavalry scouring
the woods around . . . 200 versts to traverse before we and our
Division can be in safety. . . .' The words rang in our ears, but a
dull apathy of mind rendered them scarcely intelligible. Still
200 versts to traverse? If that were true then, indeed, the end
must be very near at hand. What would happen to us? What
would happen to our men?

The night was less wild, but the rain was still steadily falling.
The slushy highway and side tracks were covered with traffic –
all creeping slowly forward in one direction. Everything and
everybody that had a covering as protection from rain had donned
that covering. The orderlies and foot-soldiers had thrown large
squares of tenting over themselves and, tying two corners on their
heads in the shape of a large knob, looked like regiments of walking
sacks. It was just as well that we could see some humour in the
grim scene around us – tragedy there was, certainly, enough and
to spare. On and on we moved, a swaying mass of men, horses and
vehicles; before us and wherever the eye turned to right or left,

we saw the same drab spectacle. Behind us, the reddened Western sky told its story; near the railway station which had been blown up while we were in Ramutsy, the glow was particularly bright, due to the large stores of timber which had been fired about the same time that the explosion had taken place.

Hour after hour we splashed and waded through the dirt and the filth. At a small, white house in the village of Geranony we stopped for an hour's rest. A German Cavalry Corps was rumoured to be at large; several tales of their merciless dealings were already known; a large forest, at no great distance from us, was said to shelter them and they might fall upon us at any moment. . . . With the exception of that one hour's respite at Geranony, we had been on the road since 3 a.m. and yet we had covered only 45 or 50 versts, but we halted at Novary, because our horses were quite worn-out.

7th September

During the night a message was brought to our *Letuchka* from Alexander Ivanovich instructing us to leave Novary without delay and join the members of our 2nd *Letuchka* who were then stationed at Kamen. We started as soon as it was light but were held up for at least an hour by a long, trailing *oboz* before we could find a place in the lines of vehicles swaying along the highway. Through the morning we followed that endless surging train. In the vicinity of the Folvark Belinshchizin we were brought to a standstill. At first we paid little attention to the fact that we were making no headway, but as one hour passed and a second drew towards its conclusion, the irritation became general and voices were raised in protest. It was at that rather critical time that the news was passed round that the General of our 38th Corps was on the road and riding in our direction. It was obvious that the news was not welcome, but rather seemed to increase the uneasiness felt among most of our members.

The General was considered a hard man, we knew, and addicted to the use of severe measures in dealing with the rank and file; as Kuzmin, our driver, added: he was a '*gospodin bez serdtsa* [gentleman without heart]'. It was rumoured that the General's temper that day was far from angelic: finding fault with everyone whom he met and not refraining from using his whip when he thought it necessary. We lifted our tired heads and straightened our drooping backs; if we were to defy hostility, we would have to put on as war-like an appearance as possible. He came at last, riding on a magnificent horse; several officers formed his escort and a *sotnya* [100] of Cossacks clattered behind them. There was no doubt about his mood; he was on the lookout for defects. His eye caught the line of hooded vans and he demanded the name of the *Otryad*. One of our orderlies pulled himself up smartly, saluted and gave the information. He passed our *furmanka*, looked keenly at us . . . and rode on.

We ate our frugal dinner where we were; it was impossible to move either to the right or left of the road so great was the throng. An artillery park was ranged alongside, and, as was to be expected, the long train of cannon, gunners, equipment, ammunition monopolised considerably more than their share of the track. As we demolished the cold *grechnaya kasha* [buckwheat gruel], we could take a good long look at the elongated guns on their lumbering carriages. I managed to snap a couple of them and the stalwart gunners, noting my camera pointed towards them, posed like well-drilled models. After the gruel, we were given bowls of soldiers' soup and lumps of black rusk-like bread; our meal was by no means appetising, but we were too hungry to be fastidious.

I must have fallen asleep, for a sudden jolt brought me back to my senses and I realised that we were moving. My veil and rug were damp to my touch; it must have rained while I slept. We continued moving slowly forwards for the space of two or three hundred yards and then, again, we stopped. Voices seemed to shout, to call, to dispute, to order – all at one and the same time. From all sides of the vast cornfield on our left and across all the tracks on the wide plain to our right, marched, rode and drove the thousands who were fleeing. The Retreat was at its height. I studied the many faces in our immediate vicinity: courageous, dignified, defiant, resigned – all were there. And, as I looked, I knew that this picture of Russia in an hour of distress would never fade completely from my mind.

It grew dusk, then night, and still we waited; suddenly from the far-distant lines of men and vehicles ahead of us a shouting was heard; it grew louder and louder, clearer and nearer; it was one word only that they were shouting: '*Poyekhal!* [Started off!]'. The word was passed down the long lines from mouth to mouth; it reached us; we repeated it: '*Poyekhal!*' It passed us and receded gradually down the lines in our rear; we heard its echo growing fainter and fainter. Then followed a chorus of voices, a lashing of whips, a straining of girths, a creaking of numberless wheels and – we had started forward! Our vexatious, protracted delay was over.

On the outskirts of a forest lay the village of Zaberezino. In the distance the River Berezina could be seen, gleaming in the moonlight like a burnished silver ribbon.* Like myriad compass needles drawn to the north, those countless lines of artillery parks, baggage trains and convoys crept slowly over road and plain, drawn slowly but surely towards that one bridge, rising over the Berezina. *One* road and *one* bridge only and *five* Corps were forced to use that route, as the only one likely to deliver them out of the hands of the enemy. They were the 1st, 10th and 38th Corps of the 1st Army, and the 20th and 21st Corps of the 10th Army.

As we drew nearer to the River, we began to imagine the unavoidable chaos at the bridge-head. Contrary, however, to all expectations, the crossing was carried through with the utmost dexterity and discipline. The Commandant of the District was himself supervising the bridge-entrance; a chain of some half-dozen men, obviously picked for the occasion, spanned and blocked the road. Each company, convoy, detachment, etc., after being carefully questioned, was allowed over the bridge in single file. An officer, heading a squadron of cavalry, received them at the other end and sped them on their several ways. As one contingent left the bridge, another made its way on to it. Here, indeed, was a methodical orderliness which reaped its own reward – no accidents, no violence, no confusion! 'We have learnt the art of retreating!' laughed one of our officers, not without some bitterness in his voice. 'Exactly,' intervened another. 'And, God knows, the lesson has been of long enough duration!' . . . 'Long enough, in very truth,' we echoed in our hearts, for five long months had come and gone since that fateful April day in Gorlitse, and still we were retreating! When and how would it all end? Wide, desolate marsh-lands lined the river's banks and in half an hour's time we had left the bridge and the river behind us and were following in the track of our divisional *oboz* along the road which had been

*This river we were to learn was a branch of the Neman and not as we had imagined the historical Berezino, a branch of the Dnieper, famous in the great Napoleonic retreat from Moscow.

apportioned to our 38th Corps. The idea of continuing our journey to Kamen had been abandoned; the latest *prikaz* [order] ran: 'All contingents attached to a Corps must follow the same route as the Corps. . . .'

8th September

It was a little after midnight when we entered the great forest which runs like a massive woodland belt to the east of Minsk and which is said to be over 200 versts in length. For an hour or two, our vans and other vehicles journeyed slowly on in the darkness, stumbling over the rough places, jolting and swaying heavily from side to side; and ever the tall, silent, sentinel-like lines of pine trees bordered our way and the narrow strip of star-spangled sky blinked and scintillated upon us from above. Sleep would not and could not come. . . .

On and on we drove and the rain continued to fall. From forest we emerged on to marsh-land, then, after a while, again into forest. The road became wider, the traffic heavier; blockade after blockade occurred; once, during such a stoppage, one of the two horses pulling our *furmanka* slipped suddenly on to the ground – asleep. Artillery hemmed us in; cavalry rode alongside – squadrons of Uralski and Donski Cossacks among them. Companies of foot-soldiers dragged themselves slowly by shuffling along, obviously too footsore and weary to pay attention to military gait and carriage. Many of them were without their greatcoats; their uniforms were often torn and discoloured; their boots ill-shaped and slit in places.

Marsh-land again appeared and, on either side of the road, the ground was patched with large pools of standing water. The Infantry marched straight on – the muddy water splashing up and about them at every step; one man walked into a pool and one of his high boots was submerged in the water; a comrade gave him an arm and pulled him out; on they pressed, stumbling through the slush and slime. . . .

8th September

Not until 6 o'clock in the evening were we allowed to halt and rest. We had been on the road since 7 the previous morning; a cup of hot tea and a chunk of black bread had been our only nourishment. Visions of unspeakably comforting things rose before our eyes as we halted in Ponizye: the warmth of some homely hut; hot, savoury soup – and which soup could be unsavoury at this critical time? – thick slices of bread; and then, the meal over, in the warmth to sleep . . . and sleep . . . and sleep. But the homely hut was not to be found so easily! Every hut and every room in the village was already occupied. The Commandant came to our rescue and informed us that a certain hut had been placed at our disposal. We could have wept for joy, so great had been the disappointment.

Bread was the next important matter for consideration and, to the general consternation, it was discovered that the bread on hand was insufficient to go the round of the *Letuchka*. Two tired orderlies, whose eyes were bloodshot from sleeplessness, were despatched to the nearest *mestechko* [small town] of Volozhin, with an urgent message to the *Intendantstvo*. The men looked reproachfully at our Head, saluted and silently left to carry out their mission. When they returned an hour later we were told that the superintendent of military stores could furnish us with three *puds** of bread, *only* three *puds*, because his supplies were nearly exhausted and demands were hourly coming in from many quarters. So small portions were carefully doled out to each member of our Unit.

We spread our coats on the earth-floor and lay down to sleep. Twice during the night we were awakened and the Sister-on-duty called up. First was a man suffering from appendicitis, the second time it was a soldier who had been kicked severely by a horse. At 7 a.m. I finally awoke to the sound of Mamasha's voice raised in anger: the hut door was open, Mamasha was standing just outside storming at a peasant who had refused to sell his hay to our Transport at 70 kopeks per *pud*. 'You think that you will get a rouble! Fool! Don't make any mistake; it would be better if you thanked God that you were selling the hay to a Brother, rather than wait for the Germans to steal it from you, without so much as a by-your-leave. But you are all the same; fools, all of you! When the Germans come you will tell a different tale.' Mamasha's angry tirade was cut short by the stentorian voice of Ivan Nikolayevich who suddenly appeared at the door: 'Pack up! Pack up! Get up and pack at once! In half-an-hour we must be on the road.' Another long journey. When, Oh! *when* will the Retreat end? . . .

* 1 pud = 36 English pounds.

9th September
At midnight we reached Mendzhe Reshcheche, where we managed
to seize a few hours of sleep until 6.30 a.m. Only 45 versts remained
now, we were told, between us and Minsk. Surely, once in Minsk,
the long road will come to an end!

10th September
After driving for a few versts through lovely pine-forests, interlaced
here and there by broad tracks of yellow sand, the small town of
Rakov came into view. Companies of sappers were engaged in
digging new entrenchments; in some places the trenches were not
more than a foot or so deep; in others, the ground bore only the
zigzag tracing of the trenches which were to be. 'Fortifying at
the last moment, as usual,' somebody murmured.

It was at this time that we found ourselves in a very difficult
situation; our fears had been realised – the *Letuchka* was without
bread. *Intendantstvo* after *intendantstvo* had been visited and
harassed by our cooks, but to no avail; the supplies of bread were
exhausted. For two days we had been living on *sukharki*, odd
scraps of black bread in various sizes, baked or dried hard, and
guaranteed to last for years. They were, indeed, as hard as stones
and could play havoc with delicate teeth; sometimes, the only
way of demolishing them was to soak them in tea or water, until
they became a 'sop' and would easily disintegrate. 'Crumbs
from the rich man's table,' we called them jokingly and, indeed,
they often looked like partly demolished, cast-off scraps.

But there were times – and this was one of them – when our
sukharki meant all in all to us. Rakov could give us no bread;
the town was filled to overflowing with the military and all supplies
had been bought up. A bread-baking kitchen offered – after due
persuasion – to bake for us during the day and, leaving Ivan
Yakovich, our *feldsher* [pharmaceutical dispenser], behind with a
hospital-Brother and a transport van, it was decided that we should
continue the journey for another eight versts and then await the
promised bread. Following the prescribed route and keeping to the
straight road, the eight versts were traversed and we drew up on
a field by the road-side to await our meal. From 11.30 a.m. until
4 p.m. we waited, hungry, angry, tired and wet through, for the
weather had had no pity on us. What was to be done? Could
Ivan Yakovich have mistaken the road? No, that was out of the

question. The only reasonable excuse which we could think of was that the bread had not been baked, but even in that case he would have sent the Brother to inform us.

Our soldiers combed the surrounding villages, but in vain; at last in the small hamlet of Petrovshchizna, one *pud* of bread was collected for the *komanda* [rank and file], while we had to be content with potatoes. We were more than content! We boiled some, roasted others in the hot ashes of our fire and, then, under shelter of overhanging trees, which kept the fine rain from our heads, for lack of something better to do, we lay down on the damp earth and dozed.

All hope of seeing Ivan Yakovich again that evening had disappeared, but the potatoes had helped us forget the disappointment and, the keen edge of appetite once smoothed away, we began to look upon the day's escapade in the light of a joke.

11th September

As soon as the sun was up, we started for Minsk. Far off in the distance we saw the old town and we were as glad as if it had been the Promised Land. Minsk was our chosen destination; the one which we had been striving to reach for more than a month; now it was within sight, almost within our reach! In it, we were convinced, we should find rest, security and bread. When we reached its outskirts, we set up our tents in a cornfield where the stubbly growth made it difficult to walk at ease. Not far from us, the equipment train of the 1st Caucasian Corps was stationed. The sight brought back memories of our favourite Caucasian Corps – the 3rd, the men of which had with such fearless intrepidity stood between our divisions and death at the height of the Retreat from Gorlitse.

In Minsk all was movement; every house, hut and barn was thronging with military and the streets were moving masses of uniformed men and wartime vehicles. Soldiers from the trenches were quickly recognised; dirty, dusty and footsore, they shambled with unsteady gait among the crowds; whereas, the town soldiers passed, spick and span, with highly polished *sapoghy* [high boots] and their military caps set at a jaunty angle.

Officers were numerous, especially *praporshchiki* [sublieutenants], many of whom were walking with Sisters of Mercy at their side; or, rather, may it be said, with ladies who wore the uniform of

Sisters. It was strange to look upon some of these women with their painted faces and long gold chains hanging down over the Red Cross on their breast. For many months past, we had been accustomed to the restless, drab existence of field-life, seeing always the dreary colourings of battered earth and darkened skies, and moving always among convulsed, apprehensive soldiers, clad in earth-coloured garments; small wonder was it then that we looked on these dandy young officers and on these pink and white, befrilled and becurled women with something akin to awe and perplexity. They, too, were Sisters of Mercy – it was a strange thought! We tried to picture them out there where we had been: passing the long night hours in the open, buffeted by rain and wind; veiled with curtains of thick dust; wearing vermin-infested clothing for days on end; sleeping on benches, floors, under haystacks, on open fields; hunger stricken and thankful beyond measure for dried, black crusts. We looked at our hands; they were rough, reddened, scratched and weatherbeaten; our boots were clumsy, shapeless, lumbering; our black leather coats, torn, scraped and discoloured; and our faces! Ah! surely our faces had suffered the most! The tiny, pocket-mirrors which we carried in our knapsacks, could show us only a small part, but we could fill in the rest! We knew without being told, or shown, that our faces were bronzed, freckled, lined by lack of sleep and hardened by the endless effort to endure discomfort and to alleviate pain.

That night both Anna and I confessed to each other that, since arriving in Minsk and seeing the lovely displays in the many shop-windows, we had experienced a great longing to taste once again the comforts of home-life. I saw myself sitting on a soft-cushioned chair, feeling the warm smoothness of silken material under my fingers, seeing flowers around me, and all the beautiful things which art and taste can produce. 'Not yet,' I told myself. 'Not yet; there is still much work to be done; after the war is over . . . *and* if God wills.' . . . The shop-windows were gaily dressed; articles of clothing were plentiful and some of them very beautiful, but all very expensive. Food was scarce and bread – to our surprise and consternation – almost unobtainable, owing to the sudden influx of soldiers and civilians who had been sent to, or had sought refuge in the town.

We had been in Minsk just three days when we heard that the enemy's advance had suddenly been checked and that the

Russians had begun to dig themselves in for the winter. All thoughts of evacuation having thus been dismissed, the town took on a livelier aspect and its numbers increased daily. Prices rose to startlingly high figures and the scarcity of all food commodities grew in proportion. Grain was impossible to find, and smaller items, such as salt and jam, were nowhere to be bought for love or money. Hand to hand fights around the Jewish bread-shops were no unusual sights. Many of the owners of these shops were accused of having large supplies of white flour hidden away and were forced to make it into small loaves, which they sold at 30 kopeks [about 7½d.] each. The soldiers were constantly fighting their way into these shops, scuffling angrily with each other in their haste to obtain the bread; even during the Hebrew holidays the bread shops were not allowed to be shut, and ever an unruly crowd was to be seen outside their doors. The 62nd Division was still in reserve at a distance of 86 versts from Minsk. As soon as the repairing and replenishing had been completed in our *Letuchka* we were to rejoin them.

The day before we left, Mamasha had been in town purchasing some goods for her housekeeping store and had arrived back very hot and bothered. 'What do you think?' she ejaculated, looking from one to the other of us. 'They are actually here in the town, walking about as bold as brass; and to think that they came to us then, so meek and mild, such *ladies*!'

Little by little we learnt that Mamasha had come across two Polish ladies whom we had met and helped on our journey to Minsk. 'And in such an attire,' she added. 'All silks and jewels, feathers and smiles; their faces all painted and powdered, and hanging, each of them, on the arm of an officer. And they called themselves refugees! Fine refugees in that get-up! No! I've seen that war-paint before! And to make things easier for them, they will, tomorrow, wear a Sister's uniform and veil and be at liberty to go anywhere they please. And so, Sofiya Stepanovna,' she turned abruptly to our new Sister, 'you see what we Sisters at the Front have to put up with; any woman under the patronage of an officer may put on our uniform and parade the streets with her painted cheeks. Half a dozen of these painted creatures are enough to ruin the reputation of all the Sisters at the Front! Did you know that the general run of Sisters at the Front had a bad name?' Sofiya's face was a study. 'Yes,' she answered haltingly,

'I heard.' 'Then, why did you come here?' flared Mamasha
wrathfully.

A flood of colour passed over Sofiya's face, leaving it very pale;
for a moment or two she was silent and then, very slowly and
distinctly, she said: 'I came to the Front because I felt that I
had to come. War seemed too far away in Moscow and I wanted to
help where help was most needed. . . . I wanted to share in the
hardship, in the suffering. I had heard that some of the women at
the Front were doing their best to ruin the reputation of the
Red Cross Sisterhood, but surely similar women are doing the same
thing in our towns at home? . . . Somehow, although I know that
they are *there*, that they *exist*, they seem to me but imaginary
people, so far are they removed from the heart of our work and
from the ideals and high principles which inspire our work. I
am sure that if a Sister – whether she be working at the Front
or in a town or city of Russia – holds fast to these ideals and sets
them clearly before her eyes, no evil reputation could possibly
overshadow her or evil influence affect her.' We wanted to app-
laud, to show her in some way that we acclaimed her words,
but her expression stopped us; she was pale and very serene, with
great earnestness on her face. And even Mamasha was silent. . . .

20th September
Our exit from Minsk was made to the deep, reverberating booming
of our guns. An enemy plane was encircling Minsk and the anti-
aircraft guns were giving it a warm reception. The aeroplanes
had been troublesome of late, dropping incendiary bombs on
many of the towns; Molodechno was said to have come off badly
on more than one occasion. Some of the people who had been our
neighbours during our nine-day stay in Minsk came from their
houses to say goodbye. Several of them were deeply affected at
our departure, but would not wish us a 'speedy return', knowing full
well that our sojourn at the Front depended entirely on the enemy's
movements. When our guns started a vigorous attack on the
winged intruder, they took leave of our party and retired in haste
to their homes. The tiny speck in the sky still wheeled above the
town, but the persistent challenge of the guns forced it to remain
too high to gain any useful information about the town below. . . .

We were all in rollicking mood: off to work and off to our
beloved Division again and – most important of all – away from

the irritating influence of Minsk. We felt like new beings! The Retreat was ended!

So hopes ran high and the beauty of the scenery through which we drove helped to heighten our spirits. Lovely little villages peeped at us from the occasional clearing in the autumn woods. . . . We drove straight towards the sunset – a massed collection of fleecy pink clouds on an eau-de-nil sky. Then came a valley, with a fresh green expanse of grassland on either side, and a patchwork of recently ploughed brown earth showed where the young corn of next year's reaping was nestling in its winter-bed. The hill in front of us loomed high, a water-mill on its summit darkly silhouetted against the sunset sky.

We passed the night at the Folvark Mikulino, near the village of Dulichi; the noise of the guns falling like a greeting on our ears. Up at 5 o'clock the next morning, we breakfasted and were away again by six. The holiday in Minsk had spoilt us; we were loath to leave our beds, for the grey mist in the outdoor world looked bleak and chill.

21st September

At the village of Yurzhiski, in an orchard-garden, carpeted thickly with yellow-brown leaves, we sat awhile and ate our cold luncheon; we piled and pressed the leaves around us, made nests in them and lay back on our soft leafy cushions. . . . Our old dog, Sabak, who had followed in our footsteps with such loyalty for more than three months, came and burrowed a hole among the leaves at my side and sprawled full length in it, blinking at me with his intelligent though sleepy eyes. . . . The world around, bathed in the warmth of the golden sunshine, was very beautiful. . . .

The 2nd *Letuchka* was also on the road, not far from us; we caught it up finally and joined its long line of swinging vehicles. Petro, the cowman, was making his way along the roadside, driving his beloved cow before him. Petro stood only five feet in his high boots – which were several inches too large for him. He was a popular figure was Petro, noted for his affection and care for all animals, but cows by preference. For many months past, the 2nd *Letuchka* had kept a cow. Mamasha did not approve of it and would not hear of buying one for our *Letuchka*. 'When we have settled in for the winter, there will be time to think of starting

a farm,' she stated in her usual decisive manner, and the matter
was left at that.

But the 2nd *Letuchka* vowed that they could not do without a
cow, and Petro backed them up to the best of his ability. This was
the third cow that had been given into his care; the other two
had been killed at critical moments when the Unit had been
without meat. At the slaughter of each animal, Petro had taken
the prominent role of chief mourner, and long and bitterly had
he wept as he watched the beloved cow being transformed into
beef-steaks. It was said that he had been inconsolable until a new
animal had been bought and placed under his care. . . .

*We moved slowly at the rate of 30 versts a day. On our way we
came across the 2nd* Letuchka, *which had left some hours before
us, stuck fast in bogland.*

23rd September, Pershaye

Little by little, the vehicles were extricated and, in order not to
share the same plight, our men set to work with axes and saws
and cut off innumerable branches of the nearby fir-trees, which
they strewed on to the marshy track – thus making transit possible,
though by no means enjoyable.

Dead animals were lying here and there about the fields and
roadsides; cows, sheep, pigs, all in various stages of decomposition.
I remembered having seen many large droves, in which more than
one suffering animal was panting from exhaustion; while many
limped painfully. I remembered seeing a horse fall during the
early months of the Retreat; I think it was in the dreadful sands
of Molodychi. The men cut it hastily out of the gun-carriage harness
and left it lying by the roadside, without so much as a word of
regret. As we passed, I remember how its sides heaved and its
eyes looked at us like the eyes of a human being being forsaken,
and left to suffer and die in solitude. . . .

A molar which had been worrying me of late started suddenly to
ache violently and persistently. I covered my face with my black
travelling veil and nursed the pain in silence. Only once I un-
covered it – and that for a fraction of a minute – when an indescribably repugnant odour permeated the air and penetrated to
my nostrils. 'What is that dreadful smell?' asked more than one

voice. 'Carcasses!' answered our Tatar driver phlegmatically. Later, we were told by a Divisional Doctor that the plain was a pitiful sight to behold; near the spot where we had noticed the offensive smell, some twenty dead animals were lying, among them several horses; they had been there for more than two weeks.

25th September, Chertoviche

The news which reached us from Russia was far from good; rumours of internal disturbances were wafted to us as on an ill wind. Bread, it was said, was growing scarce; in some parts famine already threatened to engulf the masses. The thousands of refugees swarming into the cities and towns were followed by pestilence and crime. In ministerial circles, confusion also reigned; many government executives had relinquished their posts; some, it was whispered, because they would not hold with treason; others, because they had been found guilty of treason.

The nights were growing longer and colder, and frost made its unwelcome appearance. One morning, at the beginning of October, the windows were thickly covered with the delicate fern-like tracery of hoar frost; outside, the earth looked white and numb, waiting for the coming of the snow to protect and warm it. Soldiers with frost-bite began to appear; some of them right glad to have been chosen as victims. 'We want to have a thorough rest in Russia,' they admitted frankly. 'We are all feeling completely exhausted after the Retreat.' Food, they told us, had been very scarce for some time; only one pound and a quarter of bread was distributed to each soldier daily and sugar had not been seen for more than a month.

A *sotnya* of Orenburgski Cossacks was stationed on the outskirts of Chertoviche. Their Commanding Officer, Colonel Mikhaylov, a grand old veteran well into his sixties, hearing that I possessed a camera, asked me to take a photograph of his men; accordingly I set out, armed for the fray with a goodly supply of plates. The men were rounded up and in a few minutes they were assembled in the field, mounted on their sturdy horses and wearing full fighting equipment. Then, for my benefit, they enacted their famous *dzhigitovka*, performing most remarkable feats of horsemanship with the utmost ease and skill.

Colonel Mikhaylov, not to be outdone, joined them, old campaigner that he was, and his acrobatic display was no whit less brilliant than that of his athletic men of the younger generations. I snapped them in groups, drawn up to attention; I snapped them as, with their swords, they cut an apple poised on a stick in half, at full gallop; I snapped them on their galloping horses as they stood upright on the saddle, or bent low to snatch up a handkerchief from the field.

Our life in Chertoviche had become, more or less, a real holiday; sick and wounded were few and far between and sewing, reading, card-playing formed the principal part of each day's programme. Every evening brought visits from our Divisional Doctors and officers, who sat around in our common-room, or general dining-room, discussed the newspapers' reports and the events of the day, or joined in the card games. They were, for the most part, kindhearted, cheery men, wonderfully optimistic – considering the reverses which they had experienced – and ever ready to tell a joke or relate a pleasing story. . . .

I am to have a month's leave and have already received all documents necessary for my journey to Moscow.

5th October
It was 5th October, the Name Day of the Tsarevich and military parades were the order of the morning hours. After driving some 45 versts, the station of Polochany came into view, but, learning that no trains were then running from there, I tried to continue the drive to Molodechno. There I was lucky enough to find a hospital train about to depart and was conveyed to Minsk in comparative comfort. On the Alexander-Brest station all was disorder and confusion. The town had been lately raided by a German Zeppelin and near the station two or three houses had been entirely destroyed, while, in the town itself, considerable havoc had been caused by incendiary bombs. Planes were even then hovering over the town and the anti-aircraft guns were doing their best to frighten them.

Hundreds of refugees were gathered on and around the station and it was with great difficulty that I managed to push my way slowly on to the platform where the train was standing. I reached the train, got a foothold on the steps and, with the help of pressure from behind, was able to lurch forward into the corridor. Somehow, I found a seat in a third-class carriage; I began to breathe

freely once again and felt more than thankful that my knapsack
was large enough to hold all the essentials for my journey. *After*
we had left the station, I learnt with great joy and relief that we
were bound for Moscow, via Smolensk. I was, indeed, lucky!

As the minutes sped past, my conflicting thoughts finally called
a truce. The enforced immobility and the rhythmic whir of the
wheels induced a more dispassionate frame of mind. My fellow-
travellers claimed my attention. They were a motley throng of the
peasant class, several were refugees, but all of them were laden
with bags, sacks, blankets and baskets, bulging over with precious
belongings – remnants of the homesteads which, in an evil hour,
they had been compelled to abandon. My knowledge of Russian
and smattering of Polish were enough, they plied me with questions and more than once offered to share their scraps of food with
me. I accepted a piece of home-made black bread and cheese,
but politely refused their offer of raw garlic which, despite its
health-giving properties, I had always detested.

So, for the time being, my Red Cross work was at an end.
Had I been successful? Had I fulfilled my vows and coped to the
best of my ability? God knows, I had *tried*. It was all so terribly
difficult when the world around was crumbling. And I knew that
the great weariness within me was mainly due to the persistent
suppression of tenderness and sympathy – feelings which were ever
uppermost in the face of human suffering. This month of complete
rest and freedom would speedily set me on my feet again and restore
my balance. Waiting to welcome me would be my friends – my
Russian 'family' so dear to me – with whom I would find peace
and comfort. And suddenly a longing – surprising in its crudeness,
its keenness – rose in me: a desire, a physical thirst, for the light
and colour of life. I longed to fling off this cloak of suffering, to
wrap myself round with music, art, poetry, flowers.

8th October

Moscow came at noon on the second day. Once again I glimpsed
its golden domes and ancient battlements, and I knew that the
first chapter of my war experiences had been brought to a close.

Moscow

*My holiday in Moscow came up to all my expectations; all that I
had hoped and longed for came to pass. The welcome of my Russian*

friends was deeply affectionate and sincere. Although I would have given much for a few days with my family in England, I knew I was lucky to have such genuine, kindly people to receive me with open arms, insisting that their home was mine.

The Doctor, with his usual cordiality, said he was glad that, after my gruelling experiences, I had come back to enjoy a well-deserved rest. Anna Ivanovna, my Russian 'Mother', held me close and whispered that she had never ceased to pray for me and that my safe arrival was an answer to prayer. Asya and Nadya were full of chatter – there was so much to ask and tell – but I noticed a trace of sadness in them which had not been there before.

Asya had suffered considerably during the many reverses of the past months and, being of a somewhat pessimistic nature, brooded over the calamities that had struck and was convinced that there were worse to come. I did my best to hearten her with tales of the prowess of our men, and their unwavering belief that 1916 would hold victory for them and for Russia.

Nadya's heartache was of a different variety. I had long known that she was very fond of her first cousin, Kolya, a young student at Moscow University. In my absence, Kolya had been recruited into the Army and, as Nadya confided to me in a trembling voice, had been sent somewhere south, before being drafted into his regiment and sent to the Front. She had not heard from him for two or three weeks, but his family had assured her that all was well.

Although I loved the life with my friends, it palled quickly; so quickly, indeed, that ten days had scarcely passed when I found myself actually counting the days which were left before my return to the Front. The light, the colour, the warmth, which I had so wished for – all were there: opera, ballet, drama. During the morning my Russian 'sisters' had their hospital duties, but the afternoons and evenings were given to me. Despite a definite sobriety of tone – only natural in wartime – which moderated social gatherings, there were still days on which could be heard laughter, melody, the swirl of soft silken garments, and dancing feet. The quiet evenings spent at home were a delight in themselves: softly lighted rooms, cosy cushions and Asya singing at the *royal* [grand piano]. But it palled! There was something lacking in the serenity of home-life. Gradually it was borne to me that to be happy while the world was unhappy, to laugh while the world was in pain, was incongruous; in fact, impossible. I realised that my happiness lay with my duty, and, as a Red Cross nurse, I had no need to be told where that was.

I had heard that Anna had arrived in Moscow on leave and it was suggested that I should extend my holiday by a few days so that my departure would coincide with hers.

6th December

Annushka and I met on the station-platform and, after bidding farewell to the many friends who had come to wish us God Speed, found seats opposite each other in the comfortable coupé of a train bound for Minsk. As we slowly steamed out of Nikolayevski Station, I noticed that both Asya and Nadya were holding hand-kerchiefs – now to wave to me, now to dry their eyes. I too shed tears. Strange to say, for Anna too, the novelty of life in peaceful surroundings had faded quickly; she, too, was aware that her work was calling for her. We smiled at each other in sympathy. There was no doubt about it; we had both derived much benefit from the holiday, and we were happy, because we knew that our work would not find us lacking.

At Polochany, we were met by the chief of our unit's equipment base and started off in a *troika* to his encampment. It was a white world; in the moon's clear rays, the snow-laden trees and fields shivered and gleamed. Wrapped in my thick, fur-collared coat, only my eyes showing from out of the *bashlyk* [Caucasian hood], I watched the fabulous landscape skim past, my heart full of happiness. A long stretch of wire entanglements lay across the wide expanse of white; they, too, were flecked with snow, and the moon catching their wooden supports sideways, threw shadows like crosses on to the snow. Soldiers were passing; dark, weird-looking men, treading softly in the thick snow; silent, because they were weary and still had far to go. When I saw them I thanked God that I had come back to my work.

The huts of a village lay squat and snug under the snow – like dolls' houses. Lights were burning in some of the rooms; now and then a figure moved across the window, or the sound of some musical instrument could be faintly heard. As we left the village a burst of voices suddenly filled the air. I could see a group of soldiers standing together in a courtyard. 'Oh Lord,' they sang, 'Oh Lord! help Thy people. . . .' And then, echoing fainter and fainter into the night, as we moved away: '*Bozhe Tsarya khrani!* [God save the Tsar!].'

9th December. Chertoviche

Mamasha came out to welcome us. '*Moyi dyeti priyekhali obratno!* [My children have come back!]' she laughed and, putting an arm round each of our muffled forms, she led us into the hut. It was good to be back with our *Letuchka*; the warm greetings from the Sisters and from all the surgical personnel made it a real home-coming; they praised our looks and declared that Moscow had rejuvenated us beyond recognition. So eager were we to commence work again that on the following day we squabbled as to which of us should be on duty, but as Anna was celebrating her name-day, the verdict was given in my favour. A new surgery had been equipped in my absence; it was a clean, whitewashed, homely little room; I looked round it with pride. As night fell, I found myself strangely wide awake. I sat reading in the candle-light, ears alert to the slightest sound outside – although wounded, I knew, were unlikely to come, for the Front was peaceful.

End of December. Chertoviche

Christmas has come and gone. Amongst us we collected a sub-stantial sum to give a party to all the men of our unit and a second one for the children of the village and of the refugees. There are many refugees in the huts – the peasant-owners making places for them on the stove and at table with their own children. Countless small refugees are living in the neighbouring woods with their relatives, huddled like sheep into old dug-outs. The scenes which we witnessed when making the round of the woods to issue invitations to the children were indescribable. Bread was scarce and so was water; the snow around these holes was crushed into evil-smelling slush; the floors were no better. Fir-branches were the only protection from the mud; on them men, women and children squatted and slept, and the oozy slime gurgled and slopped beneath them. Looking at their eager, expectant faces, pinched from hunger and cold, we rejoiced that we had good news to tell them. Bread and grain, we announced, were to be distributed to each family regularly three times a week after the New Year.

(This is a new mission which the *Letuchka* has taken upon itself; large supplies of bread, grain, rice, sugar and salt are to be sent weekly from the large *Zemski* depot in the Base.) They clasped their hands and bowed their heads and the children stared at us as though we were creatures from another world. But there were some whose infirmities kept them prostrate; good news was slow to penetrate the barriers built up by hardship and homelessness. A few of these elderly beings, with twisted limbs and frames racked with rheumatism, we were able to send to a base hospital. One old man refused categorically to leave his dug-out. He was lying on his sheepskin coat, spread over fir-branches on the bare earth. We told him that a warm bed awaited him and good, nourishing food. 'I will not go away,' he said, 'not away from my Maniya. No one shall make me.' Maniya, his daughter-in-law, was a woman of middle age from Grodno; her husband had been taken away during the first months of the war. She could not tell what had happened to him; she only knew that he had been in the Army under General Samsonov and had taken part in the Retreat from East Prussia. Two of her three children died a few weeks ago from typhoid; her youngest, a boy of ten, and her husband's old father were all she had to care for now in the world. We made no further mention of hospital or warm bed, we knew that she was fulfilling a sacred trust. We told her that regular rations would be forthcoming in a few days' time; she bowed to us, crossed herself and muttered some inarticulate words of thanks.

Then the children of Chertoviche had to be counted and those under twelve years invited to our Christmas party. The fun we derived from those counting-expeditions was tremendous! A divisional doctor came with us to act as interpreter; their dialect seems to be made up of a mixture of Polish and Russian, combined with strange interlocutory matter pertaining strictly to the Ruthenian temperament. We sallied forth in high spirits to the outskirts of the village. In the first huts no difficulties presented themselves; in each case, the '*Pan*' rose to the occasion, grasped the reason for our visit and obligingly gave us all the details we required, sometimes repeating them a dozen times over. Then came a hut in which there was no '*Pan*', but a '*Panya*'. She eyed us suspiciously and vehemently denied having any children in the hut. 'How many have you *outside* the hut?' 'Nobody outside, nobody inside,' she retorted angrily. We turned to go, when two

shaggy-haired little urchins darted into the room and made a
bee-line for the stove. The woman's face was a study! She stood
between us and the stove like a tigress at bay. The doctor was at
his wits' end. 'But they will have a present; there is a Christmas
tree for them!' In vain! We left her, fully aware that she regarded
us as officials sent to waylay, kidnap – even murder – her offspring.

In another hut the scene was less dramatic and more comical.
The poor, daft old Pan could not remember how many children
he had! 'Let me see,' he kept repeating. 'There are Sasha, Grisha
and Petrushka,' (counting on his fingers) 'then, Vasya, Grisha and
. . . ' 'Stop!' cried the Doctor. 'You have named Grisha twice!'
The counting began again: 'Sasha, Grisha, Petrushka, Petiya and
Vasya. . . . Seven in all!' 'Only five!' laughed the Doctor. 'Seven!'
the Pan repeated obstinately – and the counting began again.

The parties were a great success. Large dug-outs were draped
with fir-branches, brightly decorated with tinsel, coloured streamers
and shining ornaments. The *yolka*, or Christmas-tree, stood in the
centre, glowing with light and colour. How the children loved
that tree! Their hands clasped and unclasped in the excitement of
the moment and their eyes shone with delight at the wonder of
the coloured lanterns and dazzling lights. And one little lad, overcome by the beauty of the decorated *yolka*, gasped, 'If only they
grew like *that* in the forest!' There were cakes, sweets and a gift
for everyone of them, and their happiness and delight were imparted to us.

Winter has come to us in the guise of a friend; the blizzards and
snowdrifts have made military operations quite impossible. Even
the advancing Germans realise it is time to call a halt. So it is a
God-sent lull for us all. Now and again we treat a soldier with
frost-bitten hands or feet, or a man caught by a sniper's bullet;
for our young dare-devils often volunteer for reconnaissance,
and although they wear white overalls to make their movements
less perceptible in the snow the ever-wakeful enemy sometimes
spots them.

Some of our orderlies decided to build a small wooden Church.
In a very short time, strong young arms had felled fir trees, sawn
the trunks into sizeable planks, and set them up to form walls and
roof. The finished structure was exceedingly attractive; no detail
had been overlooked. A wooden cross was set aloft on the roof

and a wooden table served as an altar, on which stood a small icon of Christ the Redeemer. In this rustic building a regimental Chaplain, or our Red Cross *Batyushka*, would officiate. It was surprising how fervently the Russian soldiers took part in these simple, improvised services. But the Church precincts were limited and our enthusiastic master-builders determined to launch out on another and more unusual structure. They planned and designed it in secret and one day it was erected in the open air for all the world to see. It was a large Cross, rising from a pedestal – the whole made of ICE. Near it stood a small ice altar. This was the new open-air Church – open indeed! It was a veritable work of art and drew large congregations of soldiers, peasants and refugees. In the sunlight, the Cross was ablaze; and it gleamed with a silvery, ethereal radiance in the moonlight. The services seemed to take on a more reverent tone in the open air. Once, when a special prayer for the Mother-Country was being offered up, the soldiers knelt side by side on the frozen snow; they were, indeed, brothers, linked together by a common cause: the Tsar and their Homeland.

PART THREE

1916, The Advance

2nd January

Our doctors went to visit an invalid soldier in a remote corner of the village and to their horror found lodged in one small hut no fewer than 17 soldiers. There was no room even to move, they said, and the air was so foul and thick one could have cut it with a knife. The soldiers pointed out that they preferred to be huddled together and warm under a roof to being frozen outside under a tree. We knew that accommodation was very scarce; we knew, too, that there were refugees who at night would crowd twenty or thirty into one dug-out. The District Commandant was approached, but seemed powerless to help. 'It is only for a time,' he repeated, 'only while the soldiers are in reserve. In a few days' time, they will be back with their regiments and there will be room enough and to spare.' Some of the poorer peasants' huts were in a disgraceful condition; hygiene was totally lacking; pigs and hens, taken under cover for the winter, lived with the family and spread dirt and discomfort on every side. Rightly or wrongly, these terribly unhealthy conditions are being accepted as inevitable in wartime. No one can, or dare, raise a finger to change them.

3rd January

At any moment first aid work might be awaiting us in the trenches. The New Year has brought renewed hope. We trust implicitly in the loyalty and patriotism of our soldiers; we know that they are longing for an opportunity to win back all the fertile territory which the enemy has succeeded in wrenching from Russia. They are now rested and their ranks reinforced; the future seems reassuringly bright. 'Wait!' we tell each other. 'Wait! a little more patience and we shall see the victories which 1916 has in store for us.'

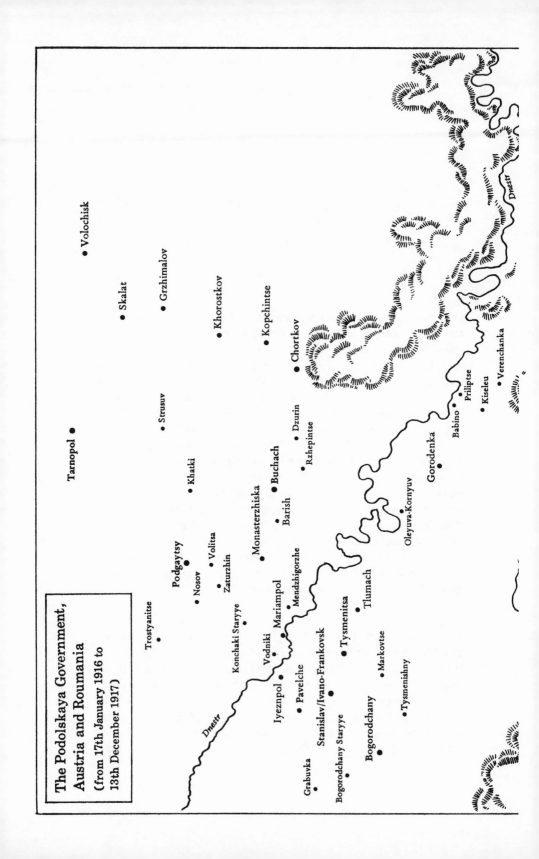

The Podolskaya Government,
Austria and Roumania

(from 17th January 1916 to
13th December 1917)

Volochisk

Skalat

Grzhimalov

Khorostkov

Kopchintse

Chortkov

Verenchanka

Kiseleu

Priliptse

Babino

Tarnopol

Strusuv

Khatki

Dzurin

Rzhepintse

Buchach

Monasterzhiska

Barish

Gorodenka

Podgaytsy

Nosov

Volitsa

Zaturzhin

Oleyuva-Kornyuv

Trostyanitse

Mendzhigorzhe

Mariampol

Vodniki

Tysmenitsa

Tlumach

Konchaki Staryye

Iyeznpol

Pavelche

Stanislav/Ivano-Frankovsk

Markovtse

Tysmenishny

Dnestr

Grabuvka

Bogorodchany Staryye

Bogorodchany

Dnestr

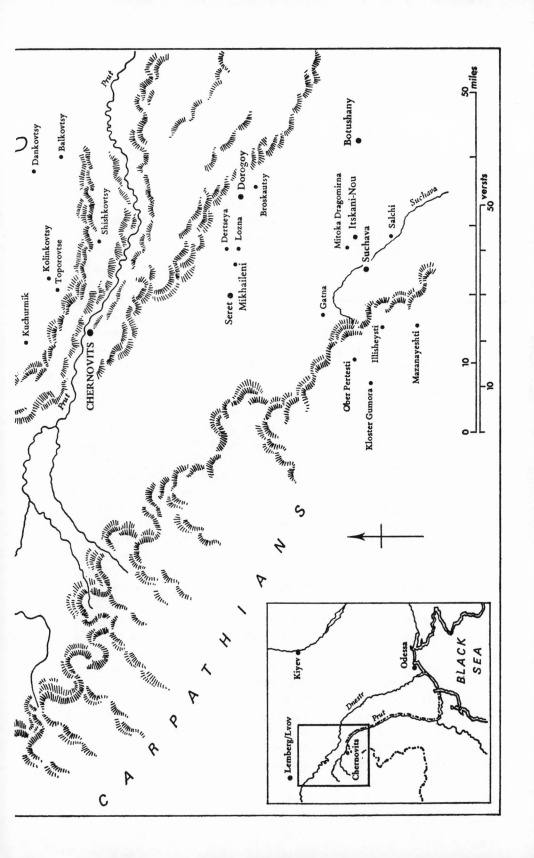

We had known for some days past that an important military operation was afoot; we had seen our doctors in deep discussion with army officers and gathered that we were to go to a Front Line station when the summons came. The prospect pleased us, for although there was always plenty of work to be done among the villagers and refugees in Chertoviche, we knew that our real activities should be centred on the needs of our fighting-men. It seemed that two battalions were about to occupy a strategic sector of our Defence Lines and would begin with a reconnaissance operation to gauge the enemy's strength and, if possible, capture one or two prisoners. Our scouts would go ahead to cut the wire. During a dinner given by the divisional staff we were told that we should be leaving next day to set up a first aid station nearer the Front Lines. We were fully prepared from early morning, but it was not until 10.30 p.m. that we were called upon to start.

We arrived at a small wood in which we found a wooden hut, where we were told we could prepare our equipment. We had hoped to attend to our wounded in a tent, but we were thankful to take shelter in the hut, for a driving wind swept rain and sleet battering against our door. Our doctors were nervous, expecting strong counter-attacks. Although we were only one and a half versts from the trenches, everything was very quiet, not a single rifle shot was heard. Midnight came and firing had not yet started. We waited patiently, wondering what our men were up to and hoping that the scouts' raids would be successful. The Divisional Commander entered and drank a cup of tea with us. We waited and waited and still no sound came from the trenches. Then about 2 a.m., the Commander was called outside to a telephone message. The news was not good: the first attempt had been spotted by the enemy and repulsed. A second attempt was now in progress. All was very quiet. Then, over the telephone, came the news that the scouts were already at the wire and that all was going according to plan. 'Good news!' we repeated to each other, and we smiled and drew deep breaths of relief.

We waited and waited. Three o'clock came and we were still waiting. Strange suspicions began to gather in my mind – suspicions that things were going perhaps too well. Then, on the stroke of four, the stillness was shattered. The roar of guns blasted the air – cannon, machine-guns, rifles, all at once. And our men were out there, cutting their way through into the enemy's camp.

The waiting became more trying and the hideous din continued unabated. The telephone delivered its latest message. Bad news. The enemy had spied the scouts and showered them with shells. The operation had met with disaster! We knew that soon they must come, and so they did, carried on stretchers, supported by a comrade's arms, limping, they were still in their white overalls and caps; their young faces were white too, but, like their loose over-garments, spotted and splashed with scarlet. One clutched a grenade in his right hand and would not give it up. Then a batch of a dozen or so were brought; one already dead, shot through the stomach, with intestines hanging out, his face the face of a young boy. But they were all young. They had volunteered for this risky work, knowing full well all that it entailed; but to these reckless youngsters it was just a lark – with a spice of daring in it. Alas! most of them would never dare again. Batyushka administered the Sacraments to them; some could scarcely swallow the Holy Bread. Several were brought straight from the trenches; they too had been strafed by the avenging Germans. One soldier was shot through the lungs; his gasping breathing was dreadful to hear! I tried to help, so did Ekaterina; but there was so little that we could do. At such times, one is so helpless.

We waited for the next set of wounded to appear; they dribbled in, but their wounds were slight and required little treatment. One or two of our party were lounging about aimlessly; I went outside the hut for a breath of air. All was terribly still. A few versts farther down the Front, the Krasnostavski Regiment of the 61st Division had taken up position; distant firing was heard now and then in that direction. Later it was said that the regiment had had 75 men killed that evening and over 200 wounded. The Regimental Commander had been severely wounded and remained, helpless, by the wire entanglement. So the effort had failed miserably all down the Line.

The Commander had taken his leave and was about to depart, when some more wounded arrived, among them a young soldier who – the orderlies admitted – had not been wounded and had left the trenches of his own accord. The Commander rounded on him fiercely and demanded the reason for his absence from his regiment. The man replied sheepishly that his head had 'turned'

and he had felt that he could not go on. The officer swore angrily
and enquired sarcastically if the soldier were a 'pretty girl' that
his head should be 'turned' so easily. In that case, the harsh
voice continued, he shall be sent to the staff headquarters of his
regiment and there dealt with as his superiors thought fit. The
soldier's face whitened and twitched: in his imagination he had
seen a firing-squad! 'Your Honour!' he stuttered, 'now I am
feeling myself again; nothing is the matter with me. I am not a
deserter. I am ready to return to my post.' But the Commander's
word was law; the young soldier was despatched then and there.
One could not help feeling sorry for him; it was so obvious that he
was a very raw recruit.

At 7 a.m. we packed up and made our way back to our lodgings
in Chertoviche. It had been a sad, useless journey and our hearts
were heavy. Sister Ekaterina and I slept till midday. Later we were
told that the two battalions which had occupied that sector had
had astonishingly few wounded in the trenches; only the young
scouts had been penalised.

The days slipped by quietly, peaceably; the memory of the recent
abortive attack faded; other plans were being prepared by the
High Command. We were feeling rested and the future seemed
brighter. Sometimes we would indulge in winter sports, go for
long walks on the snow-clad hills, and visit other Red Cross units
in the vicinity. Apart from the regular and widely attended open-
air services which were held around the large Ice Cross, we would
sometimes be invited to open-air concerts. I enjoyed watching the
soldiers who came from many a remote corner of the vast Russian
Empire. They had remarkably good voices; one and all sang with
great feeling. Some of the simple folk-songs were sung in such a
truly tender way as to bring a glint of nostalgia to many a hard-
set, furrowed face. The accordion was always in demand at these
military concerts and accordion players always received a special
ovation.

12th January
We left Chertoviche at 1.80 a.m., and took the train for Chortkov,
quite in the dark as to the kind of work awaiting us. But we did
know that for the second time we were travelling south towards
East Galicia on the Yugo-Zapadnui (South-West) Front. For the
Germans, the Eastern Front had obviously become devoid of

menace.* I have noticed more than once that the Russians never class the Austrian soldier on the same level as the German. They consider him less skilful, less cunning, less bloodthirsty. An enemy he is to be sure; anyone who dares to take up arms against Holy Russia is an arch-enemy; but, they feel that the Austrians are gentlemen, and fight as such.

We have often heard, too, of the daring exploits of Alexei Alexeiyevich Brusilov, the General who successfully broke through the Austrian defences in the early months of the War. The fact that we are going to work in Galicia where he is Commander-in-Chief has done much to boost our morale. His soldiers will be all afire to advance – we will be with them; we, too, will advance!

Thursday, 14th January
Yesterday was a bad day for me: my head ached and my heart ached, and both these aches did their best to torment me. The weather was gloomy and grey; it did not help to dispel my sorry feelings. The notorious Pinski Swamps came into view, a vast, desolate region of boggy marsh-land, much of it still frozen, known as the 'man-eating marshes'.

The railway by which we were travelling was a new one specially constructed for military purposes. In front of us were many ammunition and troop trains and halts were not infrequent en route.

We may arrive at Volochisk tomorrow; so far, we are well up to time. My head feels better; I think it is because the weather has changed. When we awoke, it was as though we had come into another world; snow was only to be seen in odd, lonely, little heaps, and in its place was a pale, sleek-looking earth covered with dull brownish grass.

Something very green has just attracted my attention; it can only be fresh grass. No, I am told, it is the young corn which was sown last autumn. This miracle of resurrection in Nature must surely bring new hope to many a heavy, downcast heart.

*Later we learned that they had transferred the bulk of men and weapons to the Western Front where, according to the newspapers, Verdun, heavily fortified by the French, was being harassed by the Kaiser's Generals. Our Russian Generals were already planning to take advantage of the absence of those heavy German cannon to seize large slices of land from the Austrian Army.

The warm sunshine instils energy; we feel its influence; we want to be 'up and doing'! We feel the strong urge to be in the thick of things, to accept the challenge of hardship, if only it will ensure work for us. Now we are passing forests of silver birch. Their slender white trunks gleam in the sunshine, and their long, delicate twigs, hanging down like fine hair, stand out against the blue sky. Before long those same fine twigs will be wreathed in tiny leaf-buds and a flush of young, green life will spread over every branch.

It is strange to think that we are already halfway through January; that means that most of the winter has gone. The two months spent in Moscow helped me wonderfully over the coldest spell; now the warmth of the sun is daily gaining strength; the farther south we go, the warmer it will become. I cannot help feeling deeply thankful to the spring for the new hope that it brings to heavy hearts.

Saturday, 16th January
We shall arrive at Volochisk this evening, and our Head is going to try and arrange that we stay in the train until the early morning, instead of turning out into the town at midnight.

Our meals provide a pleasant relief from our somewhat hum-drum daily life in the train. When it halts we jump out of our carriage on to the line and then scramble into the truck tacked on behind, which – not unlike an English horse-van – serves as a dining-room for ourselves and the Medical Personnel. A long wooden table and benches have been arranged here; we sit at our ease and are served with dinner and tea by our orderlies. Once, when I was late for the first halt, about 9.30 a.m., I was obliged to wait until 2 p.m. without so much as a bite of bread or a drop of tea. It was a practical way of enforcing punctuality! But Mamasha, poor soul, had a worse ordeal; she had neglected to jump out of the truck at the psychological moment in order to return to our compartment, and was held prisoner by the train, which puffed steadily forwards until dinner – by which time, flustered and upset by the unexpected confinement, she had lost her appetite.

Sunday, 17th January
We arrived at Volochisk about 2 a.m. At 6 o'clock, we were called and by 7.30 we were all ready, breakfast was finished and we were once more packed securely in our old, familiar four-wheeler, with

Galaef, our Tatar driver, sitting serenely in front. The station had been much battered and we drove past ruined walls and derelict buildings. It was pleasant to be out in the open again and driving on hardened, frosty roads. With the exception of a few white patches here and there, the snow had completely disappeared. Driving through the town we came across a Sister of our 2nd Flying Detachment. She guided us to the house where her *Letuchka* was stationed and a small room was allotted to us. With some difficulty we managed to get our four camp-beds into it – it was really a very tight squeeze, but we consoled ourselves with the thought that it was only a temporary arrangement, for our Chief Alexander Ivanovich might arrive at any minute and we would then be despatched to the Fighting Line without delay.

About 11 a.m. I went with Sister Ekaterina to the dentist, for she was almost beside herself with tooth-ache. The traffic was intense, pedestrians were legion, and the horses were quite upset by the puffing, snorting cars, and especially by the deafening hoot of the motor-horn. It was difficult to obtain the smallest thing in the town, but I managed to find a few respectable-looking grey envelopes. Goloshes were selling at five roubles a pair, but wood was one rouble a *pud*.

In our tight little room, still damp and chilly despite the fact that the stove was full of burning, crackling wood, we reminded ourselves nostalgically of Chertoviche and the fragrant pinewood which had always been there for the asking. We remembered, too, the warm, comfortable cottage which was always ready to welcome us after a cold walk or drive. 'Yes,' we all agreed, 'there's nowhere like Chertoviche.'

Monday, 18th January
We have just returned from a walk, in splendid spirits and health. Although a miserable, dirty little place, Volochisk has really beautiful surroundings. We turned off across the open fields, keeping a small pine forest before our eyes as our final objective. The ground was frozen hard and the air keen and pure. My companions, Anna and Ekaterina, grew gay under its bracing influence, and Ekaterina began to sing quaint old Russian songs. We reached the forest and walked slowly through its glades. Straw and old tins of preserved meat were littered about; it was plain that the forest had once been a shelter for man and horse. A little

farther on, amid snow and withered leaves, we came across some
daisies – real live daisies! In delight we dropped to our knees and
began rooting about among leaves and twigs until we had found
a good collection. 'Daisies in January! Surely it's a miracle!'
Anna exclaimed. 'Certainly, spring seems to be earlier this year,'
said Ekaterina, in her practical way.

We passed into an alley which led up to a large estate, hoping
to enter the grounds; but a soldier with a gun stood at the entrance
and told us that no one was allowed inside the gates, for the Staff
of the 11th Army was stationed there. We made a circuit of the
estate; to the right and left ran a triple line of wire and to the
south a magnificent lake – still covered with a thick coating of
ice. Far away, on the other side of the lake, one could dimly see
some figures skating. (Later I was told that the estate belonged to
a Graf Ledokhovski and what I had imagined to be a lake was in
reality a river, a branch of the River Zbrouch.) The sun was
sinking and the western sky reddening as we turned our faces
homeward. A transparent, blue-grey haze enveloped the icy lake
and the villages on the banks.

Friday, 22nd January
We are once more on the road; this morning we packed up our
belongings and left Volochisk for Chortkov. Frost was very sharp
during the early morning and my hair was soon stiffened and
whitened with it. 'You have grown grey at the thought of the
100-verst journey in front of you!' laughed our jovial Tatar driver.
But he too had whitened perceptibly; in fact, everything was
white: our fur collars, the soldiers' long coats, the horses; and the
telegraph wires on each side of the road were gracefully festooned
as though for some festival.

Soon we were to cross the erstwhile Austrian frontier which
had fallen to our men in 1914. From the beginning, our men had
had success on this Front; now, rested and strengthened, they
would – pray Heaven! – follow up their success and continue
their advance. Passing from Volochisk into Pod-Volochisk, a very
different scene met our eyes. In the former town, little or no
damage was noticeable; in the latter, it was difficult to find a house
or building which had not suffered. Here and there, among heaps
of brick débris, a tall chimney would be seen, rising up in solitary
state completely unscathed. It was surprising to note that in

several houses where soldiers were still living, the windows had not been mended and the apertures had been merely stuffed with bricks, or covered with sacking.

Outside the town the Ismailovski Regiment, 1st Guards Division from St Petersburg, was stationed. They looked a fine set of men, easily distinguished from the ordinary soldier by their elegant white belt and straps and their tall, manly figures. There were several of them lolling about as though time was entirely at their disposal. I could not help comparing their seemingly comfortable existence with that of the Infantry. No matter where we drove, these latter were always to be seen, trudging along with their heavy equipment over their shoulders, or engrossed in hard manual labour. We passed many of them digging ditches by the side of the road; the ground was very hard and there were picks and spear-like implements in their hands.

After some 24 versts, we halted at Skalat for a meal. Alas! the soldiers' cabbage soup and buck-wheat *kasha* had started again! If only one could get accustomed to things as quickly as one can get unaccustomed to them! The last part of the journey was colder than ever and the fog penetrated into every chink and corner.

On our arrival at the small town of Grzhimalov, we were met by our officer and guided to a little white house on the outskirts. We began to unpack and set up our camp-beds in a pleasant, fair-sized room, where everything seemed spick and span. The call to supper came; we answered it with alacrity, for we were all as hungry as hunters. But we did not retire as early as we had expected, for one of our Medical Staff, endowed with superfluous energy, suggested that a concert should be arranged that same evening. In a few minutes chairs were being set out in rows and a suitable programme drawn up.

It was a modest concert, but, as we all agreed, we were a modest company! One of our Sisters did a little bit of strumming and then our Austrian hostess came forward, settled herself placidly on the music-stool, arranged her skirts and opened a faded music-album. She was no great musician, but the old-world waltzes and other dances she played met with instant applause. One of our younger officers was then asked to sing; he had a fine tenor voice, untrained but pleasing; but the *pièce de résistance* came when a young soldier of the 2nd *Letuchka* was brought in and led to the music-stool. He came in rather shyly, but the sight of the old grand piano seemed to reassure him, for he ran his fingers over the keyboard and began to play. He played mostly from memory and his répertoire was a wide and classical one. I have since heard that he had almost finished at the Conservatoire in Moscow, when the war intervened and snatched him away from his beloved studies.

Saturday, 23rd January

This morning we left Grzhimalov at 8.15, we are putting up for the night at a Jew's house; the room is small and very dirty. On a wooden table there are still signs of the ritual prescribed by Jewish law for the celebration of the Sabbath, and the white table-cloth and brass candlesticks have not yet been packed away. In the adjoining room an animated conversation is being carried on in the nasal twang of Polish Jewry. If only they would stop jabbering and let us sleep. If only the walls were not so dreadfully thin.

Sunday, 24th January

We are in Chortkov at last! Yesterday we were complaining of the absence of fortifications; today there is no need for such complaints. Trenches, guarded by wire meet us at every corner; the wire entanglements themselves seem of an especially complicated pattern. In some places there are six to ten rows, one behind the other, with the wire bent to form large, empty spaces, like loopholes. Perhaps these are a new device for entrapping the unwary soldier; they certainly do not make for ease of action.

Now that the fog has lifted, we have beautiful views of the surrounding hills. Cutting across them are dark lines in the snow, which mark the site of trenches, and in front of them jagged rows of barbed wire.

The rooms chosen for us, the Sisters of the 1st and 2nd *Letuchkas* had not been heated for weeks, for the owner of the house, a Jewess, lived with her baby boy, her mother and a servant-girl in the kitchen. The spacious end-room has been assigned to the Sisters and the lady-doctor of the 2nd *Letuchka*; our room comes next and then the kitchen. To bring water to the occupants of the end-room, the orderly is obliged to walk through all the rooms, beginning with the kitchen; so an unexpected intrusion is liable to take place at any time. We are wondering how long we shall stay here; some say a week or ten days at the least. At present, our chief anxiety is to make our rooms a little warmer; the stoves, though well stacked with wood, seem disinclined to impart their warmth to us poor, chilly creatures. The best we can do is to sit with our thick coats on and a plaid round our legs and feet, or go for a walk – and see what exercise will do for our frozen limbs.

Wednesday, 24th February. Chortkov
It is just a month ago today that we arrived in this town. The hope of leaving on the morrow and starting work with our new division was very bright during the first week here; the second week it paled somewhat; the third, it waned entirely; and this last week we have grown reconciled to the fact that we may have to remain here for many weeks to come. The town itself has not suffered so much as might have been expected from the wave of war which swept over it. It was in 1914, during the second month of warfare, that the Russian troops marched into it, they occupied it so quickly that the Austrians had no time to do anything else but make themselves scarce; consequently, the Russians found everything in good order, with comfortable lodgings and plenty of food at their disposal. In 1915, however, at the height of the Great Retreat, the Russians, knowing that Germany was concentrating formidable armed forces in the Carpathian region, and fearing to be driven out of Galicia, began to destroy many of the houses, bridges and railway stations. Just in front of our present abode, a fine-looking building stands in ruins; it was the house of the Jewish Rabbi; he happened to be in Karlsbad at the outset of the war and nothing has been heard of him since. Only the roof and walls remain, and they have for some time been used as stables. In the garden, several ammunition-wagons are standing in a row with other equipment belonging to an artillery park.

The Synagogue, which stands a little to the right of the Rabbi's house, has a handsome exterior in the villa style. The interior is a disappointment, and resembles more a lumber-room than a house of prayer. Books are scattered about the room – some even on the floor – all of them dirty, musty and worn-out. I feel sure vandals must have assailed this place of worship, knowing that no practising Jew would ever allow his sacred books to be treated with disrespect.

The position of the Hebrews living in Chortkov is most pitiful.

They are being treated with vindictive animosity. As Austrian
subjects they enjoyed almost complete liberty, experiencing none
of the cruel oppression constantly poured out on to the Russian
Jew. But under the new Government their rights and freedom have
disappeared and it is obvious that they resent the change keenly.
Our hostess, a black-eyed, sweet-faced Rebecca, sometimes im-
parts a few of her woes to me.

A few days ago we had a very heavy fall of snow, which continued incessantly for three days and nights. When the blizzard
had blown itself out, the roads were blocked up, wall-high, by
enormous drifts. The Jews were at once ordered out to clear the
snow and every family was forced to send at least one representative to take his share in the task. Should a family consist only of
females – as was the case with our hostess – and there was no man
they could send, the penalty for that family would be one rouble
per diem. No matter how rich the family, money would not
exonerate them from work; *one* male was forced to join the labour-
squad. This explains the unusual scene I noticed yesterday –
among the groups of Jewish townsfolk clearing the snow off the
streets, that there were several well-dressed men whose faces
revealed their intelligent and cultured background, working,
shovel in hand, side by side with disreputable-looking old Hebrews
in long kaftans and conventional side-curls. Near them stand
Russian soldiers, knout in hand, whose sharp reprimand – and still
sharper lash – provide effective guarantees against negligence or
slackness.

Yesterday I was commissioned by Mamasha to buy a few
arshins of coarse white cloth; accordingly, I walked to town and
went into a small draper's shop. The Jewish owner was cleaning
away the snow from the pavement, but, seeing a customer, he put
down his spade. Just as he was pulling down a roll of the material
from a shelf, the shop-door opened and a fierce, bearded Russian
face, with a fierce, thundering Russian voice, ordered him out into
the street – 'immediately!' to continue sweeping the snow. I was
annoyed at the Russian's rude interference; so I, too, suddenly
became loud and rude. Facing the infuriated soldier, I told him that
I would not allow the Jew to leave the shop until my purchase was
made. '*Durak!* [Fool!]' I cried. 'What right have you to interfere?
I am carrying out an official commission. When I am ready, and
not before, this man shall leave the shop.' It worked! The soldier

turned and walked out into the street. Thinking it over afterwards, I was puzzled to decide what I should have done if it had *not* worked!

It is no easy matter to buy things in Chortkov. Writing paper, shoe-laces, pins, needles, cotton, etc., are unobtainable; though corsets, white kid-gloves, silk ribbons and high-heeled shoes, are to be found in abundance and at very reasonable prices! Yeast is said to command a very high price – someone mentioned that he had heard that it could fetch 60 roubles for a quarter of a pound, but we told him that that was exaggeration; on the other hand white bread is cheap. Butter is only two roubles per pound, but it is daily growing scarce. Eggs are going at seven kopeks each, which is certainly not cheap, but then the egg season has not yet commenced. Mamasha searched the town the other day for a hen, to make soup for a sick officer; the cheapest was three roubles and Mamasha, in great indignation, told us that one villain actually had the audacity to ask four. It rankled for a long time, until one of our doctors informed her that he had just bought a pair of goloshes for six roubles; this piece of news quietened her at once, for, she said, she now realised that she was not the only person who was obliged to have dealings with thieves!

This morning, our little Jewish dressmaker brought my new grey cotton dress. I noticed that she was agitated and enquired why. It seemed that, last evening, three Cossacks had come to the house, seeking, they declared, a lodging for the night. She told them that all the rooms were occupied, but they forced themselves into the room where she and her husband were sitting and began looking round as though in search of something important. Suddenly one of them pulled an object out of a cupboard and, shouting fiercely at her husband, demanded an explanation as to the presence there of a revolver. (Weapons of every description are strictly forbidden among the town inhabitants.) The Jew and his wife began to protest loudly, disowning the revolver. 'We have never had a revolver in our lives,' the woman said tearfully. I believed her implicitly and realised it was all a plot on the part of the Cossacks. They had thundered out a demand for ten roubles, or, as an alternative, an immediate journey to the house of the Town Commandant! The Jews were fully aware that if the latter happened the resulting punishment would, at best, mean a severe flogging; at worst, death! So the ten roubles were scraped together and handed over to the Cossacks who, as they left, commented in loud, scandalised voices on the treachery of the heathen Jewish race. Such tales of injustice are commonplace in this part of the world; it would seem the very name 'Jew' is, to Russian soldiers, a word of scorn.

Chortkov is a clean-looking town. The cleanliness of the inhabitants is, however, another matter and no interest is shown, or trouble taken, to ensure their health. During the cold, wintry weather, the houses are literally packed with lodgers and, in some of the smaller Jewish huts, as many as twenty to thirty soldiers find refuge at night. This unhealthy mode of living tells, naturally, and illness is increasing. Typhoid and spotted fever are prevalent and, in one quarter of the town, smallpox has scarcely left a house untouched. For the last month or so we have had an *ambulatoriya* [dispensary] on the hill where our Transport vans are stationed. Our receiving hours are from 10 a.m. to 12.30 p.m. daily, when our doors are open to all inhabitants. As might be expected, our patients are numerous. Infectious diseases are despatched immediately to isolation hospitals. In different parts of the town, I also have a few 'private' patients who, on account of their weak state, are unable to drag themselves up the hill to our dispensary.

Last year the death-rate among children here was appallingly high and, during an epidemic of typhoid, ten to twenty little ones died almost daily. Even now, there are many children ill. Sometimes it seems to me that not one of those dreadful wounds which I saw and treated during last year's retreat touched me so deeply as the sight of these suffering children, with their small wan faces and limp little bodies.

One of my small out-patients is little Vassiliy, the son of Ruthenian peasants on the outskirts of Chortkov. The family is very poor, the father was taken into the Army at the beginning of the war and the mother earns bread by doing washing for the soldiers. Vasiliy caught smallpox last October. Consequently, although only four he has left off growing – in fact, he is diminishing. His little body has scarcely a pound of flesh on it and his legs and arms are mere sticks. I felt sure that no medicines could help the child and was not surprised when the doctor declared the case hopeless; but we both do our best – and it comforts the mother. Vasya knows me well; he knows the English word 'love' too, for I always tell him that I love him and that he must get well quickly and come and see me; very often he looks at me and I hear a muffled 'louv' coming from his baby lips. I took him on to my knee yesterday and I still remember the shock I felt on touching those thin little sticks of arms and legs. At any other time except war-time, one might have been able to do something for him but now – what can one do? – when it is impossible even to get a cup of milk for love or money!

Another case was a young Ruthenian girl; she gave her age as eighteen, but looked much younger. She had come to ask for some soothing ointment for sores and, after answering the doctor's questions in sullen fashion, was told to wait outside until the other patients had been attended to. The first thing the doctor did was to order her hair, which was matted and dirty, to be cut off; he then gave her a packet of *sapo viridis*, told her to wash her body with the green soap and return for further treatment on the morrow. Her body, full of sores, told its own sorry story of prostitution. Contrary to our expectations, she came back to us on the following day; she looked better and certainly cleaner; I think she must have realised that we were anxious to help her, for her sullenness had vanished and she answered questions in a quiet and ready way. I was standing by the door as she went out; she turned and bent her head towards our doctor, murmuring a word of thanks. As she passed me, I had a momentary glimpse of tears below her tightly compressed eyelids. She, too, was a victim of War.

24th March

The day before yesterday, Chortkov, usually so peaceful, was full of stir and commotion. The 2nd Armeiski Corps had come to replace the 5th Kavkazki Corps, and regiments and artillery were passing through the narrow streets from early morning until late night. There had been talk for some weeks past of the possible attachment of our *Otryad* to this new Corps, but probably it will be no more than talk, seeing that several Red Cross units are already serving it. Not far away from here, in the 9th Army, is the famous *Dikaya Diviziya* [Wild Division], of which so many fantastic stories are told. It is said to be under the command of Michael Alexandrovich, the Tsar's brother, and consists mainly of Caucasian-born types of wild, youthful manhood, who have bound themselves together in a reckless, dare-devil band, pledged to obey the common law of warfare – to kill the foe, or die in the attempt.

The days passed and throughout March we waited in Chortkov. But no significant military operations took place, and the constantly talked-of 'offensive' never materialised.

Meanwhile some of the medical staff, including myself, set up a makeshift hospital in a deserted monastery nearby. The wards were full and the work hard and long. I began to feel the strain and was sent back to Chortkov to rest and relax.

April. Chortkov

Easter is the greatest religious festival of the Orthodox Church. Into our little church, the soldiers streamed, cheek by jowl with officers of all ranks. Rank, birth, grade, these did not exist; plebeian rubbed shoulders with patrician. It was a happy and deeply emotional service. Lighted candles blazed; reverent heads were bowed; devout fingers traced the sign of the cross. And then came the culmination: '*Khristos voskres!* [Christ is risen!]' and the loud, triumphant reply: '*Voystinu voskrece!* [He is indeed risen!]' Congratulations followed: warm-hearted wishes from warm-hearted people. And then the three kisses – on brow, on either cheek – evoking God's Blessing: the Father, the Son, the Holy Spirit!

But the festival was not complete without the feasting! Refreshments were many and varied, including, of course, the traditional *kulich* and *paskha*, and the time-honoured Easter eggs, painted in the customary brilliant colours. So Eastertide came and went; it was a welcome respite.

Rumours of a possible advance were rife. We packed our essential belongings and prepared ourselves for departure. But days passed and no orders came, nor was there any unusual activity along our Front. But our hands were far from idle. One highly appreciated achievement was the construction of a *banya*, or bath-house, where up to 500 soldiers could bath daily; another was the *chaynaya*, or tea-house. A general-store was opened, where various goods supplied by the *Zemstvo* were available at a low price. A second *ambulatoriya*, specially equipped for soldiers, was inaugurated and the services of a woman-dentist were engaged, much to the relief of many a young recruit.

8th April. Dzurin

We have said goodbye to Chortkov and removed to a new station at the village of Dzurin. The transfer came as a great surprise but as we are still quite near Chortkov, it has not been found necessary to cut off all ties. We were a little perturbed at the suddenness of the removal. Life had been running very smoothly in Chortkov and our work had been so well organised that it was quite a complicated task to pack up and leave our various posts at a couple of hours' notice. Fully two and a half months had been spent there and we had spread our Red Cross activities over a wide area. I must admit that we all experienced a feeling of frustration; nevertheless, we could not grumble; in the first place we were soldiers and, secondly, we were acutely aware that the imminent offensive of our fighting-men demanded that we should be well prepared for the nomadic life which might at any moment confront us. But all was quiet on our Front and the enemy gave no sign of any desire to disturb the reigning peace.

While we were having our midday dinner, one of our doctors broke some bad news to us. The 10th Army had recently been engaged in sharp skirmishes with the enemy and, among the casualties, he had read two familiar names. Both were officers known to the personnel of our unit and it was to one of them that I had written when in the train after leaving Chertoviche. Despite the brilliant sunshine, the afternoon seemed very cold and grey.

22nd April. Dzurin

Sister Anna and I strolled off into the countryside in the afternoon and to our delight we came across quite a number of trees already in flower. Under a wild cherry tree, the long branches of which were flecked with white-pink blossom, we sat and looked around at the bright sunlit scene. A swarm of May beetles made an un-expected appearance buzzing around our heads. Far away, we heard a sporadic burst of rifle fire. Firing became fiercer during the night.

25th April

Today enemy aeroplanes were seen wheeling slowly overhead. Last night the guns were barking so loudly and consistently that, unable to sleep, Anna and I got up and went out of doors. Rockets were rearing their flaming heads; shrapnel, rifle and machine-gun fire filled the air. 'This *is* the beginning,' we told each other.

With the coming of spring has come an epidemic of sickness. Our patients have become so numerous that we have had to enlist the services of hospital-orderlies from our divisional units. Sickness is widespread in the trenches and our regiments are constantly sending us some poor fellow whose high fever has left him *hors de combat*. All infectious diseases are immediately despatched to Base hospitals in transport vans set aside for this purpose. In the neighbouring villages there are so many cases of contagious illness that it has become dangerous for our soldiers to accept local lodgings.

We were told today that our division may be withdrawn from this sector of the Front; we, of course, would go with them. We have to be packed and in readiness.

28th April

We hear that our Corps is to be transferred after some military engagements; our *Letuchka* must be prepared to follow without delay. But when? and where? This evening some shells fell very near our village and one was found, unexploded, in a village street. We went to have a look at the *voronki* [craters] and were horrified to see where the unexploded shell had fallen. It was surrounded by quite a dozen huts, all of which had been packed that evening with lodgers.

29th April

The latest war news is that the Austrian Army is about to launch an offensive and that great battles may now be expected at any time. We can only wait and see.

1st May

All is still very quiet on our Front; we hear that the expected battles have been postponed; how, when and by whom this news was gleaned, it is difficult to say. We accept it for what it is worth.

18th May

We have been told that tomorrow, the 19th, may be the *great day,* and that the early morning will see the beginning of our offensive.

The constant postponements have unnerved us and we are daily awaiting the coming of a momentous event – which never comes! Meanwhile, we are packed and in readiness. In the late evening, a message was sent to us that the offensive had been again postponed.

21st May

I was told that in Hut 131 a sick woman needed attention. At length I found her, a young mother, sick with typhoid, and her baby. We Sisters are doing our level best to instil into the village-folk the urgent need to boil all their drinking-water – an idea which seems unable to take root in the peasant mind. The same old argument is raised: his parents never drank boiled water, why should he? But we persist. They listen attentively, but their minds are quite impervious to the meaning of 'pollution' and 'contamination'.

Before retiring for the night, it was whispered around that a great battle was expected within the next twenty-four hours, but we sceptically went off to sleep, having heard it so often before.

22nd May

At 2 a.m. we were awakened by a heavy barrage of firing which continued until 5.20 a.m. We left our beds at early dawn; the noise of the guns and the voracity of the fleas prevented us from sleeping; standing outside in the cool air we listened to the uproar. How were our men faring? Could this at long last be the outset of the Great Offensive?

I made my customary round and found the majority of our patients cheerful. They did not appear to be unduly disturbed about the night's firing and, had they asked, I could not have given them any information. A few wounded men turned up in the afternoon, but they were not from our Division. Two guests from a neighbouring Unit came to visit us. I snapped a photograph of them on our *blindage*, a cleverly-designed armoured dugout which our men had constructed. I went into the village to look up two sick patients and when I returned, a woman-doctor had arrived. We had been expecting her for the last two days, but she had been held up en route. Firing has been continuing in spasmodic outbursts throughout the day, but no official news has yet reached us.

It was just after supper when the orderly announced that three

officers wished to speak with us. We guessed immediately from
their alert carriage and smiling faces that it was *good* news! We
gasped as we listened! *This* was what we had been waiting for all
those long days and weeks and months. The 9th Army had broken
through the Austrian defences along a strongly fortified Line
stretching for more than 16 versts [about 12 miles] and our cavalry
had advanced some 25 versts into Austrian territory; over 10,000
prisoners had been taken and 25 guns captured. . . . We could
scarcely believe our ears! Could it really be true? We looked hard
at the messengers and then at each other. We read in every face a
great relief – the suspense was over! It was difficult for us to speak;
the profound gladness within us seemed to stifle our voices. We
talked for a short time and then accompanied our visitors to the
road. We were chatting merrily in the open air – some dozen of
our personnel had joined us – when suddenly came a long-drawn-
out 'svee . . . ee . . . eest!' and over our heads flew a fierce, hissing
thing which exploded in the air a short distance away. 'Shrapnel!'
cried several voices. One of the officers called out to us to disperse –
not to stand in a group. Several of us made our way quickly to the
blindage. Again a distant boom! 'Firing again!' someone shouted
and, bending low, they all ran towards the *blindage*. Again the
long whistling screech . . . again a violent explosion! We waited a
short while, but no further whistles or explosions were heard, so
we dispersed. I went into the house to pack away my photographic
plates and then on to the bandaging tent. We were all expecting a
few more shells that evening, but none came. Before dusk fell, we
had a look at the *voronki*. 'Only light shells!' said a soldier dis-
paragingly, and handed me a jagged piece of thinnish metal. The
men began to make jokes about the desultory firing: 'The Austrians
know of our victory and send us greetings!' 'Or,' added another,
'they want to show us that they still have enough strength left to
fire a couple of shells!'

That evening shouts of *'Ura! Ura!'* resounded from village
encampments. Soldiers passing by said that they had heard
triumphant cries of *'Ura'* from the trenches. Somewhere an
orchestral band was playing gay, marching tunes; the accordion
piped up; here and there the soldiers broke into a rollicking song.
But at midnight the drowsy air was shaken for a while by an
Austrian aeroplane which flew overhead and a machine-gun
stuttered its challenge to village and bivouac. 'Perhaps it was the

Austrian way of saying *"Lebewohl!"* ' one of our doctors remarked, over his morning cup of tea.

It was difficult to sleep that night. The fleas were unusually rampant; perhaps they, too, felt that it was an occasion for special activity. The firing started again about 1 a.m. and grew in severity. I was sorry for the lady-doctor; one could hear that she was very restless. The previous evening when the shells had begun to explode she had wished to return to the Base; later, however, when the guns had quietened, she decided to stay on. 'I can't sleep a wink for the noise,' she said pathetically.

Monday, 23rd May

The day dawned cloudy and windy. The lady-doctor, accompanied by our Head, drove off to visit the 2nd *Letuchka*. The firing continued, but grew more and more distant. The funeral service of three scouts took place in the little church. A comrade who escorted them described how a party of six from the Vyatski Regiment had set out with hand-grenades to explore the land. The Austrians had spied them and quickly retaliated, killing three. Five of the grenades thrown by the scouts failed to explode; in despair, they threw their last one; it exploded and in haste they had seized their dying companions and managed to drag them to safety.

News was coming in now and we learned that the Advance was continuing successfully along the whole of our Front. On the far-off Western Front, our Allies, too, were gaining ground and a general advance was in progress. All seemed well with our world and hopes were running high. A peasant-woman called in the morning with a gift of two dozen eggs; Mamasha rewarded the donor by offering to buy her eggs regularly.

Tuesday, 24th May

The guns have been terribly active all night. It had rained heavily towards dawn and I found the outside world very wet and dirty when I set off to relieve the Sister on duty at 8 a.m. There had been a few wounded during the night, but as the morning lengthened they came in their numbers. We were all working steadily; no time to waste in useless commiseration; compassion would prove only a hindrance; so, numbly, we worked on and on. By 2.30 a.m. most of the severest cases had been dealt with. There had been four stomach operations (laparotomy) and two head (trepanning). The men came mostly from the 103rd Regiment which had borne the brunt of the enemy's counter-attacks. One of our orderlies, shot while helping to lift a dead soldier out of the trenches, died during the night.

Wednesday, 25th May

I remained on duty until 8 a.m. for our new regulations laid down a 24-hour duty, followed by a 24-hour period of rest. A doctor and Brother remained with me on duty, in case of emergency. Six wounded men were brought in about 5 a.m.; I cleaned and bandaged them and, as no operation was necessary, I did not wake the two exhausted men who were sleeping soundly. A seventh soldier was carried in and set down on the ground in a corner; his head was bowed and he was asleep so I did not approach him until I had bandaged the other men. Then I touched him; he did not move. I spoke to him, but he made no response. I dropped on to my knees and looked into his face. He was dead. I called the two orderlies; 'He was like that when we picked him up,' they said. 'He felt warm; we thought he was asleep.' Now he felt cold. I felt a sudden stab of compunction. Could I have revived him had I attended to him without delay?

All next day we worked and still the wounded streamed in. There was little time to ask questions, but we did glean that the Russian troops were sweeping onwards, driving the routed enemy before them. We heard that prisoners now numbered over 40,000 – in two and a half days! After dinner, I slept from 2.30 until 5.30. In the evening we attended the funeral of the men who had died; nine from our division; three from the Vyatski Regiment. There was no time for coffins to be made. We wrapped the dead soldiers in white sheets and covered them with springtime offerings of flowers and green leaves. A communal 'brothers' grave' received them. Our chaplain officiated and recited prayers; a divisional band played the sad, haunting melody of *'Kol Slaven'*. It was a lovely twilight; warm and peaceful. In the heavens, a moon rose slowly, and one large, brilliant star looked down upon us.

We hear that the Austrians are retreating rapidly. Firing was going on all the time while I was eating my supper in solitary state; I could distinctly hear the rifles interspersed with the barking of the guns. I felt unutterably weary; the odd hour of rest seemed to have done me more harm than good, but the wounded were still coming in and hands were badly needed. We worked all night. Several badly wounded and exhausted Austrians were among our men; one young Austrian officer had a smashed skull and had died in transit; a second had received such a dreadful head-wound that his face was thickly covered with clotted black blood – he, too, died before we could attempt to clean and dress his wound.

Thursday, 26th May
It has been another hard-working night. Some of the wounds have been dreadful to look at. Several men were dead on arrival; seven died during the night. Two were so badly mauled by shell-fire that I marvelled to hear them still able to speak. Here was a man with half-a-dozen fatal wounds on his body and his strength of will is such that he can ask the time of day, the exact location of our Red Cross unit, even the latest news from his sector of the Front. And, having received the answers, he turns his face to the wall and quietly surrenders his wounded body to Death. Is there in our language no greater, more laudatory word than 'hero' for a man of this calibre?

I feel terribly tired today and my back aches acutely; I am afraid that there is not much of the 'hero' about me – not a scratch on my body and yet I can scarcely walk!

An adjutant from our divisional staff came in the evening. He affirmed that the Austrians were retreating fast before our advancing troops. Our men were now bent on taking Buchach; the 41st Division was fighting hard in the vicinity of the town and the Vyatski Regiment, on the left, was giving tremendous support. We asked when we were to leave and follow our men in their advance; he told us that the staff would be leaving on the following morning and we should, in all probability, receive our marching-orders at the same time. We sorted out our wounded and sent nearly all of them to the Base, with the exception of those too severely injured to be moved. The word was passed round the unit that all members should sleep that night, in readiness for the journey on the morrow and for the strenuous work which would be awaiting us.

In the midst of our elation at the success of our fighting-men, there came a flash of bad news from England. Lord Kitchener, the great English General, had died: drowned off the northern coast of Scotland when the cruiser on which he was sailing was torpedoed.*

Friday, 27th May. Rzhepintse

Saying goodbye to our wounded patients was a difficult task. They could not understand why we were leaving them and the idea of new nurses and doctors coming to look after them did not appeal to them in the least. 'Little Mother,' one of them said. 'You told me that you would look after me, and now you go and leave me.' And another: 'How can you go, *Sestritsa*? Don't you see how I am suffering?' And a third: 'Nothing but unhappiness! I came to the Regiment at Easter; now, I have no Regiment and no strength left. And there is no one to dress my wounds!' When I returned to our house, I found that all was bustle and excitement. Marching-orders had come! We were off! We too were advancing! We packed our last oddments and gleefully took our seats in the wagons allotted to us.

To our left, black smudges of smoke appeared at short intervals on the clear sky; the enemy, still intent on wasting his shrapnel, was firing vigorously. Soon we turned south and passed near the aerostat which was under the supervision of our friend Vasiliy Ivanovich; there were four aerostats, all grounded at that time. The trenches then came into view; they looked drab and inhospitable and many were badly damaged. The trenches, winding one behind the other, had been protected by wire, now torn and shattered in the fiery struggle. Not far away came the Austrian Front Line trenches, in many parts battered into shapeless débris. We were quick to notice, however, the difference in construction. They were remarkably well-made, with wire entanglements running protectively alongside; there were several rows of these entanglements – in one section we counted no fewer than twelve. In and around the devastated trenches enormous craters were visible – the Russian shells had, indeed, been most effective. As we drove slowly onwards we came across another line of battered trenches, and then a third; here, the 'communication passage' was more than three *arshins* deep. The Austrians certainly believed in taking precautions.

It was a wonderful journey; something quite novel for us all and, remembering the countless despairing journeys of the pre-

*General Kitchener was, in fact on his way to Russia.

At the Usovs' dacha near Moscow, before the war.
Above left *Asya*, above right *Nadya*, below *Asya, Florence and Nadya dressed as peasant girls*

Princess Golitsin's hospital, Moscow, 1914
The medical staff and VADs. Nadya, Florence and Asya are 3rd, 6th and
7th from right, top row *Dr Usov is 4th from left,* middle row

A group of Russia's first wounded men

Detrainment of the Red Cross Otryad *at Grodzisko, East Galicia, March 1915*

Florence Farmborough in a makeshift dispensary

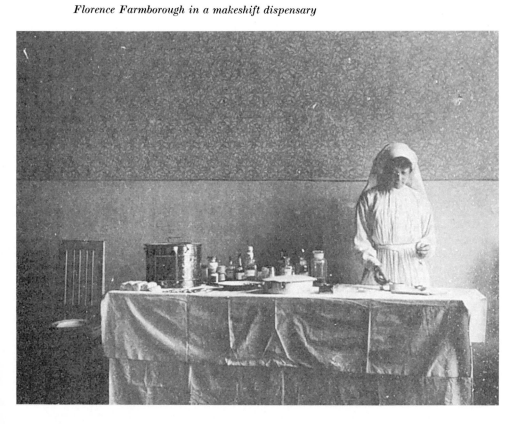

Tea by a cottage door on a quiet day at the Front

Soldiers too badly wounded to be moved to the Base.
In the background a coffin is ready for use

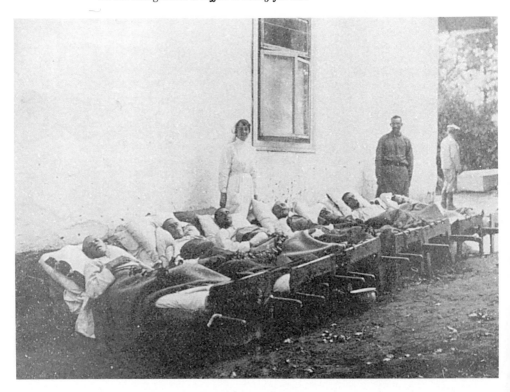

A tent can be a delightful summer residence

Sleeping under a hedge

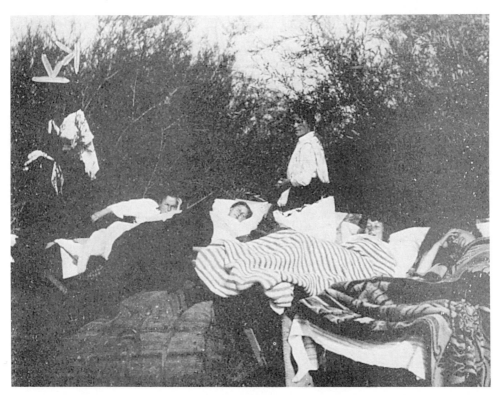

*Refugees take the road to the unknown,
their carts packed with household goods*

A stranded family. Their horse died from exhaustion

Russian trenches at Krasnobroda, June 1915
Above left *Trenches dug in rock*, above right *Trenches dug in sand*

Deserted Austrian trenches, 1916

Burial service for an officer in the open field

Dead friend and foe lie side by side in a hastily dug trench on the battlefield

Off to Front Line work in summer transport

Travelling in winter to a distant dressing-station

Setting out for a new destination on the Galician Front

Conference of staff surgeons in a peasant hut, 1916
Note the icons on the wall

A Russian armoured car, 1915

Artillery men find a safe corner for their weapon

Open-air Mass on the Russian Front

An ice cross made by soldiers, January 1917
In the background stands the wooden church which they built

Russian trenches dug through a village street

Russian soldiers with gas-masks, 1916

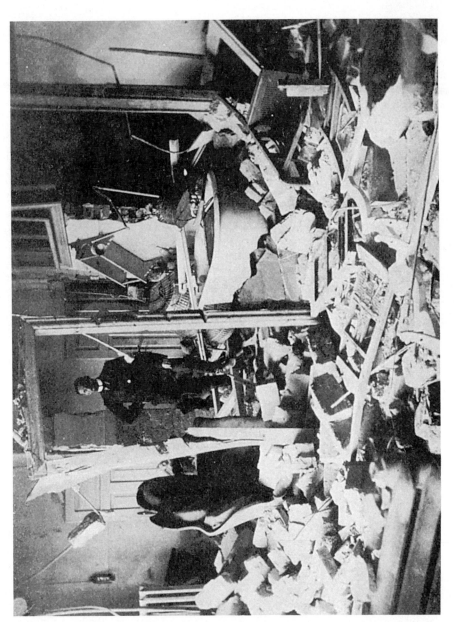

After one chemodan a Polish house is completely destroyed

Florence Farmborough on duty at a forest station

The famous Orenburg Cossack Regiment

Nomads from the Kirghiz Steppes in Turkestan, recruited in mid-1917

Machine-gunners relaxing
Note the accordion and their mascots: a monkey and a dog

A cowbarn provides shelter from wind and rain

Burial of an elderly priest of the Greek Orthodox Church killed on active service

The 'Unknown Soldier' lies on the battlefield

Inside a Russian peasant's hut. Father is away at war. The child has consumption. Strings of onions hang from the ceiling

A typical Roumanian homestead with a wooden veranda, 1917
The wife is proudly wearing her husband's boots

Hay harvesting in the Bukovina, Roumania

Three generations of Roumanian shepherds and their hut, 1917

Yasha Bachkarova who commanded the famous Women's Death Battalion, Siberia

A Communist agent haranguing soldiers, 1917

*Trench warfare is over; the Retreat of 1917 has begun
Bolshevism has spread through all Russia's Front Line*

Peasants waiting for food rations

A young Communist intent on destruction

Deserting soldiers call a halt on their way home and to 'Freedom'

End of a journey: Vladivostok, 1918

Florence Farmborough taking a photograph

vious year, we could but rejoice at the comforting thought that the tables had been turned and that we, at long last, were gaining the upper hand.

A small house was finally found for us at the cross-roads in the village of Rzhepintse. We arranged a bandaging-room without delay and then prepared for rest. It was already 2 a.m. and, because our camp-beds had not been unpacked from the *oboz*, we lay down on stretchers. Sleep came but fitfully; here, too, fleas proved a discomforting adversary.

Saturday, 28th May

It was a hot, rather sultry day. In the morning, Alexander Alexandrovich, one of our Transport Heads, offered to drive us to see the deserted Austrian trenches; we gladly consented. One excelled all others in luxury and cosiness: we decided that it must have been the *blindage* of an artillery officer. It contained chairs, tables, pictures on the armoured walls and books; there was even an English grammar.

We toured some of the smaller trenches; these, too, were amazingly well-constructed. I thought of the shallow ditches with which our soldiers had to be content; even their most comfortable dug-outs were but hovels compared with these, they were so ingeniously built and arranged: plaited strips of wood covered the walls which were upheld by large bags of earth; iron shields surrounded the loopholes for the guns, and the cupboards which held the rifles were covered with tarred matting. Outside the trenches, small plots of land had been converted into gardens in which flowers and vegetables were growing; in one quite a big patch was devoted to spring onions! A notice was nailed up on the wall of one dug-out: 'Austria kaput! 47,000 prisoners captured! 77 guns surrendered!' Obviously, an important bulletin, issued by a jubilant Russian soldier *en passant*!

We drove on through a wood and a large park. Craters pitted the earth every few yards; several dead horses lay near a coppice, their carcasses looking strangely swollen and deformed. The trees were bent and broken, their branches hanging limply earthwards. On our way back, we passed through the village of Svestova. Frightened women and children peered at us surreptitiously through windows and doorways before disappearing. It was said that all their menfolk had been taken away with the retreating troops.

We made our way back to our quarters as quickly as possible,
lest marching-orders should have been received, for we were aware
that Rzhepintse was only a temporary halting-place. Dinner came
in the shape of soldiers' soup and *kasha* – not very savoury, but
definitely appreciated by all our hungry members. Our beds had
not yet been unpacked – a good omen we felt sure. After tea we
discovered a small summerhouse in the garden. It was so clean
and dainty that we were not surprised to find from a date carved
over the entrance that it had been erected only three weeks
previously.

A Brigadier-General called for a short while and told us that
the Offensive is progressing beyond all expectation and that our
division might go into reserve for a time, but that our Red Cross
unit would go forward with our troops; in that case, he added, he
would take us under his wing. We were ready to take to the road
again when the orders reached our *Letuchka*. We were to go to
Buchach and open a first aid post there without delay; we were
more than thankful and the idea of being stationed in the town
which only a few days before had been wrenched from the enemy
filled us with enthusiasm.

28th May. Buchach
We arrived in Buchach at 6 p.m. We passed many Austrian trenches, interspersed with the trenches hastily dug by the pursuing
Russians; they, needless to say, were recognisable by their general
untidiness and slight depth. A great battle must have raged here,
for the earth looked blackened and bruised and the trees too bore
the marks of devastation. On one side of the road there stood what
once had been two mighty oaks, their heads slashed off and their
riven trunks splintered. A little farther along, we witnessed a sad
scene. Some 50 men of the 164th Zakatalski Regiment, 41st Division, had just been buried in a 'brothers' grave'. A group of soldiers
was sorting out their belongings and placing them in small heaps:
high boots, belts, mess-cans, etc.

As we neared the centre of Buchach, the flowering acacias
presented a pleasing sight after the desolate scenes along the
town-approach. Buchach was a most attractive place built on
either side of the River Stripa; there was more than one large
sanatorium and, on the hillside, were several big hospitals, displaying the Red Cross on their roofs.

Several houses were still burning fitfully and a sickly odour of smouldering paint and worsteds pervaded the air. An ancient castle reared its hoary head to our left. Soldiers were lolling idly about the streets; some of them so drunk that they were reeling. Now and then, a drunken voice shouted out to us – its owner quietened instantly by comrades as they spied our uniformed doctors following in the rear. It was a long time since we had seen a drunken soldier; the sight saddened us. It was not the best way to celebrate victory, but perhaps those poor, illiterate recruits knew no better.

Driving past two large storehouses, we noticed soldiers with rifles standing on guard. The wine-shops, we were told, had been besieged by our tired, wayworn men, with disastrous results, so that all the bigger wine-stores had been placed under strict military supervision.

We reached our quarters and prepared the bandaging-room without delay. Three or four wounded were brought before we were actually ready for them. We had bandaged those men and were busily engaged in unpacking our own necessary belongings and the first aid equipment, when an urgent message reached us: 'Prepare for burnt soldiers.' Laconic wording, but elaborated in some detail by the staff messenger. A disastrous fire had gutted a wine-cellar; several soldiers had been burnt to death; some were being brought for instant treatment. It seems that the men of the 101st Permski Regiment had that day marched through Buchach, singing lustily, on their way into reserve. During the evening, several had gone on a tour of exploration. They found a distillery in which casks of alcohol were still stored. They drank their fill and then, inebriated and elated, turned on the taps. But someone must have struck a match, for the cellar was suddenly swept with fierce flames. About a dozen men perished on the spot; others crawled out, but collapsed and died soon afterwards. Only two of them were able to stand and they were brought to us.

They came, both of them, *walking*: two naked red figures! Their clothes had been burnt off their bodies. They stood side by side in the large barn which we had converted into a dressing-station, raw from head to foot. Injections were immediately ordered, but we could find no skin and had to put the needle straight into the flesh. Their arms were hanging stiffly at their sides and from the finger-tips of the men were suspended what looked like leather gloves; these we were told to cut off which we did with surgical scissors. They were the skin of the hand and fingers which had peeled off and was hanging from the raw flesh of the finger-tips. Then we showered them with bicarbonate of soda and swathed their poor, burnt bodies with layers of cotton-wool and surgical lint. We laid them down upon straw in an adjoining shed. In an hour or two, the cotton-wool was completely saturated, but we could help them no further, save with oft-repeated injections of morphia which, we prayed, would deaden their sufferings. They died, both of them, before morning. And neither of them had spoken a single word! I don't think that anything which I had ever seen touched me so keenly.

The Sisters' room was small and the night brought little rest. I dozed off at intervals, but the thought of those two suffering, burnt bodies would not leave me. There was, too, a horrible smell: some dead horses lay not far from the house – and the wind was blowing in the wrong direction. In the distance one could hear noisy singing and faint accordion music. So many soldiers had perished in that foolhardy escapade and yet – here were their comrades once again drinking and revelling! Victory must have deprived them of their senses!

In the room next to ours, several members of the *Letuchka* were resting. It must have been well after midnight when shouts were heard outside. The drivers of our motor and horse vehicles were disputing their rights to certain extra payments. Captain V., the officer in charge of the transport, jumped up from his resting-place and stormed at the men; but, somehow, a few of them managed to enter the house. Our youngest doctor, a fine athlete and eloquent speaker, brought both these faculties into play – he sprang up, struck out with his fists and poured out such a torrent of invective that the intruders hurriedly made their exit. They stood for a few minutes shouting and swearing in the street and then wandered off into the town. These were our own men, all belonging to our *Letuchka*! Could victory and wine have changed these loyal soldiers so quickly?

Trinity Sunday, 29th May

During the morning, many cavalry regiments passed through the streets of Buchach; among them the regiments of the 9th Donski Cossacks and the 8th Uralski Cossacks, both making a grand show, their banners flying in the wind. They brought much animation into the town; the mere sight of these stalwart men on their sturdy, sinewy horses inspired optimism.

Unexpected instructions were sent to us. We were to open and equip a new *lazaret* for wounded in another district of Buchach. We left after dinner and drove to the appointed premises, where all the rooms were in a terrible state of disorder. It had been the home of the School Director, who had left the town with the retreating Austrian troops. Plainly their departure had been decided at the eleventh hour. Pictures, books, ornaments, geological specimens and dried flowers were scattered about the floors. It took us some time to get everything straight and clean. At last all was ready; and not a minute too soon, for ambulance-vans were making their way up the street; about thirty wounded men were deposited in and around our station. We unpacked all the necessary equipment and prepared ourselves for some hard work.

During the evening we saw to our surprise companies of cavalry-men returning to Buchach; their *oboz* followed them. Some of the wounded told us there had been a severe counter-attack and certain sectors of the Russian Front Line had been forced to withdraw. We listened in consternation. Withdraw! Does that mean *retreat?* We asked first one man, then another, but no one knew what had happened. Our doctors thought it wise to despatch all our wounded to Dzurin. After they had left we felt better; at least one great responsibility had been lifted from our shoulders. As far as we were concerned, we must remain at our posts. We finished cleaning the rooms and then, all very tired, we decided to retire. The divans were hard and pillowless, but they provided make-shift beds.

Monday, 30th May

We have heard that only one Regiment has withdrawn. The reason given was that the Germans had arrived and manned the Austrian Defence Lines. We also heard that many of our men in the trenches had succumbed to the influence of alcohol which they had managed to take with them, and the Austrians took advantage of the fact to launch an attack. A second piece of rather surprising news has reached us. The Red Cross *Otryads*, stationed in Buchach, are leaving and our Unit will be the only one left in the town. We already have requests from the 41st and 47th Divisions to accept and attend to their wounds. Firing is continuing intermittently, but there is no further news from our Front.

I went into the garden for half-an-hour this morning. It was a brief respite, but in those thirty minutes I had seen something which steadied my nerves and refreshed my mind. . . . It was the flowering beauty of the Austrian countryside. How strange that men should want to kill each other in springtime! . . . How monstrous that war can exist when all the world is in blossom! . . .

More wounded have arrived. One look at them lying on stretchers or on the grass, was sufficient to tell one that they were suffering intolerably and that many of them were dying. Doctors, Brothers and hospital orderlies gathered in full force and we worked hard and steadily for some hours. Fatal injuries to head, lungs or stomach, predominated; several were dying on arrival; nevertheless, they, too, received the injection necessary to bolster up the failing heart. Once, I had questioned our head doctor about these injections. 'Alexander Mikhaylovich, this man is dying; he is already in a coma. If I inject camphor or caffeine, he will only revive to feel intense pain. Shall I leave him to die in peace?' Alexander Mikhaylovich had glared at me and his wrathful voice made answer: 'Sister Florence! Do your duty! What right have you to dispute orders? Have you forgotten the supreme duty of Red Cross work: to do everything in one's power to *preserve* and *restore* life? While a spark of life remains, we must strive to preserve it.' I knew that he was right; he always was. But when, after an injection, an almost lifeless body had begun to moan and twist piteously, I could not but feel that I had helped to augment his anguish. Over two hundred men had passed through our hands at the end of the day; the majority of whom had been bandaged, fed and then despatched to the Base hospitals.

Tuesday, 31st May

Last night, when most of the bandaging had been done, several of our company went back to the house where we had lodged after arriving in Buchach; Sister Sofiya and I remained on duty with the dying men. A few wounded came during the night and, as several of our vans had returned empty, we were able to send the new-comers and some of the soldiers off to the Base. At 8 o'clock this morning, Sofiya and I were relieved by the day-duty Sister; we were very tired and thankful for a few hours' sleep. We were back

at our posts in the early afternoon. Some forty wounded had
come during our absence; they had received treatment and had
been despatched to safety.

During the afternoon the news was flashed round the Unit that,
on our Southern Front, a great victory had been won. Whole
regiments of Austrian soldiers had given themselves up and the
town of Chernovits, in the Austrian province of Bukovina, was
about to surrender to General Lechitski, the Commander-in-Chief
of Russia's 9th Army. The good news was, naturally, very heartening; we went about our work in high spirits.

Late in the evening a message was received that about 100
wounded were on their way to us. They arrived around 11.30 p.m.
We bandaged them, fed them and sent them off in our motor
vehicles. Some of them were so exhausted that they fell asleep
while we were still cleaning their wounds. A thunderstorm shook
the quiet of midnight; the thunder-claps played a noisy duet with
spasmodic explosions of shells for more than an hour. Our work
finished about 3.30 a.m.

Friday, 3rd June

I drove with a Brother to Dzurin this morning. Intensive work was
in progress on the main road. We were told that some 2,000
prisoners, including 500 Germans, were digging new trenches and
destroying the old ones used by the Austrians. The weather was
bad and stormy. In our dressing-tent, I sterilised material and lint
for future use. At noon, dinner was brought to me and I demolished
it like a true soldier – dipping the black bread into the soup and
drinking the remaining liquid from the bowl. A wooden spoon
accompanied the buckwheat *kasha* which I found most appetising,
with succulent bits of meat in it here and there.

Dzurin was teeming with soldiers; their tents were pitched
everywhere. I noticed a crowd of people waiting near a shop,
hoping perhaps to purchase some eatable, or useful object the
Zemski Soyuz had sent. The *Zemski* Administration had also
opened an eating-house especially for the men working on the
trenches. Some of the newly dug trenches were an improvement on
the former ones. It was possible that a lesson had been learnt from
the trenches of the Austrians, whose skill in constructing such a
variety of earthen encampments had aroused interest and admiration. Shells and hand-grenades had been collected and were

lying about in small heaps; rifles, abandoned or broken, were
standing, trussed together, on their butt-ends.

Saturday, 4th June, Buchach

Rain has persisted, on and off, the whole day, and the firewood is
wet. Our doctors are rather perturbed; some of our orderlies, in
company with other soldiers, have been caught stealing in Dzurin.
In the late evening, news was flashed to us by a Cossack despatch-
rider that Chernovits had fallen to our troops. Pray Heaven that
the news be true!

Sunday, 5th June, Buchach

The good news was confirmed this morning! Chernovits was
occupied by the 9th Army after a bitter struggle. Wounded and
sick have been coming at intervals all the morning and early afternoon. There was a lull in our work at about 5 p.m. and a cup of tea
has helped to banish much of my tiredness. Firing is still continuing,
but becoming more subdued and distant as the day goes on.

Sunday, 12th June, Buchach

During the last week work has been strenuous at times. We have
had several deaths, but many of the men were fatally wounded and
only came to us to die. I was on duty all day yesterday. Two of our
operated patients died; both operations – one head, the other,
stomach – were exceedingly difficult, but there was just a slender
chance. Once again, the valour of the men of the 102nd Vyatski
Regiment has come to our notice; the Regiment has sustained
dreadful injuries and nearly a whole *rota* [company] has been
wiped out. The enemy had broken in on both flanks and our men,
practically surrounded, were fighting the Austrians face to face;
many of the wounds we dressed were inflicted by bayonets and the
butts of rifles. An under-officer, who had been a patient of ours at
Dzurin, was brought in wounded in the leg; he moaned and groaned
so continuously, twisting his body this way and that and making
it difficult for the Sister to bandage him, that one of our doctors
called him cantankerous and told him that many a raw recruit
would bear pain better than he. The reprimand must have struck
home, for the man's groans ceased and he became more amenable.
It was a very busy time for us all; major operations were frequently essential.

When the operations were over, the patients would be set apart in a room, tent, or barn, with a Sister and orderly in attendance. One of our ambulance-drivers was brought to us yesterday evening with a very badly wounded leg. When I saw him I sensed that there would be trouble, for he was a Tatar and I knew that Tatars had many strong convictions and strange prejudices.

Among our transport-drivers were several Tatars, sturdy, reliable men, who kept themselves somewhat apart from their Russian comrades. Being Moslems, they were scrupulous in observing their holy days and their diet. There were so many of them in our *Letuchka* that at times special food would be prepared, and one of the large 'drums-on-wheels', our mobile kitchens, allotted to these soldiers, who would go hungry rather than eat the food forbidden by their religion.

Kulja, our driver, was a quiet middle-aged man, a very devout Moslem. When he came to himself, our head doctor told him quietly that his leg would have to come off. He shook his head: 'No!' emphatically 'No!' He would *never* allow his leg to be amputated. The doctor told him that he would wait until the next morning and hoped that by then he would have changed his mind; otherwise his life would be in jeopardy. Had he been a Russian, the situation would have been easier, but with a Moslem it was a different matter; they had rules which might prevent the amputation of a limb against the owner's will. The morning came and the doctors told Kulja in plain words that, unless his leg were taken off, he would certainly die, for gangrene had set in. Again he steadfastly refused an amputation. 'Good,' he said, 'I will die willingly, if Allah so wishes. The will of Allah be done.' He died in the evening, exactly 24 hours after he had been brought to us. I was with him at the end. He was quite happy: his simple Faith never wavered for a moment.

We hear that one of our Base hospitals is to be transferred to Buchach; we are glad, because our wounded men will be spared a long journey. A new *prekaz* [order] has been issued to the effect that all Austrians in the districts near the Russian Front Lines are to leave their homes and go eastwards to Trebunovski. All must go – old and young. I watched a sad procession of them pass through Buchach; their carts were overladen; they carried what they could, driving their cows before them. I had often seen such endless streams of broken-hearted homeless people during 1915;

nevertheless, I once again felt compassion for these helpless multitudes, driven from their native villages and forced willy-nilly into strange surroundings under a strange, hostile Government.

Monday, 13th June, Buchach

There were two major operations late last night, both stomach wounds; the intestines had been severely perforated and it was by no means easy to cleanse the abdominal cavity of the blood and impurities which had flowed into it. The Surgeons' skilled hands were able to cut away the torn intestinal tubes and join the healthy ends together once again. It would seem a miracle if the patient survived such an intricate operation, but a high percentage *did* survive and our Surgeons, who kept in touch with many of the Base hospitals, often heard that such and such a soldier was being slowly restored to health. It was a difficult time for us Sisters while these 'stomach' patients were under our care, for they were constantly crying out for water – their thirst must have exceeded their pain – and we knew that nothing must pass through those injured intestines until they had healed. It was even forbidden to allow a drop of water to pass through those parched lips.

Tuesday, 14th June

I was told that well over 200 men had passed through our Unit today; I was also told something that almost took my breath away: that some 3,000 men are to come to us during the next few days to be fed, as the *Zemski Soyuz* has arranged that enormous supplies of food should be stored in the town under our unit's supervision. This will entail a vast amount of extra work for our *Letuchka*; luckily, however, the regiments concerned have agreed to send us extra help.

I sat in the operating-room, awaiting further newcomers. I think that I must have slept, for when I opened my eyes, my watch was pointing to midnight, and all around was very quiet. At 6 a.m. more wounded arrived. One of them had a most unusual wound; a bullet had entered his body at the shoulder-blade, gone down his right side and lodged in his thigh. After an early breakfast, we resumed our work. I extracted a bullet from the upper left arm of a young soldier; it was not a difficult extraction, for the tail-end of the bullet was visible, but even after the wound was cleansed and bandaged, he continued to weep and moan: *'Sestritsa, bolit!*

bolit! [Little Sister, it hurts!].' I was washing the face of another young soldier, a face covered with grime, dust and dried blood. '*Sestritsa*,' my patient said, with an attempt at a smile. 'Leave it dirty! I shall not go visiting any more.' At first I thought that he was joking and some light-hearted repartee was on the tip of my tongue; then I saw the ugly gash on his head and I understood what he meant.

One of the stomach patients had deteriorated greatly in the last few hours. The craving for water was on him; it was all that a Brother and I could do to prevent him from throwing himself off his straw mattress. In his delirium he cried out that he and his comrades were drinking from a great river, and that he was drinking, drinking, always drinking.

In the tent which housed the sick, the patients were less restless. One soldier refused to drink because the water given to him had been boiled; he vowed that boiled water always gave him colic. A young Tatar assured me that if only I would allow him to sit up and smoke, in two days' time he would be up and about again; but as things were, he said that it was *Plokhoye delo! Ochen plokhoye delo!* [Bad business! Very bad business!].

Friday, 17th June
The night had been a fairly quiet one, despite the many onslaughts of fleas. We had been told that a cigarette would keep away bed vermin; so we purchased some *makhorka*, the cheapest and strongest tobacco available. Rupertsov, our room-orderly, undertook to roll the cigarettes for us. We smoked our *makhorka* bravely and vigorously, puffing clouds of smoke among the bed-clothes, but the strong tobacco made us feel so sick that we decided the remedy was worse than the insects.

Saturday, 18th June
The best news of the day was brought to us at dinner-time; it announced that Kolomea had been captured by our men and over 6,000 prisoners taken. What joyous news! Kolomea is considered a prize of considerable importance; this is the second time that it has passed into Russian hands, having been recaptured by the Austrians in the early part of 1915. Not only is it a notable railway-junction, but also a key-town in the rich oil-producing district of East Galicia. Among our Brothers there is a young Jew from

Kolomea – where his grandparents are still living. He told me that he had had more than one sleepless night wondering what was happening to his aged relatives. 'That town is full of Jews,' he said despondently, 'God only knows what is going to happen to them all.'

Sunday, 19th June

News from the Western Front continues to be excellent: the French and English Armies have broken through the German Lines, gained a decisive victory and taken more than 3,000 prisoners. Another welcome piece of news was that our doctors have agreed to open a first aid post near the Fighting Line, so that help would be immediately forthcoming for the wounded. I heard of this arrangement with tremendous satisfaction.

Tuesday, 21st June

At dinner-time, I looked outside and saw shell after shell exploding in front of Buchach. Three of our aerostats were in the air; the hum of enemy aeroplanes was heard; the whole atmosphere was charged with activity. The wounded began to arrive. We cleansed their bodies of caked mud and blood, bandaged their wounds and sent them on without delay. About 500 passed through our hands before dusk. Some of them were from our gallant Vyatski Regiment; they told us that over 2,000 prisoners had been taken and that the 3rd Line of enemy trenches had been occupied.

Groups of Austrian prisoners, under mounted escort, were passing through Buchach. A few were brought to our unit for bandaging; they were dirty and dusty and dejected, but we could dress their wounds only – the escorts would not wait.

Thursday, 23rd June

Many wounded arrived – both Russian and Austrian. I was struck by the stoical attitude of the latter. Few of them cried out aloud but now and then a low, gasping moan would escape them. I spoke to them in German; that evening, our head dispenser took me to task about it. 'Keep to the Russian language, Sister Florence,' he said. 'Don't let the prisoners think that they are welcome here! I'd rather see a bullet through their head any day than a bandage round it! And' – looking at me slyly – 'keep in mind that a long talk with prisoners in their own language might arouse *suspicion*!'

'What do you mean, Ivan Ivanovich?' I burst out. 'There is nothing suspicious about my conversation; how could there be? If English or French were among our wounded, I should speak with them in their own languages.' 'Yes,' he interrupted, 'all well and good; they are our Allies. I am only suggesting that you remember that these men are our enemies. A word to the wise!' he added significantly. I was downcast for some little time afterwards; indignant, too, that such a mean thought could have entered the man's head and found utterance in the way it did.

A doctor and a Sister have already gone to our new *punkt* [post] near the Fighting Line. They may send for a few more of our *Letuchka* tomorrow. I am living in hopes that I shall be included. My work finished for the time being, I retired to a corner of our operating-room, sat down on the hard, wooden chair, leant my head against the hard wooden wall and went to sleep. The fleas awakened me; I could not rest for long. Where those wretched insects-of-prey came from, it was difficult to say, for the floor and walls had often been washed and disinfected with strong carbolic. Dust, too, accumulated rapidly from nowhere! I had dusted everything again most meticulously in the early afternoon and now all over the furniture was a fine layer. What an operating-room! But I suppose we had to be thankful for a roof over our heads; there had been times when Alexander Mikhaylovich had been forced to operate in the open air.

Friday, 24th June. Barish

The much-wished-for summons came; I was called to join our team at the new first aid post. I hastened to arrange everything before departure. Some Brothers and orderlies were to remain with the patients until the arrival of the Surgical Unit which had been appointed to take our place.

After dinner, we started off in our motor to Barish, an hour from Buchach. Arriving at 4.30 p.m. we found the forerunners of our *Letuchka* installed in a partly demolished house near some devastated Austrian trenches. We distributed among them their belongings which we had brought with us, replenished the drums of sterilised material and filled the ample cupboards with lint-rolls, bandages, surgical instruments, first aid packets and general equipment. The Austrian trenches, as ever remarkably well-constructed, were smashed and shattered; wire entanglements tangled and trampled;

strips of uniform-cloth were still caught up in the barbs. Craters
pitted the ground on all sides; shells were piled here and there in
heaps; a motor-plough stood derelict in a nearby field. There were
patches of dark-stained earth where men's blood had drenched
the soil; bits of torn paper, oddments of cloth, battered mess-tins, a
crushed *furashka* [peak-cap] littered the ground. And there was one
corner, canopied by the broken branches of decapitated trees,
where stood many groups of wooden crosses. No names were
inscribed – there had been no time.

Saturday, 25th June
News reached us early this morning that our 37th Division had
twice broken through the enemy Lines only to be beaten back
each time. Intermittently, news filtered through from the various
Fronts. A great victory was reported near Balanovich, with many
Germans taken prisoner. On the far-Western Front, the English
and French Armies were still advancing. All was going well!
Only a couple of wounded have come; we may expect others at
any moment, but we are already well-prepared.

Sunday, 26th June
We have been under fire since midday; some twenty shells have
fallen in and around Barish, most of them to the right, near our
Transport, and not far from the estate where the Divisional
Surgical Staff is stationed. Our Unit has had another casualty – a
van-driver, hit by shrapnel while sitting near his van; he died
almost immediately. Among the few wounded who passed through
our hands this morning was a soldier shot through the throat; he
was subjected to tracheotomy. His face and neck were dreadfully
swollen and his difficulty in breathing was painful to hear, despite
the successful placing in the windpipe of the tube to allow passage
of air to the lungs.

Monday, 27th June
The soldier with the dreadful throat-wound died this morning
about 7 o'clock. We hear that our men are holding on to the
territory which they have taken, determined not to cede an inch.
This evening, Sofiya and I walked for a while in the park; the air
was fresh and invigorating, but the scenes around us were littered
with the 'left-overs' of the recent conflict. Once again we were quick

to note the deplorable effect of gun-fire upon the trees; one could tell that they had once been such delicate silver-birches, such tall, shapely firs; now, they were wasted and withered, as though the searing breath of a typhoon had swept over them, robbing them of all form and beauty.

Tuesday, 28th June

Late last night there came news of English and French successes in and around the valley of the River Somme; but German armies are gathered there for some supreme effort, and we trust and pray that our Allies will be able to resist the challenge. A severe thunderstorm during the night drenched the world about us and transformed it into a quagmire; the weather is definitely adverse to warfare. It is rumoured that an advance has been planned for our men tomorrow and it is possible that a small number of our Unit will follow them with first aid equipment.

At a distance of less than six versts from Barish we have already four divisions along the Front; they are the 41st, 43rd, 37th and 26th Divisions. As usual before an important field-operation there is a strained feeling pervading the atmosphere.

The 37th Division has gone by and, in the evening, the Samarski Regiment went swinging along the road, singing lustily. Newspapers have been sent to me and it is with great joy that I have read of the Allied advance in France; later, I was told that English and French troops had broken through three of the German Front Lines, forcing the enemy to retreat. It is wonderful to hear such excellent news! We, too, have great hopes for further success tomorrow on our Front.

Wednesday, 29th June

The guns were firing in a desultory way most of the night. Some wounded have come; they said that the great attack has not yet taken place. About half-a-dozen came from a regiment in reserve; it seems that a stray shell found its way into their camp. After treatment the men were packed snugly into our new wagonettes and removed to a place of safety. These new vehicles are a practical addition to our transport. The rain continues unabated. It was said that 4 p.m. was the hour fixed for the attack, but, according to the vehement activity of the guns, it must have begun earlier.

Then we heard that the 103rd Petrozavodski Regiment had

broken the enemy resistance and driven him back for several
versts, but casualties were great. We waited for the wounded. All
the evening and late into the night they came. There was no respite.
The men were brought straight from the trenches; some with
gaping wounds exposed; others with torn arms and legs, roughly
bound with cloth, tied clumsily by themselves or comrades.
Five dead men were among a cart-load of eleven.

A couple of surgeons from a neighbouring divisional *Otryad*
joined our unit. One of them, a surgical specialist from a Russian
University, known informally as 'the Professor', helped with the
most severe wounds. That night, he performed two operations of
laparotomy, one of trepanning and three of amputation. We
separated the dead from the dying and stacked their poor, lifeless
bodies in a shed to await burial. Some looked mere boys. My eyes
were full of tears as I looked at them.

So the attack had come and gone! It was said to be very successful. Some of the soldiers, in half-hysterical fashion, insisted on
relating all that they had seen. I tried to soothe them, but they
seemed to find relief in telling their tale, despite the fact that it
was quite incoherent. There was one very wide, very open field,
they said; it had been necessary to cross it and the only way to
do so was by crawling along on one's stomach. But the enemy
could see every movement and the crawling men would be mown
down, as it were, by a giant *kosa* [scythe] all along the line. They
had seen their comrades scrambling over the piled bodies of our
dead soldiers. They, too, had tried to crawl, but they had only got
half-way. We heard of this death-trap from many quarters and
we marvelled at the courage of our men who had gained the day.
From 6 to 8 a.m. the firing continued incessantly, and the Austrian
shells shrieked out their fury and vengeance.

Friday, 1st July
It was a lovely, sunny morning. Vladimir Alexandrovich came for
a brief visit and then went on to the 6th Battery. He told us that
many people in the Base can't believe that our successes will last
long, for they consider them too good to be true. Although he
came from Base Headquarters, he brought no letters for me,
which was not only surprising, but very disappointing. I have not
heard from home for several weeks and yet I know well that my
Mother writes regularly.

We hear that the British Army has smashed through the German First Line in the Somme territory, advanced many miles and taken over 14,000 prisoners. Important instructions have just reached our Unit: two Sisters, two Brothers, two surgeons and a dozen hospital orderlies are to be sent to the Front tomorrow. To my indescribable joy, I am to be one of the two Sisters.

Saturday, 9th July
We returned to Barish this morning and a relay team of workers has taken our place. It will be difficult to give a coherent account of the happenings of the past week. We were in the thick of it and there was no time to think, much less to write. We turned day into night, night into day; and only a level head like the one on Alexander Mikhaylovich's broad shoulders could tell which day of the week it was – and he had to consult his pocket-calendar more than once!

The past, gloomy year of 1915, with its hopeless defeats, culminating in the great Spring and Summer Retreat of the Russian Armies, was stamped with unspeakable tragedy, suffering and frustration. It was warfare at its cruellest and worst. Now the tables have been reversed. Instead of retreat, it is ADVANCE! We traversed the Austrian countryside – still showing signs of springtime's generous flowering – and we revelled in the knowledge that our Russian armies, and those of our brave Allies on the far-Western Front, were gaining success after success. But as we followed in the rear of our advancing troops, the trail of devastation left by war was painfully visible: we passed through deserted villages and hamlets, many of them riddled by shells and blackened by fire; an isolated chimney or half-demolished wall stood mutely forlorn on a devastated landscape. Dead, or dying, horses were lying by the wayside. Broken gun-carriages, or other vehicles, blocked parts of the roads. Trampled wire-entanglements and shell craters studded the ground on every side. Often the trees themselves would indicate the proximity of a recent battlefield; blasted, bent and broken, with their branches drooping in untimely decay, their trunks seared and jagged – dumb victims of man's inhumanity to man . . . and to Nature. And the battlefield! – I saw the battlefield in all its grim reality, for we were following closely in the footsteps of our advancing troops and ever ready to tend the wounded and dying left behind in their wake. We did not enquire as to the nationality of the helpless man, nor did we seek to distinguish the colour of his uniform; we saw – and I thank God for it – we saw only a suffering human being, who needed *our* help; and we gave it of our best, without discrimination.

I cannot pretend to describe all that I experienced at the small Red Cross station alongside the vanguard of our troops, for it was there that I became acquainted with a new aspect of warfare which, although savouring of victory, was no less savage and terrifying than the dark days of disastrous defeat. On the battle-fields, all natural features had been blasted into nothingness and there remained only scattered vestiges of the hideous scars inflicted by lethal weapons and the spoors of wild, flying feet and staggering, stumbling bodies.

Twice had our men rushed headlong into the attack; twice had they been beaten back; yet a third attempt had left them free to occupy the deserted trenches of the enemy. But the loss of life had been appalling. Some had received no outward visible wound; their hurt had been inflicted on mind and spirit; and those we were powerless to aid.

The badly-wounded received an injection without delay and were carried to the 'sorting-house', where operations were immediately performed – stomach and head operations being in the majority. As the fighting became more intense, the wounded lay massed outside our temporary dressing-station, waiting for attention – countless stretcher cases among them. A few would crawl inside, beseeching the care they so urgently needed.

We were working day and night, snatching a brief hour here and there for sleep. In the evening the dead would be collected and placed side by side in the pit-like graves dug for them on the battlefield. German, Austrian, Russian, they lay there, at peace, in a 'brothers' grave'. Swarms of flies added to the horror of the battlefields and covered the dead brothers, waiting in their open ditches for burial, as with a thick, black pall. I remember the feeling of horror when I first saw that black pall of flies *moving*.

Sunday, 10th July
I was glad to be back in Barish for a few days; and thankful to have a good wash and see to my laundry; my hair, too, needed attention. All these were but small items in a crisis; nevertheless, each one added to personal comfort after days of hard work and

complete neglect of personal appearance. During my absence, a liaison-officer had brought a packet of letters for me. I almost danced for joy! I was especially thankful to hear that all my family were well and that the food rations, doled out to them weekly, were sufficient for their needs.

Our doctors' plans had not materialised. We were still stationed in Barish and no hospital had been opened. Members of our transport-train were hard put to find accommodation for the countless wounded men we were forced to evacuate. It was heartening to read the newspapers, jubilant at the continuous success of our troops; but we, at the Front, knew that the battle was not yet won. The weather has changed again and rainstorms are the order of the day; the mud is hourly growing thicker.

I have just read the news-sheet of the 7th Army and am thrilled at the good reports which it contains. The Arabs have captured Mecca from the Turks; and the Russian 11th Army under General Sakharov has had remarkable success in the north of Galicia. Just one regrettable item: our good acquaintance, General Dragomirov, had been wounded by shrapnel. The paper also reported that, on the Allied Front, English cavalry – Dragoon Guards – had taken part in military operations for the first time since 1914; over 10,000 prisoners had been taken by our Allies in the last two weeks; the Germans are suffering defeat on all Fronts and 400,000 Germans shed their blood in vain at Verdun.

A boy-soldier was brought in, shot through the lungs; he died soon after arrival. He was about fourteen – a volunteer! I was amazed that the Military Command would permit lads of such tender age to be in the trenches, but I was told that it was not unusual, that the soldiers looked after them well and sometimes regarded them as mascots.

The rain continues and is causing much concern. The waters of the River Stripa have swollen three *arshines* above their normal height and our men in the trenches are standing in water above their knees. At night, we received more than twenty wounded; two or three of them with dreadful wounds in stomach and chest.

Thursday, 14th July
Yesterday, something happened which touched me deeply. Among the few wounded brought to us in the morning was a

young officer of the Vyatski Regiment. We were exceedingly
proud of this regiment; it had fought so long and so valiantly, and
several of its wounded had passed through our hands. This
young officer was found to be severely wounded in both legs. One
leg demanded immediate amputation; the wound was jagged and
torn and fragments of rusty metal were extracted from the swollen,
discoloured flesh. The leg was amputated high above the knee.
Our surgeons were very worried, and the ominous word 'gangrene'
was bandied from mouth to mouth. 'We might have saved him
had they brought him here 24 hours earlier,' said one of them
ruefully. But those 24 hours had been spent on the cold, muddy
earth, near the enemy's wire defences. He was placed on a narrow
bed in a small, empty room. Smirnov and I kept vigil at his bedside. His wandering mind was often on the battlefield, leading his
men to victory and, in a frenzy of patriotic fervour, he would
swing himself from side to side and his strong arms would pound
the air, while Smirnov and another stalwart orderly would seek to
prevent him from crashing on to the floor. We knew that he could
not last another day; the first stage of mortification was well-
advanced. The terrible odour of putrefaction which accompanies
that form of gangrene was harassing us desperately, but we knew
that it would not be for long. Before Death came to release him,
he became calmer – he was back at home, among those whom he
loved. Suddenly he seized my arm and cried, 'I knew that you
would come! Elena, little dove, I knew that you would come!
Kiss me, Elena, kiss me!' I realised that in his delirium he had
mistaken me for the girl he loved. I bent and kissed his damp, hot
face, and he became more tranquil. Death claimed him while he
was still in a state of tranquillity. How I longed to be able to tell
that unknown Elena that her unseen presence had helped him to
die in peace.

Friday, 15th July
Our troops have crossed the river and captured a village on the
other side; they praised the sappers and said that their bridge
had been quickly and firmly constructed. We had seen some of
them hurrying by the previous evening, carrying boards and bags
for the bridge. It had not been an easy task; shrapnel had peppered and delayed them more than once. It is said that the advance
may take place tonight or tomorrow. At 4 p.m. artillery pre-

parations started and firing continued for some hours. It is still raining; if it goes on like this, we may be in for a flood.

Saturday, 16th July

The advance has been postponed again because of the bad weather. The mud is so thick that high boots get sucked off the owner's legs. Each day brings more and more shells over Barish. On the 12th a couple of bombs killed two officers and a Sister of the 80th Red Cross Transport Column, stationed less than two versts from us. Yesterday, a bomb fell straight on to a house where two Sisters were sitting; one was killed instantaneously, the other received a severe stomach wound. That same afternoon, a shell wrecked half of the staff-building, where Mamasha and Anna happened to be staying; we were most thankful to hear that both had escaped injury. We only felt the repercussion; our windows splintered and our house rocked.

We have often heard distant cries of '*Ura!*' Practically always, those lusty shouts acclaim the victories of our General Sakharov. So frequently do we hear of the daring and gallantry of this General's Army that when the joyful '*Ura!*' reaches our ears, we invariably exclaim: 'There's Sakharov again!' An attack has been fixed for this evening by the 103rd Regiment and, in the early morning, the whole Line of our South-West Front will spring into action. The Germans have transferred men and guns from the Allied Western Front to bolster up the morale of the Austrians. We know that the German heavy guns and long-range, high-explosive shells are a more formidable opponent than anything which our batteries could present, so our secret thoughts are burdened with misgivings.

The weather has definitely cleared and the roads have dried. It would appear from the papers that our long spell of shocking weather has transferred itself to our Allied Front in France.

Sunday, 17th July

About 70 wounded came during the night while I was on duty. I have heard that the 103rd Regiment has managed to cross the River Koronez and occupy Dubenko, half of which town had been in its possession for several days past. The 102nd Regiment has gone into reserve for three days after three and a half months in the trenches.

Our next attack is timed for 4 p.m. The guns have been blazing
away. Mamasha and I slipped away for a few minutes, climbed a
small hill and crouched on its summit among waving corn and
wild flowers. From our vantage point, we could see the Front
spread before us. Shells were falling, throwing up blackish clouds
of earth about our trenches; farther away, our shells were engaged
in similar action near the enemy's defensive ramparts. Shrapnel
was exploding in mid-air, leaving puffs of slowly dissolving smoke
behind, and scattering bullets and metal particles to right and
left. We picked a few flowers and returned to our quarters.

Dusk had scarcely descended when cartload after cartload of
wounded made their appearance. Difficulty arose regarding transport; the highways round Barish were under fire and our ambulance-vans in urgent request alongside the Fighting Lines.
We placed the men on the straw-strewn earth in the empty sheds,
told them to rest awhile and, at the earliest opportunity, they
should be driven to the Base. A young Tatar, heavily wounded,
was carried to the operating-table. He could speak no Russian and
vainly tried to whisper something to us which we could not understand. One of our Tatar drivers was sent for; he stooped low over
the prostrate form, but no answer came to his eager questioning.
'He's gone!' said a voice. The weather-beaten face of the older
tribesman stiffened with emotion as he walked away. An infantry
officer whose thigh-wound had been dressed and bandaged, declared that he could walk without difficulty; he was most anxious
to help and assured us that he had taken a first aid course before
joining the Army. He was allowed to tend the more lightly
wounded and this he did with considerable skill, but insisted on
wearing rubber gloves which, he said, gave him greater confidence
and grip.

Monday, 18th July
We continued work until 4 o'clock this morning. I got up at 6.30
a.m. and went to work. Few wounded came that morning, but the
fury of the guns never ceased. I managed to write a couple of
letters to Moscow; one to my Russian 'family', the other to be
forwarded to England. Conflicting reports have reached us from
the Front Line. First came news of a slight advance of our men;
then, that they had been beaten back to their former position. An
official news-sheet states that the Germans are keeping well in the

background and, at the same time, urging the Austrian soldiers to repel the Russian attacks. It is certainly not an enviable situation for the Austrian soldier, knowing that he is being prodded from before and behind!

Wednesday, 20th July
We have all been working round the clock. Yesterday, we started at 5 a.m. and went on steadily until 5 o'clock this morning. We have been told that over 1,130 wounded have passed through our Unit in the last two days.

Thursday, 21st July
Yesterday, too, we worked all day with only a few minutes' respite to drink tea or swallow a few mouthfuls of food. I am very tired and my feet and legs are aching so much that I am wondering just how long they will be able to support me. Both Annushka and I have had bad stomach-ache, so we strap a hot water-bottle about our middle; under our white overall it is not at all conspicuous. It was Mamasha's idea, and she is nothing if not practical.

The patience, the sustained endurance of the heavily-wounded is heart-rending. They may be in the same position for hours, seldom asking for anything, unless it be 'Water! Water!' If anyone should ask me what I consider the outstanding qualities of the Russian soldier, I would have no hesitation in replying: patience and endurance. Sometimes, as I watch them lying there on their beds of straw, so still and composed, despite the pain which their wounds must be causing them, I try to imagine what they are thinking; I am sure that in spirit they are back in their homeland, surrounded by those whom they love.

We have to be thankful for the lovely, dry weather, otherwise we should be at a loss to know where to put all our wounded for transport is still a great problem. In one nearby yard, some 800 men are awaiting transport; it is, we know, dangerous to keep them so close to the Front Lines, but there is no alternative. They, poor souls, seem content enough; they think that, because they are in the hands of Red Cross Sisters and doctors, their safety is assured. We are grateful for their simple faith in us and pray that it may never be diminished, for in our memories lie those ghastly days when we were forced to forsake our wounded and leave them to the mercy of the German invaders. Here, in Austria, we feel that such a débâcle could never happen. A Colonel Bisgubski, the Head of an ambulance transport train on the South Front has come to our aid by promising to send some 50 ambulance carts for our wounded.

The wounded are still coming in. We do not regard the men with an amputated limb with the same deep pity; we know that their lives are not in great danger compared with those who have had operations on intestine or brain. I was terribly thirsty all the evening, but had no time to go back to the house for a drink. Our surgeons looked quite exhausted, but their stamina was astonishing; they just carried on.

We have been told some exciting news: that Tsar Nicholas may be coming to our Front. I am sure our soldiers will go wild with joy at seeing their 'Little Father' in their midst. It is said that he is anxious to thank them in person for their wonderful loyalty and courage. We hear that, on more than one occasion, he has ordered that special prayers be offered up in Russian cathedrals and churches in thanksgiving to God for the bravery and successful efforts of his soldiers. There is a report that Alexei, Grand Duke of All the Russias, who is now twelve years old, may be accompanying him, but our doctors say that it is most unlikely, seeing that the boy's health is far from strong.

Ten more men have died in the last 24 hours. Our surgeons say that the deaths at our Red Cross station must be considered few, taking into account the vast number of severely wounded brought to us. There are funerals here every evening; we seldom have time to attend them. Our orderlies lay the bodies side by side, cover their faces with their military coats, or with strips of white sheeting, strew on them leafy twigs and wild flowers and, when the earth has been flattened over them, often drop to their knees and bow their heads in prayer. Batyushka, our Chaplain, is usually at hand to officiate at the burials, but in his absence, Smirnov, our head orderly, conducts the short, open-air service and reads the prayers.

The soldiers, themselves, have not seemed over-elated by the success of their recent attacks; they say that, in reality, very little has been achieved. In one engagement, they succeeded in occupying three lines of the enemy's trenches, but were beaten back; they pressed forward and occupied them for the second time; again they were driven back. They describe the enemy's gunfire as being terrible and devastating; but in some sectors our shells and grenades had managed to destroy many complicated lines of the Austrian wire-entanglements.

We hear that our losses have been terrible during the recent fighting. The 103rd Regiment has only a few hundred men left; the 101st Regiment has suffered great losses. The Vyatski Regiment back again in the trenches. The 43rd Division has done well, has advanced and not been repulsed. Our division has sustained very heavy losses; the Corpus General has issued an order stating that, if the Austrian Defence Lines are not occupied by our soldiers, all the regimental commanders will be deprived of their rank. . . . And so this dreary war drags on: success and failure! victory and defeat!

At night a young boy is brought to us with a bullet wound in his head; some of his brain is showing outside the wound. He talks all the time and nothing can quieten him. In his delirium, he sees all the battlefield as his own home, and his family and friends as enemies intent on killing him. He shouts at the surgeon who is cleaning his wound, and accuses him of pulling out his hair.

A van drove up to our door and two soldiers were escorted into the house. They had no wounds, but their minds were a blank and they could neither eat nor sleep. One of them could not keep still and was dancing from side to side. Their empty, wooden faces and staring, vacant eyes made a pitiful impression.

Friday, 22nd July
At 9 a.m., Ekaterina and I had breakfast and then went to sleep until 3 in the afternoon. I had begged Mamasha not to wake me for dinner; but when I got up I found her waiting for me with a bowl of hot soup and *kasha*, which under her eagle eye I was forced to demolish before leaving the house. It was a remarkably quiet night; I slept like a log from 10.30 p.m. until 9 a.m. When I awoke, I found my face covered with flies! I must have slept very soundly!

Saturday, 23rd July
We have begun to notice the rapid development of both gangrene and tetanus resulting from flesh-wounds. It has been confirmed that enemy shrapnel are often filled not only with bullets, but with particles of rusty metal, nails, even fragments of shrapnel picked up on the battlefield. These, covered with any filthy substance,

become more than ordinarily lethal. Even a small flesh-wound,
little more than a scratch or graze, can prove fatal; and once the
jaw is firmly locked and the spasms become more frequent, there
is little medical skill can do, except to keep the doomed man under
morphia sedation. We have had several bad cases in recent weeks
of lockjaw; one of them had laughed at his slightly-gashed left
arm – already showing signs of inflammation – and said that he
was lucky that his arm had caught the splinter and not his heart!
He said that he had had dozens of similar scratches at home and
had taken no notice of them, but he had come to us, because his
Sergeant-Major had sent him; and, he joked: 'You know what
sergeant-majors are!' But after three days he had ceased to laugh
and his frightened eyes were dumbly asking what had happened
to him. It had been such a small scratch. We placed a wedge
between his upper and lower teeth, so that his tongue could be
moistened at times with a tiny swab. He died silently. So, from
now on, every soldier with a flesh wound will receive an injection
of serum anti-tetanicum. Should they rebel, we shall warn them
of the grim alternative! We hear that this new treatment will
save thousands of lives and we thank God that such a remedy
has been found *in time*.

Cholera and typhoid have taken toll of many, both military and
civilian; even a smallpox scare flared up for a few days. Special
precautionary measures were instituted and hundreds of soldiers
passed through the Red Cross units for the necessary injections.
Each one was vaccinated against smallpox and then received two
injections – one against typhoid, the other against cholera. It was
amusing to see this long queue of shirtless soldiers lined up outside
our tent; some of them laughingly said that they were about to
go to the *kino* [cinema], while others declared that they were being
driven 'like lambs to the slaughter'. The majority of them however
– not unlike the English Tommies – made light of the occasion and
faced their three 'executioners', armed with the appropriate
'weapons', in a jovial spirit; a few merry-faced recruits reminded
us that all 'good boys' should be rewarded with a sweet or cigarette.
Our orderlies are always at hand ready to help the wounded: they
are very gentle with them and wave branches over the dying heads
to cool them and prevent flies from worrying them unduly.

We are saddened at the thought that there has been no advance
and that the valiant efforts of our men have met with no results –

only casualties, casualties, hundreds and hundreds of them. A report recently stated that the men of the 104th Regiment were lying 200 paces away from the enemy's lines in shallow holes which they had dug for themselves. Between them and the Austrian trenches there were many rows of dead men who had crawled out to shoot at the enemy; they had been mown down by machine-gun fire, and lay there, their rifles still in their hands. No one can collect them, for no one dares move. The dead are beginning to smell and the taint of corruption is heavy in the air. Their comrades in their hastily-dug holes must be suffering intolerably; they have nothing to eat or drink – and dare not move. It is said that only 700 men are left in the 104th Regiment and that the 103rd can muster very few more.

Tuesday, 26th July
Three major operations took place in the morning. At nightfall, very many wounded arrived. All night long we were working. Some 75 men were attended to, bandaged and sent on. Five urgent operations have just taken place. The men were still coming in after midnight, but the cases were lighter. In several instances, I was able to carry the operation through alone, with the help of an orderly. When time allowed, we would visit the tent or shed where the men were lying, already bandaged, prior to despatch to hospital.

Wednesday, 27th July
It is true that the Austrians have retreated, but only for a distance of two or three versts. Three lines of Austrian trenches have, however, been definitely captured by the 102nd and 103rd Regiments. Some friends visited us this morning and presented me with a German *kasca* (helmet); it belonged to a prisoner, they said, who died. I don't think I shall want to keep it.

Thursday, 28th July
More than 100 wounded came during the night. They have been arriving in numbers all day and in the late evening were still being brought in. We have all been working in tremendous haste; most of the bandaging has been left to our hospital-orderlies; we, the surgical staff, have been cleaning, operating, dressing. Austrians

of all ranks were among the wounded. All night long, the operating-
table was occupied: eight major operations had been performed
before daylight. Candles, kerosene lamps and torches supplied the
only available light. Stomach wounds were by far in the majority.
Our surgeons never flagged; they were chain-workers. Prostrate
form replaced prostrate form on the table. The room was filled
with agonising groans, stertorous breathing, the rustle of moving
arms, the murmur of voices, the clink of surgical instruments, the
slash and click of surgical scissors, and always the deeply-drawn
breathing of men performing a task of intense importance.

Friday, 29th July
Reports from the Front Lines were astonishingly good; our men
were still advancing and the enemy was in full retreat. Our
batteries and aerostats were constantly moving forwards. More
than 800 wounded have passed through our hands in the last 24
hours. Despite our experienced hands, to place in correct position
a *shina* [splint] and bandage it securely to a broken thigh, must
take nearly half-an-hour, but one dare not hurry, lest extra pain
and discomfort should be added to the already intolerable suffering
of the wounded man. The head surgeon of No. I *Lazaret* has come.
Our head surgeon, after more than 36 hours of non-stop work, has
retired to his tent to rest.

There are no on-duty or off-duty regulations now; all hands are
needed. Amputations of arms and legs have been many; one leg
was so heavy that I could not lift it from the table and, the
orderlies being occupied, a Brother helped me carry it to the tiny
shed where a stack of amputated limbs awaited burial. I had not
been in that shed before and I turned away hastily; I went to our
room, drank some water and swallowed two aspirins; the choking
feeling disappeared and I was myself again. But my thoughts would
not adjust themselves so easily: after the war, what would happen
to these limbless men?

We were called to dinner; afterwards, Annushka and I went to
our room and slept until 6 p.m.; a military band was playing
'*Kol Slaven*'; the beautiful yet mournful strains worked on my
emotions and I began to wonder how long my physical strength
would hold out under the heavy burden of these never-ending
sorrows. And there seemed no end to these tragic days. Mamasha
had said only that very morning: 'The worst has still to come!' ...

Saturday, 30th July

Only a few wounded have come today, but there has been heartening news: the towns of Monasterzhiska and Stanislav have been occupied. In the former, it is said, there is widespread destruction, but the town of Stanislav is said to be untouched. Once again we are concerned to hear that our troops are intent on celebrating their victory by drinking bouts and unruly behaviour. The greatest news of all has just reached us in the shape of marching-orders! We are to leave Barish tomorrow and follow our victorious troops to Monasterzhiska. So the dream of a successful Great Offensive in the South-West Front has now become a reality! Praise be to God!

Sunday, 31st July. Monasterzhiska

As we journeyed [from Barish] the scenery became more and more beautiful; to the right and left ran long, undulating ranges of wooded hills; behind them rose majestic mountain-peaks. We came to various places where enemy batteries had stood; and to other sites where our cannon had been hastily stationed. We drove through the little villages of Bertniki and Cherkhov, where the narrow streets had been disfigured and rent asunder by makeshift trenches and where buildings of every description had been demolished, or so badly mutilated as to leave them mere piles of disintegrated brick and wood. We saw the 'ditches' where our men had dug themselves in before the attack. The attack itself must have been of a most terrifying kind on account of the difficult terrain on all three sides. On the hill facing our hastily-contrived 'trenches', were the fortified, many-lined Austrian escarpments, and to occupy those enemy strongholds much dangerous manoeuvring would have been necessary, seeing that our men were obliged to descend their hill and ascend the one opposite *in full sight of the enemy*. All over the downward and upward sides of the two opposing hills were branches of trees which, in their own poor way, had helped to disguise the attack and to shelter the attacker. We drove on and came to the upper slopes of the fortified hill; they were spread with mangled heaps of the Austrian barbed-wire protective fences which had lost all their protective capacity under the powerful battering which they had received from our guns. Enormous craters had churned up the earth and left gaping, jagged holes on all sides and a medley of indescribable objects littered the ruptured ground.

On a levelled piece of land near the lower spur of the hill,
several small wooden crosses were seen; it was, obviously, a
temporary cemetery for the Austrian dead. We walked among the
débris caused by the recent conflict and in some of the trenches we
saw – scarcely believing our eyes – human figures. They were, we
felt sure, Austrian soldiers, whom retreating comrades were unable
to remove, and whom the pursuing Russians would have neither
time nor will to heed. In one trench there were three men huddled
together, their contorted forms proving beyond doubt that they
were lifeless; in another lay the figure of a soldier stretched at full
length among the broken fragments of a once strongly-constructed
dug-out. His face was unmarked and his skin still clear; he might
have been resting, were it not for the chaotic condition of his
surroundings. So this was ADVANCE! Wherein lay its glory? Only
these forsaken, mouldering bodies could testify to the Russian
Victory.

As we continued our journey, we passed more than one battlefield. The dead were still lying around, in strange, unnatural
postures – remaining where they had fallen: crouching, doubled
up, stretched out, prostrate, prone . . . Austrians and Russians
lying side by side. And there were lacerated, crushed bodies lying
on darkly-stained patches of earth. There was one Austrian without
a leg and with blackened, swollen face; another with a smashed
face, terrible to look at; a Russian soldier, with legs doubled
under him, leaning against the barbed wire. And on more than one
open wound flies were crawling and there were other moving,
thread-like things. I was glad Anna and Ekaterina were with me;
they, too, were silent; they, too, were sorely shaken. Those
'heaps' were once human beings: men who were young, strong and
vigorous; now they lay lifeless and inert; shapeless forms of what
had been living flesh and bone. What a frail and fragile thing is
human life! A bullet passes through the living flesh and it ceases
to live. But a bullet cannot kill the soul; one knows, most assuredly,
that the Spirit – God's breath in man – returns to God Who gave
it. Oh! one *must* believe and trust in God's mercy, otherwise these
frightful sights would work havoc with one's brain; and one's
heart would faint with the depth of its despair.

Dinner was brought to us soon after our arrival. We Sisters
were still feeling affected by the awful sights which we had witnessed during that memorable journey. There was a heaviness

within us difficult to throw off and although the menfolk of our contingent carried on a cheerful conversation we could take but little part in it. We had received instructions to delay the unpacking of all surgical equipment because we might have to continue the journey on the following day. We were still surrounded by gruesome remnants of the recent conflict. Not far from our tent, there was a slight incline with a couple of dug-outs; a dead man was lying near them, half-buried in the piled earth thrown up by a shell. Mamasha took a cloth and threw it over the discoloured face. To our right was a plain; there, too, was a litter of bombs, hand-grenades, cartridges, rifles, spades, pick-axes, gas-masks, shells exploded and unexploded. From where we stood, we could clearly espy the crumpled forms of dead soldiers. I took one or two photographs, but a feeling of shame assailed me – as though I were intruding on the tragic privacy of Death.

On another part of the plain, many bodies were strewn; all in different attitudes – many on knees; others lying prone, with arms flung out; some had fallen head-first and buried their face in the soil; while still others were lying on their side, arms crossed as though they had found time to compose themselves before Death had released them from their sufferings. . . . It was a terrible battlefield; a sight which one could never erase from one's memory. There was another dreadful aspect – that of the ghastly smell of decaying human flesh. The sight of so many dead soldiers, left to decay in the hot sun and at the mercy of marauding flies, made a deep impression on us all. Our medical staff were highly indignant; they were taking the matter up immediately with the military authorities of the district and insisting that these forsaken bodies should be buried at once.

Farther away one could see long rows of devastated houses; another village laid desolate by our shells. God help the inhabitants! There was not one home left standing. It seems that some effort had been made to bury the dead, for to the north of that village a pit had been dug, in which some 50 soldiers had been deposited; the pit had not yet been filled in and here too the sight and smell of the decaying bodies were terrible. We left this gloomy halting-place and on the road, we passed a strikingly beautiful Austrian cemetery. The Austrians were particularly solicitous over their war-graves. This one was a neatly fenced-in plot with a rustic gateway, surmounted by a wooden cross and an inscription reading: '*Hier*

ruhen die für ihr Vaterland gefallenen Helden' [Here rest the heroes
fallen for their Fatherland]. Each grave bore a cross on which
was inscribed the name of the soldier. Russian and German soldiers
were buried there too. And a grave of a Jewish soldier bore a
Star of David which the Austrians had scrupulously erected
instead of a cross.

After supper, we heard that the Austrians were retreating
rapidly, and our regiments pursuing them so quickly that in some
sectors they had lost touch with each other! Later we heard the
heartening news that the whole of the Austrian Front was giving
way, that the Austrian armies appeared to be completely demoralised and that the Russian forces were pressing forward and
meeting with little or no opposition. With Austria beaten, Germany
would stand little chance of gaining a firm hold on our Front; and
our new ally, Italy, was at hand, ready to advance. Our doctors,
too, were greatly impressed and gladdened by the wonderful news,
and advised us to be ready to start away at a moment's notice;
consequently, we unpacked no luggage, but remained for the rest
of the day in our travelling garments, buoyed up by the knowledge
that marching-orders could reach us at any moment.

Alexander Ivanovich, head of our *Otryad*, arrived just before
dark; he corroborated the good news and told us that we were
leaving for Khutanova on the following day. I heard with joy that
an English officer, Sykes by name, had helped to restore order in
Persia and to prevent English and Russian communities from
being driven out of the country by the Germans who had gained
the support of the Persian police.

Monday, 1st August. Khutanova
A few wounded men found their way to us; we bandaged them,
fed them and sent them eastwards to the Base. We started the
journey in our *dvukolka* and found the highroad surprisingly full
of traffic, all moving west. Having arrived at Khutanova, we lost
no time in setting out our equipment. Mamasha arrived a little
later and arranged our camp-beds in the tent. Scarcely an hour
had passed before the ambulance-vans were at our doors and the
orderlies were bringing in the wounded; some 40 to 50 came with
the first batch. While we were attending to the broken arm of an
under-officer, he told us that Halisch and Mariampol had been
occupied by the Russians; the Austrians, he said joyfully, had

astonished everybody by their continuous retreat, but, he added, did we know that the Germans had taken their place? There was, however, nothing to fear; our troops were in such high spirits that no one, German or Austrian, could halt their advance; some of our regiments could not keep up with the pace at which the enemy was fleeing!

Tuesday, 2nd August

We are to remain in Khutanova for the time being. The enemy has called a halt and is resisting the Russian pressure. After dark, some 140 men were gathered in and around our first aid hut; by midnight, we had despatched the majority of them and found ourselves free to rest for an hour or so. But soon after 3 a.m. we were called to the Emergency Shed to another contingent of wounded, and our work continued until well into the morning. The news-sheet informed us that the 3rd Sharpshooters' Regiment of the Turkestanski Division, together with the Finlandski, would be obliged to advance before our Division would be called upon to move. So, for a week or so, we should be stationary.

Wednesday, 3rd August

Firing became fierce during the evening, and a thunderstorm arose, adding its uproar to the challenge of the guns; I could feel the rain beating on my bed and face; Ekaterina got up quickly, too, and we moved our beds away from the tent walls. Water was streaming down the slope outside and forcing its way into the tent, splashing high and wide as it accumulated in rivulets and pools on the uneven ground.

Thursday, 4th August

It was difficult to believe, but the tumultuous firing of the past night had been all in vain. The enemy's lines were still intact and our men had been beaten back every time. We had been so sure that now the tide had turned all would be plain sailing, and that the armies of our hero, General Brusilov, would have little difficulty in sweeping the Austrian forces out of Galicia and taking possession of the strategic passes of the Carpathian Mountains. So, here was a deadlock! Perhaps it was indeed true that German guns were behind this sudden repulse.

A young artillery-officer came to seek advice from our medical staff. He was downcast by the recent catastrophe and criticised the High Command who, he declared indignantly, were ordering our troops to continue the advance along the whole of the South-West Front, no matter what the cost. 'They do not realise how exhausted our men are,' he cried. 'In their comfortable armchairs in the Base hotels, with the war-maps stretched before them, they put their finger on a town – "Ah," they say, "that is a grand strategic site. That town must be seized by our men within the next three days." And the *prekaz* goes forth! And our men, hungry, cold and tired to death, are expected to spring into action . . . and sweep everything before them – no matter what the cost!' We listened despondently.

Saturday, 6th August

News from the Front has remained the same; our men have not moved. The Germans have taken over the Austrian trenches and obliged the Austrians to retire into the hinterland. It is rumoured that the Germans are preparing an 'unpleasant surprise' for us; we await it with some trepidation. Few men have been left in our decimated Division; in Vyatski Regiment only 500, and 700 in Petrozavodski; one Company can muster only 50. In our Corps, 17,000 men are said to have taken part in the last battles.

Wednesday, 10th August

Mamasha was full of news concerning the Sisters of the Saratovski Hospital; she had been told, in confidence, that they had been ordering sweets, eau-de-Cologne, and flowers from the doctors and officers of the 104th Regiment; she had also heard that the Sisters disliked our *Letuchka* and had no wish to be friendly with any of us.

Our lady-doctor wants to return to her hospital in Moscow.

Thursday, 11th August

Several priests came to recite prayers at the coffin of the dead priest [brought from the trenches with severe head-wounds the day before]; he lies clothed in his vestments with a crucifix in his hands and the Sacred Book upon his breast. Gregoriy Ivanovich told us that the Germans had poured a hurricane of shells on to our trenches, but to the consternation of our men no orders had been received from the battery. Later it was ascertained that the battery telephone had been smashed by a splinter. The soldiers had feared the worst and fled from the trenches. Then there were scenes of panic. Grigoriy Ivanovich managed to crawl out as the last men were leaving the trenches; he told us that he almost went mad. During the morning several groups of deserting men were seen in the vicinity. Everyone was under the impression that our trenches were by now in the hands of the Germans, but, to the general amazement, it was discovered that they were still empty, so the deserters were rounded up and sent back to their posts. It was, indeed, a miraculous escape, for there had been no one between the German troops and our batteries! It is known that the escaping men belonged to the 101st Regiment and had just taken over the trenches from the men of the 103rd; also that the officers were not with the men. Grigoriy Ivanovich told us that it may even be necessary to punish some of the men by shooting them.

We learnt that a peasant woman in a neighbouring village had been shot as a traitor. It seems that a *bronirovanuy avtomobil* [armoured car] stationed near her village had been destroyed by some German shells. She had been seen to leave her hut every time a shell had exploded; gradually the explosions crept nearer and nearer; finally a shell found its target. The woman's hut was searched and a hidden telephone discovered. Our batteries were often quickly located by the enemy; this might have been due to the clarity and range of their observing instruments; but it was generally acknowledged as being the result of treachery. Not long ago, Nos. 1 and 2 Batteries were hit and yesterday shells were bursting in and around Nos. 5 and 6. 'Undoubtedly, the work of spies,' we were told, and many a poor family was roughly treated owing to the suspicion of treachery.

This afternoon I carried out a distressing mission. A message had reached me from the divisional staff requesting me to photograph the dead priest; a photograph, so ran the message, would be deeply appreciated by the sorrowing relatives in Moscow. On approaching the military cemetery, I realised that full military honours were being accorded to the dead man; to my dismay, I found myself obliged to walk down an avenue of soldiers, drawn up on either side of the road. It was no easy thing to run the gauntlet of so many curious eyes, but I summed up courage and at last arrived at the small shed which served as a mortuary-chapel. Here were assembled several priests, officers, Red Cross doctors and Sisters and a large company of sympathising onlookers. My knees were shaking and I had begun to feel desperately afraid lest I should fail to focus clearly or even to make the correct exposure. The coffin was open and the dead priest's face exposed; except for its pallor, he might have been sleeping, so composed and peaceful was his expression. My tripod, as ever, was my salvation; it steadied my camera and my nerves at one and the same time. I took three photographs.

The service was a long one – fully an hour and a half. Many people came to pay their respects to the dead priest; among them army officers of high rank. One was outstanding by reason of his handsome face and wooden leg; the latter, although invisible to the eye, was certainly not to the ear, for it creaked at its owner's every movement and, of course, refused to oblige when the congregation knelt in prayer. A second was conspicuous on account of his corpulence. He was the head of a division, I was told later, and the same informant added: 'They say that he has not seen his own feet for ten years.' A small piece of paper, on which was a written prayer, was placed on the dead man's hands, and the beautiful old dirge-like hymn *'Kol slaven nash Gospod'* was sung.

Shingarov, a Member of the Duma, spent several hours with us in the evening. He was well versed in military statistics and told us that England had already one million men on the French front and that two more million were in England, ready to leave for France. The French had five million men along their front, but they were facing a German force numbering over five and a half million. On the Russian front, Germany had stationed only two and a half million; one could, therefore, conclude that she considered this front, in comparison with that of the French and British, as *detskaya zabava* [child's play].

Friday, 12th August
There was a major operation on a stomach case during the night. We have heard that the 102nd Regiment has gone back to the Front Line trenches. Grigoriy Ivanovich suddenly appeared with his newly-awarded decoration – St George's Cross for Valour. He is the first in our detachment to receive that honour, so we did our best to show him how proud we all were of him. He is rather a shy man and would, I am sure, have preferred to escape from our clutches, but we were determined that he should not. The doctors,

Brothers and other members of our *Letuchka* showed their appreciation by throwing him up several times into the air. He seemed thankful enough when their enthusiasm had quietened and their boisterous demonstrations given way to more peaceful activity, such as eating sweets and fruit-salad, which Mamasha had prepared in secret and which, despite the late hour, were accepted as a fitting celebration.

Saturday, 13th August

I was at my post by 8 a.m. Two men have died, one after a trepanning operation, the other when he was being carried to the operating-table. It has been an unhappy day for me, because I have been through a very trying experience. Perhaps, by writing down all the facts clearly, my mind may be eased of some of its guilt. 'Guilt' is a strong word to use, but I was told during the afternoon by Ivan Ivanovich, our head dispenser, that I could consider myself 'guilty of murder'. It seems strange to write these words, but the whole scene was strange. I was watching over three men who had recently been operated on, but were gradually losing their hold on life. Our surgeons had seen them in the morning, had said that there was nothing more that one could do for them, only 'tend them to the end'. One of the three was the stomach case, operated on during the previous night. He had regained consciousness, but found it difficult to speak; he could articulate only one word: *Voda* [water]. I would shake my head; tell him gently that he must not drink; when he would be stronger, water would be given to him. I could see that he was dying, but his cries for water were insistent; he was beseeching, imploring; his thirst must have been agonising. Near one of the other men, a mug of water was standing. He had seen it and, raising an arm, pointed towards it. His eyes challenged mine; they were dying eyes, but fiercely alight with the greatness of his thirst. I reasoned with myself: if I give no water, he will die tormented by his great thirst; if I give him water, he will die, but his torment will be lessened. In my weakness and compassion, I reached for the mug; his burning eyes were watching me; they held suspense and gratitude. I put the mug to his lips, but he seized my arm and tilted the mug upwards. The water splashed into his open mouth, sprayed his face and pillow, but he was swallowing it in noisy gulps. When I could free my arm from his grasp, the mug was empty.

I was deeply distressed and knew that I was trembling. I wiped his face dry and he opened his eyes and looked at me; in them, I saw a great thankfulness, an immense relief. But, before I could replace the mug, a strange, gurgling sound came from him, and, out of his mouth, there poured a stream of thick, greenish fluid; it spread over the stretcher-bed and flowed on to the floor. His eyes were closed and . . . he had stopped breathing. I ran to the door; in the yard stood a Brother and Ivan Ivanovich. 'Come quickly,' I begged them. They followed me in, but there was nothing that one could do, for he was dead. Ivan Ivanovich seemed to take in the whole picture at a glance. 'Have you given him water to drink?' he asked. 'Yes,' I nodded. 'His thirst was terrible.' 'Then you have killed him,' he said, and added: 'Quite simply, you have killed him.' 'He was dying,' I gasped. 'So you thought you would put the finishing touch!' Shrugging his shoulders, he left the room. The Brother called an orderly and together they washed the dead man and carried him to the mortuary-shed.

I remained in the room until one of them returned. I felt cold and lifeless; as though some violent thing had struck me unawares. Only Mamasha was in our room; she was the last person whom I wished to see; she was so practical and undemonstrative, but I felt that I *had* to tell *somebody*. She listened patiently. Then she said: 'You are very silly to let these things prey on your mind. You were certainly wrong in disobeying orders, but this kind of thing is happening every day in our abnormal world at the Front. As to Ivan Ivanovich, I have always said that the man is a knave or a fool, or both. In the circumstances, and knowing that death was near, I am sure that, had I been in your place, I should have done exactly the same thing.' 'Mamasha,' I sobbed. And then for the first time in our long acquaintance, Mamasha took me into her arms and I could feel the throbbing of her motherly heart, comforting and consoling. It didn't hurt half so much after that. I knew that all my life I should have the grievous memory of hastening a soldier's death through my disobedience; but, at the same time, there would be another less grievous memory: that of a pair of dying eyes looking at me with infinite gratitude. Throughout the evening, the wounded were being brought to us. We buried our many dead as dusk fell, with prayers, music and the silent homage of soldiers who were stationed in the vicinity.

Sunday, 14th August

Another lovely day. Aeroplanes have been flying constantly overhead; now and then a tremendous explosion has warned us that they are seeking nearby targets. We have heard that there is soon to be an advance by the Russian troops along the whole Front from north to south. The 33rd Corps now occupies the left flank of our division. Some Artillery friends have been and given us news from Russia. They say that the young Grand Duke Alexei is far from well, and we were interested to hear from one of them who had recently returned from Petrograd that a monk, well-known in social circles, but regarded by many with suspicion, had worked his way into the affections of the Imperial Family to such an extent that he was able to influence both the Tsar and the Tsarina. It seems he had found favour with them by reason of some special treatment which had had a beneficial effect on the health of the young Alexei. There was much dissatisfaction both in Petrograd and Moscow at this man's growing power and it was whispered that because of him the Tsarina herself was becoming increasingly unpopular, for people were reminding each other that she was of German birth and would, therefore, naturally uphold the cause of Germany rather than that of Russia. We were shocked and grieved to hear this, but paid little attention, realising that it could be only sheer gossip, for we well knew that the Tsarina was devoted to Russia and the Russian people. There was general dissatisfaction, we also heard, at the enormous number of casualties in the Russian Armies. There were complaints from all over the Empire that the Russian Generals were using their soldiers to bolster their own reputations, that they regarded life among the rank-and-file as cheap; and that Russian soldiers were daily dying like flies – and little or no success had been reaped by their sacrifice. The owners of those voices, we were told, kept well in the background; no names were ever mentioned – it was all hearsay – but it was definitely *said* and just as definitely *heard*. Even the newspapers dared not print adverse criticism. One Moscow newspaper had printed an article from the English Press in which the successful Offensive on the Russian South-West Front had been described as a tremendous strategic achievement, employing 'steam-roller tactics'.

Monday, 15th August

We have heard many loud 'Hurrahs', and the military bands have been playing rousing marches since early morning. The news from abroad is most welcome: Roumania has declared war on Austria-Hungary, and Italy, already at war with Austria, Bulgaria and Turkey since 1915, has at last declared war on Germany. So two Allies have been added to our Entente in the last 24 hours.

Wednesday, 17th August

The firing has been very intense. We have heard that the 103rd Regiment has advanced a verst or two and captured the wood just in front of the enemy's trenches. Only 147 men have come during the day. But at night many more bad cases were brought and we all worked without ceasing until 5 a.m. The doctors told me before they went to their tent that Germany had just declared war on Roumania; so they had retaliated quickly – which was only to be expected. Soon they will have to do the same with our Ally Italy. Surely this demoralising war must now soon come to an end.

Thursday, 18th August

A terribly hot day. From the small hours our batteries have been in action; the *podgotovka*, or preparation, had begun. Shells, bombs, shrapnel, rifles, machine-guns! It was really terribly unnerving; such an overpowering clamour.

Around 6 p.m. the first wounded appeared; they had attacked only three hours earlier. We were all at work. Our orderlies were busily cutting away the stained garments. Only the heavily-wounded had been brought, and their injuries were indescribably terrible: heads, chests, stomachs, arms, legs, every kind of wound was there and we found body after body smashed, broken, lacerated. The operating hut became intolerably hot and the flies, too, gave us no peace. There were many deaths. . . .

Supper came at midnight! – and after supper we returned to our posts. The wounded were still slowly coming in. There were so many now that we did not know where to put them. Finally, we gave up our tent and, like so many others of our unit, transferred our beds and baggage into the open air. But a fine rain continued until dawn, and we, wet and chilled and unable to sleep, felt as miserable as the weather. I really was dreadfully tired, for I had not slept for two nights, and rest by day was almost impossible.

Saturday, 20th August

To our surprise, we heard that we were to leave Khutanova for Serednie; but, when everything was packed, we were told that Serednie was under enemy fire. Some of our members started off to find out what was happening and to look for suitable lodgings. The sun was shining brightly and I felt so invigorated after my long rest of yesterday that I decided to go for a walk. I made for the forest, thinking that I might, perhaps, come across some flowers and ripe berries. I had taken my letters with me and re-read them, leaning against the trunk of a pine. My mother's words were so warm and comforting that a great longing for home enveloped me. I picked a few flowers and found a couple of ripe berries and then, leaving the forest, I crossed a cornfield. As I walked, I suddenly became aware of a nauseating smell. I hurried on, anxious to be clear of it when, unexpectedly, I stumbled upon the cause. A dead soldier lay at my feet. Swollen and blackened by exposure, his features had disappeared. He was lying on his back, with arms extended, and his uniform had burst with the pressure of his swollen, decaying body. . . . Then I saw something moving where his heart had once been: a mass of crawling, writhing worms. Sickened, terrified, I turned and ran. Back at the Unit, I told them, somewhat incoherently, what I had seen. A couple of orderlies went off at once with spades to dig him a grave. His identity disc was never found.

However, we did not go to Serednie, but were sent to Volitsa – a village a long way from the Front Line.

Tuesday, 23rd August. Volitsa

Newcomers have told us many stories of life in the heart of Russia. In some places there is such a shortage of foodstuffs that, unless the authorities build up sufficient stocks, there could be famine during the coming winter. Dissatisfaction is still rife in many cities. There have been rumours of strikes and even riots in Moscow, but nothing has been officially confirmed. In the city of Petrograd, there is such unrest; and there is severe criticism regarding the Imperial Family. The Empress comes in for a big share of it and in certain cliques is referred to openly as the *Nemka* [German woman]. The Tsar – 'God bless and preserve him,' they said – is doing his best to please his family, to whom he is devoted; his

household, composed of so many different elements – many at
variance with each other; his people, who are – to his great grief –
becoming estranged from him; and his Allies, whom he holds in
the highest esteem and whose just Cause will always be that of
Russia. 'And what does he say about his armies?' we asked. 'He
is, of course, most enthusiastic about their prowess; refers to them
always as his "valiant, loyal armies", and says he is convinced
that they will continue to fight for the honour of Russia and to
support their Country's Cause to its victorious end.' We devoured
all the news our visitors could give us, as well as the newspapers
which they always brought with them. Those newspapers held, of
course, special interest for me, for they gave news of the Allied
Front in France. Some of the Russian commentaries were cursorily
written; then, I would instantly suspect some catastrophe among
the British and French troops that the Press had thought fit to
screen, lest the morale of the Russian soldiers should suffer. I
knew that the Battle of the Somme had been raging for more
than two months and that British and French casualties were
great.

Thursday, 25th August. Nosov
Marching-orders have come! We are in our hearts relieved that our
idle, restful holiday is not, after all, to be long. We collected our
belongings and departed for Nosov, where we found the medical
staff of the 103rd Regiment; they were exceedingly kind and
insisted on sharing their dinner with us. But our waiter-orderly
suddenly appeared from nowhere and informed us that dinner had
been set out for us in the open-air. So we sat on the grass, delighting
in the picnic and in the warm sunshine. The soup was most appetising, though no one could guess what was in it. We had never
been able to name the ingredients of our army soups – except once,
when we were bivouacking in a pine forest infested by earwigs, and
then we knew, only too well, that it was *real* earwig soup! After
dinner, we investigated our new surroundings. While strolling in
the valley, we came across a new wooden shed. There was no
furniture, but the floor was compactly covered with clean straw.
Here was a first-class shelter for a good night's rest! The five of us
took instant possession! That night, we slept in the shed on the
thick, straw mattress and all agreed that it was a marvellously
comfortable bedroom.

Friday, 26th August

In the early morning we went for a walk on the hills around Nosov. The delectable Carpathian mountains were spread before our eyes. In the foreground lay a long, low chain of tree-covered ranges; and in the dim, blue blackground towered lofty peaks. Near at hand were Austrian trenches – marked and outlined, but unfinished. Barbed wire lay about, still bound in bundles. We came across two graves, one of an Austrian officer, the other of a Russian soldier, side by side. On the soldier's cross were the following words: *'Hier ruht ein Russischer Held* [Here lies a Russian Hero].' This was one more instance of the fellow-feeling of the Austrian soldiers towards their adversaries. Some trenches had obviously been occupied by Austrian Red Cross workers, for blood-stained bandages were on the earth floor, together with rolls of lint, pads of wadding, and dozens of empty bottles. We went to bed soon after supper. It was still light enough to read and I began a German novel which I had picked up in the wood. The novel was interesting and it was not until 8.30 p.m. that I blew my candle out and shut my eyes.

Saturday, 27th August

It was just after midnight when a loud voice outside the door shouted: 'Wake up! Get up at once! We are starting in twenty minutes.' What had happened? Was it perhaps a joke? But no! The noisy movements in the valley; lights flashing here and there; men's voices calling; it was real enough. There was no time to be lost; we dressed in haste, packed our beds into their bags and went out. We could hear Mamasha's loud, angry voice demanding – not the reason for our departure, but why *she* had not been informed the previous evening. Well, it wasn't her fault that the Surgical Personnel would have to leave on empty stomachs; no breakfast could be forthcoming at that unearthly hour; so that was that! We started off in the dark, tired and disgruntled. We enquired repeatedly: 'What has happened?' But no one knew. We asked anxiously: 'Is it Retreat?' Was there nobody who could tell us what was happening and why we were being rushed away from Nosov at dead of night? Finally a doctor, informed of our lamentations, told us that an order had been received instructing us to remove without delay to the Folvark Ponora.

Sunday, 28th August. Folvark Ponora

We were awakened by a sudden blast of discordant sounds: a military band, indulging in an early-morning practice. Who could possibly sleep through such pandemonium!

The large Red Cross placard, bearing the inscription that First Aid was at hand, was hoisted near the road for all passers-by to see. On the main road, coming towards us, was a distant mass of baggage-trains, carts, vans and soldiers; among them a *Letuchka* from the Saratovski *Lazaret* and its Red Cross *oboz*. We were mystified, the more so when a woman-doctor on horseback shouted out: 'Save yourselves! We are retreating!' She rode on out of sight. We watched the long lines of vehicles, and noticed baggage-wagons of the 103rd and 104th Regiments; all moving slowly away from the Fighting Lines. The sullen faces of the soldiers betrayed their mixed feelings; we, too, experienced to the full their perplexity and bitter disappointment. So that was why we had been so heartlessly awakened in the middle of the night!

Conflicting versions began to reach us. It was said that large forces of Turkish soldiers had broken through our right flank and were swarming across the countryside, killing everything in their way. We heard alas! too, that it was our 103rd Regiment which had been forced out of their trenches and driven backwards. We had received no orders, so were obliged to remain where we were. In about three hours' time we noted that the great wave of movement on the road had dwindled into small, fitful groups. Soon news was brought that the Turkestanski Division had swept up in the nick of time, suppressed the enemy encroachment and reoccupied our trenches. A feeling of great thankfulness spread among us; we smiled and chatted cheerfully again. The Retreat was at an end!

Some three hundred wounded came towards evening. We finished our work about midnight. It was cold in our tent and the dull ache in my legs and back had returned.

Monday, 29th August

We were awakened at 6 a.m. Many new wounded had come and we were so busy that it was 10 o'clock before we could steal a few minutes to drink a cup of tea.

My legs and back were aching so acutely that, at times, I could scarcely walk. It was probably an attack of rheumatism, I told myself; I must have caught a chill sleeping out in the open – and yet I had done it so often! After dinner, we attended to a few more wounded and then I went to bed; wrapped myself round tightly like a cocoon, for I was still very cold, and slept for a couple of hours. I awoke with a splitting headache and my legs were hurting in a strange, unnatural way. Our *Doktorsha* [woman-doctor], Lydya Alexeiyevna was in our tent; I asked her for some *pyramidon*; she gave me some and it brought much relief to my head.

We hear that the Tsar had conferred with his Generals as to the advisability of discontinuing the advance into Austrian territory, in view of the tremendous human sacrifice which it involved. The successes in the Galician Campaign had aroused the patriotic spirit of the masses to the highest levels. Should the Generals be persuaded to cease further offensives in Austria, it was feared that the people – ever ready to find a flaw in Government rule – might ascribe it to lack of ammunition, to weakness in the High Command, to the soldiers' loss of stamina, or to the treachery of the Empress. 'How is she accepting the criticism?' we asked eagerly. 'With complete indifference,' our informant replied, 'but she is definitely withdrawing herself more and more from social life and public scrutiny.' 'And what about that man whom they call the mad monk?' 'Oh! he is living in the lap of luxury and is hated by all in Petrograd; in fact, some of the Empress's own courtiers are his worst enemies. But Alexandra Feodorovna will not hear a word against him, and he, this dissolute *Sibiryak* [Siberian], Rasputin by name and *rasputnie* [licentious] by nature, walks the Royal Palace at will and expects everyone to dance attendance on him.' 'And what would the people in Russia do if the Galician Offensive were officially suspended?' 'What the outcome would be, one could not predict, but all Russia knows that Brusilov would be the last man to be dictated to and told "Hold back your men," when he knows for a surety that Victory is there for the taking.' 'And, Sister Florence,' he added, 'there is news which will interest you. The British Army is reported to have crossed the River Struma in the Salonika Expedition, captured considerable territory from the Bulgarians and is now on its way to join the combined forces of Russia, France and Serbia in an attempt to capture Monastir.'

Tuesday, 30th August

This morning I could not eat and dared not move my head for it ached so furiously. Lydya Alexeiyevna took my temperature; it was 37·9°; she gave me some quinine. They said it might be an attack of rheumatic fever, or even influenza. Because of the pain in my legs, I suggested that it might be gout! At least, I could still make them laugh! . . .

The weather grew cooler and I agreed to sleep in the house. In the afternoon, I got up, dressed and went for a short walk in the wood; it didn't seem to do much good, so I returned to bed. My temperature that evening was 39·2°. Lydya Alexeiyevna ordered me to remain in bed and gave me more quinine. Despite my aching head, I tried to work out a plan which would enable me to remain in the *Letuchka* until the attack, whatever it might be, had burnt itself out.

Wednesday, 31st August

My temperature this morning was 38·1°. Marching-orders have reached us and our *Letuchka* is to leave on the morrow! I feel desperate. Could anything be worse for me at the present moment? Two staff doctors came to see me. I was to be transferred without delay to the Base hospital in Podgaytsy. I knew the name; it was miles away and long, long miles from the Fighting Lines. I wept bitterly and protested vehemently, but tears and protests were of no avail. So this was the end; a miserable, humiliating end to all my longed-for Red Cross work. I lay helpless in my bed, torn by misery and fever.

Thursday, 1st September. Podgaytsy

My temperature was only 38·1°. The *Letuchka* will leave Folvark Ponora in the evening and I am to go after dinner to Podgaytsy. The Sisters have tried to impress upon me that, because I am feverish, I must be under a roof; they will be sleeping tonight, they assured me, in the open-air and it would be cold and rough. I felt sick at heart at the thought of losing my beloved Unit. I knew that I could bear heat exceedingly well; suppose I got up and dressed, would they, I wondered, believe me to be better? I tried to raise myself but my back was too painful. It was a dreadful thing to be so weak that one could not dress oneself. Dinner came and I was able to take the warm soup. Elizabeth Hopper, my compatriot from the 2nd *Letuchka*, had in some unexpected way appeared that morning; she announced that she was accompanying me to hospital. She was a sweet, quiet girl and I knew I should be glad of her company. I asked about my conveyance and was told that it would be a *dvukolka*. Again I protested – I was *not* a wounded soldier; surely I could be driven in one of the more comfortable carts? Here again, my lamentations aroused no response. I was lifted from my bed by Smirnov and carried to one of our two-wheeled, horse-drawn ambulance-vans; there I was placed on straw and driven uphill and downhill, through wood and valley, over rocky and uneven roads, far, far away into the background of the remote Base.

Some weeks later I was able to note down a few of my impressions of those first days of my illness.

Despite my disgruntled state of mind, I found the welcome awaiting me at the Podgaytsy *Lazaret* very acceptable. A lady-doctor, with a sweet, serene face was in charge.

I looked round the little, bare room; my narrow bed, a wooden armchair and a small table comprised the furniture. The small, square window was high up on the whitewashed wall; I could see nothing through it but a grey emptiness. The only bit of colour was the frieze all round the room. It was composed of large, yellow daisies, I thought; then I decided that they were sunflowers. I looked at them with contentment.

The night passed slowly; the doctor came in early and told me some Staff Doctors were coming to see me. One of them was a very tall man; with his thick fur-coat, he completely blocked the doorway as he entered. They tapped me, listened to heart and lungs and seemed to find nothing wrong. I told them that it was only the ache in my head and back which made me so weak; they smiled and told me that with a temperature of 40·2°, I could expect to feel just a little weak. They took my blood to analyse and said that they would return in a day or two.

For the next few days, my temperature was less high. The doctors assured me that, had it not been for the inoculation I had received in the *Letuchka*, I should have been feeling a great deal worse. 'An English sportswoman!' they said and nodded their heads approvingly. They took blood for the second time, to be quite sure that it was not *typhus abdominalis*; later, I was told that it was only *parateef B* [paratyphoid], thanks to the inoculation.

One afternoon, Mamasha paid me a visit; my temperature was still high, but the aches and pains had diminished. I saw to it that some silly joke of mine should now and then provoke a hearty laugh from her. 'So you see, Mamasha,' I informed her, 'it was only a rheumatic chill after all, and I shall be back at my post in a few days.' 'Yes,' she acquiesced, 'I can see you are better; but you must rest and we shall expect you when we see you.' Mamasha was always of a practical frame of mind.

A burly young orderly, named Ivan, waited upon me; he occupied the next room and was always alert. But despite every care and attention, my temperature persisted and I found myself daily growing weaker. The doctor came to see me more often and once she must have heard me call out in English, for she tried to find an English nurse to look after me in case I grew delirious. Failing to find a compatriot, she enlisted a young French Sister. At the time I was oblivious to the fact that my delirium was expected to be voiced in French! She was exceedingly kind and I loved her face as much as that of the doctor, and enjoyed watching her as she sponged my hot body with that glorious cold water, or changed the sheets on my bed while Ivan lifted me in his strong arms. As the crisis approached – needless to say, I was unaware that a crisis had to approach! – my mood worsened; I hated the sight of strangers and turned my face to the wall when the doctors made an appearance. Only my French nurse and the doctor were welcome because of their quiet, beautiful faces. As to delirium, I am not sure what was really expected of me. I may have called out once or twice in English, but as no one understood that language it didn't matter a brass farthing; in any case, I was not giving any State secrets away. But there was one definite indication that things were not all as they should be, but I kept that fact to myself, although it worried me considerably. Strange as it may seem, it was the sunflowers which turned against me! Whenever I looked at them, their golden faces began grimacing, laughing, leering; they would shut their eyes and distort their features. I began to hate them, and then to fear them. I feared them so much that I dared not raise my eyes, and, if I turned away from the wall, I would keep my eyes tightly shut, or cover my head with the sheet.

Mamasha came a second time, but I lay with my eyes shut, not wishing to speak. She gave me messages from friends in the *Letuchka*, but they held no interest for me. And when she whispered: 'Florence, you will be coming back to us soon,' the idea was abhorrent to me. 'No! No!' I moaned. I caught a glimpse of her face and it was all screwed up and wrinkled with perplexity. I shut my eyes and turned away. I had seen that grimace before. Mamasha and the sunflowers were my worst enemies.

For several nights, I slept only fitfully; the lady-doctor tried to help and gave me injections of *pantapon*, but they were ineffectual and succeeded only in suspending me midway between earth and heaven. Then a new difficulty arose: I could not turn myself in bed without help. The Sister, or Ivan, was continually lifting me from side to side, for I was very restless. I remember the night of the crisis clearly, for I could not sleep at all, because I was hard at work. It was a strange kind of work. I knew that I had one body, but three faces; these faces were mine, but only one belonged to me; the second was that of one of my sisters and the third belonged to a wounded soldier. All three faces were perspiring profusely and it was my duty to wipe them dry. I lay on my back in one position all night long and my body became cold and immovable. The faces grew colder and colder; the perspiration heavier and heavier. I worked and worked; it grew terribly difficult, but I knew that, did I cease to work and wipe the perspiration from off the faces, the faces and body would die. I felt the blood stop flowing in the body; only the faces were still alive and perspiring dreadfully. I worked on and on. . . . It was so difficult, I felt that I had to have help. I tried to call the Sister, but could not, because I had no voice. And all the time I was working hard – wiping, wiping.

I must have called, for she came. I begged her to feel my face to know if it were still alive. She felt it; took my temperature; gave me brandy. In the morning, I had a normal temperature. The doctor came and bent over me. I was cold, inert, almost lifeless. She laid her hand on my forehead; felt my pulse. '*Slava Bogu!*' I heard her whisper.

I recovered slowly, for I had been very tired. The days passed and my strength gradually returned. My thoughts began to centre once again on the work of my *Letuchka* and I welcomed every item of news brought from them.

It was on Saturday, 17th September, that the distant guns seemed to be especially active and the firing at night became more ominous. I began to want to be up and about again, to return to my post, to be in the thick of it with my fellow-workers. The cannon-fire worried me; it was such a baffling position – just to lie there and listen, knowing that the wounded were being brought in and needed help. I grew so restless and miserable that my French nurse reprimanded me gently: '*Ecoutez-moi, Florence,*' she protested. 'You are only making things worse for yourself. Just accept the fact that you are an invalid and have to go through the convalescent stage before you can get well.' I ignored the wisdom of her words; in any case, she could not understand the ignominy of my position. I couldn't bear to think that work was going on without me; it had never happened before that I was absent in times of stress. That evening, I had a slight fever. The Sister told the doctor that I was very nervous; he came, had a good look at me, felt my pulse, told me that I must remain quietly in bed and not think of getting up until I was stronger, and he reproached me for being so nervous. 'Nervous!' I cried. 'I don't know what you mean; I have never been nervous in my life!' He had another look. 'You have a very angry face,' he said.

Monday, 19th September
It was all well-planned beforehand. I waited until my nurse was out of the room, then I threw the bedclothes off, slowly raised myself and tried to stand; my knees doubled up under me and I fell back on to the bed. I waited for a few moments and then, very carefully and deliberately, placed one foot on to the mat . . . then the other . . . all was well! Slowly I raised myself to my feet – but once again something happened to my knees, and I fell backwards on to the bed. So the doctor and Sister were right after all. It was a bitter disappointment; I had not realised that one's strength could evaporate so quickly. I had thought that an English constitution would have come to my aid in this hour of need.

Thursday, 22nd September
For the first time, I dressed myself alone. What a joy it is to be independent again! The cannon are still barking loudly in the distance. No news today, but the incessant firing tells its own story.

Friday, 23rd September

I have been told some wonderful news. The head of our *Otryad* has arranged that I shall be sent to the Crimea to recuperate for a whole month. I rejoiced at the prospect, knowing that, in that paradise of sunshine and beauty, I should rapidly recover strength and be ready to return to my post. I already knew the fascination of that marvellous peninsula, for I had twice visited the Crimea before the War. And what was more, I had heard from my Russian 'family' that Anna Ivanovna and her daughters were planning to spend two months in Alupka, for Asya was far from well. And so it was arranged. My French nurse would accompany me, see me safely installed and then return to her *Lazaret*. How kind everyone was to me! In their kindness and thoughtfulness, they had planned every comfort for me, and I just sat back and accepted it all.

It was a long and tiring journey to the Crimea; we arrived in Yalta on 2nd October, and on the 6th left for the Sanatorium at Novy Semeitz

7th October–16th November. The Crimea

The Sanatorium turned out to be a Military Hospital for tubercular patients! The medical staff discovered that I had been sent there by *mistake*, but not before they had examined, thumped and knocked, pummelled and sounded me, several times during the first few days. One of the older doctors, hearing me cough, ordered the application of those little glass bulbs – the old-fashioned cupping remedy which superseded the still older-fashioned leech-treatment. But the intensive search proved negative. The doctors were, I am sure, very disappointed in me, but they told me that, although my lungs were in perfect condition, I might remain in their Sanatorium. And so began lovely, tranquil weeks amid the glorious flowers and trees, steeped in golden sunshine, of the Crimean countryside. It was a God-given rest for mind, body and soul. . . . I responded with amazing rapidity.

My hair was in bad condition and coming out in handfuls. So, one day, the barber came to my room and not only cut off my hair, but shaved my head! I was assured that I should never regret it, and that it would grow again stronger and thicker than it had ever been before. From that time, I wore my nurse's veil round my head and no one – save the few initiated – could ever guess that the veil covered a bald pate – devoid of even a single hair! Needless to say, I caught a severe head-cold, which, in the warm sunshine of the Crimea, impelled the doctors to regard me with a certain amount of suspicion and concern.

My Russian 'family' in Alupka soon heard of my arrival and there was a joyful reunion. A colleague of Doctor Usov, holidaying in the Crimea, joined our party and we had some wonderful walks together; both the man and his wife said that they intended to keep an eagle eye on me, which amounted to feeling my pulse whenever we met and forbidding me to climb up any steep hill. When they heard of my bald head, they agreed that it was an excellent idea, but, 'Watch out!' said the doctors. 'The new growth may be quite a different colour. It might even be bright red!'

In two weeks' time, I was feeling on the top of the world. Flowers were everywhere; roses were growing in profusion outside my window and their exquisite fragrance filled the air. And the fruit! Every kind of fruit imaginable was to be found. The vineyards were being despoiled of their rich harvest and on all sides there were baskets heaped with luscious grapes. These famous vineyards produced the wines so sought after by the Russian aristocracy. Melons, too, were prolific and large piles of this rich, golden fruit were stacked in the several market-places. Having read so often of the severe winters which had increased the disasters of the Crimean War, it had always seemed incongruous that fruit and flowers should be so prolific during the winter in certain parts of the peninsula. But I soon learnt the reason. Rising high above the fertile southern slopes, ran a wall of mountains, a natural barrier against the bitter north winds.

Early in November Anna Ivanovna heard from Moscow that her husband was ill; she and her daughters started packing at once, anxious to reach home as soon as possible. I decided to return to my unit without delay, but my Russian 'family' would not hear of it. They begged me to stay with them until my *otpusk* [leave] was at an end. 'Come,' they urged me. 'Come, if only for a few days.' So, having received permission from the Red Cross Authorities and the approval of the Sanatorium, I gladly agreed to go with them. We said goodbye to the sunshine and the flowers and left the Crimea.

19th–end of November. Moscow

Anna Ivanovna and the girls had no details of the doctor's illness, and in their agitation imagined that they would find him in a very grave condition. So our relief was great when, entering the house, we were told that the doctor was sitting in the drawing-room. He had been at some medical conference, when he had suddenly suffered a severe heart attack. Luckily, he had been in good hands, for his colleagues were all doctors. He had been resting at home for the last few days, and was already beginning to feel more himself.

It was very cold in Moscow. What a contrast was this white, frozen world with the glowing, colourful Crimea! We noticed, too, how cold the house seemed, but the stoves were soon crackling away in all the bedrooms; and the doctor was up and about again and that was all that mattered. In the morning, we were told that he had had a good night, but had been persuaded to stay in bed until the afternoon. About 10 a.m. a call was heard. Anna Ivanovna rushed at once to his room. It was a second heart attack! A doctor was quickly on the scene and, after a little while, he came to say that Pavel Sergeyevich was already easier, but must remain in bed. We took it in turns to sit by his bedside. I felt thankful to be of use and to take a share of the nursing. Being a heart-specialist, Doctor Usov knew all about his own illness and followed its progress closely. Sometimes he would feel his own pulse; then, with a sigh, or shake of the head, he would shut his eyes – knowing full well that his was a critical case. One evening, his colleague whom we had met in the Crimea was sitting in his room and I was called in to give him the injection. I had given him similar injections several times, but that day I was feeling tired and nervous; consequently my hand shook and I did it so clumsily that he cried out. I was terribly ashamed and made my exit as quickly as possible – but not before I had seen Pavel Sergeyevich shake his fist after my retreating figure. Later, our doctor friend came to me, felt my pulse, and said kindly: 'You are overdoing things, my dear; you must rest more, otherwise I shall not give you permission to return to the Front.'

Although I did not venture far from the house, I could see that Moscow was not the same. And yet it was difficult to say just what was wrong. Of course, as was only natural after more than two years' war, food had become very expensive, and supplies sometimes failed. Some seasonal festivities were in progress, but they

were ill-attended, and a pall of despondency seemed to hang over
the population. People expressed dismay at the way things were
going at the Front. They told me that the Russian Offensive in
Galicia had come to an abrupt end. This was news for me. One man
told us that his two sons had written of this inexplicable cessation
of military operations on the Austrian Front. Food was sufficient,
ammunition plentiful, the soldiers' morale high; and yet no further
attacks had been made. They begged their father to enquire what
plans were afoot for the coming months; why the High Command
had sanctioned such a halt. 'There is little that we in Moscow can
do in the matter,' he said dejectedly. 'The power lies in Petrograd.'

Others related – in an undertone – that disputes and denuncia-
tions were daily occurrences both in Court and Ministerial Circles;
that the strange pro-German behaviour of the Empress had been
openly condemned; it was widely known that she had come under
the influence of the mad monk Rasputin, due, it was said, to the
hypnotic power exercised in his efforts to heal the sick Tsarevich.
He was now doing his best to corrupt the Church dignitaries and
force them to acknowledge him as a prophet and a 'man of God'.
He had been heard to declare that he had been sent to the Capital
to preserve the Romanov Dynasty, and boasted that he was in a
position to promote or impede the progress of the Russian Armies
at the Seat of War. 'And is there no one who could challenge him
as an impostor?' we asked. 'There are such men,' our friends
replied; 'for he has many enemies. But their hands are tied.' One
of the names mentioned was that of Alexander Kerensky, a young
Socialist barrister, still in his thirties, who was wielding considerable influence among members of the Duma and other legislative
bodies. 'He is a coming man,' declared Vladimir Nikolayevich, one
of Doctor Usov's medical colleagues, and, after a moment's pause,
added: 'Mark my words! There will have to be a great *perevorot*
[upheaval] in Russia, before Russia can recover her sanity and equili-
brium again.' He uttered these words very slowly and deliberately.

After a week or so I returned to the Front.

Beginning of December. Trebukhovtsy
I received a very warm-hearted welcome, with many an embrace
thrown in for good measure. Even our unit's rank-and-file, in-

cluding our sturdy Tatar drivers, bowed and scraped their welcome; one old Tatar told me that he knew that I should return in
health, because he had prayed to Allah for me.

There had been several changes in our *Letuchka* but Mamasha,
Annushka, Ekaterina and Sofiya were still there, and they, for me,
constituted the mainstay of our Flying Detachment. The lack of
military operations provided us with little work of importance. I
was told that, in various sectors of the Fighting Lines, confusion
and bewilderment were rampant. Orders were slow in coming in
and, when they did arrive, they were so vague and ambiguous
as to cause grave concern. Only one conclusion became obvious:
all military operations on the Southern Front had been completely
suspended.

My shaven head caused considerable merriment among the
Sisters. It was a dreadful sight, but I took care to have it well-
covered when any male member of our personnel was at hand.
For weeks, I did not dare look in a mirror. I knew that it was only
a question of time, but what a long time it was before it began to
grow even the most miniature hairs! Even at night I twisted a
nurse's veil round my head, for it is amazing how warm a head of
hair can be. During the day, with this twisted turban-wise, and
the larger veil enveloping it and pinned under my chin, the
camouflage was complete.

18th December

A great sorrow was awaiting me in letters I now had from home.
My Father had died on 6th December. He was 84 and had married
my Mother, 20 years his junior, when he was 50. It was a dreadful
shock for me; it seemed incredible that I should never see him
again, but I was comforted by the tone of my Mother's letters.
My Father was of a strong, kindly character; in his ample pockets
there were always fruit-drops or bull's eyes to regale any child who
happened to cross his path. He was deeply religious, too; though
he would never 'preach' to anybody. I once heard him say that his
favourite quotation was: 'Not more than others I deserve, but
God has given me more.' When we were young, every Sunday
afternoon Father would read to us one of our favourite Bible
stories. My elder brother told me, 'I never once heard our Father
swear, nor did he ever say an unkind word about anybody.' [What
an old-fashioned type he would be considered nowadays! But a

more gracious, nobler nature it would be difficult to meet.] I don't think I cried much, the grief seemed too deep; but Mamasha and Annushka were especially understanding; they made me take a soothing valerian drink and insisted on my remaining in bed until dinner-time on the following day.

Although all is quiet on our Front, events are seething in the heart of Russia. Rumours are constantly coming to our ears of political and domestic troubles at Court. It is said that the Grand Duke Nicholas, cousin of the Emperor, and Commander-in-Chief of the Russian Armies, has remonstrated with the Tsar and warned him against his several pro-German Courtiers and Ministers who, it is alleged, are engaged in stirring up the people. The Tsar is – according to rumour – fully aware of Rasputin's ability to perform mock-miracles, but deeply influenced by the trust placed in the charlatan monk by the Tsarina and certain Court officials, he has been known to request Rasputin's advice in more than one instance connected with State Administration. Of late, reports from the Capital and from Moscow have become more involved, and heated discussions often take place among our Red Cross personnel as to what the Council of the Empire and the Duma are doing – or not doing. But I must confess they seldom register very deeply in my mind. I am not at all politically inclined; I know that the Tsar wields complete power; that his word can make or break laws; that an *ukaz* [decree] from him will be accepted and obeyed blindly. And we all know that criticism of his private and public life exists on a large scale, together with much grumbling and backbiting. But we ask ourselves: 'When was a man vested with supreme power *not* the target for venomous speculation?'

End of December

We were sitting quietly in our common-room when a knock came on the door. An officer appeared. 'Ah! here you are!' he ejaculated, 'I have some news for you! Grigoriy Rasputin has been murdered.'*
We were all looking at him, agape with curiosity and suspense, and not a word was spoken. 'Yes,' he said slowly, 'strange as it may sound, it is true. We received the news from a reliable source this afternoon.' In the buzz of conversation which followed, question after question was asked; everyone was eager to hear every available detail of such an amazing crime. We heard that

*Rasputin was murdered on the night of 16th/17th December.

the monk had been missing for several days, but his disappearance had been hushed up; nevertheless, it was known that the Secret Police, together with Rasputin's friends and the Court Officials who had openly supported him, had been searching for him high and low. Now his body had been discovered, half-embedded in ice in the River Neva. The newspapers referred to the 'mysterious crime' in guarded terms; they dared not do otherwise; and the names of the conspirators – even that of Rasputin himself – had not been mentioned. 'Have you any idea who the murderers might be?' someone asked. Our friend hesitated and then replied: 'We all have our suspicions, but it would not be right to brand a couple of patriotic men as murderers until we have proof. One thing we do know – the world is well rid of this treacherous man, who was doing all in his power to bring about the downfall of Russia and to sell his country to the enemy.'

During the winter days that followed we had many visitors from the neighbouring regiments and Red Cross Otryads, and, because of the cessation of military operations along the Front, our conversation would invariably turn to Russia and to the many reports of insubordination and treachery said to be prevalent in both town and countryside. We were able to learn some of the circumstances which had led to the murder of Rasputin. It seemed that, in Petrograd, towards the autumn of 1916, the monk had become so notorious for his dissolute life and the influence he had gained over the Imperial Family, that strong antipathy had been growing against him among a clique of young aristocrats. So violent did their hatred become that they planned, in secret, a scheme by which they could destroy him. They had obviously succeeded, but who they were and how they had managed to slay him no one could tell. Perhaps details of the crime and criminals may never be known, but there seemed to be no doubt that the absence of the Staretz [saintly person] had cleared the air in Petrograd and many a public-spirited Russian was able to breathe freely once again.

PART FOUR

1917, The Undoing

On 3rd January, 1917, I received a telegram from Anna Ivanovna: Doctor Usov had had a third heart attack and was rapidly sinking. Our head doctor gave me permission to return to Moscow, and I arrived at my friends' home in the morning of 7th January. The doctor had died on the 4th and was to be buried that same afternoon. I had not been able to notify them of my arrival and their joy at seeing me again amply repaid all the inconvenience of my rushed and disorganised journey. . . .

How deeply and sincerely my friends and I could sympathise with each other's sorrow. I told them of my great loss, and in our mutual grief we found much comfort. The doctor's death-chamber was adorned with sacred pictures and icons, draped in black crêpe. The coffin was on a raised pedestal in the centre of the room; on and around it were wreaths and sheaves of flowers – roses, lilies, carnations, chrysanthemums; the scent was almost overpowering. Pavel Sergeyevich lay embedded in flowers; his face was serene, like an ivory mask. At the head of the coffin sat a nun reading in a hushed voice prayer after prayer from the book in her hands. From time to time she was relieved by another, so that the recitation of prayers continued night and day. The front door was always ajar; relatives, friends and colleagues were continually entering to pay tribute to the dead man. And all the time the sweet-toned orisons, in the majestic Russian language, rose and fell.

With the funeral over, on the evening before my departure, Vladimir Nikolayevich, one of the doctor's best friends, dined with us. He was a staunch upholder of the Duma and had been deeply indignant when all its Sessions had been prohibited during the autumn of 1916. He spoke highly of the statesman Pavel Milyukov, Leader of the Liberals, who, in November 1916, had, with remarkable courage, denounced the sinister 'camarilla' which was leading Russia to her doom, and had singled out the infamous Siberian monk as its ringleader. He had further exposed the ex-Premier Stürmer, referring to him as the traitor Judas, who, with his pro-German confederates, was intent on betraying his country for shekels. It was not the first time we had heard the word 'camarilla' mentioned in connection with Court Circles in Petrograd and we begged Vladimir Nikolayevich to explain it more fully. It seems that it was a fairly new word coined into the Russian language as *kamarílya*, from the Spanish, meaning a small room or coterie of influential persons. But of late, the word had taken on a much more sinister meaning: it was applied to the group of courtiers and ministers who had rallied round Rasputin, fully aware that he was in direct communication with the German High Command and anxious to see Russia dominated by Germany.

I left Moscow on 17th January and on the 23rd left Trebukhovtsy with the rest of my unit for Trostyanitse where we opened a dressing-station. War at the Front seemed to lose some of its significance and the mysterious happenings in Petrograd loomed in men's minds.

Discontent among the masses in Russia is daily becoming more marked. Disparaging statements concerning the Government are being voiced – at first, they were surreptitious, and now, more bold and brazen, at meetings and street-corners. We feel sorry for the Imperial Family and especially for the Tsar. He, it is said, wishes to please everybody and succeeds in pleasing nobody. As time goes on, rumours of disorder become more persistent. Sabotage has become the order of the day. Railroads are damaged; industrial plants destroyed; large factories and mills burnt down; workshops and laboratories looted. Now, rancour is turning towards the military chiefs. Why are the armies at a standstill? Why are the soldiers allowed to rot in the snow-filled trenches? Why continue the stalemate war? 'Bring the men home!' 'Conclude peace!' 'Finish this interminable war once and for all!' Cries such as these penetrate to the cold and hungry soldiers in their bleak earthworks, and begin to echo among them.

Now that food has grown scarce in Petrograd and Moscow, disorder takes the shape of riots and insurrections. We are told that mobs of the lower classes parade the streets shouting 'Peace and Bread!' They are aware that the war is at the root of their hardships. So it is: 'Peace and Bread!' But as the days pass, hunger gains primary place and the erstwhile docile rabble grow unruly and rampageous. They no longer bother about peace; their empty stomachs warrant no rival. So it is only 'Bread!' 'Give us Bread!'

We devour the newspapers and are amazed to find that some of them openly describe details of the turmoil in the cities. The Moscow papers are unusually candid; one of them referred to the disaffection which prevails among Muscovites of all classes. A few months ago, such an article would have been instantly condemned as subversive, its writer arrested and the newspaper which printed it banned. But now – what is happening? Some enigmatic movement is afoot in Russia. Who can gauge its meaning and determine its goal?

It is a dull, oppressive winter; the frost and ice do their best to numb our thoughts and hamper our movements. There is no settled work; now and then a couple of wounded are brought in, or a few sick men, but for the most part we are experiencing complete inaction. Tempers become fractious, nerves frayed, and it is no unusual thing to hear lengthy disputes, or peevish, irritable words. We seem to be waiting for *something* to happen. Things cannot continue as they are. Many questions are asked, but none can answer them. 'Will the war continue?' 'Will a separate peace be arranged between Russia and Germany?' 'What will our Allies do in such an emergency?'

It is a grievous situation for us all; I, too, share the tension. My general health has greatly improved, but my father's death in December and the death of Doctor Usov in January seem to minimise the importance of other events. Even Rasputin's murder has made little impact upon me; I know that everyone has considered him an arrant scoundrel and – he has met a scoundrel's death.

4th March

THE TSAR HAS ABDICATED!* Nicholas II, Emperor and Tsar of All the Russias, has renounced his Imperial Throne. Is it voluntarily? – or involuntarily? It matters little; what does matter is that Russia, the mighty Empire which stretches from Central Europe across the whole vast continent of Asia to the far shores of the

*The Tsar had abdicated on 2nd March.

Pacific, is now without a ruler; without the august figure of a
Romanov Emperor to steer the Ship of State through the turbulent
waters of war. We are all stupefied by such an unheard-of con-
tingency. Today everyone has been unnaturally quiet.

Then reaction set in, everybody wanted to speak.

Argument has been raging on the question of 'What will happen
now?' And no one can, or dare, give an answer. Gradually authen-
tic news has crept through to us in our remote dwelling here in
Trostyanitse. The Tsar abdicated against his will; in a word, was
forced to do so by certain Ministers who saw in the continuation of
the Tsarist Régime an administration of corruption and betrayal.
So it *is* Revolution! But Revolution in its most benign aspect:
no violence, no bloodshed. It is, in fact, a *Bloodless Revolution* –
the first of its kind ever known in the troubled history of the
Russian Empire.

And who are the men who could have brought about this remarkable *coup d'état*? Foremost among the names mentioned have
been those of a well-known Statesman, Prince George Lvov, and
of Alexander Kerensky. These men, it is said, were determined at
all cost to rid their Mother-Country of the evil influences at work
in the Imperial Court. They realised that there was only one way
by which they could achieve this and that was to remove the Tsar
and to cleanse the Court of its pro-German satellites. All had been
well-thought out and prepared by these courageous, public-spirited
men. Success crowned their efforts. The Tsar abdicated, the Tsarist
Government fell, the Romanov Dynasty ceased to exist.

We have been told that Nicholas II, before signing his abdication, did his best to persuade his brother, the Grand Duke
Michael Alexandrovich, to accept the crown. The Grand Duke was
not entirely against this proposition, but, aware of the widespread
discontent in Russia, he decided to accept only if the masses
would acknowledge him as their Tsar. That the rightful Heir, the
Grand Duke Alexei, should succeed is, at the present time, quite
out of the question; the young Tsarevich is a weakling of thirteen,
whose health is so precarious, due to his incurable disease, that his
death might occur at any moment.

This evening, I found Annushka in our bedroom weeping. I
knew the reason. She is a firm Royalist; so am I. We cannot bear

to think that the Tsar had been deposed and degraded. Surely it would have been sufficient just to dissolve the Tsarist Government? Surely one cannot destroy a Dynasty by the mere stroke of a pen? We feel deeply for the Tsar and for his young children; they must suffer torments to find themselves in such an ignominious position. Where are they now – the anxious, humiliated parents, those sweet young girls and the delicate small boy? Will they be driven out of the Palace? Will they be deprived of all their Imperial rights and heritage? Will a reign of terror and intimidation begin for them?

Some of our personnel are deeply disturbed by all that has taken place. 'A Russia without a ruler is like a living body without a head,' said one of them. But others pointed out that history never stands still, and when a great Empire shows signs of deterioration, it is high time for reforms. 'These patriotic men,' said another, 'were great reformers, intent on bringing about the regeneration of Russia.' He applauded their courageous action and would pray for their success, as all right-minded, Orthodox Russians should do. 'Let us keep our criticisms to ourselves,' he continued. 'This is a great historic moment. And let us bide our time, before we break into invectives against the new Régime.' New Régime! Who would have thought of such a thing? As he was speaking, I recalled the words uttered by Vladimir Nikolayevich in Moscow, not many weeks previously. Is this the *perevorot* which he predicted?

There are so many conflicting reports from Russia that it is impossible to know which are true and which false, but I shall note them down, as the mood takes me. I add this last clause purposely, because for some days past I have not wished to touch my diary. The explanation is simple: there has been nothing definite to write about. We are living in a state of expectancy waiting for something to happen; what it will be, no one can tell. We can but wait.

On 26th February, we have been told, the Tsar, realising that power was slipping out of his hands, made an attempt to abrogate the State Duma. Rumour had it that Parliament was, indeed, dissolved, but it proved false, for not only did the Duma refuse to accept such an order from the Emperor, but determined to assert its legal rights and remain open. That decision obviously hastened the crisis, for, on the following day, 27th February, several arrests were made in Petrograd and many of the leading men in Tsarist circles were placed under lock and key by the revolutionaries. The

Leaders of the Duma, to meet this emergency, took the government
of the Empire into their own hands.

On 2nd March, from the town of Pskov, the Tsar issued a Manifesto. It is a sorrowful document – probably the last issued by the
Emperor to his people – and reads like the confession of a man,
sorely tried, who feels that he is powerless to face the problems
confronting him. He begins in the customary way: 'By the Grace
of God, We, Nicholas II, Emperor and Supreme Ruler of All the
Russias, Tsar of Poland, Grand Duke of Finland,' etc. etc. He
refers to Russia's struggle with a foreign foe, to the internal disorder which might threaten the victorious end of the War, but
assures them that the hour is approaching when the heroic Russian
soldiers, together with the glorious Allies, will definitely crush the
cruel enemy. The most poignant part of the Manifesto comes when
the Tsar asserts that, in order to unify all the forces of the Nation
to bring about a speedy Victory, he has decided – in agreement
with the State Duma – to renounce the Throne of Russia, but, not
wishing to be separated from his beloved son, he is prepared to
hand over the Imperial inheritance to his brother, the Grand Duke
Michael Alexandrovich. He calls on all the loyal sons of Russia to
rally round their new Tsar and to assist him in all ways to lead
Russia to victory, prosperity and glory. He finishes with the
prayer: 'May the Lord God help Russia!'

On the same document is a Manifesto from the Grand Duke
Michael, drawn up on 3rd March in Petrograd. He acknowledges
that his brother's wish to relinquish the Imperial Throne in his
favour will, in these days of warfare and national unrest, lay a
heavy burden upon him; but, placing the welfare of Russia above
all else, he is prepared to accept the offer. Nevertheless, before his
final acceptance, he has decided to appeal to the Russian people
themselves to give the casting vote, for he is determined that he
will ascend the Throne only if he has the unanimous support of
the whole Nation.

There is a third announcement on that document. It is the
prekaz [Order] addressed to the Troops on the South-Western
Front by General Brusilov, and dated 4th March, 1917. It includes
a solemn reminder to his 'glorious and unconquerable troops' of
their sacred duty towards God and towards their beloved Mother-
Country. He points out that any kind of disorder in their ranks
would give the enemy cause for rejoicing. We are standing guard

against the enemy, he continues, and must remember that it is our duty towards our mothers, wives, sisters, children, to protect them from invasion; otherwise, posterity will curse us and Holy Russia will be held in contempt. He demands from all his soldiers unflagging discipline and unflinching calm. He concludes: 'May the Lord help us!' At the foot of his *prekaz* are the words: 'This Order is to be read in all Regiments, Squadrons, Cossack *Sotnyas*, Batteries and Military Detachments.'

As I held this document in my hands, a wave of emotion swept over me. I knew that this sudden change in the administration of Russia must have repercussions throughout the world. Here were three great Russians, true lovers of their country; each with enormous power in his hands. Each knew that the future of the Russian Empire depended on the *will* of the *people*. Each in his own way was stretching out imploring hands to the people: those multitudinous, heterogeneous races which compose the population of the Empire, saying: 'It is *you* who can help Russia in this hour of her dire need. On *you* depend the success of our armies, the safety of our homes, the security of our Faith and the guarantee of peace and prosperity for our Country.' This document was sent to me personally by the military staff in the Base. I am hoping to preserve it; for it is not every day that the Ruler of a mighty Empire proclaims that he is about to relinquish his Imperial Throne.

Events are now moving at a rapid pace. The Grand Duke Michael's appeal for support to the people of Russia received little encouragement and he decided not to press his claim. The New Régime has lost no time in making itself felt. Immediately after the Tsar's abdication, a *Vremenoye Pravitelstvo* [Temporary Government] was set up by Prince Lvov, who, as the new Prime Minister, together with Alexander Kerensky as Minister of Justice, Pavel Miliukov as Minister for Foreign Affairs, and other prominent men, has exerted every effort to establish a constitutional system. Prince Lvov's name is already a household word in the *Zemski Soyuz*, for ever since 1904, he has been prominent in the *Zemstvo* Congresses, has done useful work on behalf of the Red Cross Society, and has always been an untiring campaigner for the education and betterment of the peasantry.

These Constitutional Reformers, as they are called, are sup-

ported by the military chiefs, notably Generals Alexei Brusilov
and Platon Lechitsky. It was our General Brusilov who led the
Great Offensive during the summer of 1916, conquered wide
stretches of Austria and, with General Lechitsky, the whole of the
Bukovina. Their victories were bought at a heavy price; Russian
casualties have been said to be over 1,200,000. Brusilov, as a loyal
soldier, is prepared to obey his Emperor to the last and, despite
bitter resentment, he has halted his advancing armies and ordered
all operations to cease. His loyalty is illustrated, too, by his
prekaz to his troops. I notice that, in it, he carefully omits all
reference to the Tsar's abdication, although he does mention that,
in accordance with God's Will, Russia has entered upon a new
historical course in the administrative life of the State. But for
Brusilov and Lechitsky prospects of further success in Galicia
seem very much brighter now.

Manifestoes from the new Government have begun to be distributed widely along the Russian Front. Our *Letuchka* is well supplied with them; many are addressed to me by the military staff –
a courtesy which I greatly appreciate. The main trend of these
proclamations, directed especially to the fighting-men, is FREEDOM.
'Russia is a free Country now,' the Manifestoes announce. 'Russia
is free and *you*, Russian soldiers, are free men. If you, before being
freed, could fight for your Mother-Country, how much more
loyally will you fight now, when, as free men, you will carry on the
successful conflict on behalf of your free Country.' So the great
perevorot has come! Russia is a free country! The Russians are a
free people! Tremendous excitement reigns on all sides; much
vociferous enthusiasm, tinged with not a little awe. What will
happen now? Newspapers are seized and treasured as though made
of gold, read, and re-read. 'The Dawn of Russian Freedom!' 'The
Daybreak of the New Epoch!' rhapsodise the romancer-reporters.
A *prekaz* has been sent to the Front Line soldiers describing the
otkaz [dismissal] of the Emperor. We were told that in some sectors
the news has been received with noisy gratification; in others, the
men have sat silent and confused.

We were all very relieved to learn that the Imperial Family have
left Petrograd and gone to their summer-residence at Livadia in
the Crimea. At one time it was said that the Tsar had been arrested
and might be imprisoned in the Fortress of SS. Peter and Paul.
Criticism of him is rife, but we Sisters are always pleased when we

hear a voice raised in his behalf. He had been only 26 when his father, Alexander III, suddenly died in 1894, and now, after 23 years, he has been forced to renounce the Throne. 'A weak man,' several declare; but another challenges: 'How could he assert his will when the Court was composed mainly of foreigners, of whom the majority was pro-German?' Unlike the giant figure of Alexander III, 6 ft 4 inches in his socks, Nicholas was of slight build. They say that he was shy too; no wonder, with that father overshadowing him. There is no doubt that his father's reign, cut short after only thirteen years, did little to prepare him for the boundless responsibilities which surrounded him after his Coronation in 1896.

Another interesting document has been sent to me. It is entitled: 'Text of Oath for Orthodox and Catholics', and signed by Prince Lvov. It begins:

I swear by the honour of an officer (soldier, citizen) and promise before God and my own conscience to be faithful and steadfastly loyal to the Russian Government, as to my Fatherland. I swear to serve it to my last drop of blood. . . . I pledge obedience to the Provisional Government, at present proclaimed the Russian Government, until the establishment of the System of Government sanctioned by the will of the People, through the instrumentality of the Constituent Assembly. . . . I swear obedience to all who are stationed above me as superior in rank. . . . I swear to be an honest, conscientious and courageous officer (soldier) and not to violate my vow on account of greed, kindred, friendship or animosity. To conclude the Oath given by me, I make the Sign of the Cross and add my signature. . . .

The document ends as follows: 'Ratified by the Council of Ministers of the Provisional Government; 7th March 1917. Prince Lvov.' This Oath of Allegiance has been sent to the armies along the Galician Front. We were told that the soldiers were assembled into groups and, after hearing the text, the men repeated it word for word, holding up their arm the while. Russians, Jews, Moslems, all pledged their loyalty to the Provisional Government; then they cried a loud 'Ura'. A new era has begun for them. In the background, there is still a WAR to be waged, and a formidable foe is still lurking in the vanquished territory of their own land.

March has slipped past, the general commotion slowly eased. It soon became obvious that Alexander Feodorovich Kerensky,

Minister of Justice, was the man of the moment. His name seemed
to be in everyone's mouth; in fact, it was rumoured that Kerensky
himself was instrumental in bringing about the abdication. So
much is rumoured in these exciting days that it is difficult to
distinguish truth from fiction.

I saw a picture of Kerensky this morning and was surprised to
see how young he looked; clean-shaven, with an oval face, his
appearance was in striking contrast with those heavily bewhiskered
and bearded generals and politicians. One of our doctors, who had
been a fellow-undergraduate with him at St Petersburg University
at the beginning of the century, told us that he had a way with
him which made even his tutors 'sit up and think'. He had always
been interested in politics and, after becoming a barrister, in
Moscow, had, on several occasions, defended men accused of sub-
version. He had strong sympathies with the working-classes and
had entered the 4th Duma* as a 'moderate' Socialist.

There had been no fewer than four Prime Ministers since the
war started and not one of them, declared our doctor, had shown
any outstanding genius. Now, however, in these early days of the
Revolution, the Duma had a very special role to play. Prince
Lvov, now the Prime Minister in the Provisional Government, had
taken a leading part in the formation of the 1st Duma; and the
Socialist member, Kerensky, was now Minister of Justice. All eyes
were now riveted on the Provisional Government. Would the
power wielded by that handful of brave men spread its kindly
influence throughout that vast country, bringing new hope to the
despondent, allaying the fears of the pessimistic, and assuring one
and all of the advent of a new era of hope, peace and prosperity?

April

It was the first week in April and some slightly wounded soldiers
had come in. We were anxious to hear what was going on in the
trenches and how the men had received the news of the abdication.

*The Duma came into existence in 1906; as a Representative State
Council, it had been expected to bring about much-needed reforms,
but like many other newly-engendered organisations, it had done little;
'there had been much talk and little action'. It was composed of some
400 members, chosen from the delegates sent to the Electoral Assembly
from various towns and districts. Despite its power as a part of the
Legislature, it was not permitted to meddle with the Imperial Administration; and could be dissolved by a simple *ukaz* of the Tsar.

But they volunteered little information. We asked if they had taken the Oath of Allegiance. Yes, they had, with many other comrades; they were told what to do and they did it. We could not get them to talk – so we ceased to ply them with questions. But they revealed one item of news which seemed to interest our medical staff. They told us that leaflets from the enemy had been dropped into the Russian trenches. They were printed in Russian, but as there were few among them who were sufficiently *gramotnie* [literate], they had been unable to understand them. Some of the leaflets had been handed to the officers, who had used savage language and told their men to tear the papers up, or burn them. When they had enquired what the enemy had said on the leaflets, the officers told them that the enemy wished to dupe them by offering to fraternise with them and visit them in the trenches.

Today, two staff officers showed me a lengthy paper, printed in large Russian type, from the enemy; or, rather, from the enemies. On one side was a long extract from the Berlin newspaper, *Norddeutsche Allgemeine Zeitung,* dated 2nd [15th] April 1917, and on the reverse the reply of the Austro-Hungarian Government to the Proclamation of the Russian Provisional Government dated 1st [14th] April 1917. The German statement refers to the Proclamation issued by the Provisional Government in Petrograd on 28th March [10th April] 1917. This, it affirms, agrees with the repeatedly expressed views of Germany and her Allies that they are striving only to obtain the guarantee of existence, honour and free progress of their peoples.

> The Central European Powers are by no means desirous of bringing about the downfall of the Russian Nation. . . . They do not intend to infringe the honour or liberty of the Russian people and are anxious only to hasten the time when they can live in peace and harmony with a contented neighbour. Germany has never dreamt of interfering in the internal re-organisation of Russia, much less to menace her at the moment of the birth of her freedom. If the Russian people are still obliged to suffer and to shed their blood, instead of dedicating – peacefully and unhindered – all their strength to the widespread development of their newly-won liberty, then the fault does not lie with Germany. Who hinders the Russian people from realising their

yearning for peace, expressed on the 28th March [10th April]?
Their Allies. England, France, Italy and the States adhering to
them, in reply to peace proposals, openly indicated their own
terms: to seize the vast provinces rightly belonging to Germany,
to divide Austria-Hungary, to thrust Turkey out of Europe and
to parcel out Asia Minor.

I turned over the paper and read the reply of the Austro-
Hungarian Government to the Proclamation of the Russian
Provisional Government. It pointed out that the contents of the
Proclamation had come to the knowledge of the Austro-Hungarian
Government on 29th March 1917.

> From them, it ensues that Russia's aim is not to dominate foreign
> nations or forcibly occupy foreign territory; that she, on the
> contrary, is striving to conclude a lasting peace, based on the
> fundamental right of nations to determine their own destiny. It
> is, therefore, plain to see that the aims of the Russian Pro-
> visional Government coincide with the aims of Austria-Hungary,
> expressed by her Minister of Foreign Affairs on 18th March 1917.
> In other words, the Austro-Hungarian and Russian Provisional
> Governments have similar yearnings to conclude an honourable
> peace for both sides, as has already been proposed by Austria-
> Hungary and her Allies in December 1916. From all this, the
> whole world and especially the people of Russia can clearly see
> that Russia has no further need to continue the war . . . and that,
> in view of the complete similarity of the aims of our Allies and
> those of the Provisional Government, there can be no obstacle
> in arriving at a mutual agreement; all the more so, seeing that
> the Austro-Hungarian Monarch, together with his Allies,
> cherishes the wish to live in peaceful harmony and in friendship
> with the free Russian people. . . .

So it is at this moment that both Germany and Austria have
embarked on an artful ruse to spread unrest among Russia's
fighting men in the trenches. Fully aware of the upheaval caused
in Russia by the Tsar's abdication, they hoped to take advantage
of the debilitated morale of the soldiers; so their wily leaflets,
promising peace and friendship, have been showered into the
Russian trenches. A good thing for the soldiers that so few were
gramotnie! A good thing for the soldiers that their simple, loyal

minds could not grasp all the implications of those deceptive over-tures! Nevertheless, these long-winded leaflets roused within us certain fears. There was said to be considerable dilly-dallying on the part of the Provisional Government in making definite deci-sions about the war. One or two of our members, noted for their pessimistic views, hinted that the time was now ripe for a separate peace to be concluded; but the majority stood firm by the Alliance and declared that Russia should fulfil her sacred promise and re-main a faithful Ally until the war should be brought to a successful end. Sometimes, in moments of perplexity, we ask ourselves what will happen to our Red Cross *Otryad* should peace be concluded? Shall we be dissolved?

There is no doubt that the Revolution has been acclaimed as a victory for democracy. Intellectuals declare loudly that now is the moment to reconstruct political, social, educational and industrial systems throughout the country. Now is the great opportunity to deal vigorously with land-ownership. 'Free Russia must see to it that the people of Russia shall be free to rejoice in their freedom.' But how can those problems be solved while the enemy is still hammering at the door? The patriots answer: 'It is the primary duty of all Free Russians to oust the enemy from Russian territory. Then, and only then, can fundamental reforms be carried out.'

As the days pass, the Provisional Government comes increasingly under attack. Its members, say critics, are new to administration and lack both time and experience to deal adequately with the enormous problems confronting them.

14th April
We left Trostyanitse for Strusuv, all of us pleased at the prospect of renewed work and – we hoped – renewed success for our fighting-men. We journeyed through Podgaytsy, where I caught a glimpse of the hospital, and arrived at Khatki for the night. On the morning of the 15th we continued our journey to Strusuv, a quaint little Galician hamlet where we learnt to our surprise that our Division had been ordered into the countryside for a brief rest. So Strusuv was destined to provide us with relaxation; the work which we had hoped for was yet to come our way.

Early May. Strusuv

Some regimental doctors arrived for supper. One of our guests
refused the plate of meat offered to him; he was at once teased for
his loss of appetite. He said that it was true, he had little appetite,
but would explain more fully later, adding in a low voice that he
did not wish the orderlies to hear the conversation. When the meal
had been cleared away and the orderlies had retired, he said he
had heard that strange things were happening in Petrograd.
Kerensky was taking it into his own hands to bring about drastic
reforms in the army. He had declared that army discipline was too
rigid, that the soldiers should be treated in a more liberal, friendly
manner by their officers. As an instance of the new attitude which
he desired to see he had abolished the use of the condescending,
patronising 'thou', employed to those of inferior rank. An officer,
when addressing the rank-and-file, would now be obliged to use the
more polite 'you'. This order had, naturally, caused dismay among
all officers, for they feared – and not without reason, said the
doctor – that it would lessen the authority of officers over soldiers
in the ranks. One and all declared this new reform to be grossly
out of place. 'Impossible!' they decided indignantly. It would be
the end of all discipline.

Kerensky had never been an advocate of capital punishment, so
his new law to abolish the death sentence aroused little surprise,
although it did excite resentment. Men began asking: 'Who is this
Socialist Minister who holds the destiny of Russia in his hands?'
There is no doubt that Kerensky, despite his youth and lack of
political experience, is acknowledged the most powerful politician
in the New Russia. The Provisional Government is undergoing
reconstruction and Kerensky has been given the post of Minister
of War and Marine. At the age of 36, he has already climbed to the
top of the ladder, firmly holding the reins of Government and
controlling the fortunes of the war as well.

11th May. Podgaytsy

Today we left Strusuv for Podgaytsy. Our division is back at the
Front and two of its regiments are already in the trenches. Now
and then unexpected skirmishes take place – the initiative always
with the Austrians – and a few wounded are brought to us. We
notice a strange apathy about them; they lack the spark of loyalty,
of devotion to God and their mother-country which has so dis-

tinguished the fighting-men in the previous two years. It worries us; we do not need to be told that the Russian soldier has changed; we see the change with our own eyes.

There is an English hospital in Podgaytsy, run by a group of English nurses, under the leadership of an English lady-doctor. I was very glad to chat with them in my mother-tongue and above all to learn the latest news of the allied front in France. It was certainly comforting to hear that the Germans had been forced to retreat to the Hindenburg Line, which has been regarded by the German High Command as completely impregnable. A great Offensive is in progress at Vimy Ridge, where Canadian soldiers have stormed and held important enemy sectors. The English hospital has English newspapers, too; outdated, but, nevertheless, full of interest for me. They are very nice women, those English and Scottish nurses. They all have several years of training behind them. I feel distinctly raw in comparison, knowing that a mere six-months' course as a VAD in a military hospital would, in England, never have been considered sufficient to graduate to a Front Line Red Cross Unit. They could not believe that I had experienced all those nightmare months of the Great Retreat of 1915, as well as the Offensive of 1916. 'You don't look strong enough to have gone through all that,' said the lady-doctor, 'and too young,' she added, 'I don't think that I should have chosen you for my team.' I secretly rejoiced that I had had my training in Russia!

Some of the medical terms they used were Greek to me! I consoled myself with the thought that my Russian was Greek to them! Not one of them spoke Russian – perhaps an isolated word here and there, but quite inadequate to meet the simplest emergency. They invited me to spend my free time with them; I was glad to do so, although my 'work' consists principally in soothing the wounded. The men betray a certain anxiety when they find themselves at the mercy of nurses whose language they cannot understand. I explained to them that they were from England, *my* country, *their* ally; but I saw that suspicion still crept into their untutored minds. So I felt pleased and gratified when some of them whispered to me: 'Stay with me, *Sestritsa*. Don't go away! Don't leave me alone!'

Their methods, too, are new to me. I was surprised to note that saline solutions are frequently used, but I was still more surprised and not a little perturbed when I saw that tiny bags, containing pure salt, are sometimes deposited into the open wound and bandaged tightly into place. It is probably a new method; I wonder if it has been tried out on the Allied Front. We treat an ordinary light injury in quite a different way, using *perekis* [peroxide] to cleanse the wound, and paint it around with *iod* [iodine] before the sterilised dressing is applied. These bags of salt – small though they are – must inflict excruciating pain; no wonder the soldiers kick and yell; the salt must burn fiercely into the lacerated flesh. It is certainly a purifier, but surely a very harsh one! At an operation performed by the lady-doctor, at which I was called upon to help, the man had a large open wound in his left thigh. All went well until *two* tiny bags of salt were placed within it, and then the uproar began. I thought the man's cries would lift the roof off; even the lady-doctor looked discomforted. 'Silly fellow!' she ejaculated. 'Stop it! It's only a momentary pain. Foolish fellow! He doesn't know what is good for him.'

The reforms initiated by Kerensky are meeting with little success. They were intended to create a closer relationship, a more friendly atmosphere; they seem, however, to be doing exactly the reverse. Strangely enough, it is the soldiers who appear disgruntled; they are moody, even morose, and often astonish their officers by pertness and effrontery. Soldiers can now sit – even smoke – in the presence of their officers. They are free men now and they insist on every new privilege as their bounden right. But even privileges, never before dreamt of in military service, produce a rapid deterioration in morale and discipline quite foreign to the rigid military training of the Russian rank-and-file.

Kerensky must have been made aware of the indignation among the officers and, in his impetuous energetic way, resolved that the best course of action would be for him to approach the soldiers in person; he would parley with them, and find out just where things had gone wrong. So he has begun what is described as an 'oratorical campaign'. Wherever he goes, we hear with very real thankfulness, he meets unbounded enthusiasm. He is a born orator; he sways his audiences as no other politician has ever been able to sway them. The soldiers know that he is on their side; they have already had proof of his fellow-feeling and sympathy; so they are willing to listen to him.

13th May, 1917

During breakfast the Order was brought to us: Kerensky was coming to Podgaytsy! He would come and harangue our soldiers with heartening words. Pray Heaven that his influence would succeed in re-organising the already disorganised Front Line troops. We had no doubt that at Podgaytsy he would be given as hearty a welcome as on other sections of the Front. We were all most eager to hear him. In small groups we wended our way through the dusty streets and up the hill outside the town. What an enormous mass of military! It was amazing that so many could collect together in so short a time! Our first thought was, 'We shall never catch a glimpse of him in such a crowd.' But we pushed our way forward and fortune favoured us. Some regimental doctors of our acquaintance spied us and helped us through into the very front row.

The hill-top spread out like a wide arena and on all sides were tightly-packed masses of soldiers. The hill-slopes were literally bristling with military. I noticed cameras in the hands of some officers, who, every now and then, would look anxiously skywards. My eyes followed theirs – dark clouds were slowly rising, drawing nearer the sun. I studied my camera; it was in order. 'If he comes now,' I thought, 'I can get a snapshot before the sun disappears.' But in the excitement of his arrival I forgot all about my camera! As he stepped out of the car, a great roar of welcome rose. He approached the high platform, mounted it and stood there confronting the multitudinous assembly. At first glance, he looked small and insignificant. He wore a darkish uniform and there was nothing about him to indicate the magnetic power he was able to wield. I remember clearly a feeling of disappointment. Was *this* man really *the* Kerensky? He looked less than his 36 years and his beardless face made him even younger. For a while he stood in silence; then he began to speak, slowly at first and very clearly. As he spoke, one realised immediately the source of his power. His sincerity was unquestionable; and his eloquence literally hypnotised us.

He spoke for about twenty minutes, but time seemed to stand still. His main theme was freedom; that great, mystical Freedom which had come to Russia. His words were often interrupted by wild applause, and, when he pointed out that the war must, at all costs, continue to a victorious end, they acclaimed him to the echo. 'You will fight to a victorious end!' he adjured them. 'We will!' the soldiers shouted as one man. 'You will drive the enemy off Russian soil!' 'We will!' they shouted again with boundless enthusiasm. 'You, free men of a Free Country; you will fight for Russia, your Mother-Country. You will go into battle with joy in your hearts!' 'We are free men,' they roared. 'We will follow you into battle. Let us go now! Let us go now!'

When he left, they carried him on their shoulders to his car. They kissed him, his uniform, his car, the ground on which he walked. Many of them were on their knees praying; others were weeping. Some of them cheering; others singing patriotic songs. To the accompaniment of this hysterical outburst of patriotic fervour, Kerensky drove away. His car was soon lost to sight. We were told that more than 12,000 soldiers had gathered to acclaim him. We were all greatly impressed by him and his marvellous influence over the men. He had promised them that the Offensive would not be long delayed and had assured them of the renewed strength of batteries, heavy artillery and ammunition at their disposal. We had heard that a General Polivanov had succeeded General Sukhomlinov who had been held responsible for the complete lack of equipment which had brought about the Great Retreat of 1915. It was General Polivanov who supplied manpower, guns and munition for the Offensive in Galicia which, in June 1916, met with such extraordinary success. So we felt confident that, with Kerensky and Polivanov at the helm, all would go well.

Nearly a month has passed and no Orders from the Russian High Command have been received. The exultation of the troops on the South-West Front has gradually weakened. Had Orders to start the Offensive come at once, the soldiers would have risen to the occasion with magnificent zeal; they were all afire to go. But weeks have passed and no Orders come. These leisured weeks have given the men – 50 per cent of whom are illiterate – time to think. Their thinking has been their undoing, for their thoughts were concerned – not with Russia, nor with the foe confronting them – but with their new-found liberty. Freedom, for them, is a wonderful, inexplicable thing which has suddenly been thrust upon their country and upon them. 'Freedom,' they argue, 'implies liberty to say, think and act as each individual thinks fit.' 'Freedom gives us the privilege of deciding things for ourselves.'

And so they have thought things over among themselves, and the word 'freedom' is bandied from mouth to mouth, and ever the taste of it to these simple, credulous peasant-soldiers becomes sweeter and sweeter. So ignorant are many of them, that they cannot even pronounce the word properly. 'Freedom,' in Russian is *svoboda*, but these poor, uneducated men called it *slaboda* and *slabada*, and so corrupted the word in their own mother-tongue that it was scarcely recognisable.

And still no Orders come and army officers look at each other blankly and ask the same question: 'What, in God's name, is happening?' Criticism of Kerensky and of his ruling respecting army reforms becomes more frequent and sharp. The majority of officers agree that he has overstepped the bounds. Discipline is tottering in the trenches. 'How shall we lead our men into attack now?' they ask. One officer told us that, in earlier days, it had sometimes been done with the revolver; now that was impossible. Authority had been taken out of their hands. Some regimental doctors who attended another mass welcome of Kerensky on the Galician Front related how Kerensky had described his visit to a Front Line after a skirmish with the Austrians. With tears in his eyes he had said: 'I saw my compatriots dying, numbers of them; and nothing could save them.' The doctors agreed that for an ordinary man to shed tears 'in the proper place and at the proper time' was understandable, even praiseworthy; but for the War Minister of the Russian Government, it was a sign of weakness. Kerensky, they said, might have become a great man in Russian history, in fact, one of the greatest, but he had forfeited that position by losing control over himself in public. . . .

After his abdication, Nicholas II had insisted on saying goodbye to his officers and troops in Galicia. We were told that, with the permission of the Provisional Government, he had journeyed to Mogilev, the Army Headquarters, where he and the Tsarevich had spent many weeks in the autumn of 1915. In 1916 the Tsar himself took over the command of all his Armies and visited Mogilev again, where he inspected the Regiments of his Imperial Guards. Now, however, deprived of Throne and Power, his visit was sorrowful in the extreme. He spent only a few days there and was visited by his mother, the Dowager Empress Marie. There they parted; she, to return to her home in Kiyev; he, to return as a prisoner to his family in Tsarskoe Selo [the Village of the Tsar]. Those who saw him in Mogilev were amazed at the self-control and courage with which he carried out the final ceremonies. He wrote to his fighting-men on the various Fronts and addressed the troops in person. He told them that he was leaving them because he felt that he was no longer necessary; thanked them for their never-failing loyalty; praised them for their unwavering patriotism and be-sought them to obey the Provisional Government, to continue the war and to lead Russia to Victory. Only his mournful, hollow eyes, and extreme pallor told of the effort he was making to preserve the calm demanded of him.

Even before he left Mogilev, vociferous celebrations were taking place in the town; large red flags blazed in the streets; all photo-graphs of himself and family had disappeared; Imperial emblems were being pulled down from walls, cut off uniforms; and, while the ex-Tsar sat alone in his room, the officers who had visited him, cheered his brave words and bowed low – many in tears – before him as he bid them farewell, were at that moment queuing up in the open-air, outside his window, to take the Oath of Allegiance to the Provisional Government.

We had heard some days before that the Tsar and his family had been transferred from the Crimea to Tsarskoe Selo. This was some 20 versts south of Petrograd, and the beautiful Alexander Palace had been built by an Italian architect in the eighteenth century. We learned that Kerensky had organised this transfer and had undertaken to protect the Tsar and his family from intrusion. They could not, we decided, be in better hands.

The abdication had, by now, been received by the general public with a certain amount of equanimity. At first it had stunned them, but gradually they came to accept it. Nevertheless there were still those whose loyalty was unshaken and who were anxious to gauge the why and wherefore of the Tsar's fall from grace. 'What shall we do without him?' it was often asked. And some stupid clown would reply: 'Exactly the same that you did *with* him. Pray, what did he do for you?' As might be expected, a series of spiteful rumours played around the figure of the deposed monarch, and more than one facetious recruit expressed the hope that a term of imprisonment on bread and water might bring him to his senses. 'He has to travel in an ordinary train now, like any ordinary man. No more Imperial transport for him! And he will have to pay for his ticket into the bargain.'

One of our doctors heard that the Tsar and his family might be sent to England *for safety*. Those last ominous words aroused fear in our hearts. Were they in danger from their own people? That was an idea so horrible that one refused even to think of it. If only they would go to England! How glad and proud I should be!

Wednesday, 7th June, 1917. Loschina
Yesterday I returned to my unit in Loschina after spending some days with the English nurses in Podgaytsy. When I saw the familiar *dvukolki*, standing stiffly side by side, and the tents, partly hidden by branches, dotted here and there on the hillside, a feeling of gladness came over me. Our *Letuchka* had just moved nearer the Front Line, for we had been warned that our men were preparing to launch an assault. In a day or two, we should be in the thick of it again and within a verst and a half of the Fighting Lines. We are stationed on a gentle slope: the heaviest vehicles of our baggage-train are in the valley below; the lighter carts and *dvukolki* a little higher up, while our tents are above them. The few trees have been taken by our drivers to protect their horses from the blazing sun. The small hamlet of Bojikov is nearly two versts away on the right. Our 2nd *Letuchka* is stationed there; also the Staff of our 23rd Division and the 108th Division which has just returned from reserve. Across the open plain winds the River 'Golden Lepa' and one can see soldiers taking a cooling bath in its somewhat muddy waters, or trying to wash the dust and grime out of their shirts and trousers. Their small figures look like flies and the horses and cows grazing on the plain like tiny wooden animals.

The air is wonderful, strong and clean; real mountain air. But the heat is intense for the sun blazes down on our shelterless quarters with a pitiless glare. Thunderstorms are about.

At dinner I must confess I felt dismayed when I saw the large bowl of soup and dish of *kasha* brought from the soldiers' kitchen. I remembered the appetising food at the English Hospital; but I told myself: 'This is no town hospital; this is a front line dressing-station!' Mamasha must have read my thoughts, for, looking at me, she said in a firm voice: 'We eat soldiers' rations now.' In spite of my hunger, I found it difficult to swallow that salt-fish soup; and the *kasha* contained so many lumps of fat that I was obliged to give it up and turn to black bread and tea. The conversation, too, was distasteful: it was principally fault-finding and petty arguing.

Again I found myself comparing my companions with the quietly-spoken, affable English nurses. 'Comparisons are odious!' said the decisive voice of one of our party. I was startled. The remark might have been directed at me! . . .

It was rumoured that a Russian assault would take place about 15th June. Our Allies were pressing the Provisional Government to start an Offensive as soon as possible, and it was expected to be a successful one. Even Mamasha seemed in a most optimistic frame of mind. 'I am badly in need of a new pair of shoes,' she announced, 'but I hope before the end of the month to be able to buy a pair in Lemberg!'

After dinner, I walked up to the top of our hill with Sofiya. In the far distance were the high mountain peaks, bathed in a soft, cobalt haze. The small villages of Saranchuki, Kotov and Ribniki were lying far below us in their respective valleys; we could see that the homesteads were ruined and deserted. The enemy's trenches were visible; they seemed perilously near the Russian lines – only 70 feet away, Sofiya said she had heard. There are scarlet patches of poppies in the fields around, marguerites too and a few cornflowers. There is something so comforting, so home-like, about a field of poppies.

At 4 p.m. we started off to Bojikov, where a Conference had been arranged with the 2nd *Letuchka*. We sat in a small room from 5 to 10 p.m. and talked and talked, mainly about Red Cross tactics along the South-West Front. Back at our hillside tents, the spirit-lamp was brought to boil the soup which had been awaiting us since 6, but the lamp refused to ignite. For 20 minutes Mamasha cleaned it patiently, but it remained obdurate; finally, a bit of wire broke off, blocking the primus tube. That was the end. We tried the soup cold but the fat was obnoxious. We decided to go to bed and forget our troubles in sleep.

Thursday, 8th June
Enemy aeroplanes had been over about 4 a.m. and awakened us; discontented murmurings came from most beds. We took turns in washing, with as little water as possible. Once or twice we had tried to persuade Rupertsov, our tent-boy, to scrounge another bucketful for us. He would screw his face up and shake his head. Smirnov's tent was next door to the water-cart and woe betide the person who tried to steal more than his share, for Smirnov

knew each one's quota to a spoonful. Our water-cart had to go to Bojikov to be filled, so we had been warned not to be extravagant.

Friday, 9th June
Enemy aeroplanes came over again soon after dawn and a couple of shells were dropped near our bivouac; but no harm was done. But we lost two aerostats that bright June morning; and two valiant Russian aeronauts, who had not had enough time to escape, perished in the flames.

Sunday, 18th June
At 6 a.m. a burst of firing came from our artillery, and we knew, instinctively, that the hour was at hand. We grew very restless and Mamasha proposed that we should make our way through the undergrowth to some old trenches higher up on our hill; we might catch a glimpse of the fighting from there. Our men were advancing! Rifle and machine-gun fire spurted and spluttered; shells shrieked and shrapnel exploded, flashing and flaming like fireworks. The interchange of heavy gunfire was ferocious. I felt myself shivering from head to foot; Mamasha's face was pale and her lips tightly compressed; Anna kept covering her eyes with trembling hands. We turned away distraught, speechless, and tumbled our way mechanically downhill towards our tent. Our Offensive had begun! We had witnessed its beginning with our own eyes! And our hearts were sick with fear.

By noon, the wounded had reached us and our hands and, thank God! our minds were kept busy. The Offensive was more successful than one had dared to hope. Three lines of trenches had already been captured and hundreds of prisoners taken. The wounded were in good heart, but dazed by the suddenness of it all. There were several operations, but we all worked with a will. During dinner, a couple of shrapnel exploded near our camp – a farewell salute from the Austrians! We worked until 2 a.m. without ceasing, and the firing continued unabated – slowly becoming more and more distant. That was a good sign, for the less distinct the gunfire, the deeper our advance into enemy territory.

Monday, 19th June
They sent me to rest at 2 o'clock this morning and said they would call me in two hours' time. I awoke at 5, startled to see the hour.

The Sisters reassured me. They said that we had been told to sleep while it was possible. The firing was still intense. A tremendous battle must have been in progress. The earth was shaking under our feet, convulsed by thunderous detonations. Someone wanted to call Mamasha; she was still asleep. 'Let her sleep,' they said. 'Breakfast can go on without her.' A strong, acrid tang was in the air; the Sisters on duty came to fetch their gas-masks. The soldiers had told them there had been more than one scare. The wounded were still being brought in in batches of a dozen or so at a time. Many very heavily wounded came about midday. We have heard that Alexander Alexandrovich has been killed, and Mischa and Mak, two of our transport-van officers, badly wounded. We postponed dinner until after 4 p.m., in order to finish the bandaging. Afterwards, Mamasha and I walked a little way up the hill. All the western world was in tumult. Red, grey and yellow rockets glowed for a few seconds and then died away. The cracking and rapping of rifle-fire was still audible, with the crash and bang of shells. Volley after volley resounded among the hills. The most dreaded sound of all was the hollow thud of a heavy shell tearing into earth. A shrill whistling above our heads – and a couple of shrapnel exploded between our camp and the road. We thought it wiser to return to shelter. The wounded continued to come and we bandaged them until about 10 p.m. The doctors then sent me to rest, for I was to be on duty all next day. The guns were roaring more loudly than ever: I covered my head with my blanket and tried to obliterate that fearful clamour.

Tuesday, 20th June
The Sister on night-duty returned to our tent at 6 a.m. and lay down, exhausted, in her underclothes. 'Sleep, Tamara,' I told her. 'I can't sleep any more. I am going on duty.' Our dressing-tent was packed with wounded; they were lying on the ground outside, the hillside was covered with them. I don't think I sat down all that morning until dinner at 2 and then for only 10 minutes. Shells came hissing over our camp. The soldiers heard them and begged us to send them on to the Base and not expose them to further injury. One large tent had been set apart for the severely wounded. One had only to step inside and their pain-racked voices would be raised – beseeching, imploring: 'Little Sister! come to me!' 'Oh! little Sister! Water!' 'Little Sister! for the love of God!' I was too

busy to stay with them, but I promised I would look after them at night. When I went to our dining-tent for black bread and cheese and a cup of hot tea, one of our doctors was there; I begged him for the latest news from the Front. He told me that our division had been forced to retreat a few versts; it had been so devastated that it would have to go into reserve. 'Would that mean our departure from Loschina?' I asked. 'More than likely,' he answered. Although we had made a small advance, our casualties were so enormous that several regiments had to be withdrawn and patched up before they could return to the position. It was a night of noise and horror; more than one attack was launched by our soldiers and the raging of the guns never ceased.

I went into the large tent where the heavily wounded were lying. Two torches provided a dim illumination and a lighted candle flickered on the small table in the middle of the tent. I sat at the little wooden table and tried not to be upset by the groans and cries of pain. There was a dreadful smell of pus and gangrene. Two men with smashed stomachs had just died; I called the orderlies to take them away, but they were busy in another tent. Now and then, I got up from my chair to give an injection, to pick up a blanket or sheet which had been thrown off by some restless form, to pour out a dose of medicine, or to feel the pulse of some poor man whose life was ebbing fast. From various corners of the tent came the repeated cries: '*Sestritsa*, please give water.' 'For the love of God, water!' 'Water, or I die!' I shut my ears to this living pain and tried to write a few words in my notebook, but I could not concentrate. The men with head wounds and whole stomachs were allowed to drink; but if a laparotomy patient lay alongside, I had to resort to strategy – hiding the mug in a fold of my overall, or kneeling between them. But it availed little. '*Sestritsa*, darling, give water!' the cry is taken up. '*Sestritsa*, my *rodnaya* [own dear] Mother, water!' 'Water! one drop! You can't refuse *one* drop!' I got up, pretending not to hear, and walked to the other side of the tent. A soldier with a smashed skull was breathing heavily with a funny, gurgling noise; his nostrils spouted out foamy matter with each gasping breath. An orderly, squatting by him, was constantly wiping his swollen face. Not far from him was a little stout man in a half-sitting position; the rattling noise in his throat was dreadful to hear. He had been shot through the right lung and his open wound was big enough to insert my fingers.

The usual injection of morphia had had little or no effect and his frightened eyes were now gazing at me with a great pleading in them. . . . If only I could help them! If only I possessed that magic 'healing touch' to sooth their anguish! '*Sestritsa*, don't you hear how I pray to you?' came a voice behind me. I hardened my heart and walked on.

I have explained to them times without number that water is poison to them in their present state. I have moistened their burning lips, their parched tongues, but no! they are not content. The water must be swallowed, for, they say, their chest and stomach are on fire. I kept special watch over the rubber-bags – to know if the small lumps of ice had melted. Those ice-bags were a sore temptation: more than once a dying soldier had summoned up sufficient strength to bite through the rubber and get at the ice. There was one man who, I remember, succeeded in holing his rubber-bag and placing a piece of ice in his mouth. A doctor had noticed it and, shouting at him, told him that death would surely be his punishment. I remember, too, the man's hopeless, despairing face: 'Better death than this living torture!' he had said; then there had come the doctor's curt, rough rebuke: 'Fool! I tell you; you're a fool!'

Next to the wall, a man is stretched out unconscious, but so restless that an orderly has to be at hand to hold him down. In his delirium, he is crying out; sometimes he is supping with comrades round a camp fire, then he is in the trenches under enemy fire. A wounded Turk is wailing out something in his mother-tongue. I returned to my seat and began again on my notebook; but the cries for water came again. I got up and moistened the lips of the sufferer; but his cries started a chorus. How I longed to get away from them; they were breaking my heart. If they continued much longer, I, too, should begin to cry. These living beings so shattered and smashed – how can one help them? How comfort them? When I see some of those gaping wounds, it would be heartless mockery to say 'Patience!' or 'It will soon be better', for I know only too well that it will take long, weary months before the pain will pass.

'*Sestritsa*, for the love of the Blessed Mother of God! *One* drop!' I went to him and I saw that he was dying; the face, the eyes bore the positive unmistakable stamp of Death. I had seen it so often . . . I could not make a mistake. . . . His dying eyes were fixed on my face: 'One dr-op!' he breathed. A great determining resolve came over me. I rose from my knees, took a small mug, half filled with water, and held it to his lips. He drank feverishly, wildly; then, his head sank back, his eyes closed; a deep, long-drawn sighing breath came from him . . . he was at peace.

I needed air and went outside for a few minutes. The guns were still booming in the distance, the shrapnel still bursting over the nearby hills. I gazed up into that vast, starlit vault of Heaven and drank in the peace of those immeasurable spaces. Oh God! when will it all end? – Perhaps He does not know, I thought. Perhaps He cannot understand our human torment. And yet were we not told that not even a sparrow can fall unknown to the Father's Will? Oh God! rise up in Thy Might and Mercy and end this ghastly human carnage! As I stood on the hillside, enveloped by the night's deep calm, the line of a poem – or was it a hymn? – came to my mind: 'And in the wondrous stillness, He sent strength to me.' The stars blinked down at me unperturbed. The cool breeze made me shiver slightly. A shell exploded in the valley below. I walked back into the tent.

Wednesday, 21st June
Marching-orders had been received and we were to leave Loschina in the afternoon. Those wounded too frail to stand the jolting of the *dvukolki* were carefully packed on stretchers attached to horses. Horse-drawn stretchers have proved to be an excellent way of traversing the well-trodden mountain-paths, too narrow to admit any vehicle. Both Mak and Misha – the wounded transport men – were sent off early. Just before Mak was lifted into the *dvukolka* a shrapnel exploded near our camp and a largish piece of metal fell into his tent, while another bit wounded our horse *Lebed* [Swan]. Two more stomach cases had died; mercifully they had passed away quietly under heavy sedation. Our soldiers, under Smirnov's Christian guidance, buried the dead men, seven in all, and a wooden cross inscribed with their names was placed at the head of the brothers' grave. Our packing took time, as we had been stationed in Loschina since 6th June, but at 12.30 p.m. we set off. We drove to a lovely wood, some four versts from Bojikov and seven from Podgaytsy. It was a beautiful day, but I was still so tired that I lay down and fell asleep while the tents were being erected. A light supper of eggs, black bread and cheese

was served in picnic fashion. As twilight was falling, we Sisters
decided to seize the opportunity of a long night's sleep. In that
tranquil spot, with the sweet, clean air of beech and pine trees
around us, it was not difficult to find rest.

Thursday, 22nd June. Outside Bojikov

This morning, we were all rested and in good spirits. Camp-fires
have been lit and water is plentiful. One or two of us Sisters
washed and ironed our laundry. But before long our peace was
disturbed by shouting and the noise of creaking vehicles.
Rupertsov our tent-boy brought us the news: there were soldiers
everywhere, hundreds of them. The ground was covered with
their tents. The 45th and 46th Siberian Regiments have encamped
in our wood, awaiting reinforcements.

Once or twice we have heard the call of the cuckoo. We often
see wood-pigeons too; their soft cooing-notes come down to us
from the thickly intertwined branches overhead, sweet and low
like a lullaby.

Sunday, 25th June

Two Staff Officers paid us a flying visit in the evening. Both
Alexander Andreyevich and Alexander Sergeyevich were old
friends and we eagerly welcomed them and anxiously awaited all
their news. They confirmed that the Offensive, under our intrepid
General Brusilov, might, so far, be regarded as highly successful.
It had taken place along a 50 – or more – verst line and the many
divisions concentrated on that part of the Galician Front had had
little difficulty in ousting the Austrians from their trenches and
driving them far back into their hinterland. The Russians had
better guns, more men and enormous supplies of ammunition.
Everything was in our favour; if only the morale of the soldiers
endured, Russia might soon see the complete collapse of the
Austrian Army.

The morale of our men was, on the whole, they affirmed, very
good. One battalion captain had sent in a report to the effect
that if the Generals would not allow his men to launch an attack
soon, he could not answer for the success of the Offensive in his
sector of the Front. When at last his men were told that an
advance was about to begin, they had jumped out of their trenches
some minutes before the given time. In most cases, the officers

would go first, leading their men. But there were instances when officers had met with defiance, soldiers had shown great unwillingness to leave the trenches, and officers had been obliged to beg the men to attack; then, perhaps, six men would run out; then ten; but never – as in former days – all together, as one man. Such insuboidination was attributed to the ill-advised and irrational reforms introduced into the Army by Kerensky. We heard of a case where an officer had actually been arrested by his own soldiers for slapping the face of one of the men. In another sector, the soldiers had instituted what they called the Order of Field Court Martial and already an officer had been seen escoited by soldiers with drawn swords. Whenever the regimental flag was carried, the men insisted that it should be preceded by the Red Flag of Freedom. 'Things are bad enough as they are now,' said one of our guests, 'but they will get worse unless the Provisional Government repeals some of these ridiculous reforms. Only a Military Council should have the right to introduce changes in Military Administration. What can a civilian know about the Army?'

Monday, 26th June
Alexander Andreyevich appeared again in the afternoon and told us that we were to be transferred to the 8th Army, recently reinforced and under the command of General Kornilov (General Brusilov having been appointed Commander-in-Chief). We were all thankful to be leaving the Division of the 7th Army and joining the glorious 8th.

Wednesday, 28th June. En route for Mariampol
The weather has become quite cold and windy. We were told that a *komanda* [body of troops] was holding a meeting and decided to go and hear what it was all about. It was a strange, depressing experience. The speeches of two officers were genial and optimistic; but when we saw the faces of the soldiers, we realised something had gone wrong. They were sullen and ill-humoured. First one and then another began to speak; they were not good speakers, but their words were forceful and made an impression on the listening comrades. Their Commanding Officer, they said, had deliberately ridden through wire entanglements which had torn out the eye of one horse and so lacerated another that it had to be

shot. There was no doubt that the majority of soldiers present
nursed resentment against their c.o.; a third soldier complained
angrily that it was only because of his rank that no punishment
had been meted out, and that had a soldier committed such a
crime he would have been instantly shot. Another soldier demanded that blankets be distributed among the troops without
delay, and all disabled soldiers receive special compensation
without any discrimination whatsoever. We were all ears; it was
such an unusual scene. Since when had our soldiers acquired the
right to denounce their Commanding Officer in public? They had
repeatedly been told that they were Free men in a Free Country,
with free speech and action. But it made one tremble to think
what freedom might do to Russia if all her fighting-men followed
the example of this *komanda*. In the midst of the speech-making,
a despatch-rider appeared and delivered some documents to one
of the officers. He read them aloud: Halicz had been occupied by
the 8th Army under General Kornilov. The victorious Army was
pushing onwards towards Kalusz and other strategic points. We
all breathed a deep sigh of relief and thanksgiving. The second
Official Order said that the Russians had captured Kalusz; 60
guns and 10,000 prisoners had been taken. This news could not
have come at a more opportune moment. All the wrathful and
revengeful feelings smouldering among the soldiers seemed suddenly
to melt away. A buzz of excited voices followed and then a mighty
'Ura!' from the entire assembly.

Thursday, 29th June. A barn at Mendtzikhortse
... We heard that many soldiers of the 91st Regiment had refused to
return to the trenches; some of them had left their regiment and
were making their way eastwards towards Russia. Motors with
maxim-guns were being sent after them, with orders to force
them to return, or to fire at them on the road. It was said that
certain regiments had refused to take runaways back into their
ranks; and one regiment, in reserve and awaiting reinforcements,
had refused point blank to accept any new recruits.

Sunday, 2nd July
By midday our Flying Column was making its way through driving
rain towards Stanislav. We got stuck more than once in the boggy
woodlands, but the boredom of delay was relieved by one of our

doctors who read aloud to us some comical stories by Chekov. Slowly the rain-clouds dispersed, the sun came out and the whole scene – and our hearts – took on new life. We crossed the Dnestr; the roads on either side were dreadful, our carts and vans literally wading through mud, in places up to the horses' knees. At Iyezupol, taken only a week before by Kornilov's 8th Army, we found several houses still smoking. Some little children were sitting on piles of bricks and mortar, and there was one old *Pan* intently searching for something among the ruins.

From Stanislav, we journeyed on to Novy Bogorodchany and Grabuvka where we occupied the buildings left by the Austro-German troops.

Thursday, 6th July. Grabuvka

Before dinner, one of our doctors told us that the 90th Regiment has refused to remain in the Front Line and nearly two versts of trenches are completely unguarded. His voice was thick and unsteady. 'What can that mean?' someone asked. 'Mean?' he repeated heatedly. 'Why, any fool can see what that *means*! The enemy will occupy the empty trenches and our troops on either side will be obliged to retreat.' 'But surely reinforcements will be sent to their aid?' The doctor thought for a while and then he said – very slowly: 'Reinforcements will be sent. But *will they go*?'

But at Grabuvka, our situation was uncertain so we did not unpack.

Friday, 7th July

At an impromptu meeting of the medical staff, the question was raised as to where our Red Cross *Otryad* should go, if our soldiers refused to stem the advance of our enemies. What a tormenting predicament! Surely such a drastic step would never be necessary! It is said, too, that several crack German divisions have been transferred from the French Front to Galicia to boost the wilting morale of the Austrians. We Sisters seized a moment to wash our laundry in the river; our hands became quite sore from the rubbing and scrubbing.

Saturday, 8th July
The firing has ceased. What the silence portends, no one can tell.
We are all on the alert for marching-orders. Anna and I walked for
a brief while in the small neighbouring wood. We found a few
mushrooms, but they and the beautiful trees failed for once to
revive our spirits. We looked at each other and each saw tears in
the other's eyes, but we made no mention of them. For my part,
I was deeply downhearted for the Russians, but I was homesick
too, for no news had been received from my homefolk for a long
time.

Sunday, 9th July
They brought a noisy volunteer with a comrade's bullet in his
leg; the first thing he demanded was something to eat. I offered
him our black bread and cheese, but no! it was not good enough.
His friends went away and returned with white bread, butter
and milk, which *our* kitchen could not supply. Another told us
that things were going badly in the trenches and that he had
heard that Tarnopol had been recaptured by the Germans. He
was in very low spirits, so we did not believe his story, but when a
second soldier came, with a hand-wound, self-inflicted, and told
the same story, we were forced to believe there might be some
truth in it.

*By that evening, we were once more retreating along the chaotic
roads on a moonless night.*

Monday, 10th July
. . . The 11th Donskaya Division came riding towards us, grisly,
invulnerable Cossacks, their spears pointing skywards, sitting
like silent, carven statues astride their panting horses. They – and
they only – were bound westwards. We guessed their missions:
to check the advance of the enemy at all costs; to put the German
hordes to flight; to rally the desperately tired Russian Infantry,
and knout the cowardly deserters into submission.
    As we drove through a village, flames suddenly shot up from a
burning house; through the doorway several soldiers came
running, a glowing fire-brand lighting their way. Soon they had
set fire to another house; bits of burning timber and débris flew
up like rockets, illuminating the surroundings in brilliant relief.

It was a tragic scene. The inhabitants passed us in their flight; frightened, defenceless peasant-women, running, limping, breathing hard, uttering little smothered cries, intent on reaching the friendly woodlands, where they might find shelter. . . .

At the village of Kamenna we rested for a few hours. We noticed some Austrian prisoners being escorted by; they were walking at a leisured pace and seemed in no way subservient to the two Russian soldiers who headed the party. A bakery was in full progress; loaves of black bread were being handed round to the soldiers and to our housekeeping personnel, but Mamasha's offer to pay was steadfastly refused. Then we saw that the bread was being given away to all and sundry, and we understood. The bakers were leaving the village and this was, indeed, their last batch of loaves. When the last loaves had been brought out, we saw some soldiers take them, pocket what they could and throw the rest on to the ground – and then tread on them with their dirty high boots. This action sickened us, for we knew that the peasant-villagers were without bread. We also remembered reports of the starving multitudes in Russia, and their cry: 'Bread! Give Bread!' As the soldiers moved on, we saw the peasants who had been waiting in the background, come hastily forward, pick up the crushed loaves and drop them into sacks.

Later that day we heard that Tarnopol had fallen.

Tuesday, 11th July
It was a bad night, and the predatory incursions of flies and fleas helped to make things worse. We were awakened at 5 a.m. and on the road by 6 o'clock. It was a fine morning, but cloudy. Anna and I walked with one of our doctors for the first ten versts. It was good to have physical exercise again after being cooped up in a small space so long. We saw the Markovtse railway-station and heard that trains were no longer running to Tarnopol. We met a young doctor, who told us that whole regiments had withdrawn from the trenches. Many soldiers had given themselves up to the enemy, under the influence of alluring leaflets that assured them that men of the Austro-German armies would welcome them as brothers.

Meanwhile in the capital, he said, riots had taken place and mobs were parading the streets, demanding that the war should cease, the soldiers be brought home and bread supplied for the hungry. In some places there had been shooting and civilians had suffered. There was considerable dissension among the members of the Provisional Government: Prince Lvov was thinking of resigning the premiership and in that case, Kerensky would take it. Shingarov had already resigned from his ministerial post. But Kerensky, despite his power and popularity, had a new foe, who publicly attacked him and his Government and was stirring up the populace to rebellion. This man, Lenin, had attempted a *coup d'état*, but Kerensky's supporters and the loyal police and troops in Petrograd had suppressed it. Lenin himself had either been arrested or had fled the country.

We stopped at some huts near the station and tried to buy a few eggs, but the peasants refused point-blank, even when we showed them the money in our hands.

We halted (for the night) at a *folvark* near the town of Tysmenitsa, surrounded by a park, now split up by lines of ugly trenches. Our camp-beds were brought in and all prepared for rest. Enemy aeroplanes were flying over the house and bombs fell on Markovtse railway-station, and the troops encamping in the vicinity. Our anti-aircraft guns fired at them repeatedly.

Alexander Andreyevich told us he had heard that the death sentence was again to be pronounced lawful, as a deterrent to desertion. . . . Soon after 8 p.m., quite unexpectedly, orders reached us to pack and leave at once. In great vexation, we demolished our supper standing, for there was no time to sit down! The camp-beds, just set up, were dismantled and repacked. We started off, passing through the orchard, where the fruit trees were already stripped of every apple and pear. When we had gone some way I remembered that I had left my wrist-watch behind, but it was too late to retrieve it.

Wednesday, 12th July. Tlumach

All night long there was loud, chaotic movement. Artillery and troops were constantly overtaking us. Now and then when the soldiers saw us in our open transport-van, they called out and some of their remarks were far from agreeable. It was the first time in three years of war work that we had met rudeness from our own men; we felt dismayed and humiliated.

We found many wounded and sick en route. Some had even walked from the trenches and were terribly weak and tired. We lost no time in unpacking our first aid kit and bandaged them there at the roadside. Two or three very weak ones we placed in our van. Then we ran after our transport-carts – they could not stop for fear of putting the whole *oboz* train out of gear – and managed to find a seat here and there with our drivers. Tlumach was empty, the houses stark and bare, not a pane of glass was left; and all the shops had been ransacked. Soldiers were everywhere, entirely undisciplined, and obviously out to loot anything they could lay their hands on. They were carrying pictures, books, boxes, even rugs. A group of them had discovered some jewellery and we saw them trying on rings. Once again, our hearts sank with dismay.

The traffic on the road was becoming thicker and less controlled; wagon-wheel interlaced with wagon-wheel; frantic drivers shouted, frightened horses reared. One of our wagons broke down in the middle of the town. The soldiers of our *Letuchka* stopped to mend it; consequently the *oboz* belonging to various detachments became obstructed and curses were showered on our men and on us. It was vital to get on! After leaving Tlumach, we turned off into a field to wait for the stragglers to catch up.

The spectacle of the many struggling vehicles on the road was a dreadful one. There was a tremendous surging forward, no matter what the cost, no matter what the injury to man, horse, or cart. All was a hectic scramble, a headlong rush eastward. We were thankful to remain in the field. A group of deserting infantry was passing. Alas! they had caught sight of our Red Cross uniforms; they were making remarks which they knew we should hear. 'How many of them?' 'Now, brother, take your pick.' 'Little fools, only getting in the way.'

In the evening, at the outskirts of the village Oleyuva-Kornyuv, we turned off across a river-bed and on to a hillside. There we found some wounded men and by the flickering light of two candles we bandaged fifteen of them. We had a sack of potatoes with us and, having collected some twigs, we lighted a fire. It began to rain and, to make matters worse, the wood was not enough to make a good fire and the water would not boil. So we had to be content with black bread and salt fish, washed down by muddy, tepid tea. . . . The rain came down gently but steadily.

There were no empty carts, so we spread straw on the earth and lay down to sleep. I covered myself with my mackintosh and pulled my soft leather hat well over my head and face.

Thursday, 13th July
A *sotnya* of Cossacks rode by towards the front; we could see their outlines dimly in the grey light of dawn. Someone had discovered a potato plot in a nearby garden; Annushka, Ekaterina and I collected a spade and dug up a bucketful. We finished just in time, for our *oboz* was waiting for us. We reached the *chaussée* and, to our surprise, found it practically deserted. In fact, at that moment, the only *oboz* on the road was ours! We had journeyed for about an hour, when a horseman galloped up with the news that the enemy advance had been halted and we were to return to Oleyuva Kornyuv! With hearts relieved we retraced our way towards the village we had bypassed yesterday. In the village, we found plots of maize and potatoes, and stately, golden sunflowers.

Our drivers were denouncing the wear and tear their tired horses had endured in the hours wasted on the road. One had only to look at those patient, docile animals to see that they were exhausted. The loudest lamentations were those of the Tatar drivers who were especially devoted to their horses; they would treat them almost as human beings – even hold conversations with them.

We put up at a cottage, washed some rooms in the next-door huts and placed straw-matting on the floors. Before the day was over, we had fourteen sick and seven wounded. One of the latter had fallen off a cart while asleep; his face was badly torn and his eyes bruised and swollen. In the evening we sent all our patients off to the Base; our doctors thought it too risky to keep them with us. We Sisters lay down on the benches and floor – I found an old wooden door and, although it was a hard mattress, it did raise me up from the floor by a couple of inches. We all slept deeply until 11 o'clock! And then there came again that peremptory voice we dreaded. It roused us as no other could ever do, for it was the voice of *Retreat*. 'Wake up! Get up at once! No time to lose!' We started up, seized what we could and helped the orderlies collect the equipment. We were told it was a *proruiv* [breakthrough] on the right flank of our Front and that the enemy was pouring through the gap. The Sister-on-duty began to weep;

Mamasha rounded on her – sent her straight off to Moscow, and then – straight to the Devil! Troops were passing quickly by in the darkness; whole regiments were there.

We were given a lantern and told to stand by the gate and await transport. Some soldiers entered the yard swearing; we hoped they would not see us. But they did, and soon they were shouting ugly things about us. I too felt like weeping, but we had to keep a straight face and pretend that we had not heard. The tired Sister began to cry again; Mamasha once again raised her voice.

The soldiers who had always been our patient, grateful men, seemed to have turned against us. Now for the first time we realised that our soldiers might become our enemies and were capable of doing us harm. Could it be that our work in the three years of warfare had been useless and in vain? Perhaps it would now be necessary to disband. . . . Oh! the pity of it! I found myself wishing that these disrespectful, churlish men – most of whom were young peasant recruits – would come under fire, and then, if wounded, find how badly they would need our help!

More soldiers went by in the darkness. There were no officers with them, they too were deserters. Cursing and shouting they made their way along the highroad. We were frightened and crouched low against the fence so that they could not see us, and we dared not speak lest they should hear. Our Chief appeared, nervous and flurried. 'Take your seats at once!' he ordered. But there were no empty vans or *dvukolki*, so there were no seats to take. 'Sit where you can; find a place by the drivers.' So we left our hiding-place and went out into the road to edge our way through the disordered ranks of deserting Infantry. Again there came rude remarks and again our hearts sank.

The night was very dark and the confusion great. Wheels creaked and scrunched; frightened horses slid forwards by leaps and bounds; cart grated against cart; whips twanged and swished; and agitated voices shouted and cursed in one and the same breath.

. . . All around us were fires; even in front of us buildings were blazing. My driver said that some of the soldiers thought that they were already surrounded by the enemy. We reached the village of Gorodenka and orders were given to halt. On one side of the village the mansion of a large estate was in flames. Camp-beds and straw were brought and, by the side of a large lake, we wrapped ourselves in our plaids and tried to sleep. . . . In the half-

light of dawn, we heard heavy gun carriages thunder by, followed
by the tramping of foot soldiers. Behind them came *bronirovanny*
[armoured motors]. . . . It was very cold and damp on the lake
bank.

Our chief and head doctor arrived, bringing further news – none
of it good. German troops have taken over the Austrian trenches
and their heavy guns have caused enormous casualties among our
men. Several of our regiments have refused reinforcements and
withdrawn from their Front Line positions. The gaps were instantly
filled by the enemy and in many adjoining sectors our men were
obliged to flee, lest they be cut off. The soldiers were arranging
meetings, surreptitiously, among themselves and stipulating for
continuing to fight. Soldiers' committees were being formed,
claiming the right to dictate to their officers. There was no doubt
about it, they had mistaken the meaning of 'Freedom'. The
Germans, aware that little resistance would be forthcoming,
were sweeping forward along the whole Galician Front. Many
Russian divisions had refused to attack and the soldiers were
deserting in their hundreds. The Great Offensive had been ir-
retrievably shattered.

We all knew that many soldiers had deserted. What we did
not know was that desertion had taken on such amazing proportions that field officers, staff chiefs, even the high Command,
were powerless to stop it. The soldiers had decided that freedom
for them meant throwing down one's rifle and going home, there
to drink vodka and sleep on the large *pyechka* [stove] in their
village huts.

Our medical staff was always disposed to pass on to us any
and every item of encouraging news; they knew well how cut
off we were from the outer world. Today I heard that a number
of armoured motors had been sent to Russia from England under
the command of an officer named Locker-Lampson; they had
done splendid work in the Brzezany sector of the Front, against
German, Austro-Hungarian and Turkish troops. They had held
up the advancing enemy and covered the retreat of the 7th Army.
I was deeply gratified to hear that my country was endeavouring
to help her ally in this moment of need and that my countrymen
were actually in Galicia and putting up a tremendous fight.

Saturday, 15th July

We started away from Priliptse at an early hour. It was a lovely, clear morning. A Brother had been able to purchase butter, sugar and dried fish in Zaleshik village. We left Zaleshik on our right and journeyed on for a few versts to Kiseleu. We had hoped that the peasants would allow us to buy their eggs, but they would not sell any. We dined today off pork soup and a small roasted pig! After dinner, we were told that the piglet had actually walked up to the kitchen *komanda* on a visit! Had we known this earlier, I doubt if we should have demolished him with such gusto.

In the afternoon, Olga and I went to the village to see if we could buy some hens. But the peasants shook their heads at us; they had none, they said – though we had seen several scuttle out of the hut when they opened the door. And no! they had no eggs at all; and when we pointed to a dozen lying in a corner, we were told they could be exchanged only for tobacco, as *Tata* must smoke! A peasant girl bewailed the fact that a Russian soldier had stolen fifteen chickens from her only the day before. We pointed out that later the soldiers might take *all* her poultry and that it would be wiser to sell them before it was too late. But she would not. At another hut, Olga managed to buy a hen for four roubles and offered twenty-five roubles for a small pig, but the woman would not part with it. We came to the conclusion that word had got round to them that the Russians were re-treating and they had put two and two together and realised that when the *Moskali* had gone, their own kinsmen, the *Avstriaki*, would take their place. Who could blame them if they wanted their own folk – perhaps their husbands and sons – to enjoy the pigs and poultry which had been reared in their absence?

Artillery with heavy cannon were passing on the main road. We went to the school-house in Kiseleu. Several sick men came to us, but only a few wounded. We bandaged the wounded and placed 26 sick soldiers on straw. Orders came: we were to leave, but a small surgical detachment was to remain. We Sisters volun-teered in a body to stay, and quite a heated argument ensued, but our head doctor solved the problem by deciding that all Sisters should resume the journey and only two Brothers with orderlies be left at the schoolhouse. Our supper consisted of two hens with rice; the peasants persisted in their refusal to sell us potatoes.

Sunday, 16th July

We arrived at Kuchurmik. Many wounded were already there
and many more were brought to us. We were stationed side
by side with the 2nd *Letuchka* and in the evening I went to help
with their wounded. Then I returned to our camp, washed and
undressed. It was the first time that we had gone to bed undressed since 9th July, after leaving Grabuvka; it was a very
simple thing, but it brought us tremendous satisfaction.

Monday, 17th July

There was a quarrel about eggs at breakfast and Mamasha
reprimanded us sternly: soon afterwards, she drove off to Chernovits, only eight versts away. We found a peasant woman to wash
our laundry, so we were able to sew, read and rest; it all seemed
wonderfully luxurious. Mamasha returned with many provisions
and began distributing pears, apples and sweets among us. She
told us that Chernovits was a delightful place and full of foodstuffs,
though, of course prices were very high. Three soldiers suddenly
presented themselves, very hungry and asking for food. They
calmly informed us that they had left the trenches voluntarily,
because they had not been given enough bread. Mamasha's face
was a study.

Tuesday, 18th July

After dinner, we moved to the outskirts of Kuchurmik for the sake
of our faithful friends the horses. There were wide fields of oats,
waist-high and green. The horses ate and ate to their hearts'
content. We had just had a delicious meal of chicken, fruit and
tea; now, it was their turn.

While our doctors were discussing the problems of our itinerary,
Annushka and I lay down and rested. In my sleep, I heard a
voice calling me to get up. 'Ah,' I laughed to myself, 'that's only
a make-believe!' Then I heard it again. It was Mamasha's voice,
loud and stern: 'Florence, get up at once.' . . .

We journeyed slowly on. We had chosen a side track and our
way was comparatively clear. An aeroplane fight took place over
our heads. Suddenly our driver halted, ran into a garden, seized
several young maize-cobs and pulled up some potatoes, and returned to deposit his booty under his seat. 'It is easier to take these
things while we are still in Austria,' he explained. 'In Russia, it

will not be so easy!' In *Russia*! So we were leaving Austria behind us.

In the late evening, we arrived at the village of Kolinkaoutz. A peasant was passing, and our driver called to him: '*Pan!* come here!' The man stopped. '*Nyet,*' he said. 'I not "*Pan*"; call me *Batyushka,* or *Dyadya.*' Our driver asked: 'Where is Russia?' '*Here* is Russia,' came the answer. We were confounded: we had left Galicia behind us quite unknowingly and were actually in the Bessarabskaya Government of Russia. We had supper in Russia and, tired out by the endless journeying, lay down in a Russian *moujik's* hut and slept.

Wednesday, 19th July

We awoke in bad moods. We were all upset at the humiliation of having been driven out of Austria, and saw this as likely to be the end of our Red Cross work, and the end of our Red Cross unit! Two Sisters began an argument which flared into a quarrel; a third joined in. Soon there were harsh words and tears: two decided to leave at once. The third, offended because the lady doctor had reprimanded her for interfering, said that she too would leave. . . . But a note came from our chief, still in Chernovits, asking for our housekeeping Sister and one surgical Sister. The doctor chose me, as I was on duty. Pleased at the prospect of returning to Austria, I collected my little pillow, plaid, change of linen, brush, etc., and Mamasha and I started off after dinner in a *dvukolka*. We took a short cut, for we were wanted as quickly as possible. We met several lines of *oboz*; at first we thought that some of them belonged to our *Otryad,* for a certain number of our ambulance-vans had gone ahead. But no! we were mistaken – until, rounding a corner, we came face to face with our vans and the familiar figures of our drivers and orderlies. They began shouting at us at once: 'Go back! Turn round and go back!' In a few hurried words they explained. The enemy was hard at their heels and there was no time to be lost. We turned and followed our transport, full of disappointment and dismay.

The heat became oppressive. Both Mamasha and I were perspiring and white-coated with the thick dust raised in clouds by the thronging vehicles. From side-roads and tracks came companies of soldiers, dishevelled and dead-beat; following them, the regimental carts and wagons laden with equipment. All were

retreating, the Germans were closing in. So much for our return
visit to Austria!

We finally met up again with our *Letuchka* and continued
together to Toporovtse, where we turned off the road into a field
by a tributary of the Dnestr. Mamasha and I had fortified ourselves with bread and cheese on the road, but the other members
of our detachment had had no dinner. We collected sticks, made
a camp-fire, boiled some soup and potatoes – and tempers began
to improve all round.

There, in the open field, our sick and wounded were brought to
us. Our mobile kitchens were soon hard at work and we fed 56
sick soldiers and bandaged and fed some 15 wounded. We found
places for all in our vans and *dvukolki* and were able to despatch
them almost immediately. Anna and I went to a secluded corner
of the river to snatch a quick bathe. It was 7 p.m. but still very
hot and sultry. We had hardly disrobed, when we heard Sofiya's
voice: 'Come at once; we are just about to leave.' In great haste
and some resentment, we started to dress again; our feet got
muddy and made mud-marks on our clothing. But we managed,
somehow, to get dressed and scrambled up the river-bank. Had
they left us for a further five minutes, we should have had time
to bathe. They gave us water from our *bochka* [water-barrel] to
clean our feet, so we quickly slipped on our boots and were ready
for the journey. But we were thankful to learn from Mamasha
that it was *not* retreat this time, merely a change of camp from
the field to the village of Toporovtse. Mamasha also volunteered
the information that had she and I driven by the *chaussée* that
morning instead of taking the side-track, we should have gone
straight into German arms; or, more probably, straight on to
German bayonets!

Thursday, 20th July
It was a white night, with a huge full moon. I could see to read
quite plainly. The light and deep shadows reminded me of a sunny
day seen through blue glass. I shall be on duty until 8 a.m. It is
now 1.30 a.m. In an hour's time, the ten ambulance-vans – lent
to us – should return from the Front Lines with a fresh supply of
wounded.

I could have wished that my Mother might see me as I sat at
the little wooden table: the picture around me was so simple.

The small, white, thatched hut, in front of which I was sitting, was like a doll's house. I had lighted the candle on the table, to write a few notes for my diary. To my right, lying on their hand-woven counterpane and covered with their sheepskin coats, the owners of the hut were sleeping; a peasant woman and her little son nestling up to her, his thin, bare legs sticking out from under the bedding.

To my left, a wounded officer was lying, his high boots protruding quite half a yard over the stretcher's edge. A little farther away on another stretcher, a sick soldier lay; he had been picked up from the ditch by some artillery soldiers. Through the open gate, I could see a field of Indian corn; and behind this the dim, dark outline of mountains. In the field, not far off, was a quaint plantation of trees rising up from an isolated hill; the trees were poplars which, starkly silhouetted against the sky, resembled the stately cypress trees which had so fascinated me in Italy. It suddenly came to me that I had seen that same plantation in a picture and I realised that it reminded me of the painting by Böcklin entitled *Insel der Toten.*

While thinking of paintings, I felt a sudden craving to visit galleries, art exhibitions, to comfort myself with beauty and culture. But it was only a passing thought. I recalled that the date was 20th July (R.s.), 1917; the fourth year of warfare was about to begin, and I remembered the words of a Russian officer who had said only yesterday: 'Never has the Russian Army fallen so low. Never has its condition been so miserably abject as at the present moment.'

About 5 a.m. I called Mamasha and we made tea for the patients. Some were hungry too, and said they had not eaten for three days. More wounded were brought; one of them had his leg amputated almost immediately, we were afraid that it might already be too late. There was a second bad stomach-case: his body was slit across from side to side; all intestines were visible; we could even see *glistee* [tape worms] moving about. He asked me: 'Why don't you try to save me?' There was much to do and I stayed on duty to lend a helping hand.

After dinner, I lay down in the shade of an apple tree and fell asleep. Anna, who came to look for me, told me that some soldiers had picked apples from the tree while I slept, but had not spoken loudly in order not to disturb me. . . . Again it was Mamasha's determined voice which awakened me. I was about to fall asleep again, when a loud rumbling fell on my ears. I opened my eyes; there was no one there! I started up and met Anna rushing towards me: still half-asleep, I managed to climb into the *furgon*. I was told that both stomach-cases had died and been buried in the little cemetery among the poplar trees on 'Böcklin's Island'.

We had had orders to go to the mainroad and wait there for our regiments who were retreating before the enemy. Many regiments came marching past, but not ours. The heat and dust were tormenting. Our carts and vans picked up some more sick and wounded; then again, we were left without transport! I sat and looked at the road. Infantry, Cavalry, Artillery, Cossacks – a whole army in motion. Behind them, heaving and swaying, swept long lines of military equipment: cannon, light and heavy, maxim-guns, and all the appendages essential to modern warfare. The *oboz* followed; then again soldiers, soldiers, soldiers, slouching along, too tired to hold themselves erect. I noticed their shuffling feet, their bent backs, and a great pity swept over me for these cheerless, heartbroken men. How much they must have suffered! And, throughout that stream of men and machines, not a single *red* ribbon or *red* flag had been visible! God be praised! These, then, were *not* deserters; these were Russia's faithful sons.

Two of the passing regiments were retreating to music. At first, this offended me. Those gay, martial tunes were at variance with the disastrous time. In 1915, such music might have been welcome; but not *now*, when our trenches had been purposely emptied and handed over to the invader. But, on second thoughts, who was I to judge?

Our regiments came at last; we were ordered to fall in behind them. We arrived late at night near an old wooden church in the village of Shishkovtse. Some of us slept on straw by the *sklep* [crypt], others under the church walls.

Monday, 24th July. Bankaoutse
We washed, ironed and got our clothes in order. Our garments were getting very discoloured and old, due to the hard wear demanded of them. We had a chat with the schoolmaster-caretaker of the *folvark*. The owner was in the Russian Army and his wife had gone to relatives. Our transport-officers were badly in need of horses; they bargained with the caretaker for a couple and he,

finally, allowed them to buy the pair at 1,500 roubles. There was a nice *britchka*, a small half-covered carriage, which would have suited us Sisters admirably, but the price was too high: and we were already so accustomed to our rough and ready *dvukolki* and *furmanki*, that we decided that we should feel ill-at-ease in a smart equipage.

We heard that both the Armies, the 7th and 8th, to which we had been attached would probably go northwards and the 1st and 2nd Armies take their place. But plans are, at present, very unsettled and our High Command must find it exceedingly difficult to unravel the innumerable entanglements wrought by the unprecedented disorganisation among the rank and file. We were told to be in readiness to leave Bankaoutse on the 26th inst.; we are unaware of our destination.

Tuesday, 25th July

It was a dull morning. We packed our belongings, wrote letters and mended some of our torn clothing. Our head doctor arrived, and told us that plans had been altered and that our flying detachment was to go south into Roumania. We were delighted! Roumania was our ally and Russian troops had already joined forces with the Roumanian Army and were carrying on a slow but successful campaign. So once again, we were buoyed up with high hopes, knowing that a new period of work was about to begin for us. But we did not overlook the stern fact that the Germans had driven the Russian Armies out of Galicia and beaten them back over the Russian frontier. It was the *truth* – a terrible, *tragic truth*, and had to be faced. All day long we heard distant firing, despite the fact that the Russian retreat had reached an end.

Wednesday, 26th July. Into Roumania

We left Bankaoutse at 7 a.m. The roads were in a very muddy state after the rain, but the horses, having been well-rested and well-fed, pulled with a will. The view of the open country and hills was enchanting in its soft, morning colouring. At the River Prut, Austrian prisoners were working on the bridge. Their tents looked drenched; some of the men were sitting in the sun, drying their wet clothes. We crossed the wooden bridge and passed into Roumanian territory.

We halted in an open field and a soldiers' dinner was served:

fish and meat had been lumped together in the thick *kasha* soup, and there were strange greenish leaves which had certainly not been reared on a cabbage-plot. How true was the old Russian saying: 'To a hungry man, there is no stale bread!'

A guest from a neighbouring first aid post and our head doctor entered into a heated argument over politics. They discussed the Provisional Government, the resignation of Prince Lvov, and deplored the impending dismissal of General Brusilov by Kerensky. We had not heard that news and it filled us with indignation. Brusilov was our hero. We had heard that he had been unable to defend Tarnopol against the combined forces of Austria and Germany, due to the wholesale desertion of a division of the 11th Army, which had left the 7th Army in such a perilous position that it too was obliged to retire. Brusilov, who but a couple of months before had replaced General Alexeyev as Generalissimo, was now superseded by General Kornilov. So Brusilov was to be the scapegoat for the disasters which had driven the Russian troops out of Galicia and Bukovina. It seemed a most unjust decision, but we were told that, no matter how distinguished the General, if his army sustained defeat, he, and he only would be blamed.

It was dreadfully hot and Anna and I longed to take a cooling bathe in the river, but the soldiers seemed to have commandeered the waters. To escape the sun, we crawled under our transport-van and, in that cramped condition, managed to write one or two letters to our home-people, which our chief had promised to take with him on the morrow to Kiyev. One of our supervisors, who had returned from collecting money in Mogilev, told us that the English nurses had driven from Podgaytse in English motors to Mogilev and had there taken the train for Kiyev. I was sad that I had not been able to contact them before their departure; it would have been such a grand opportunity to send a first-hand message to my Mother.

We left at 4 p.m. and came to a high hill, where we had to wait our turn to make the ascent. A bevy of stalwart young soldiers assisted each horse and cart to reach the summit, and there was much shouting and unnecessary whipping of horses. They, poor, frightened creatures, knew what was expected of them and did their best; but their deep, spasmodic breathing and foam-streaked, perspiring bodies told of the strenuous exertion which every movement demanded of them. From then onwards, the roads were bad and the hills steep. We drove through several picturesque villages; the neat, wooden huts, with curtained windows and verandahs, made a great impression on us, as did the women and children in their richly-embroidered costumes. One old woman clasped her hands when she saw our uniforms. 'Ah! *Dio mio!*' she exclaimed.

Driving through a small town, we were surprised to see a large community of Jews, obviously shopkeepers and merchants, for all the shops belonged to them. We had yet to learn that the Roumanian population was composed of Roumanians, Russians, Serbs, Magyars, Turks, Jews and Bulgarians. We bought apples with our Russian money, not being acquainted with the Roumanian coins of *lei* and *bani*. Eggs, there were none; the soldiers had bought them all, the Jews explained. We traversed a lovely pine wood, where the air was like wine, cool and fragrant, in striking contrast to the sultry air on the open field. As we came to the highroad, we saw four German prisoners being led by under Russian escort. It was strange to see them in Roumania.

Near the village of Loupeni we encamped for the night on an open hillside. The moon came slowly riding on a clear, starlit sky. Our chief had received a Moscow newspaper dated 23rd July, and he read extracts to us over supper. Cossacks had escorted Nicholas Nicholayevich – the former Commander-in-Chief and cousin of the Tsar – to Moscow and were campaigning for him to be proclaimed Emperor. General Brusilov had been temporarily sent into retirement, because he had not gone to meet Kerensky at the railway-station, but had waited until Kerensky had sent for him. There was a twinkle in our chief's eyes when he read this, so whether it were true, or just a joke, it was difficult to decide. Personally, I didn't think that Kerensky could be so petty. But another story made a deep impression. A Siberian woman soldier had served in the Russian Army since 1915 side by side with her husband; when he had been killed, she had continued to fight. She had been wounded twice and three times decorated for valour. When she knew that the soldiers were deserting in large numbers, she made her way to Moscow and Petrograd to start recruiting for a Women's Battalion. It was reported that she had said: 'If the men refuse to fight for their country, we will show them what the *women* can do!' So this woman warrior, Yasha Bachkarova, began her campaign; it was said that it had met with singular success. Young

women, some of aristocratic families, rallied to her side; they were
given rifles and uniforms and drilled and marched vigorously. We
Sisters were of course thrilled to the core.

A woman soldier, or boy soldier, was no unusual sight in the
Russian Army. We had even come into contact with a couple of
Amazon warriors; one, in her early twenties, who had had a nasty
gash on her temple caused by a glancing bullet, had come to our
first aid post on the Galician Front. I recalled how, after bandaging and feeding her, we had had some difficulty in persuading her
to stay the night with us in our barn and return to her company
at daybreak. I think that she feared that her comrades might
think that she had absconded.

Thursday, 27th July

A shower of rain awakened us about 4 a.m. Our camp-beds
had been set up on the hillside and our clothes and beds were
soaked.

In the distance, we saw a small house, surrounded by a plantation of trees, and were very glad to find it inhabited by a friendly
family. They treated us well, made us come in and dry our clothes.
With the exception of our hostess, who was of French extraction,
they spoke only Roumanian, which, to my delight, I found greatly
resembled my smattering of Latin and Italian. We were told that
the majority of cultured people in Roumania spoke French. The
weather had cleared again and the sun was shining when we returned to our camp for dinner. Two soldiers were brought, both
with self-inflicted wounds. We bandaged them and sent them on
their way. Mamasha and I lay down to rest in a *dvukolki*; she
snored loudly until 5.30 p.m., when an orderly called her to remind
her that it was the tea-hour. It was so peaceful after she had left
that I, too, slept and only awoke when I heard voices announcing
that supper was ready.

Later, we slept again in the open air. The heavens were thickly
carpeted with myriad stars: now and then one would shoot across
the sky, dragging an incandescent tail after it, and disappear;
then another . . . and still another!

Sunday, 30th July. Broskautsy

The last three days have been spent in Loupeni. They have been
pleasant, restful ones. . . .

We had heard that we were to remain in our beloved 8th Army; the 1st Army is to be disbanded and its remaining corps and divisions will become part of the 8th.

The weather had again changed and we drove off in the rain and, still in the rain, arrived at Broskautsy. It looked a charming village, but to our surprise and chagrin, the peasantry proved to be far from friendly. The Roumanians, we knew, were our allies, so it was some time before we could explain this sudden change of attitude. It seemed that strong animosity had broken out between the Russian and Roumanian soldiers. When we begged the peasants for permission to take over a hut they vehemently objected. Neither would they sell us any goods. One woman crossed her arms and confronted us defiantly at her closed door: 'You Russians only make our lives a torment. You don't help us. We want to be left in peace.'

This morning, we witnessed the funeral of an old peasant. The priests, dressed in their vestments, wore bowler-shaped hats. A cow and a calf were led up to the coffin in which the dead man was exposed to view; holy water was sprinkled on him and on the animals; then, bread and tapers were handed to the man and girl who had brought them. A bed, complete with sheet and counterpane, was arranged on the ground and the peasants who carried the coffin walked solemnly over it. We were told that in the last two days there had been two weddings and three funerals in the village. 'What a heyday for the priests! They must have earned a lot of money!' someone remarked: but the facetious speaker was reminded that the peasants were often so poor that they could pay their debts only in kind.

Monday, 31st July
We heard of a bakery selling bread in Dorogoy. Two Sisters drove there immediately. They said that they had been just in time, for soldiers were clamouring round the door ready to purchase loaves at any price. One of our doctors predicted a famine before the winter was over, unless food was rationed. We heard that Russian soldiers had raided stores and looted property. So no wonder the Roumanians had begun to regard the Russians as enemies in disguise.

Thursday, 3rd August

A dust storm blew up during yesterday evening. It was all over us
before we had had time to be aware of its approach but with ad-
mirable speed our orderlies made fast the doors and boarded up
the windows. It blew westwards and, in the distance, took on the
form of a thick bank of fog shrouding the horizon. The huge, red
ball of the setting sun glowed like a fiery furnace through its dense
grey curtain. This morning, we Sisters of the 1st *Letuchka* were
driven to the estate where the artillery officers of the 3rd *Park* of
the 79th Brigade were stationed. Our medical staff had received
instructions to open a *Lazaret* there. We chose the necessary rooms,
cleaned them and prepared them as hospital wards. Almost immediately two 'beds' were occupied by two sick soldiers of our own
komanda. We were grieved to note that Mamasha was unbearably
nervous; she had already loudly upbraided two young orderlies for
some trifling offence. I think that they had omitted to bring with
them some kitchen utensils of importance. Smirnov, our head
hospital-attendant, must have taken their part, for Mamasha
turned and vented all her pent-up anger on him. We could do
nothing to help, although all our sympathy was definitely with
Smirnov. Mamasha was threatening to leave us; her life, she
declared, was 'sheer misery' with such stupid *negodai* [worthless
fellows]. Smirnov, with his customary, wonderful tact – I always
felt that he was wasted in our *Otryad* and should have moved in
higher 'political circles' – kept his temper and begged to be excused,
saying that work was awaiting him. Mamasha was left to
herself, smouldering. We slipped away, knowing that solitude
and her own inherent commonsense would soon restore her
equanimity.

Wednesday, 9th August

We housed fifteen wounded in our improvised *Lazaret*. Last
Monday, an ambulance-van drove up with three wounded women
soldiers. We were told that they belonged to the Bachkarova
Women's Death Battalion. We had not heard the full name before,
but we instantly guessed that it was the small army of women
recruited in Russia by the Siberian woman soldier, Yasha Bachkarova. Naturally, we were all very impatient to have news of
this remarkable battalion, but the women were sadly shocked and
we refrained from questioning them until they had rested. The

van-driver was not very helpful, but he did know that the battalion had been cut up by the enemy and had retreated.

Thursday, 10th August. Seret

Yesterday morning, Mamasha received a telegram which much upset her. She took counsel with our medical officers and decided to go on *otpusk* [furlough]. We were so sorry for her, but knew that she badly needed a change and that the holiday had come for her in the nick of time. She left us this morning and we all gathered at the door to bid her farewell. She came hurrying in; stood for a moment looking at us and then, with considerable emotion said: 'I go, my friends, but I shall not forget you. I beg you to forgive my bad temper.' There was a glint of tears in her eyes, something we had never seen before. We assured her that we had nothing to forgive and wished her safe journey and God speed, and waved as she drove away. What a stout-hearted, dynamic character she was! For two-and-a-half years she had ministered to our needs in the most appalling circumstances, never thinking of giving way under the Herculean strain; she had, indeed, been a 'tower of strength'. 'Mamasha,' we thought, 'with all your faults we love you still, and we shall miss you sorely.'

Our head surgeon told us that he was about to leave our *Otryad* and take up an appointment in Russia. Two Sisters were also anxious to return home. It seemed that our Red Cross unit was slowly crumbling! But our doctors dispelled our fears, telling us that our two flying detachments, reduced in personnel, would still be on active service and each, as earlier in the war, be attached to a different division. A new housekeeping Sister was to be sent in Mamasha's absence. We were also told that we should be leaving that evening for the Front and that our wounded must be despatched without delay.

We left about 7 p.m., for the Austrian-Roumanian frontier. At first the roads were very good and there was a pleasant feeling of exhilaration that we were moving towards a new post. An aeroplane had been circling for some minutes over our heads; suddenly a bomb exploded, killing two of our horses.

At the frontier, the roads were in a dreadful state; our *dvukolka* threatened to turn a somersault more than once. We heard that it was impossible to cross the River Seret by the bridge, because it was under fire. We forded the river in two places and were thankful that the water was not very deep. At 10 p.m. we arrived at Seret, a large town with many fine buildings. Rooms were given to us in the hospital. They were nice, spacious rooms, with comfortable furniture.

Friday, 11th August

The first thing we did after an early breakfast was to look at the hospital wards. We found there 16 wounded, Russian and Roumanian. There were three small Roumanian children too. One of them, a tiny mite, Gheorghi by name, only two-and-a-half years old, had had an arm blasted off by shrapnel. The boy's baby face still bore traces of shock and suffering. Panaria, his elder sister, had a wound in both head and stomach; Melania, the younger sister, had sustained a fractured thigh. The old grandmother, Babka, as they called her, came daily to see them and, inevitably, went away weeping. She too had been slightly wounded in the stomach, but, as it was little more than a graze, she was treated and allowed to return to her hut. It was a sad family story. Babka's daughter, the mother of the three children, had gone off with a soldier and had not been heard of for several months. Poor Babka! Her son-in-law in the Roumanian Army was reported missing. Another young war-victim was a Jewish girl, Fransichka, with a wound in thigh and leg.

I was on duty. A soldier's leg had to be amputated; he was a young Roumanian and I expected to see and hear signs of deep despair; but no! he took his crippled condition stoically. He had a happy face, so I was sure that he had a happy home. A Jew died of gangrene; his smashed arm had been amputated too late; he would not allow it to be done earlier. Guns were firing constantly; sometimes in strange, spasmodic bursts. Now and then our hospital and grounds would shake with an unusually heavy 'thud' and the windows were continually rattling. A young Russian had had to undergo an operation on his ribs, in order to drain fluid from his lung. His name was Andrei; he was very patient, but suffering great pain and discomfort.

Sunday, 13th August

There was much work in the hospital. Each of us Sisters had her own ward. At dinner we heard more of the Women's Death Battalion. It was true; Bachkarova had brought her small battalion down south to the Austrian Front, and they had manned part of the trenches which had been abandoned by the Russian Infantry. The size of the Battalion had considerably decreased since the first weeks of recruitment, when some 2,000 women and girls had rallied to the call of their Leader. Many of them, painted and powdered, had joined the Battalion as an exciting and romantic adventure; she loudly condemned their behaviour and demanded iron discipline. Gradually the patriotic enthusiasm had spent itself; the 2,000 slowly dwindled to 250. In honour to those women volunteers, it was recorded that they *did* go into the attack; they *did* go 'over the top'. But not all of them. Some remained in the trenches, fainting and hysterical; others ran or crawled back to the rear. Bachkarova retreated with her decimated battalion; she was wrathful, heartbroken, but she had learnt a great truth: women were quite unfit to be soldiers.

Tuesday, 15th August. Khatna
The 26th *Otryad* of the *Zemski Soyuz* is coming to replace us. Several shells burst during the morning; one just near the hospital. I thought the house would collapse under the thunderous reverberation. We did our best to quieten and reassure the patients. My Andrei died peacefully under sedation – Smirnov attended to his burial. After supper, we said good-bye to our patients. Little Gheorghi was asleep; his face was extraordinarily beautiful. I would not wake him, so I kissed his one tiny white hand which lay on the white sheet. His sisters smiled and nodded; I don't think that they quite knew what was happening. The Jewish girl, with whom I had always conversed in German, seemed deeply moved to hear that we were leaving. She seized my hand and kissed it, before I could stop her, and, with tears in her eyes, said: *'Sie sind meine Rettung.'*

We drove quickly over the hill, for we saw enemy foot-soldiers on the neighbouring hills. Just before Khatna, we met many Russian soldiers. I was sitting by the driver. One soldier looked at me and shouted to his companions: *'Kakoy tam zvyer sidiyt?* [What kind of wild beast is sitting there?]' And a chorus of derisive mirth greeted his words. I willed myself not to think of those offensive words but I was deeply hurt. I had thought that the bands of unruly soldiers would somehow have contrived to remain in Russia; but here they were at large in Roumania too.

Would they infect the Roumanian Infantry? What would happen then? . . . That night, we slept in our *dvukolki*; the matted straw was by no means a satisfactory mattress, but sleep gained the mastery and we might have been sleeping on feather-beds for all we knew or cared. . . . Sleep is, surely, God's own merciful sedative for those who are low-spirited and apprehensive.

Wednesday, 16th August. Izkani
We halted for dinner at Izkani on the Suchava River. Everywhere the ground had been trampled by men and horses, and it was difficult to find a clean spot. We were given white bread – a real treat! They were small round 'loaves' which a good-natured Roumanian shopman had sold us, together with some excellent butter. . . . While we were searching for a sheltered corner to bivouac for the night, many Russian soldiers passed along the highroad and made for a stretch of woodland. One of them informed our drivers that they were about to attend a meeting. It was not long before some of our rank and file asked to be allowed to join them and hear what it was all about. Our doctors readily gave permission. . . . At night we slept in the open-air, among the willows and riparian shrubs. It was another night of pure starlit glory. Annushka and I had placed our camp-beds side by side; we held a whispered conversation for a few minutes and then, too tired to speak, just lay and listened to the chorus of night sounds. A bird twittered in the nearby bushes; a frog croaked below us in the river reeds; and there was always the soft, swishing current of the river. In the river, round the bend, soldiers were bathing, their guffaws borne across to us on the breeze. In a neighbouring camp a squadron of Donski Cossacks were singing songs of their far-off homeland. On the road we heard the tramp of Russian Infantry marching by in perfect rhythm. It was not difficult to guess that those men were numbered among 'the faithful'. They, too, began to sing, a plaintive melody which I knew and loved: 'On the hill the bread [corn] is growing . . .'

Thursday, 17th August. Illisheysti
I took a snap of our riverside dormitory. A storm blew up, due, probably, to the sultry heat, and we took refuge in a peasant's hut. A woman soldier with a badly contused leg came to us for a dressing. She did not belong to the Women's Death Battalion;

she had, however, heard of them and from her curt remarks one could understand that she held them in but little respect. I drove with her to Suchava, where the 16th Surgical *Otryad* of the *Zemski Soyuz* was stationed, and left her in their care. Later, a Sister joined me on my drive to Illisheysti. Our Tatar driver was in good humour. By flicking his whip and making clucking noises, he induced his horse to swing into a staccato dance which, although amusing, bespattered us with mud. We stopped at a shop where I bought some butter for 3 roubles and a few small cakes at 25 kopeks each. I went to a hut to ask for directions; no one answered my knock, but a dog within the house began barking furiously. As I turned back towards the van, I saw that our driver had been standing behind me, whip in hand. He had heard the dog and feared that the door might have been suddenly opened. It was a kindly thought.

We reached Illisheysti as darkness was falling. Six divisions were quartered in and around the town and every available space was filled to overflowing. We waited until our *oboz* came into sight, then fell in behind it until we halted for the night near a roomy hay barn. A kind-hearted Jewess invited us Sisters into her small house, occupied by herself and her *seven* children. She showed us a room which contained three large beds; we were six, and gladly took possession of them. They were certainly comfortable, but the atmosphere was dreadfully airless and smelly, as though the room had not been aired for months. Where she and her many children slept that night, we did not like to enquire.

Friday, 18th August

From early morning, our medical staff was out searching for better accommodation. Everywhere things were chaotic and the dust and dirt which had accumulated passed description. We happened to hear that some Russian officers were leaving, so we quickly confiscated their rooms in a small Roumanian homestead. The place was tidy and well looked after, and the woman herself must have seen better days; she showed us some of her embroidered aprons and blouses, which were of exquisite workmanship. Her husband and two sons were in the Roumanian Army, and she spent her days in looking after lodgers, the house and vegetable garden, and trying to save up a few *lei* so that she could buy foodstuff to celebrate the men's homecoming. She mentioned that sometimes

she was lucky enough to sell her embroidery and we offered to buy
some. She asked so little that there was no question of bargaining.
I bought a blouse and a towel, hoping to keep them safely and
give them away as presents.

Saturday, 19th August. Kloster Gumora
We left Illisheysti and arrived here about 4 p.m., where we found
the Transport *Otryad* of the 12th Cavalry Division. They received
us well; gave us both tea and supper. Apart from white bread,
there were young potatoes, beautifully cooked with butter, and a
large dish of *kukuruza* [maize-cobs] formed the centre-piece of the
dining-table. We Sisters were given the dining-room for our
sleeping quarters, while the men ascended the rickety wooden
staircase to the attic.

Tuesday, 22nd August
The latest news from Moscow and Petrograd says the rioting has
relaxed somewhat, but there are outbreaks of violence among the
workers in the large factories and mills. . . .
    On the Russian North-West Front, the Russians, aided by
Lettish troops, were unable to check a fierce offensive by Prussian
forces on the Baltic seaport of Riga and the ancient city had been
occupied by the enemy. A wounded man walked up to our dressing-
station and asked for assistance, and we saw at once that his
lower arm had received a self-inflicted wound: in the circumstances,
we thought it best to bandage him and leave him to continue his
homeward journey – it would have done no good if we had accused
him of cowardice. The evenings in these Roumanian highlands are
steadily growing colder. It is good to be able to sleep in a comfortable room.

Wednesday, 23rd August
Rumour has it that Riga was not *taken* by the Germans, but *given*
to them; and we read that near Chernovits the Front Lines were
left open and the Austro-German troops lost no time in occupying
the Russian trenches and advancing on Novovesilits. These terrible
tales of desertion and treachery reach us almost daily. They
distress us deeply and there are moments when we feel that our
work has really reached an end. I begin to wonder whether it
would be better for me to return to England.

Thursday, 24th August

Anna and I walked for a while up a steep mountain path. The panorama was very beautiful, although the far distant view was blocked by wooded hills on all sides. Over one hill shrapnel was bursting at intervals and we knew that the rival armies were lurking there. Some recent newspapers were being passed from hand to hand among our personnel. How impatient we were to read them and to hear the latest news of the situation in Russia and the news-bulletins from the various Fronts! It was mostly dreary, dismal reading. One newspaper affirmed that hundreds of deserters were in the woods and marshlands surrounding Riga and that demoralised companies of soldiers could be seen retreating in all directions.

One or two of our Brothers predicted that the Prussians would now make straight from Riga to Petrograd. More than one newspaper said that many residents were already leaving their homes in the capital. We Sisters went about our duties with glum faces and aching hearts. That the death sentence for desertion had been restored was nothing but a farce – a meaningless absurdity! One could not shoot down thousands of one's own countrymen!

Saturday, 26th August

We have been told that a meeting is to be held in the neighbourhood. Although meetings organised by the rank and file are strictly prohibited unless sanctioned by the Commanding Officer, there is no doubt that they are taking place.

Strange-looking men – some in uniform, others in civilian clothes – have been seen combing the Russian Fronts, section by section, and organising informal meetings with the troops. So now that such a personage is due to visit our Front, we Sisters are extremely anxious to hear for ourselves the 'message of good-will' which he is supposed to deliver.

Sunday, 27th August

It was a most extraordinary meeting! Never, in our wildest dreams did we imagine that we should listen to such an outpouring of treachery. We sat in a group among the trees, surrounded on all sides by soldiers. Some of our hospital Brothers were there and I caught sight of several of our transport drivers.

The man who had come to speak to the soldiers had an ordinary

face and was dressed in ordinary Russian clothes: dark trousers
and a dark shirt, buttoned on the left and worn outside his
trousers, with a black belt round the waist. His face was serious
and pale, but he smiled and nodded once or twice to one or another
of the audience, as though he recognised friends. He spoke for a
time about Russia, her vast territory, her wealth and the many
overlords who, possessing enormous estates and resources, were
revered on account of their riches throughout the western world.
Then he described the impoverished peasantry who, unschooled,
uncared-for and half-starved, were eking out a miserable existence
by tilling and cultivating the land belonging to those same overlords. War had burst upon Russia and enemies had invaded her
territory, and who were the men who had sacrified themselves to
fight the ruthless invaders and drive them off Russian soil? Not
the wealthy overlords, not the despotic land-owners; no! – they
were safely installed in their fortress-homes. It was those down-
trodden countrymen who had been roped in in their thousands,
in their millions, to stem the tide of invasion; when they had been
killed, others had been quickly collected and sent to replace them.
There had been no end to the slaughter and sacrifice of the
Russian peasant. Enemy guns had devoured them daily, hourly;
every minute of the day and night, the heavy guns had feasted
on them and every minute new recruits were being seized and
thrust like fodder into the voracious jaws of the enemy's cannon.
But now a miraculous event had taken place! The Tsar – that
arch-potentate, that arch-tyrant – had been dethroned and dismissed. Russia had been pronounced a free country! – the Russian
citizens a free people! Freedom had come at last to the down-
trodden people of Russia.

Our doctors were moving restlessly. They were, as always, in
officers' uniform. I wondered if they were thinking it was high
time to leave, but they stayed. Undoubtedly, it was the wisest
thing to do. I glanced around. Most of the soldiers were young and
raw, inexperienced and impressionable; all of them drawn from
far-off corners of what, until recently, had been known as the
Russian Empire. What easy prey they would be for seditious
guile! New ideas could so readily take hold of their gullible minds
and a cunning speaker would soon be aware that he could sway
them this way and that with his oratory.

The speaker was still harping on the theme of freedom. Freedom, he declared, was a possession so great, so precious, one dared not treat it lightly. But war was an enemy of freedom, because it destroyed peace, and without peace there could be no freedom. It was up to the Russian soldier to do all in his power to procure peace. And the best and quickest way to bring about a guaranteed peace was to *refuse to fight*. War could not be fought if there were no soldiers to fight! War was never a one-sided operation! Then, when peace had at last come to Russia, freedom could be enjoyed. The free men of Free Russia would own their own land. The great tracts of privately-owned territory would be split up and divided fairly among the peasantry. There would be common ownership of all properties and possessions. Once the Russian soldier had established peace in his homeland, he would reap benefits undreamt of. Peace above all else! Down with war!

The soldiers were all astir; they were whispering, coughing, muttering. But they were all in full accord with the orator; he held them in his hand! Their stolid faces were animated and jubilant. *'Tovarishchi!* [Comrades!]' he was calling them. *'Tovarishchi!* You free men of Free Russia! You will demand peace!' 'We will!' they shouted in reply. 'You will assert your rights as free Russian citizens!' 'We will assert our rights,' they echoed with one voice. 'You will never allow yourselves to be pushed into the trenches to sacrifice your lives in vain!' 'Never!' they roared in unison.

There swept through my mind the memory of another meeting, where the enthusiasm of thousands of loyal soldiers had been kindled by the patriotic words of Kerensky. That was only some three short months ago.

When we got back that evening we were all very nervous. Our doctors were grinding their teeth, and our head doctor resolved to bring the matter to the attention of military headquarters. 'The man is a shameless traitor.' 'He deserves to be shot!' *'Now* one can understand why there is so much disobedience and desertion.' There were questions too: Who were these men? Who had sent them on these subversive missions? They were, we were quite sure, German agents in disguise, for who else would have the audacity to incite insurrection in the Russian Armies?

We were more than thankful that Mamasha had not been present. She would doubtless have challenged the speaker, and, had the soldiers intervened, not even Mamasha's courage could have saved her from insulting language! We dared not think what would happen if all soldiers on the Russian Fronts rebelled. There could be only one sequel: the Austro-German Armies would sweep across Russia, occupying Kiyev, Moscow, Petrograd, and enslaving millions of innocent people.

Monday, 28th August
Today, something has happened which has spread dismay and consternation in our unit. Two official telegrams have reached our medical staff, containing instructions which have completely mystified us. One was from Alexander Kerensky, Prime Minister of the Coalition Government; the other from General Kornilov, Commander-in-Chief of the Russian Armies. Some dissension must have flared up between these two great men, for – sad to relate – each has denounced the other as a *traitor*. It seems incredible, but alas! it lies before us in black and white. What could have happened to cause these two famous Russians to fly at each other's throats and condemn each other publicly? In the despatch signed by Kerensky there were strict injunctions not to obey any orders issued by Kornilov, who had proved himself a traitor to his country, had been deprived of his military rank and dismissed from the Army.

It directed that all military telegraph and telephone services should be supervised by special delegates, to prevent any suspicious communication from being distributed among Russian troops. The second telegram, signed by Kornilov, denounced Kerensky as a traitor and accused him of being in league with the enemies of Russia. What irony that these telegrams should arrive at the same time! To us it all seemed quite inexplicable; but *there* were the telegrams, lying side by side on the table, for all the members of our *Letuchka* to read!

Very soon it was confirmed that Kornilov, on account of differences between himself and Kerensky, had been charged with treacherous conspiracy against the Government and dismissed. 'Conspiracy' was a hard word; perhaps it had been coined by Kerensky himself, for it was known that the General, embittered by the demoralisation of the forces, had attributed this to the reforms instituted by Kerensky: moreover, he had accused the Prime Minister of being responsible for the desertions which had brought about the fall of Riga. Kornilov was supported by

Milyukov, former Minister for Foreign Affairs and Leader of the Constitutional Democrats: he, too, was vehement in his denunciation of the Kerensky reforms. It must have been a bitter pill for Kerensky to swallow. He was an idealist; but was there room in Russia, in the present harrowing days, for idealists?

An orderly, returned from a meeting in a neighbouring town, said that the men who came to harangue the troops belonged to a secret society in Petrograd and that they were paid to spread dissension. The speaker advised the men to desert, assuring them that by so doing peace would come quickly and their own freedom would be established. We asked: 'And how did the soldiers accept such advice?' 'They were pleased,' he answered, 'and agreed among themselves that they would not return to the trenches.' But a few of the older soldiers had admonished the younger ones, calling them bastards and cowards, telling them that they would bring ignominy upon their country and that *Batyushka* God would punish them for neglecting their duty. The young fools had replied by calling them 'old asses' and telling them that God had had no hand in sending away the Tsar and in bringing freedom to Russia. 'We are free men now,' they had cried. 'And neither the Tsar nor God can interfere with our lives.' There were still loyal soldiers, however, who refused to be influenced by the infamous propaganda. They were, of course, old stagers: some of them perhaps even veterans from the early days of warfare. I clearly recalled those fine men, with their strong, bearded faces and giant stature; they were the 'flower' of the Russian Army; their faith in God was unfaltering and their courage was of bulldog tenacity. But those calamitous years had destroyed them in their thousands. They were the stout-hearted men who, possessing no ammunition, had fought the well-equipped Germans with the butts of their rifles, cudgels and bare fists in 1915.

When the news of Kornilov's fall had spread, many soldiers were bewildered and vowed that they were ready to man the trenches if only they had *someone* in whom they could put their trust. 'Whom can we believe?' they asked. And the uncertainty fostered despair. The Divisional Commander was called in. He met his soldiers face to face, answered all their questions as best he could and, after much hesitation, accompanied by many a 'hem' and a 'ha', finally told the men that he sided with Kerensky. So a telegram was drawn up and sent from our division to the Prime

Minister, indicating that the soldiers were ready to support the
Government. It was, we were assured, the right thing to do:
nevertheless a sense of disloyalty towards our valiant General
caused us much uneasiness.

Tuesday, 29th August
It was rumoured that our Army Commander would be arriving
in Kloster Gumora; no hour had been fixed and, although we
were prepared to receive him, he did not turn up. . . . It is thought
that we shall soon be leaving, transferred, perhaps, to another
Front. Tonight our regiments will depart and be replaced by the
166th Division. I took a few snapshots of Roumanian peasants.
One woman quickly collected her family, arranged them to her
liking, then, disappearing into the hut, returned wearing her
husband's enormous working-boots. She was so proud that he
had possessed a pair of boots of his own, and was most anxious to
display them!

   In the evening, a document was brought confirming that
General Kornilov was advancing with an army on Petrograd,
intent on seizing the capital. The Government, therefore, issued
orders that he should be arrested without delay.

Wednesday, 30th August
The 2nd *Otryad* of the *Zemski Soyuz*, attached to the 166th
Division, has arrived. There are six Sisters, two doctors – one a
woman and a woman dentist.

On 31st August we left Kloster Gumora for Mazanayeshti.

Friday, 1st September. Mazanayeshti.
We scoured the village for food but there was little to be had and
that little sold unwillingly. We made no attempt at bargaining,
just handed over the money demanded. Eggs were 20 kopeks each,
a goose was 8 roubles and a little pig 30 roubles. Only plums and
pears were cheap. We did manage, however, to buy a newspaper;
so anxious were we for news that we started devouring it while
standing in the road. We read that General Kornilov had gathered
an army of 120,000 men; that the men of the *Dikaya* [Wild]
Division were rallying round him. We wondered whether the
Grand Duke Michael was still their leader and recalled the glimpse

we had had of him when, in the gorgeous trappings of a Caucasian commander, he had galloped at the head of a squadron through a Galician village in the Carpathian highlands. We read that there had already been fighting on the road to Petrograd between Kerensky's supporters and Kornilov's men. After one sharp skirmish, Kornilov had continued the march towards the capital.

Railway-lines had been purposely sabotaged in order to prevent them being used by Kornilov's troops. Things seemed to be daily growing more complicated. How our hearts bled for Russia! Should enmity continue between those two powerful leaders it might even end in civil war. That would be the downfall of Free Russia. How Germany would rejoice to see her foe so weakened by internal strife!

Monday, 4th September

There has been no news of our departure. A few sick have been to us for treatment and yesterday, to our surprise, a batch of vociferous, mud-caked Turkish prisoners was brought in. They were a sorry group, dirty and ill-kempt beyond description. We had, literally, to scrape the mud and vermin off their hairy bodies. Many of them actually resented the treatment, as though reluctant to part from their wartime crust, preferring it even to the clean shirt and pants provided for them. Then we fed them and gave them hot tea; and only then did they nod their heads and look at us with gratitude. We fed the two armed Russian guards as well and, noting that their eyes were heavy for lack of sleep, suggested that they should all rest a couple of hours before continuing on their way. They assented readily and lay down just as they were in the small yard adjoining our dressing-room: within minutes they were fast asleep – guard and prisoners lying prostrate side by side.

We hear that Kornilov has been arrested, and do not know whether to be sad or glad; our loyalties are so evenly divided. Kerensky has been our hero since the political revolution in March 1917, but it was thanks to Kornilov that our Armies – especially our beloved 8th Army – achieved such success in Galicia during the recent summer campaigns. The divisional doctor came to tell us that we might take over their hospital as we should not be moving from Mazanayeshti before 18th September.

Tuesday, 5th September

We got up early and took possession of the divisional hospital,
with the exception of the ward which had been set apart for syphilis
patients. Anna, who was on duty, said that it was in an awful
state, that she had seen the *feldsher* wiping wounds with dirty
cloths and when she had remonstrated he had replied: 'Why
should we trouble to have sterilised material here?' I did not go
near the hospital in the afternoon: I was feeling far from well. But
I knew what was wrong with me. It was that my love for my Red
Cross work was slowly fading; I was becoming sick of wounds,
illness, dirt and filth. That was the dreadful truth, and I had to
face it. The daily fears about Russia; her ghastly predicament; the
wholesale desertion by her soldiers; the hatred and insolence of the
deserters; the unfriendliness of the Roumanians; the absence of
news from home – all had combined to unnerve me. I felt deeply
ashamed to think that I was growing tired of my work; where had
my passionate enthusiasm gone? And my vows? Sick at heart, I
sat for many long minutes a prey to dejection and grievous
reflection. Annushka's sudden appearance brought me to myself.
'Florence,' she cried, 'news has just come that we are leaving
tomorrow. You can begin packing at once!' I jumped up and a
strange feeling of thankfulness swept over me; this was like an
answer to some inarticulate prayer.

Wednesday, 6th September. Salchi

We told our hosts that we were leaving and paid our bill. They
demanded money for wood which they vowed we had used, but,
as we had never touched their wood-pile, we refused to pay.
Again they demanded payment for other items we had not taken;
they were really very ill-natured and spiteful. We remembered
that our old friend, Alexander Andreyevich, had said we must
always be courteous to the peasants, but not over-generous; that
it would be wise not to ask the price of ordinary things, but just
to put down the money and take them. This seemed a distinctly
arbitrary way of transacting business, but, knowing that he was of
a generous nature, we realised he would be the last person to give
such advice unless he had just reason.

A drive of 35 versts was before us. We packed ourselves into the
Sisters' *voz*. It was a hot and dusty drive and we went slowly on
until we met with our *oboz* near Izkani. We halted on the roadside,

opposite the spot where we had been stationed in August, and which was now occupied by a regimental bakery. Thick vegetable soup with rice was doled out to all members of our unit. It was, we heard, the soldiers' favourite soup, so it was good to know that most of our people were enjoying it. After dinner, we sat in the shade of some tall pines. At 3.30 p.m. we started off again and at 5 o'clock arrived at Salchi, where we were allocated a nice-looking schoolhouse, with large, pleasant and very clean rooms.

Thursday, 7th September
I was feeling more like my ordinary self and was thankful to remember that I had not mentioned to a soul about those dark, gloomy moments of dejection. I felt happy and deeply-rooted in the life of my *Letuchka* once again. . . .

Newspapers were found and passed from hand to hand. Kerensky had recently proclaimed Russia to be a republic but the arrest of General Kornilov made the headlines. We still remembered our General Brusilov, Commander-in-Chief during the successful summer in Austria, 1916. Where was this great soldier now? No one could tell: one knew only that he too had incurred Kerensky's displeasure and had retired – or been dismissed.

Saturday, 9th September
This morning our chief and a doctor have arrived from Kiyev – the same doctor who had left us to take up an appointment in Russia. We heard of the difficult conditions in Kiyev: many people were nearly starving. The arrival of our chief and doctor started the ball of political controversy rolling, for politics formed the main topic of conversation all evening.

Saturday, 16th September
Typhoid has broken out among the peasants, and our doctors predict that there will be many infectious diseases during the coming months. But I notice that the Roumanian peasants, although as poor and illiterate as their counterparts in Galicia and Poland, are given to cleaner ways. They are constantly white-washing the walls of their little huts; the interiors, too, are neat and wholesome. Of course, it is really unjust to make such com-parisons. War has so cruelly ravaged those Galician and Polish

peasants! Roumania has suffered, but not to the same extent, though her Government was forced to retire to Yassy when Bucharest was occupied by German troops during the winter of 1916–17.

We visited the nearby villages to purchase, if possible, a few provisions, but the peasants either would not sell, or would demand exorbitant prices. There were no eggs for sale, not even at 25 kopeks each; and yet every peasant kept hens! We were offered two undersized ducks at 15 roubles and a small goose for 12 roubles. We mentioned the high price to some Roumanian officers: they quietly but firmly told us that they had not enough food for themselves. One of our Sisters rather rudely retorted: 'So, *we* are expected to die of hunger!' I was ashamed of her, but they were too polite to retaliate.

The food question became more and more acute. The Roumanians were feeling the pinch; and some of them foretold a famine. Crops had been despoiled; herds of cattle and sheep stolen; towns and villages ransacked. Only the maize crops seemed to have endured. As the days went by, we were forced to rely mainly on *kukuruza* for our staple food. Ground into flour, mixed with a little water and salt – the latter already precious – and boiled, the maize made a very palatable porridge; mixed with sugar and then baked hard, it provided an excellent cake or pudding. There was *mamaliga* too, coarsely-ground maize, boiled with water. And when we were hungry, we would go into the fields, wrench off the young, ripe cobs and demolish them on the spot with great relish. The peasants raised no objections; they knew they had enough and to spare.

A *Prekaz* [Order] has been circulated; it directs that, in the event of withdrawal from Roumanian territory, Russian soldiers are strictly forbidden to ill-treat the peasantry, or to steal from them. Another *Prekaz*, this time from the Roumanian High Command, forbids all sales of foodstuffs to Russians. I must admit that my sympathies lie with the Roumanians; the Russians are really bad allies, they have lived so long in Galicia, where they considered everything theirs by right. Here, some of the under-officers send the soldiers out at night to steal hay or oats; the soldiers return with sacks of the booty, muttering: 'We saw no owner, so we didn't know whom to pay!'

The newspapers hint that Kerensky may resign, as so many

people – including some of his own supporters – are advocating a
military dictatorship.

Our unit may be stationed here for the winter. The 2nd
Letuchka will soon be leaving, there being little necessity for a
large Red Cross *Otryad* in Roumania. I have not yet had letters
from home and feel very disquieted. The salary of Red Cross
Sisters at the Front is to be raised from 50 roubles (£5) per month
to 75 roubles for all who have served for more than one-and-a-half
years. This is gratifying news, for even a pair of boots now costs
about 100 roubles (£10).

Our soldiers' head cook, Stepan Belikov, may have smallpox.
He has been sent to an isolation hospital in Russia. If it turns
out to be smallpox, then one can accept as positive that vaccina-
tion is a sure preventive; for little more than a year ago, when our
regiment was vaccinated, Belikov stoutly refused.

Wednesday, 20th September
Our Caucasian Sister has returned from holiday. She said that
even there, among the fertile valleys of Caucasia, crops were bad
and food was scarce. Tea and sugar were obtainable only by
ticket. But there was plenty of black bread, at 15 kopeks a pound
(white bread was available only for hospitals); and butter could
be bought anywhere at 3 roubles 50 kopeks a pound. We were
paying 6 roubles for it here in Salchi, if we were lucky enough to
find any. A letter from a former Sister of our *Letuchka* says there
is famine in Moscow and shops are being raided. Clothes are at
excessively high prices; an ordinary fur coat, formerly sold at 80
roubles, would now fetch 500 roubles, or more. Shoes, too, cost
from 90 to over 100 roubles per pair. There are no fashionably-
dressed people now; everyone wears old clothes. Fuel, too, is
scarce. What will it be like when winter descends?

Stepan Belikov *is* suffering from smallpox, and from a very
virulent kind called *chyornaya ospa* [black smallpox]. Our poor
Belikov is paying dearly for his obstinacy. . . .

Saturday, 23rd September
We were told that the American ambassador had visited our
division and spoken to our soldiers, asking them to continue to
fight.

Sunday, 24th September
A newspaper printed a report that the English and French armies, on account of the disorder in Russia, wished to sever the alliance. I refused to believe such a thing. In another newspaper I read that the report had been denied. I read also that the British Army had gained much territory in Mesopotamia.

Wednesday, 27th September
A railway strike has dislocated rail-transport throughout Russia. Finland has proclaimed herself a republic. Strikes and riots are still rampant, while famine is augmenting the general hardship. At supper there was a pessimistic feeling among us that our Red Cross *Otryad* was slowly but surely closing down. Alas! for our hopes and ambitions! Alas! for poor, suffering Russia.

We heard of a party of Social Democrats in Petrograd, who had coined for themselves the name of *Bolshevik* – meaning one who forms the majority. Being such a small party, the name *Menshevik* [minority] would have been more appropriate! The members professed to be 'apostles' of the doctrine of Communism and declared that their objectives were to bring peace to Russia by negotiation; to abolish capitalism; to establish a proletariat dictatorship and to equalise all classes. In a word, the *Bolsheviki* called upon all the 'down-trodden multitudes' to rally around their new 'Socialist Organisation', promising them a common ownership of the immense lands now privately owned, joint control of all industrial and commercial concerns, with full legislative and social rights. They began forming groups, parties, committees, councils, in towns and country districts and, although they professed to be pacifists and upholders of democracy, they preached insubordination in the army and navy, and upheld their right to organise armed resistance, both military and civilian.

It was not difficult for us now to guess the origin and aims of those suspicious men who for some weeks past had been inspecting Russian Front Lines and delivering speeches to the troops. It was now quite clear that the *Bolsheviki* had started an extensive subversive movement.

Thursday, 28th September. Mitoka Dragomirna
We were called early, but our departure was postponed until after dinner. At 2 p.m. we were on the road, bound for Mitoka Drago-

mirna, where we arrived in time for tea. Three of us Sisters were accepted in a peasant hut owned by two German-speaking women who had once lived on the borders of Austria. We heard that we might be staying here for two weeks. I have not yet had news from my compatriot, Elizabeth Hopper, who promised to write after her arrival in Moscow; am afraid that the prevailing chaos may have prevented her from carrying out many of her plans.

Monday, 2nd October

We slept late, but managed to reach the Polish church in time to attend the service commemorating the hundred years' anniversary of the death of the famous Polish soldier Tadeusz Kosciusko. The black cassock worn by the old priest was covered by a white robe, which looked as though it had been made out of a lace curtain. He described the adventurous life of Kosciusko, who had dedicated his life to his country's welfare; and the bitter strife he and thousands of his countrymen had endured; but wisely refrained from mentioning that Russia had been the arch-enemy! He besought the soldiers to be faithful to God, country and ideals; to be just and honest to each other and to their neighbours. Freedom was theirs, it was true: freedom of action and of speech; freedom of will and of religion; but freedom could be brought to nought if abused.

Tuesday, 3rd October

We were asked to attend a sick woman and her daughter. It was a sad household: each member seemed to be bowed down by tragedy. We found the elderly woman very ill: we helped to mitigate some of the excruciating pain, but the large hard swelling in the lower abdomen indicated plainly that there was little hope of recovery. One of her two daughters had recently died and the little child whom she had left behind was suffering from hydrocephalus. The husbands of both of the daughters were still in the army and had not been heard of for more than a year. The remaining daughter told us that her husband had been reported a prisoner in the Austrian Army, her first baby had died soon after he had been called up, and she was now carrying another child, though she knew neither the name nor nationality of the father. We asked no questions, for we saw from her strained, worn face that she had passed through much mental suffering.

Wednesday, 4th October
The 2nd *Letuchka* has left us to take up its position with the 189th
Division. We were grieved to see them go: we had worked well
together and had become good friends.

Friday, 6th October
The sick woman was still dreadfully ill, but she had refused to go
to the Suchava Hospital where arrangements had been made to
receive her. Her severe pain seemed in no way to weaken her will-
power; she explained to us in broken German and Russian that
she would rather suffer and die in her home than be treated in a
foreign hospital and live.

Sunday, 8th October
We have been told that we are to leave for the Front.

Monday, 9th October. Ober Pertesti
We left Mitoka Dragomirna at 8 a.m.; drove to Illisheysti and had
dinner in a peasant hut. It was very cold and the peasants did not
like the idea of relinquishing their warm, one-roomed hut, so they
stayed and we packed ourselves into it with them. Our men ate
their dinner on the open field; the east wind was fierce and we
could hear them grumbling. We drove off into the full blast of
the bitter wind and reached Ober Pertesti where an empty school-
house was assigned to us. We thought regretfully of our rank and
file left without shelter to face the cold winds of an autumn night;
but we went joyfully into a warm, pleasant room, had our camp-
beds brought in and began to prepare for supper. No sooner had
we succeeded in getting everything well under control, than a
doctor hurried in to say that our room had housed patients
suffering from dysentery and had not yet been disinfected. We
were thoroughly upset and voiced our disappointment in loud,
disgruntled language. But go we had to and in about ten minutes
had taken over another room, similarly large, but as cold as an
ice-house. The stove was soon heated, but the cold persisted;
none of us slept well.

Tuesday, 10th October
Much of our equipment, as well as our personal belongings, had
been left with our *oboz* in Illisheysti. We came across Viktor

Viktorovich, the head of our automobile service, and begged him to get the necessary items sent to Ober Pertesti. He told us bluntly that we were 'capricious' and 'impatient' and that he was far too busy to attend to matters which did not concern him. After our cold and cheerless night, our nerves were somewhat frayed, and we accused him of lack of consideration. I too joined in the fray and was quite surprised to hear myself express my feelings in such voluble Russian. I told him that I deeply regretted that he did not understand English, for there were several English words which could convey more clearly my resentment at his ill manners. He retorted that he had not the slightest wish to speak English, that the Russians were in no way beholden to England, seeing that England had not raised a little finger to assist Russia in her hour of need. I seethed with indignation, but having delivered this parting shot Viktor Viktorovich deemed it wise to make his exit.

In the morning, we were called to the railway station, where we found some wounded and a few sick soldiers. Only one hospital orderly was in charge and he had not even attempted to dress any of the wounds. He told us that he had sent a message, requesting a doctor and a *feldsher*, but the young lady doctor declared that no message had been delivered to her, so we felt sure that the orderly had deceived us. We got to work at once and by the time some of the ambulances had reached us our patients were ready to be despatched to the Base. The lady doctor, new to our *Letuchka*, seemed to go about her work in a dreamy manner: she was young and very pretty and liked to engage an officer or doctor in conversation. Anna whispered to me: 'She is better at flirting than dressing wounds!'

When we returned to the house, we found that in our absence our room had been allotted to the crew of our armoured motors, despite the fact that our beds and belongings were still there. We were deeply offended and went off in a body to our head doctor. He suggested that we might find comfortable accommodation in some of the peasants' huts. But we would have none of it, and insisted that we Sisters had a better right to the room than the newcomers. Finally he gave way and it was with a decisive sense of victory that we returned to our room and saw to it that the orderlies removed every vestige of their baggage. A note from the divisional head doctor came, asking us to prepare a *lazaret* for

about 100 beds; he pointed out that the divisional *Otryad* could
not accept so many, but that they would help us to cope with both
wounded and sick. We started to clean the rooms without delay.

Wednesday, 11th October

Many sick men came to us and were put straight to bed. But we
were far from content at the way these sick soldiers had been
classified. Angina and dysentery were mixed with rheumatic fever
and sprained ankles; there was even a case of typhus and one of
spotted-fever. We were at our wits' end to know how to arrange
them. The divisional doctor visited us, and instantly saw the
predicament. The only solution to the problem, he decided, was
for us to take over the railway station house; but we found that
was impossible.

Now that we had been separated from our 2nd *Letuchka*, we
were only four surgical Sisters, and two Sisters could not possibly
run either the *lazaret* or the station house.

Thursday, 12th October

There were 17 men in one ward and others were coming and going
all the time. Seven wounded were brought in a cart, injured by
the explosion of their own bomb. When night fell, I had been on
my feet all day and was very tired. Another cart rolled up: six
wounded, two of them very weak. A young officer had been holding
the headpiece of a shell in his hand; he knocked it against a tree
and it exploded. He and two soldiers were killed instantaneously
and these six were wounded. One died during the night. We
carried him on his straw-matting – for there were no stretchers –
across the yard to the barn mortuary. There was only one candle,
so we had to be very careful as we traversed the yard. A sick man
was brought in with a very high temperature; we could find no
room for him in the ward and, as he was unconscious, we wrapped
him in a sheet and carried him, too, to the barn for shelter. All
night I worried about him; I thought that he might wake up
sufficiently to realise that he had been considered dead. Once or
twice it seemed to me that I heard him knocking on the barn door.

Friday, 13th October

Work was plentiful, so I helped bandage until the dinner-hour.
When, after a good sleep, I returned to the *lazaret*, I found a

young peasant lad in the ward. A piece of shrapnel had ripped through his stomach and what seemed to be the spleen was hanging out; the doctor cut it away. But the boy died very soon. His sister, who was sitting by him, would not believe that he was dead. *'Nyet! Nyet!'* she kept repeating, shaking her head. His father arrived in the evening; he kissed my hand and thanked me over and over again. I dared not tell him. I watched him approach; he bent and looked at the boy's still, white face. The girl moaned: *'On umer!* [He died!]' *'Umer?'* cried the father and, clutching his head with both hands, leant against the wall for support. It was a heart-rending scene. We gave them permission to leave the dead lad with us for the night.

Saturday, 14th October
I was still dressing when the father returned. Outside in the street a little group of mourners stood; two were carrying an empty coffin; another was holding a discoloured banner. There was no priest. They took the boy's body, which we had wrapped in a sheet, and laid it in the coffin. The father came hastily toward me, bowed low and kissed my hand. I do not know whether he saw the tears in my eyes. As they moved away, they began to sing a dirge-like chant.

In the evening, we were told that all the Red Cross *Otryads* of the *Zemski Soyuz* would be disbanded, with three exceptions: the 1st, 5th and 10th. So we, the 10th, would, thank God, remain!

Sunday, 15th October
In the early evening, a man was led in who had been wounded by a German bullet. He soon came to know that he was the only soldier in that ward who had received a wound from an enemy. He strutted up and down feeling quite a hero among the many who had self-inflicted or accidental wounds.

Monday, 16th October
It was a very quiet morning and I was able to enjoy a really good rest. A divisional doctor had monopolised the services of the surgical staff. He had fallen from his horse and seemed to think that his brain might have been badly injured. Several regimental surgeons put in an appearance at his urgent request, and he was finally made to understand that his recovery would be a matter

of only a few days. We were all thankful when he was transferred
to the divisional *Otryad*.

Tuesday, 17th October
Vladimir Nikolayevich will be returning to our *Letuchka* from
Kiyev; we are very pleased. Another report has caused me considerable dismay; it is said that the ambassadors of our allies are
to leave Russia. If so, there must be some grave reason. Could it
be that the methods of the *Bolsheviki* in Petrograd have made life
too dangerous? Could it be that the widespread desertions have
proved that Russia is unable to maintain the alliance? Could it
be that England and France foresee the downfall of Russia?

Wednesday, 18th October
My compatriot Elizabeth will not be returning to our *Otryad*: a
bitter disappointment, and I am wondering what will happen to
my letters which she was going to bring with her. We seem to be
cut off from all friendly contacts.

Thursday, 19th October
We have had news of a great French victory, on 13th October.

A little later, we heard of another victory; this time, it was the
German Army which had defeated the Italians.

I saw one of our young doctors dressing a wound before the dirt
and grime around it had been washed off. I gave way to my wrath
and told him that he was asking for serious trouble if he had
dressed the wound before first cleansing it. He rudely told me to
mind my own business; I told him that it *was* my business to see
that our soldiers' wounds were cleaned before bandaging. We
exchanged many angry, resentful words. I knew that I was right;
he knew that he was wrong. But he was a doctor! I was only a
Sister!

That night, I worked it out before I went to sleep. I knew that
I was growing coarse, bad-humoured and fault-finding. At first,
I ascribed it to the pressure of warfare, the many hardships and
humiliations, the conditions of our everyday life at the Front,
when for days we could not undress, or even have a good wash. I
decided that there were, indeed, good reasons for my bad temper;
yet I began to feel ashamed of myself. Before I became a Red Cross
nurse, I had been fully aware that there would be many exasperat-

ing moments, but I had been certain that I would overcome them – even welcome them in order to prove the strength of my will. I would often repeat those words of Goethe: *'Es bildet ein Talent sich in der Stille und ein Charakter im Strom der Welt.'** I had wanted my character to be strengthened and to come through, as victor, in the struggle. But recently there had been three times when the knowledge that I was rude and ill-tempered did not even bother me. I remembered the ugly row with Viktor Viktorovich; then, that same day, the resentful words with the head doctor, concerning our room; and now I had criticised one of our doctors and started a wrathful dispute.

Some of our Sisters and Brothers were not noted for their self-control and when they began to throw nasty, biting words at each other, I would tell myself: 'It is lack of education,' or 'It is the Russian temperament.' And now, I am doing the same thing! And I am English! We English have a reputation here for having our feelings well under control. I really am ashamed of myself and must take myself in hand.

I am wondering if my nerves are beginning to fray. If only I could go to Moscow for two or three days! I will broach the matter to our head doctor tomorrow and see what he says.

Tuesday, 24th October
Our chief is going to Russia on the 26th. I had a sudden urge to beg him to allow me to accompany him, so that I might stay a day or two with my 'family' in Moscow. But I heard him say that he was travelling with a staff officer and his programme had to coincide with that of his friend. So I suppressed my longing.

Friday, 27th October
There has been a big uprising of the *Bolsheviki* in Petrograd. A telegram has come containing the news that some members of the Provisional Government have been arrested by the rioters and that their so-called 'Socialist Organisation' intends to overthrow the Government and take power into its own hands. It seems that the man Lenin, who, with his accomplice Trotsky, had been worsted in July by Kerensky's supporters, had reappeared and assumed complete control of the Organisation. Will Kerensky

---

*'Talent is developed in tranquillity, but character is moulded in the tumult of the world.'

prove strong enough to withstand him? If not, a civil war will be inevitable!

Tonight, the head doctor summoned our *Komanda* to a meeting. He told them of the violence and rebellion in Petrograd, and assured them of his complete faith in their loyalty. Our soldiers were obviously perturbed by what they had heard. One or two of their spokesmen, after a whispered confabulation, rose and asked permission to say a few words; the doctor's encouraging response put them at their ease. They declared that they would remain loyal to the *Otryad*; that all they wanted was the best for their families and themselves; the best for Free Russia. But where could they find the 'best'? One soldier, with a fine, open face, affirmed that he spoke on behalf of all his comrades. 'We are *malogramotnie* [half-educated],' he said, 'and they tell us that we are free men, but we do not know what this freedom means or how we can use it. We are unable to decide what is best for us. Tell us plainly how we can serve our country and how we can bring peace to it. It is difficult to know whom to trust. But what we all want is *peace*. Tell us how we can bring peace quickly. They say that England and France can carry on the war for another ten or fifteen years; but we, in Russia, cannot. Russia must have peace. *'Da! Da!'* assented the soldiers. *'Nam nuczno mir!* [We need peace!].' *'Mir! . . . mir! . . . preczde vsevo!* [Peace above all else!].'

Saturday, 28th October

During the day, gunfire started again. Two shells fell perilously near our *Lazaret* and our cow received a small leg wound. By 10 p.m. five wounded men had arrived.

Sunday, 29th October

Sofiya confessed early this morning that she had had a trying night. The soldiers had slept fairly well, but a young officer, brought in with a stomach wound the previous day, had been continually restless, his mind constantly wandering. His orderly had told her that he knew the family, which consisted of seven children – four girls and three boys. The wounded man, Sergey by name, was the eldest and he was only 20 years old. Early in 1915 he had joined the army as a volunteer, but had soon been picked out and sent to a military academy, which he had left in 1916 with the rank of *podporuchik* [second-lieutenant]. He was quickly promoted to *poruchik* [lieutenant] and his orderly had told her with great pride that, during the recent fighting, his name had been placed on the honours list.

At last we have news from Russia. It is rumoured that the *Bolsheviki* have gained the upper hand in Petrograd, but Kerensky's troops are slowly restoring order. Moscow is under the control of the Government but the railway stations are in the hands of the *Bolsheviki*. Negotiations are taking place between the rival factions. Our worst fears have been realised: *a civil war is in progress in Free Russia!*

My thoughts are constantly in Moscow with my good friends and, especially, with my Russian 'family'. How they must be suffering: no food, no fuel, and strife and bloodshed outside their very windows! Our doctors have recommended me to wait a week or two before travelling to Moscow; they say that the situation there is too precarious. . . .

The young officer's case was hopeless from the beginning. Our surgeons did their best – as they always do; they knew that there was just a slight chance, so they operated. Alas! the bladder had been shot through and the *kishki* [intestines] severed in more than one place. When they brought him to us, I noticed the regular, classical features of the southern Russian; dark, curly hair; light grey eyes, heavily-fringed with long dark lashes. He was indeed very handsome, with a finely-built figure. His orderly was devoted to him; he would have sat by his bedside night and day, had he not been ordered away to rest.

Sometimes he called to me: 'Zina, lift me up.' I told him gently that the doctor had forbidden movement. Then he shouted: 'Lift me up at once. Zina! I tell you – at once! You won't? Then, away from me! I never want to see your face again! . . . Egor,' he called to his orderly. 'Here, your Honour.' 'Bring me cord and strong hook; I'll show what I can do.' He turned his face to the wall and began moaning. Some ten minutes had passed; he had sipped some water and seemed to have forgotten his request. But, suddenly, again: 'Egor, have you a cord and hook?' 'Certainly, your Honour, I have.' 'Give them me; give immediately!' And the orderly, who had not left the bedside, started to stammer: 'But, your Honour, they not here. I go fetch them.' The patient's anger increased: 'You blackguard!' he shouted and in his most authoritative voice. 'Away to the trenches, scoundrel! Away to the very foremost

fighting line!' The orderly wisely disappeared through the doorway,
to wait in the next ward until his master's wrath had abated. The
angry face of the wounded boy turned towards me: 'Zina,' he said
penitently, 'was I right to send Egor away to the trenches? He's
a good fellow on the whole.'

Early this afternoon – Sergey's second day with us – we discovered the dreadful truth that his body was decaying; the abdomen was already discoloured. There was now no chance of saving
his life. I sat by his bedside nearly all night while the medical men
on duty received and bandaged any stragglers who happened to
come to us. Once or twice came his cry for 'Mama!' and my heart's
pity would surge towards him, the boy who had played a man's
part so nobly and was doomed to die among strangers.

The end came in the morning about 5.30, peacefully, under the
blessed influence of morphia.

The guns have been firing again; the air is choked with unrest.
Sergey is lying in a small room, with folded hands and shut eyes,
deaf to the sound of the guns, oblivious to the turmoil. His orderly
is sitting near him; his face, too, is set and pale. He will keep vigil
until the kindly earth is ready to receive his young master.

Monday, 30th October
I had breakfast and lay down to rest, but I could not sleep. So,
once again, I had been *chosen* to witness the cruel death of a brave
young soldier. I use the word 'chosen' deliberately, for I am
convinced that God would not have allotted that difficult task to
me had He not given me the necessary strength to accept it and
to carry it through. 'Great your strength, if great your need'. . . .
It has often seemed to me lately that I must have experienced all
the hardships and witnessed all the horrors that warfare could
offer to a non-fighter. I don't think that I could stand many more.
I had always hoped that my war experiences would, despite their
misery and bitterness, act as a stimulus to my spiritual life, would
heighten my compassion, would 'strengthen my soul in all goodness'. But now I wanted to find a quiet spot where the world was
at peace. I suddenly remembered some lines which I loved: 'Now I
will take me to a place of peace; forget my heart's desire; in
solitude and prayer work out my soul's release.' I repeated them
over and over again to myself. Like a prayer, they soothed me.

A welcome message reached us from a neighbouring *Otryad*,

telling us that a lady doctor was about to leave for Kiyev and would be pleased to accept any of our commissions. It was soon arranged that, when she went, probably on 3rd or 4th November, I should accompany her and, from Kiyev, make my way to Moscow. . . .

Smirnov, our head orderly, returned this morning from a short furlough to his village home between Zhitomir and Kiyev. His old father had died and our doctors had arranged the necessary seven-day leave for him. We were thankful to see him back with us; he was, in his quiet, unobtrusive way, one of the mainstays of our unit.

Tuesday, 31st October

We Sisters sat about, reading or sewing, for there was little work. There was still no news from Petrograd or Moscow; the absence of all news arouses many suspicions. I am still hoping to go to Moscow on 3rd November. Smirnov came to the *lazaret* and I was able to have a little chat with him. I found him looking older and thinner; the journey must have been trying and the bereavement in his family circle had naturally caused much sadness. He said that his wife and children were well and that although food was scarce, they managed to find enough to eat. 'We are really better off than the citizens in Kiyev,' he told me, 'for we have our own home-grown potatoes and maize – excellent crops this year.' 'Smirnov,' I said, 'tell me frankly, is there much unrest in Kiyev?' 'It is difficult to describe it, *sestritsa*,' he answered. 'The unrest in some parts borders on insanity. In Zhitomir, many soldiers are hiding; they are deserters and dare not show their faces in their own native villages. Only last year a soldier who heard that his wife was dangerously ill left his regiment without permission to go to her; they caught him and hanged him for desertion. But now there are hundreds of deserters, and no one dares say a word to them. In my village they told me of a soldier who, hearing that a bomb had killed his wife and child, begged for a few days' leave; it was refused him and he, in his despair, cried out that he would go to join them. And he stood straight up in the trenches, a sure target for the enemy, and was riddled with bullets. Life is very hard, *sestritsa*; sometimes one wonders why so much cruelty is allowed.' 'There are many cruel people in the world just now,' I said. 'It is they who make life so hard. Think of all those young

soldiers – mere boys – who delight in pillaging, plundering and
killing, regardless of the pain and suffering they are causing.'
'Yes,' he answered thoughtfully, 'and yet I feel sure that *at heart*
all my comrades are true and honest; it is their youth, their lack
of understanding, which lead them astray. *At heart*, believe me,
sestritsa, they are good and true.'

Wednesday, 1st November

Several wounded have come, all self-inflicted. There seems to be a
real epidemic of men who shoot a hand, or even a finger, in order
to have 'just cause' to leave the trenches. I am surprised they take
the trouble to injure themselves. In these abnormal days one
would expect them just to walk calmly away. News from Petrograd is very disturbing; it is rumoured that the Russian Navy at
Kronstadt has mutinied and, collaborating with the rebellious
army, has taken by storm all the principal buildings in the city.
There is no mention of Kerensky; one can but hope and pray that
he is still alive.

A note has been brought to me, telling me that the lady doctor
who had intended travelling to Kiyev has now with great regret
cancelled her journey. So my high hopes have been dashed to the
ground! But why should I have to depend on another person to
make the journey to Moscow? Was I not capable of travelling
alone? . . . I rushed off to the head doctor and explained the
predicament. 'Sister Florence, wait a week or two until things
have settled down.' 'No! No!' I expostulated, 'I will go now. You
have given me permission; my papers are in order. I can manage
quite well.' He saw from my eager face that I was determined to
go. 'I will see what I can do about it,' he said. So all was well. I
would go to Moscow alone. . . .

Thursday, 2nd November

I am to start tomorrow. Sandy, our liaison officer, had to carry
out several commissions for our unit at the *Zemski sklad* [store-
house] in Botushany, and I would drive with him. As the drive to
Botushany was a long one, we would be obliged to spend the
night – and rest the horses – in the hut of a Roumanian peasant
who was well-known to Sandy. In Yassy, I was to go straight to
the *Zemski Soyuz* offices, where I could rest and have my meals.
And, our doctor added, it was an amazing coincidence, but one of

the *Zemski* orderlies was being sent to Kiyev; he would await my arrival in Yassy and travel with me to Kiyev. . . . It all sounded marvellous to me. . . . The weather is bad, cold wind and rain or sleet; but for me, now, the weather is a minor detail.

Friday, 3rd November. To Moscow
The head doctor came to wish me a safe journey. 'You must not imagine that you are in for an easy time,' he said. 'I don't envy you. Travelling by train nowadays must be like purgatory. I still think you would be wise to postpone your journey.' At 4 p.m. I was dressed and waiting. Sandy appeared in the doorway and said that we would be leaving on the morrow. At my cry of dismay, he began to laugh, confessed that he had been joking and that the horses had already been ordered. They all gave me a warm send-off and at 5, I was on my way towards Moscow.

Sandy, to my surprise, told me that he had been a revolutionary and had spent one year and three months in prison in 1906–7. Now, he added laughingly, the present-day revolutionaries would not recognise him as a brother, but would classify him as a 'bourgeois', which was the name they were giving to all who refused to accept their doctrines. 'Imagine!' he laughed. 'They call me a "bourgeois", one of the "idle rich", and my father was only an ordinary workman, without money or education.' I liked Sandy, everyone liked him; he was a tall, good-looking man in the late twenties, tireless in his work, a grand organiser, and always ready for a joke.

We reached the village where we were to spend the night, and found Malukov and his wife expecting us; we excused our late arrival and got him to stir up the fire and make us some tea. Sandy and I had brought sandwiches and bread and cheese with us, and, sitting on a wooden bench, enjoyed a picnic supper. By the light of the single candle, I could see that the hut was very small but very clean. Sandy had told me that Malukov was an 'oats-merchant': possibly that was how the relationship with our Red Cross unit had been established. Nevertheless, I was surprised to see both men bringing sacks of oats into the hut; they, I was told, would serve as mattresses. Five were allotted to me and, after vigorously manipulating the 'hillocks' and 'holes', I was able to smooth them out sufficiently to make quite a comfortable mattress. The hut was cold, but I slept well.

It was still dark when I heard Malukov and his wife conversing;

then he left the hut to awaken our driver who had slept among the oats in the shed. There was a bucket of cold water from the village well, and I washed my rough, grubby hands and the dust and sleep from my face. The driver having joined us, we all drank tea, finished the sandwiches and prepared to leave. I was touched to see that neither the man nor his wife would accept the money which we wished to give them. 'Never mind,' whispered Sandy, 'I shall make it up to him with the next consignment of oats.'

Saturday, 4th November
It was still very dark. No one had a watch, but someone said that it would be nearly five o'clock; I thought it must be much earlier. Our lantern was lighted and we started off in the darkness. Malukov packed my feet round with hay. It was still raining, a light, cold drizzle, and the wind was icy. . . . An ambulance-motor swished past us, disquieting the horses; then another one rushed past; it seemed that every five minutes one would hasten by at top speed.

Then something white fell on to my knee – it was a flake of snow. Another and another; the first snow of the newly-arrived winter! I think I slept a little; holding, however, tightly on to the side of the constantly swaying cart. Sandy was humming to himself; the driver, like the horses, was snorting and making funny sounds. Many Roumanian soldiers passed us, stacked in carts, on their way to the Front. It was light enough to see that their long coats and high, fur hats were saturated; the men must have been nearly frozen.

We arrived at Botushany about 9.30 a.m. and walked to the *Upravlenie*, or railway authority's office, leaving our driver and horses at the storehouse. My feet were so cold and numb that I began to be afraid lest they should refuse to support me. I was grateful for Sandy's strong arm. The 'authority' had not yet arrived; we were asked to wait in his office. When he came, I handed in my papers and told him that I was on my way to Moscow. He looked at them and said that they were not sufficient to warrant a permit. Then, more than ever before, was I thankful that Sandy was with me! He rose to the occasion; towering above the small figure at the desk and looking most impressive in his long military coat and insignia of lieutenant, he pulled out his official *laissez-passer* of liaison officer of the 1st *Letuchka*, 10th

Front Line Surgical *Otryad* of the all-Russia *Zemski Soyuz* and stated that he had been commissioned to accompany me to Botushany to see me safely on to the train for Moscow, via Yassy, Kishinev and Kiyev. That was enough. The 'authority' took paper, wrote on it, stamped and sealed it and handed it to me. . . . Outside the office, we looked at it; it gave me full permission for a *month's* furlough in Moscow! I looked at my companion with gratitude: 'Sandy!' I said. 'Thank you! I don't know what I should have done without you!' He clicked his heels together and saluted in true soldierly fashion. 'Pleased to have been of service to you.' We returned to the *sklad* and, after dinner, were driven to the railway station. Sandy happened to say that he had a splitting headache; I opened my handbag and gave him a couple of phenacetin. 'Pleased to have been of service to you,' I said laughingly. We shook hands and wished each other *vsevo khoroshevo* [every good thing].

As I walked down the platform after Sandy's departure I passed a group of soldiers; one or two of them began to laugh and call out to me. Again I felt dispirited, but told myself that I was on my way to Moscow and must be prepared for difficulties. I sat in the tea-room until the porter came to tell me that the train was in and I could take my seat. Easier said than done! There was no empty seat to take! I pushed my way through the crowded corridor, peering into every *coupé*; at last I found a place in a third class carriage near a broken window. The compartment was full of Russian and Roumanian soldiers and a noisy conversation was being carried on among them. A Roumanian expressed surprise that the train had been filled so quickly, but a Russian informed him that he and his comrades had lined the railroad outside the station and, as the train slowed up, had scrambled on and occupied their seats. 'Ha! Ha!' he said arrogantly. 'We Russians know how to get what we want!' As time went on, their controversy became more heated. *'Nu! Nu!* [Come! Come!]' admonished a Russian. 'You don't have much left to boast of! Just Yassy left to you now!' *'Da!'* the Roumanian retorted, 'Riga gone, only the Germans' Petrograd left to you!'

It was very cold and the broken window sent draughts of icy air across me. I pulled the plaid tightly round my legs and feet, opened my leather jacket, saw to it that the fur waistcoat was pulled well round me, fastened up my jacket, turned up the collar and wrapped my black travelling veil tightly round my head and neck.

There was one old Roumanian holding two sacks on his knees, more like a peasant than a soldier; only his gun disclosed the fact that he was on active service. In answer to a Russian's question, he said that he was 43 years old. 'Time to go home,' called out a young Russian soldier. *'Da!'* the elder man assented. 'I hear that in Russia many soldiers of 40 years and over have gone home, but they didn't give me permission.' The young Russian made a quick reply: 'Oh! Permission is not now necessary!' The old soldier looked at him. 'You are very young to say such things. Haven't you heard that it is a man's duty to defend his country?' 'That's all *chepukha* [tomfoolery]. Now we are free men, our country has been freed of all bastard rulers. They made the war; we didn't. Why then should we fight?' The old Roumanian looked him up and down, but decided it was wiser not to continue the conversation. Quietly, he opened one of the sacks, took out a tin bowl containing some *mamaliga* and began to eat. The Russian soldiers continued to poke fun at him, likening him to a gypsy, or old market woman, with his sacks. One of them began to smoke a *makhorka* cigarette and held the lighted match to a corner of one sack; it would have burst into flame, had not the old soldier crushed it out with his bare hand. There was a general laugh, but the man showed no sign of anger or annoyance.

Although I had entered the train soon after 4 p.m. it did not stir from the station of Botushany until 9.30 p.m. Soldiers were coming and going all night long; the chatter of hoarse voices never ceased. They quarrelled; they swore; they shouted with anger; they roared with laughter; there was no thought of sleep. We stopped at a station. There was a sound of angry voices and the train slowly jerked forward.

Suddenly a heavy blow came on the broken window at my side; glass splinters scattered in all directions, and through the aperture scrambled a soldier head first, propelled by a comrade on the platform. He fell forward on to my knees, then made a frantic dive and landed on the floor. Then he tried to pull his comrade through but the soldiers dragged him away, at the same time giving a mighty shove to the head and shoulders of the man clinging to the broken frame. He thumped back on to the platform; the train was gathering speed and soon cleared the station.

Sunday, 5th November

A quarrel started in the early hours of this morning between a Roumanian soldier and a Russian *unter-ofitzer* [non-commissioned officer]; the latter, newly-arrived, demanded the seat of the Roumanian, but the Roumanian refused, insisting that he came first; he pleaded that he had bad feet and wounded hands. The infuriated Russian shot out with his fist and knocked off the Roumanian's hat; the Roumanian jumped up and shouted to his countrymen to help him; the Russian shouted to his comrades. Matches were struck and a candle was produced and lighted. Little by little the noisy dispute subsided. I was glad to note that the young Roumanian retained his seat. . . .

We arrived at Yassy about 8 a.m. I was thankful to move and bring the circulation back into my legs again. I went straight into the city, which seemed very large and spacious after the smaller Roumanian towns. It was, I knew, the present administrative seat of the Roumanian Government, for the capital city of Bucharest had been evacuated in December 1916. I lost no time in enquiring the location of the *Zemski Soyuz* offices and had no difficulty in finding them. I was able to enjoy a good wash and the excellent breakfast and hot tea soon revived me. A lady told me that she had heard that it was now impossible to journey by train to Kiyev, much less to Moscow. She declared that in Vinnitsa the disorder was so great that no trains were allowed to run to Kiyev. She advised me strongly not to attempt the journey. I listened to her politely and in my heart felt quite sure that she might be right. But . . . but . . . I had begun the journey; I *could not* turn back.

The *Zemski* supervisor had been informed of my arrival; we had a short chat together and he suggested that I go to the station as soon as possible, for the few trains still running filled so rapidly that it might be difficult to find a seat. He told me that the orderly who would accompany me to Kiyev was a very decent man, Kazimir by name, who had worked for some months in the offices and had been sent to Kiyev on business more than once before. Kazimir soon arrived; he was a short, stocky man, about 30, but looked clean and very capable.

When we reached the station, there was a train standing alongside the main platform. It was already overcrowded – soldiers and civilians were even standing on the steps. All doors were

locked with the exception of those of the third and fourth class;
but at last, in a fourth class compartment, two seats were cleared
by none too willing fellow travellers. I think that my nurse's
uniform might have persuaded them. I sank down thankfully on
to a hard, wooden plank near an outside window.

The dirt and grime in our coupé were dreadful; Kazimir cleared
up the floor around our feet and wiped the dirty window-pane. . . .
From my window, I saw the Red Cross train of Porushkevich
standing on a neighbouring line, and asked Kazimir to keep my
seat and look after my bag and plaid while I went to speak to the
Sisters. I asked them to allow me to wash; they gave permission,
but none too graciously, since I think they were rather dubious
about my nationality. I returned to our coupé and sent Kazimir to
dinner at the restaurant run by the *Zemski Soyuz* on the station.
It was just after midday – the soldiers' dinner-hour. The soldiers
opposite asked me where I came from and were interested to hear
that I was English. An elderly Roumanian asked me: 'Goes
England with Roumania?' 'Yes,' I answered. 'Goes England with
Roumania, Italy and Russia?' 'Yes.' 'Then all is well,' he said
complacently.

Kazimir came back and I went at once to take a ticket for my
dinner. I waited from 1 o'clock to 2.45 p.m. for the second service:
there were many people waiting and I noticed that they were
becoming more and more agitated. Would there or would there
not be any dinner? Finally, we were called to the tables, and served
with savoury rice soup, *kuritsa* [chicken] and *kapusta* [cabbage],
all very nice and appetising. The cost was 1 rouble 75 kopeks.
I did not wait to drink tea but hurried back to the train. I was
surprised to find that it was not there, but was told it had been
moved on to another line. I found it almost at once and congratulated myself that I had had the foresight to jot down the
number, which was 4781.

It was most difficult to reach my place, for the corridor was
packed with soldiers, but I managed to squeeze my way through
them, recognised my compartment and subsided thankfully on to
my seat. I looked at Kazimir and saw that he was asleep and –
horror of horrors! – his face was very red, his breathing stertorous
and saliva was oozing out of his mouth. At first I did not understand and, thinking that he was unwell, I let him sleep on. In about
half-an-hour I shook him to awaken him. There was no sight of

our bags and belongings. 'Where are the bags?' I asked. Kazimir grunted and continued his slumbers. I asked him a second time and with another shake. He began to talk nonsense, and I realised that he was drunk. For some moments I felt helpless and then anger seized me. I gave him another good shake and told him to get up at once and look for our luggage. He nodded his head: '*Tak tochno!* [Just so!]' he repeated. But a Russian soldier, sitting in front of me, leant forward and said 'They – under seat!' and pointed under *his* seat, not mine! To my great relief I saw them there! I did not enquire as to how or why they had been transferred. I was just thankful to see them.

I found myself hoping that, after his deep sleep, Kazimir would awaken in a sober condition and display a contrite understanding of his lapse from rectitude. But . . . not yet! For to my consternation he slowly inclined towards me and in a moment I found his head resting on my shoulder. I wanted to push him away with disgust: his drunken face so near mine sickened me. One or two of the younger soldiers began to giggle and I saw the faces of the older ones turned towards me, wondering how I should treat this disagreeable situation. I quickly worked it out in my mind: to repel him roughly – as he deserved – would possibly arouse the malice of the onlookers, not a few of whom were undoubtedly deserters. I must do or say something to gain their approval and confidence. I looked round the coupé, noting well the expressions on all the faces, and said 'He is an orderly in the *Zemski Soyuz* offices in Yassy and has been sent to accompany and help me on my journey to Kiyev. But he is very tired, so I must be lenient with him. I must try to imagine that he is a wounded soldier, one of the many hundreds whom I have nursed during my three years of warfare.' 'Three years, *sestritsa*?' some voices asked. I noticed the friendliness in the word '*sestritsa*' and felt that all was well. Then I told them how it was that I had been in Russia at the outbreak of the war, how in my Red Cross unit I had been without news of my family and relations during the last many months. They listened attentively, like children: those younger ones loved to hear a story. . . . Kazimir moved and his head slipped off my shoulder on to his own chest; his sleep was still deep and his snoring noisy. One soldier said to his neighbour: 'In such a condition, how easy for a man to lose the contents of his pocket!'

The coupé became dreadfully hot and the smell of the perspiring soldiers made me feel quite sick. The luggage rack above my head was creaking every time its occupants moved; there were two men on each side. How they could keep their balance was a mystery! Dust, dirt and tobacco ash were constantly falling on to us. The rack opposite not only creaked but cracked; the soldiers managed to tie it precariously to its hinges with cord.

It grew dark and a candle was produced. In its flickering light, the scene around me was remarkable. Soldiers were packed like sardines on the seats; others, standing, were braced against each other, rocking and rolling with the train. There was constant abuse: *'Ne tolkay!* [Don't push!]' *'Chort tibya vozmi!* [Devil take you!]' *'Durak!* [Fool!] do you think this train belongs to you?'

Now and again a match would be struck and the weird, uncanny picture of those sleep-befuddled, evil-smelling soldiers would dance for a few seconds before my tired eyes. They were sprawling everywhere on the seat and floor: lying across each other; doubled up in hunched, misshapen forms. An old Roumanian was sighing and groaning; at last, he managed to get his high boots off and unwind his foot-cloths. I heard his sigh of relief. The soldier in front of me stretched his legs out with a groan and they came into rough contact with mine. I tried to stretch mine out to relieve the painful numbness, but I came into hard contact with his. I must sit still, I told myself; I *must* endure the painful discomfort. I dozed a little, thanks to the small travelling-pillow Mother had made for me, but awoke every few minutes to the chorus of stertorous breathing and long drawn-out snores. Once a moan sounded; I moved slightly, and the moan came again. I suddenly realised that it came every time I moved, and it came from under my seat! I stooped and felt a breathing body! My feet were embedded in the stomach of a soldier; every time I moved, he groaned. I lifted my cramped feet and tried to balance them on the opposite seat, but there, too, was something big and moving! What could I do with my feet? I left them lightly on the human lump opposite and discovered thankfully that they did not worry the sleeper.

A sudden stir of noisy voices in the corridor and the ticket inspector appeared with a lantern. He spied me in the far corner. 'Your ticket?' 'I have no ticket, only a pass,' I said. 'Ah!' he replied scornfully, 'you are one of those who think they can travel without a ticket!' Kazimir, my inglorious 'right-hand', was again sunk in a drunken sleep. It was essential that I settle the dispute single-handed. I said loudly: 'Well, if you don't believe me, I shall ask you to accompany me to the military commandant on the next station.' Swearing and muttering, he walked away. I was upset at the man's impertinence and a little agitated. But the couple of soldiers who were sufficiently awake to understand the situation showed me their sympathy: 'He's always trying to find somebody to shout at.' And the other agreed: 'He likes to make a lot of noise about nothing!'

I tried to sleep, but could not. The smell was terrible, and insects were biting viciously. The old Roumanian began to groan and tried to move. His Russian neighbours swore at him, but he did not lose his temper, just murmured: 'Ah! *Russki! Russki!*'

Monday, 6th November
We arrived at Kishinev station. I found the ticket inspector on the platform and told him that he could now accompany me to the commandant's office. 'If you wish it, *Sestritsa*,' he replied meekly. 'Ha!' thought I. 'It's "*Sestritsa*" now!' 'Yes,' I said firmly, 'I wish it. I intend to tell the commandant about your unpardonable insolence last night.' He followed me to the commandant. I explained why I had no ticket, and how I had spent that night in a fourth class carriage. He examined my pass and Red Cross documents, then handed me a ticket for the military staff carriage! The ticket inspector had disappeared. I was rather disappointed, for I should like to have given him a tip – and parted friends!

I found the Kiyev train and the military staff carriage, and took possession of a comfortable corner in the corridor. Kazimir tried to pretend that nothing unusual had happened, but I spoke to him firmly and told him exactly what had taken place and that it must not be repeated. He was very confused: began making excuses and finally, begged my pardon. . . . I was able to wash and tidy up in the train before the majority of passengers arrived; then I stood in the corridor near an open window, breathed in the cold, clean air of an early November morning and felt more composed and contented.

A young *poruchik* [lieutenant], seeing me standing, saluted and offered me his seat. It was simply heaven to sit in a spotlessly clean, uncrowded, comfortably-upholstered coupé, with a real luggage-rack! Among the passengers was a middle-aged *Batyushka* of the

41st Division, who actually remembered our 10th *Otryad* when we had been stationed at Barish and Monasterzhiska. I talked of those early experiences with this friendly priest who had shared them. '*Batyushka*,' I asked. 'Was it all in vain? The pain and suffering and the *enormous* sacrifice?' 'No, *Sestritsa*,' he replied. 'No sacrifice is in vain if made in answer to the call of duty. God is just; those who gave up their lives for their country will receive them again, from the merciful hands of our Father in Heaven.' Before I closed my eyes that night, the priest took leave of me and gave me his blessing. When I awoke in the early morning, he had already gone.

Tuesday, 7th November
A young man in civilian clothes entered into the conversation, said his name was Goodlet and he was bound for Mogilev, where the rioting had been kept within bounds. He related that he had an estate of some 15,000 *desyatines** in the Khersonskaya Government. It had been seized by the *Bolsheviki* and only the house and 30 *desyatines* were left to him. He had, however, refused to accept the offer from such unruly scoundrels, and wished to have nothing more to do with them. It had, he admitted, been a cruel blow, for he had inherited the property from his father. He said that his grandfather was a Britisher; he had been born in Russia but he was grieved and ashamed to be Russian in these humiliating times. His voice was agreeable and his manners gentlemanly. He had brought provisions with him and offered me some *blini* [small pancakes] stuffed with *ikra* [caviare]. I took two, but not being accustomed to such rich food after weeks of nothing but maize my stomach rebelled and more than once during the night I regretted eating them.

Wednesday, 8th November
Standing in the corridor were two officers, in greatcoats of civilian cut. I had heard that some officers disguised their rank in order not to clash with the *Bolsheviki*. Perhaps, in Kiyev, these men would feel safer in civilian garb. From them I heard that in Moscow the railways and stations were still in the hands of the *Bolsheviki* and that they and they only gave permission to travellers to enter the city. In the city itself, at night, no one dared leave his home. I

* desyatina = 2·7 acres.

was very anxious to hear what was happening in Petrograd, but when I broached the subject, nobody seemed inclined to discuss it. I decided that either they knew nothing, or, knowing too much, they were loath to speak of it.

Our informants were in possession of a wide variety of news. We heard of the disastrous defeat of the Italian Army, under the Commander-in-Chief Cadorna, when the Austrian troops had been heavily reinforced by German manpower and artillery. Despite a magnificent stand by the Italians, Caporetto had fallen and a hasty retreat had followed, during which hundreds of Italian soldiers perished and hundreds more were taken prisoner. We all expressed deep concern for our gallant and trustworthy allies. We were told, too, that a strong force of Cossacks was marching towards Moscow under the command of General Kaledin, *Hetman* of the famous Cossack Cavalry Corps. He had played a brilliant role during the offensive in the summer of 1916 and had supported General Kornilov in his abortive efforts to bring back discipline into the disorganised Russian Army. Whether he and his diehards would succeed in subduing the mobs under their ringleader Lenin was a difficult question, for the doctrines of Communism had already gained enormous support from both the military and civilian population, the working-classes and the peasant communities. Kaledin had already taken Voronezh, a town in Central Russia, and was moving steadily northwards.

Hearing that I was on my way to Moscow, my fellow passengers began to advise me not to go. Kiyev, too, they said, was in turmoil and firing could be heard day and night. In the evening, our train was brought to a halt at Vinnitsa, where the line was said to have been sabotaged. After some twenty minutes, we moved slowly onwards. As we approached the ancient Ukrainian capital, we could hear faint rifle-fire.

We arrived in Kiyev just before 9 p.m. A strong, cold wind was blowing: the city was in the grip of winter. I said goodbye to Kazimir, who had now reached his destination, wished him well and told him that I should never mention the fact that he had 'slept' so long and profoundly. I went straight to the old *Zemski* offices in Alexandrovskaya *Ulitsa* [Street], but found that the site was now occupied by a Ukrainian theatre. At last, in Vladimir-skaya No. 19, I found the offices and was able to talk with the head doctor. He very kindly saw to it that my papers were in order and took me to dine with him at a friend's house, near the station. There was no time to venture into the city and, as he affirmed, it was best to keep away. Now and then there was some light spasmodic firing; otherwise everything seemed very quiet. The doctor accompanied me to the station and arranged with a porter to help me and my bag safely into the train, which was due to leave at 11 p.m.

The Moscow train was already full to overflowing. I poked my head in an open window and met the curious gaze of many eyes. 'Listen,' I said, 'I have to go to Moscow. If you will let me in, I promise not to inconvenience you in any way.' They nodded their heads but made no movement. 'It is impossible to enter by the steps; so many soldiers are clinging to them. I must come through the window,' I told them. Again they nodded their heads, but again no movement was made. I turned to my porter and gesticulating towards the window said loudly: 'Lift me up and push me through.' The miraculous happened! I sprawled through, pushed from behind and pulled from in front. It was not a dignified posture for a Red Cross Sister, but I was *in the train bound for Moscow!* My bag and plaid were thrown in after me. I gave the porter two roubles, four whole shillings! He beamed at me. I beamed at him. He deserved it, for it is not every day that a Ukrainian porter has to lift an eight-stone English Red Cross nurse and push her bodily through a train window!

I managed to scramble through legs and knees into the corridor; it was choc-a-bloc with passengers. A man in the coupé touched my arm and pointed to his seat. I shook my head. An officer in the next coupé saw me struggling and offered me his, but I would not accept it. I had promised not to inconvenience anybody. It was very cold in the corridor, despite the throng, and a great draught was blowing down from the roof.

At last, at a small wayside station, a man got out of the coupé behind me. I slipped into his place – only just in time! Oh! how good it was to sit down! I was dead tired, but things were working out well and I was deeply grateful. I clasped my hands and, in my heart, said 'Thank you, God!' The train was moving slowly through the night, slowing up and stopping often, as though suspicious of something, or somebody, on the line.

Thursday, 9th November

Two women in my coupé intended to push their way through to the lavatory. I asked if I might go with them. We made our way inch by inch to the end of the carriage. There was, of course, a queue waiting, mostly soldiers, and many disagreeable remarks were heard. The fact that I was in Red Cross uniform seemed to make me a special target for criticism. I made up my mind never to walk the length of that corridor again.

Friday, 10th November. Moscow

We steamed slowly into Moscow about 4 in the afternoon. There was a rush to descend: the soldiers were shouting, pushing, jostling each other. The platform was full of people, military and civilian: bustling and hustling, colliding with each other, gesticulating excitedly. I had expected to see armed guards parading up and down but there was none to be seen until I reached the exit. There stood some twenty of them – the men whom they called *Bolsheviki*. I looked at them critically: to me they looked exactly like any other soldiers, only they were not lolling about, with drooping shoulders and bored expressions. They were erect, with determined faces and keen eyes always on the alert; they held guns in their hands and daggers, in leather pouches, were suspended from their belts. A broad, red band was attached to their left uniform-sleeve. They barred the way, demanding the permit or pass.

They treated the soldiers lightly, sometimes even with a friendly word. But the civilian travellers' tickets and passes were carefully scrutinised, their addresses noted, and certain information written into a large book. When it was my turn, I showed them my documents, ticket and permit. The guard took them to a uniformed man at a table. He examined them meticulously and noted down the particulars in his book. 'Was I returning to the Front?' 'Yes, in a week or ten days' time.' 'Where was I staying in Moscow?' I gave the name of my friends and the number of their house in the Plushchika Ulitsa. 'Of whom did the family consist?' I told them that it was a widowed lady with two daughters. The guards were civil enough; they returned my papers and told me that, on the morrow, I must be sure to register with the police. I was allowed to pass into the street: I found a white world, still and motionless.

I stood for a minute or two, trying to collect my thoughts. So I

was in Moscow! I had arrived! But where was all the noise and
rioting I had been led to expect? It was all so quiet. The light
was beginning to fail. I must make my way quickly before darkness
fell. I saw a boy standing near the station door and asked if he
would carry my bag to Plushchika for three roubles. There were
no trams running, so there was no alternative but to walk the
snowy streets. It was very cold and I was glad of the walk to
restore circulation in my legs. The boy chattered incessantly.
There had been great fights in the streets, he said. Men had made
ambushes and fired at each other. He had seen men and soldiers
lying dead in the streets; they must have been dead, for a cart
had come later and collected them. There had been a kind of
funeral that very day of some Red Guards who had been killed.
They didn't bury them in churchyards now, and they didn't need
priests any more. Sometimes the guns made such a noise that he
was frightened to go out. All was very quiet now, but he had heard
that on the 12th, in two days' time, there would be a great battle
and, of course, many people would be killed. He had made up his
mind not to go out-of-doors that day.

I was taking it all in as best I could, for a dreadful feeling of
lassitude was creeping over me. If there was indeed to be a great
battle in two days' time, I should be with my friends, my Russian
'family'; we would keep each other good company. As we passed
into the Plushchika, we met a lady and two men: the first people I
had seen since leaving the station. The boy recognised the street
and said that a great battle had already taken place in it some days
ago. Many of the window-panes were shattered and one could see
where bullets had bespattered the walls and doors of private
houses.

We reached the house. I gave the boy three roubles. He was
jubilant. 'If I can't get any bread, I can buy potatoes,' he said
brightly. I noticed his pinched, young face, blue and red with the
cold, and gave him an extra rouble to get some hot tea.

I walked up the stairs and waited a few minutes before knocking
at the door. My heart was palpitating quickly and I could hear my
breath coming in little sharp gasps. I must control myself. I
breathed hard and deeply; that was better. . . . Then I knocked.
Soon a voice from within asked: '*Kto tam?* [Who is there?]' 'A
friend!' A chain was slipped back and a key turned. The door
opened. Nadya stood there! Her cry of surprise and joy brought

Anna Ivanovna and Asya into the hall. *'Floscenka! Dorogáya moyá! Moyá dorogáya! Moyá rodnáya!'* They asked: 'All this long, long way! *How* did you come?' I said lamely: 'I don't know. I . . . just came.'

They led me into the sitting-room and placed me in an armchair near the fire. Asya and Nadya took off my coat and boots. I leant back in the chair and closed my eyes. I wanted to cry, for sheer joy – so great was the happiness within me – but I was too tired to shed tears. Ah! it was good to be with those I loved, with those who loved me. Asya and Nadya asked me questions. I tried to answer, but my head was swimming. Anna Ivanovna rebuked them. 'Don't talk, Floscenka,' she said. 'Just rest. You are at home now!'

The following day, after a wonderful night's sleep, I felt rested and supremely happy. Anna Ivanovna had said last night: 'Tomorrow there will be time to hear all her news and to tell ours.' But first they brought me a packet of letters from England. Anna Ivanovna had feared to entrust them to any chance acquaintance travelling towards the southern front, and posting them to me was out of the question. I knew that several letters had never reached me. I revelled in my home news. Everything seemed to be going fairly well with my family. Food was rationed, but our large garden continued to provide its usual crops of fruit and vegetables. So all was well and I was deeply thankful.

I related how it had taken just seven days to reach Moscow from Ober Pertesti in Roumania; as to details, I promised that, after writing them down coherently in my diary, I would read them aloud. . . . Meanwhile, I was most anxious to hear their news. Asya and Nadya had much to tell, but before it was told I had read in their faces that it was ill tidings. Kolya, Nadya's cousin and fiancé, had been killed in the Bukovina. Asya's friend had been posted missing in Mogilev. These were tragic happenings for my young friends. I felt deeply for them both in their grief. But they were both so young; life would, please God, still hold much happiness for them.

I did not forget to visit the military police. The former civil police of Imperial Russia had, naturally, disappeared. In their place were uniformed *Bolsheviki*, morose and stern, the red armband indicating their allegiance to Lenin's dictatorship. They asked many questions and told me that I must advise them in good time of my departure, in order to get the police pass without which I should not be allowed to leave the city.

It was wonderful to sit quietly and chat with my dear friends. They told me that since the dreadful July uprising in Petrograd, things had never been the same in Moscow. It was true that Kerensky had subdued the revolt, and many people were even convinced that Lenin had been killed and that a new era of peace and prosperity was about to begin. But Lenin's doctrines had infected soldiers, workers and peasants to such a degree that they, ignorant of the true meaning and aims of the *Bolsheviki*, had declared they would follow him through thick and thin.

There had been days in Moscow, I was told, when it had not only been dangerous to walk in the street, but even to remain quietly at home. And there had been nights when no one dared sleep, for fear of the mobs which paraded the streets after dark, plundering private homes and public buildings, as their fancy led them. Yes, there had been both fighting and firing in the Plushchika about a week previously; even the *dvornik* [yard-man] had begged leave to take shelter in the house. Anna Ivanovna said: 'I am often thankful that Pasha died so peacefully in his own home, knowing nothing of the terrible conditions which exist today. He loved Moscow so much that he would have been heartbroken to see it in this desperate state. And, being so outspoken, he would have called them to account; and we have had proof that to censure these lawless rioters would be to court death.'

Word of my arrival was sent to friends and some came to greet me and hear news of the operations on the Roumanian Front. The doctor and his wife whom we had met in the Crimea gave me a warm welcome. The first thing they noticed was my hair, for they remembered my bald head, shaven after my illness. It was already about 4 inches long and, I was pleased to note, had a slight kink at the ends. Before, it had stood straight up on my head like bristles!

Another visitor was Vladimir Nikolayevich, Dr Usov's colleague. He, I remembered, had foretold a great upheaval in Russia. Now the twinkle of merriment had gone from his eyes. Asya whispered that his eldest son, Volodya, had been killed during the defence of Riga.

Anna Ivanovna said she had not heard for weeks from her relatives in Petrograd, for no news was allowed out. But it had leaked through that the capital was at the mercy of the *Bolsheviki*. I begged Vladimir Nikolayevich to tell us all that he knew. He replied that Lenin's second attempt at a *coup d'état* had succeeded beyond his wildest hopes. In July, in some mysterious way, he had managed to escape from the Government troops; but he had turned up again, and had overthrown the Provisional Government.

I asked whether the revolution had started in Petrograd, but Vladimir Nikolayevich replied that it originally started in Kronstadt, the fortress on the Island of Kotlin, near the mouth of the Neva, connected with Petrograd by a canal. Some sailors mutinied, killed their officers, and took command of their ship. The mutiny spread and soon the fleet was in the hands of the *Bolsheviki*. It was one of these ships, manned by mutineers, which had steamed up the Neva to Petrograd, enabling its crew, aided by revolutionary soldiers, to assault the Winter Palace, arrest the ministers and overthrow the Kerensky Government. Lenin then set up his own government, composed of his chosen commissaries, and proclaimed himself head of the Proletarian Communist State of Russia.

'And Kerensky?' I asked. 'It may be that he is in hiding, biding his time until the moment is ripe for him to defy the commissaries of Bolshevism. If he is still alive, he will not leave his country in the lurch.'

'And the imperial family?' While living at Tsarskoe Selo, they had been well guarded, but, noting the ever-increasing unrest in and around the capital, Kerensky had decided to arrange their departure to a quieter, safer spot. Rumour had it that they had been sent to Tobolsk in Siberia. I was astounded! Siberia! The very name conjured up monstrous hardship and misery. It was the Land of Exile, where banishment implied the renunciation of all one's hopes. I thought of Livadia, the exquisite summer residence in the Crimea. It was a far step from the Crimea to Siberia.

During my second night in Moscow, firing was heard more than once, sometimes in the southern part of the city, at other times, in the eastern. I mentioned the boy's warning to Anna Ivanovna; she did not laugh at it. She did say that it might be advisable not to leave the house. Food, although meagre, would be sufficient for two days. Shortly before my arrival a small sack of potatoes had been brought to her by one of the older men who had worked at her country house.

I enquired whether it was still being looked after in her absence. She answered that the property was no longer hers, that the house had been confiscated by the peasants of the vicinity and she would probably never see it again. She and the girls had spent two weeks there in the summer, but they had not enjoyed it; they could sense the unrest and discontent of the country people. Her own staff were not impolite, but one or two tasks which she had asked them to do in the garden had been left undone. Rather than face flagrant disobedience, she had overlooked such small *pustyaki* [trifles]. The caretaker and his wife, the cook, had left in the early autumn. Ivan the gardener and his wife were now occupying the house, and Anna Ivanovna had heard that Vasiliy was still the woodman. Vasiliy was the most grotesque little peasant I had ever seen, misshapen and hairy; we had called him the ape-man. All the logs now in the back-yard had been sawn by Vasiliy. I could picture him, ambling along in his old peaked cap, down-at-heel high boots and leather apron. His wife Dasha, an excellent washer-woman, was but a poor specimen of a country peasant; her face, small and pale, was pitted heavily with smallpox scars. Every year she was pregnant and her expression indicated both suffering and resentment. Only once did I see three of their surviving children. It was high summer and the small, brown urchins were chasing each other round the silver birches; with the exception of one small garment, they were in their birthday suits, and looked like tiny wild woodland gnomes. The doctor and Anna Ivanovna had been kindness itself to all the peasants. Vasiliy, Dasha and family had been given their own small hut and all their food.

The 'great battle' has not taken place; but stores have been looted, some were fired, and brawling has continued for many hours. Soldiers finally dispersed the rioters. It was a strange, bewildering situation: the rabble looted in the name of Bolshevism; the soldiers were *Bolsheviki* and fired at the rabble!

Lenin is playing a double game. He is preparing to open negotia-tions with Germany and Austria, but at the same time that he seeks to disarm the Russian soldiers at the Front Lines, he plans to rearm those same soldiers and to incite them to fight against their own compatriots. He is prepared to betray his own country, in order to further his own ends. So he has instigated a new system of terror and established councils and committees to suppress all political liberties.

So Russia has, within eight months, suffered two explosive revolutions. There was the political revolution of last March, which brought about the abdication of the Tsar and the formation of the Provisional Government under Prince Lvov and Alexander Kerensky; and the military revolution at the end of October, when Kerensky's Cabinet was overthrown by Lenin, Trotsky and their *Bolshevik* supporters – mainly mutinous sailors and soldiers. The old saying comes to my mind: it must get worse before it is better. It is certainly getting worse. We have heard that the German Armies are about to march towards Petrograd, and that Lenin and Trotsky are intent on devising hasty peace plans with them. Further south, thousands of deserting soldiers are handing over wide areas of Russian territory to the Austro-German forces. So news is bad from all Fronts except the Roumanian Front – my Front!

One morning, a note was brought to Asya from some friends. It was an invitation to a small, private party-dance, arranged to celebrate the coming-of-age of the daughter of the family. Asya was not keen to go, but did not like to refuse; she asked me to go with her and the thought of a gay evening with music and dancing filled me with delight. She offered to lend me one of her evening-dresses and we went to look at them. She chose a white one, with simple bodice and long, frilled skirt. It was new and had been made for her during the summer, before she had heard that her friend in Mogilev was missing. I chose a pale blue muslin frock, which was most dainty and fitted me well. . . . Asya had her moments of deep sadness. I grieved so much for her, but I hoped that the gaiety of a small family party would lighten the burden of her sorrowful thoughts.

It was in the afternoon of the day of the party that Asya entered the room where I was reading and came and sat at my side. She said: 'I can't go. It is impossible. I cannot. Really, I cannot!' I looked at her with surprise and disappointment. 'Don't be angry with me,' she whispered. 'But I cannot. Something is weighing too heavily on my heart.' At first, I tried to coax her, then I rebuked her for changing her mind at the last moment. It was very unkind of me, but I really felt that she should have kept to our arrangement. 'I shall not go without you,' I said in a peeved voice. 'Oh!

but you must! They will come for you. You *must* go. I beg you,
please go!'

I went and I wore Asya's new white frock; she insisted on it.
. . . I loved the party; for a brief time, one forgot all sadness, all
disaster, all suffering. The lights, the laughter, the music, were
so infectious. Now and then, my thoughts flew to Asya; she
would surely have enjoyed these light-hearted hours. Unconsciously, I began to reproach her for her ill-timed decision. I
would describe it all to her in detail and then she might be a little
sorry that she had missed so much that was enjoyable. When I
returned, I went to Asya's bedroom, as I had promised. She
was awake and sat up in bed. I had intended to tell all about the
joyful occasion, but when I saw her face, I stopped. Her face
was very white and her large eyes were full of a great sorrow. . . .
'Floscenka,' she whispered, 'forgive me, dear. I could not go and
enjoy myself while my country is suffering so deeply.' I looked at
her and saw the suffering in her face. A sudden revulsion of feeling
came over me; I saw it all now in its true light. She was a wounded
'soldier' too; wounded to the quick – bearing all the sorrows of her
afflicted country in her young heart. And I . . . I had been so
thoughtless and selfish; a sense of deep shame came over me. I
knew then that I should always – all my life – regret that I had
given way to my own selfish wishes and sought my own selfish
pleasure. . . . I put my arms round her. . . . 'Forgive me,' I cried.
'Forgive me! It is *I* who must beg *your* forgiveness!'

The days pass quietly enough in the comfortable Plushchika
home, but one's mind is never at peace. We are always aware that,
in the world outside, tyranny and suffering reign. Food is terribly
scarce; bread cards have been allotted to those 'worthy' to receive
them; but the bread is poor and often contains foreign bodies.
Sometimes the supplies run out and two potatoes are given instead.
Black markets are coming into existence. It is a sad sight to see
some of the food-seekers: among them are gentlewomen, often
disguised as peasants, a thick scarf round their heads, bringing a
family heirloom, a piece of jewellery, anything of value to exchange
for bread, cereals, potatoes.

On the eighth day of my stay I went to the police commissioners
for my permit for the journey back to Roumania. The police
hummed and hawed, said they would look into the matter and

told me to come again on the 10th. I told them it was quite essential that I should return and showed them all my papers and passes. They noticed the one given to me by the military commandant on the station of Botushany, entitling me to a month's furlough. 'There is no hurry,' they said. 'Perhaps in a month's time, your Red Cross unit will have ceased to exist.' I returned and told my friends. They begged me not to get upset. 'You are at home here,' they assured me. 'You must stay as long as you can.' But it was not that I wanted to leave them; I felt that I belonged to my Red Cross unit, and that, if disbandment were in store for the 10th *Otryad*, I must be there.

The war against intellectuals which began in Petrograd is now threatening to sweep over Moscow. Men and women of good families are being forced from their homes and compelled to do the most menial tasks, such as selling Bolshevist newspapers in the streets or pasting Bolshevist posters on to walls. As an old friend of the Usovs aptly put it: 'The *Bolsheviki* are trying to pull the cultured classes of Russia down to the level of the uncultured, but they will never succeed in raising the uncultured to the level of the cultured.'

From the very beginning of their régime, the *Bolsheviki* decried religion; soon they were threatening to abolish it completely and crush all those who upheld it. 'Religion is the opium of the people' was one of the many Marxian slogans emblazoned on posters and placards. Anna Ivanovna said how bewildered some of the old country-folk had been when they heard that the Tsar had abdicated and that the revolutionary forces had announced their intention to persecute the Churches. One old peasant woman exclaimed with a gesture of despair: 'If *Batyushka* Tsar can go, then *Batyushka* God can go!' But another country *baba* had cried scornfully: '*Batyushka* God cannot go; He too powerful; they persecute Him; all is same; *He* remain.'

Portraits of Lenin have begun to appear in public squares, adorned with red ribbons, while the Red Flag of Free Russia, bearing the words '*Svoboda! Ravenstvo! Bratstvo!* [Liberty! Equality! Fraternity!]', has been erected on important buildings. The *Bolsheviki* are sending out innumerable manifestoes and pamphlets. A few have come into my possession, too long-winded to translate into my diary. Their message, always couched in most inflammatory language, urges the 'free men' of the New Proletarian State to assist in the destruction of capitalism, to uphold the peace negotiations and to safeguard the Revolution by taking up arms against all those 'bourgeois' forces which seek to destroy their lawful rights.

The *Bolsheviki* are forming councils, committees, sub-committees, courts, leagues, parties, societies; they are talented talkers and gifted orators. The masses of the people flock to their call. Already they have established the nucleus of the Proletarian Republic and drawn up their political programme; and, what is more surprising, they have successfully organised the Red Army – in great part drawn from the disloyal soldiers of the Imperial Army. One and all wage war against the 'intelligentsia' and the 'bourgeoisie' – nicknames given to the educated people and to the middle-class or 'idle rich'. There is no doubt that Lenin and Trotsky are intent on exterminating the Russian intellectual classes.

Some half dozen times I approached the police commissioners for my permit; each time they told me either that no trains were running, or that it was not yet my turn. Then one morning the police informed me that they would give me a permit for the journey on 29th November, as far as Kiyev; but there I must obtain another permit to continue to Roumania. I am always careful to wear my nurse's uniform whenever I go to their office, for I feel that, despite their dislike of the middle and upper classes, they must have a certain amount of respect for the medical profession. After all, hospitals are essential even in a proletarian world. On 28th November I went for the last time and received my permit and a stamped document entitling me as a Red Cross nurse to travel without hindrance. When I left their office, I thanked them for their help and advice; they actually wished me a safe journey!

28th November

Tonight, my last evening, I sat with my Russian 'family' and we talked long and seriously about many things. They made me promise to come back to my Moscow home if I found things too difficult at the Front. As we chatted together, the sure feeling that we belonged to each other was strong within me; it was a glorious, comforting feeling. I told them that, without their love and friendship, I should have been lost in Russia; I also told them that, no matter what life had in store for me, no matter where my wandering feet would lead me, I should always remember them with love and gratitude, and that I should always thank God for guiding me to them. . . .

29th November. Back to Botushany

I parted with my family soon after 10 a.m. I showed Anna Ivanovna the tiny cross and icon which she had placed round my neck in March 1915, and which I had always worn. Once again she blessed me and whispered the mother's prayer for the departing soldier over my bowed head. Masha, the maid, accompanied me, but left me before we reached the station entrance; she did not wish to come into contact with the Red Guards. I took care to buy a ticket this time. Red Guards seemed to be everywhere – at the entrance, near the ticket office, outside the door of the station commissary, on the platforms. My police permit and stamped document seemed to satisfy them. I found a seat, and the train left at midday for Kiyev.

My train journey lasted one week.

. . . A Ukrainian on his way to Mogilev told some fellow passengers that the Ukraine had been declared a separate republic and was anxious to establish itself as an independent state. At Yassy I heard that my *Letuchka* was still stationed at Ober Pertesti, although some of its members were temporarily in Botushany. That, too, was good news, for I knew that I should have to spend the night in Botushany. A *Zemski* official gave me the address.

It was a good half-hour's walk to the address I had been given. I enjoyed the exercise after the week in the train. A woman came to the door and said there was no room and I must look for other accommodation. I told her that it was only for one night and that her present lodgers were members of my Red Cross unit.

With ill grace she allowed me in. When darkness fell, I told her I was tired and wished to go to bed. She said that she had no bed to give me, but I could share one with two of her children. I was not too pleased, but there was no alternative. I had hoped to see my colleagues to arrange an early drive to Ober Pertesti, but the woman said they might return very late. I had a few small biscuits so I gave one to each of the children. They were delighted and when bedtime came they all three wanted to sleep with me! There was not room for three, but the two smallest cuddled up to me on either side. The tiny boy was restless, tossing and scratching his matted curly head. I guessed that he had head-lice!

Suddenly I became aware that somebody was singing in the next room; a raucous voice interspersed with giant hiccups. My first thought was that some drunken soldiers had taken the room which had been let to the members of my *Letuchka*. Above the discordant sounds came a hoarse shout: 'Stop it, Ivan Ivanovich. Stop it, I tell you!' The voice made answer: 'Yuri Vasiliyevich, what do you want of me? Can't you leave me in peace to enjoy myself?' Then I knew the truth. The drunken men next door were members of my Red Cross unit.

I shivered as I lay and listened to those drunken voices. What would happen if they decided to roam the house and enter the room where we were sleeping? The even breathing of the woman and child in the next bed to mine told me that they were still asleep. The noise had not awakened our hostess; perhaps she was accustomed to it. What had come over these men? Never had they shown any inclination to drink while they were in the *Letuchka*. I made up my mind that I would get up early in the morning and go straight to the *Zemski Sklad*; they would arrange some sort of conveyance to take me back to Ober Pertesti.

7th December. Ober Pertesti
It was daylight; the children were still asleep. The woman gave me a bowl of *mamaliga*; I ate it quickly, but without appetite. I explained where I was going and told her that I would return for my bag and plaid. . . .

It was bitterly cold in the street and the snow was frozen hard. The *Sklad* had just opened at 8 a.m.; the supervisor very kindly offered to send me to Ober Pertesti in a small one-horse van, at any hour convenient to me.

I walked into the dining-room of our *Letuchka* just before the midday meal. It was a joyful moment. '*Zdrastvuitye! Moye druziya!* [Good day to you, my friends!]' I called out. And then I caught sight of a familiar figure! 'Mamasha!' I cried. 'You here?' And we were in each other's arms – a real bear-hug! Then it was the turn of all the others. That, too, was a wonderful home-coming. I was back with my *Letuchka* in Roumania!

I sat down to dinner with them. It was, as usual, just maize soup and maize porridge. Between mouthfuls, I answered question after question about life in Moscow. No one mentioned our colleagues in Botushany and I was determined not to divulge what I had heard last night. Alongside Mamasha was a stranger – a new woman doctor. She was a Jewess, and known to everybody as Doctor Rakhil. She had a strong, good face, high cheek-bones and merry dark eyes. She came from Odessa, where she had left her doctor-husband engrossed in his private practice and in supervising several hospitals.

In the afternoon I began to unpack. Where were my new boots? Where the new woollen vests and the thick new gloves? But they *were* there last night! So my Roumanian hostess . . .? I was thankful to note that the new boxes of photographic plates were untouched. Only the new articles just purchased in Moscow were missing. My hostess had been both discerning and practical.

There were only one or two wounded in our *lazaret*; the cold weather had ended our military operations temporarily. I spent most of the afternoon chatting with Mamasha; after her long absence, she had much to relate. She had met many *Bolsheviki*; at first she had called them traitors and had given them a piece of her mind, but a cousin of hers who shared her views and was similarly outspoken had one day been arrested and imprisoned as a counter-revolutionary. Not wishing to share the same fate she had decided that in the circumstances it was wiser to keep a still tongue in her head!

Mamasha had been in Ober Pertesti just a week, but that was sufficient time to realise that the Roumanian Front was in a most precarious position, and that the Russian soldiers were being slowly infected with the *disease* – as she put it – of Bolshevism, and might at any moment leave their allies in the lurch and make off to Russia. 'But, Mamasha,' I asked, 'what would happen to the Roumanians?' She shrugged her shoulders. 'They would be forced to capitulate.' 'And what would happen to our Red Cross unit?' 'It would be disbanded and we should have to fend for ourselves as best we could.' 'And then what would our allies do?' Mamasha said sternly: 'I consider that it would be *their own fault*. They have seen the obstacles which Russia has been up against during the last year and never once have they thought of intervening on our behalf.' 'But, Mamasha,' I cried. 'They have their own problems. Think of the colossal strength of the German forces on that wide extent of Front, think of . . .' 'Yes! Yes!' she interrupted. 'I have thought, and I do know that in the first two years of war it was the Russian Army and the Russian Army alone which prevented both France and England from sustaining defeat. And as for your wide Front, take your map and study the stretch of land which Russia had to defend.' She told me that a German aviator who had been taken prisoner was asked, during examination, what he thought of his allies – the Austrians and Turks, and of what they had done for the German military cause. He had answered: 'I think that, before asking me such a question, you should tell me what *your allies* have done for you.'

I had sent for the luggage I had left in our baggage van. A hold-all was missing. The van-driver and I searched for it, but it was not to be found. I called on Viktor Viktorovich, the transport officer. He wasted no time: 'It must have been stolen,' he said. 'Stolen?' I cried. 'Are things getting stolen in our *Letuchka*?' 'You would be surprised if you knew how many things disappear almost daily,' he answered nonchalantly. My high boots, leather breeches, thick woollen scarf and gloves were in that bag, so I did not intend to part with it without a fight. I went in search of Smirnov. He promised to go and look for it himself. When he came back his face was very serious. '*Sestritsa*, I regret to tell you that your hold-all has not been found. You may not have heard that, while you were away, a dozen or more soldiers of our *Letuchka* left us without permission; in other words, they deserted. They took with them several things which belonged to other members of our unit. I am afraid that your hold-all must have been among them.' 'Is it possible that some of our own men have deserted?' I asked incredulously. 'It is true, and there is nothing we can do about it.' 'Has Bolshevism come to Ober Pertesti?' 'Not yet,' he said, but I could sense that he knew it was on the way.

Are our soldiers going mad? A dreadful tragedy has taken place. I heard a commotion in the road and saw a Roumanian peasant carrying a small child, followed by a dozen men and women gesticulating and shouting. The peasant came in and, seeing me, stretched out his arms, holding the limp figure of the child. I looked at the small, white face, and realised at once the child was dead. We laid him on a bed. I saw a large blood-stained patch on the left side of his shirt. I told the orderly to fetch the head doctor, and he heard the distracted man's story. The father and son had been on the hillside above their village, collecting sticks. Some soldiers were encamped in the valley below. The father heard a rifle-report and the swift whistle of a bullet; then the child had given a loud cry and fallen to the ground. The boy had been shot by a Russian soldier.

Our doctor was furious; he ordered his horse and set off to interview the commander of the regiment stationed in the valley. The sympathising companions were told to leave; they left obediently, the men still gesticulating, the women weeping.

I enlisted the services of Smirnov; he ordered a small coffin to be made without delay. In the evening, we laid the little lad into it and tucked the long shirt and sleeves securely round the childish form. The serenity which only death can impart was stamped on the sweet baby-face.

In the morning the father will come for him and the funeral will take place in the little Roumanian church.

At dinner the doctor told us that it was unquestionably a soldier who had fired the fatal shot. The soldiers admitted that, sometimes, they did take one or two pot-shots at a sheep or goat on the hills around; but they stoutly refuted the suggestion that they had fired a random shot at a shepherd-boy. The doctor was ill at ease: we knew that he knew that the shot had been fired on purpose – for sport! The Russian soldiers have become very callous; they have for some time regarded the Roumanians as passive foes and are insensible to any pain or discomfort they might cause them. We have heard of cases where soldiers, brutalised by drink, have inflicted bodily harm on Roumanian men and women.

10th December

News was brought by a *Zemski* official from Yassy that civil war has commenced in real earnest. The *Bolsheviki* in Petrograd and Moscow have proclaimed that all aristocratic, wealthy, cultured, religious and educated people are to be classed as *bourgeoisie* and denounced as enemies of the New Proletarian State of Russia. If they show resistance to the laws laid down by the *Bolsheviki*, they will be considered counter-revolutionaries and their lives forfeited.

A meeting took place in our *Letuchka* that evening, at which all our medical and surgical members were required to be present. Our head doctor addressed us. Bolshevism, hand-in-hand with

Communism, he said, was sweeping southwards and swallowing up all who dared to defy its passage. The situation on our Front was a highly dangerous one; that same afternoon some regiments of Russian soldiers, after killing their officers, had left their trenches open to the enemy and crossed the frontier into Russia.

We listened, speechless with dismay and sick at heart. There was no doubt that our days in Roumania were numbered. Our doctor pointed out that we must be prepared for the worst; he begged us to remain calm and, if called upon suddenly to leave Roumania, to endeavour to keep together; to *keep together*, he repeated, at all costs. We would try to reach Kiyev. He could not tell when the final orders to disband would come, but meanwhile we were to be prepared. . . . He was a strong man, compassionate and understanding, but we could see from his set face and distraught manner that sorrow was weighing heavily on his heart.

We have been thinking well and deeply about the situation and the longer that we ponder over it the more grievous does it become. So, Bolshevism is slowly sweeping southwards, engulfing towns and villages *and* the *bourgeoisie* in its path. We, on the Roumanian Front, have so far been unmolested, but, now, we will have to be always on the alert, for traitors are lurking in every corner and civil war is about to descend upon us. It is clear that, at the present time, the danger does not lie with the Austro-German enemy, but with the Russian proletariat. Our enemies must know of the precarious state of affairs ruling in Russia, for they have made no attempt to attack our men and on the Front Line not a single rifle-shot has been heard. The war and the horrors of warfare are completely eclipsed by those other more hideous horrors of the savage civil war raging in the heart of Russia. A one-sided civil war, as it were, for the opponents of Bolshevism, being now in the minority and unarmed, are powerless to resist.

16th December, 1917. Odessa
How can I describe all that has happened in these last tragic days? I feel as though I have been caught up in a mighty whirlpool, battered, buffeted, and yet. . . . I am still myself, still able to walk, talk, eat and sleep. It is astounding how much a human being can endure without any outward sign of having been broken up into pieces.

I must try to remember the principal events of these last six days, for in a strange way they have provided the finishing touch to my life as a Red Cross nurse with the Russian Army.

On the day following the meeting in our *Letuchka* we heard that both Petrograd and Moscow were seething with crime. Rioting, now a daily occurrence, had taken a more dangerous form, for the mobs were attacking the homes of the *bourgeoisie,* confiscating their possessions, arresting the owners and shooting all who resisted them. No one was safe. Entire families had fallen before the blind fury of the Marxist fanatics. Kiyev, the beautiful old capital of the Ukraine, had fallen and the wave of Bolshevism was approaching our Front. It came and engulfed it. The trenches were emptied of Russian soldiers; the Roumanians were left to carry on the war as best they could.

After completely disrupting the Roumanian Front, Bolshevism sped onwards, enveloped Odessa, the Crimea, Sebastopol and other Black Sea ports. The whole of Russia was then at the mercy of the Communist Proletariat.

It was 12th December. We were hourly expecting orders, but none had arrived. We had little to fear from the war; our Front Line, being half-emptied, was quiet. The Austr. a troops were still docile, realising undoubtedly that with the coming of the Bolshevist régime the Russian Regular Army had ceased to exist and the Russian territory lay before them – theirs for the taking! When discussing the insubordination of the so-called fighting-men, the name of Kerensky was continually cropping up; all his great achievements on behalf of his country seemed to have been forgotten – only his lamentable mistakes were remembered. He it was who had insisted on closer comradeship among army ranks and less rigorous army discipline. Alas! that *one* mistake of a great and just man can stamp with indelible blemish his whole character!

When a soldier, conversing with his superior officer, omitted the salute; when he strutted before him with hands in his pockets and a cigarette between his lips, it was easy to guess that chaos must follow. A general, who had been visiting some regiments in our vicinity, had been shot dead by his orderly only the previous morning. It was said that the general called for his high boots; the orderly threw them at him. The general struck the orderly; the orderly shot the general dead. The news spread like lightning. Officers were openly defied by their men and there was no power to support them or protect them. Many were shot. Finally the soldiers, or *tovarishchi* [comrades] as they now call themselves, refused categorically to take any orders and, leaving their trenches, roamed the countryside at will. Theft and pillage were the order of the day. We heard all this with sinking hearts and we were powerless to act. So far, the Red Cross personnel had always been respected and unharmed, but whispers had reached us of units attacked, doctors shot and nurses assaulted.

On 13th December, orders reached us at last – none too soon. We were instructed to leave Ober Pertesti without delay and make our way to Moscow *as best we could*. Our rank and file had already left, taking with them anything which might be of use. Several of our orderlies had disappeared, too. Our doctors made us memorise the addresses of two centres in Moscow where we might meet again, if and when we managed to arrive.

There were warm farewells. It was a momentous occasion. We who had shared the tribulations of three long years of active service on the Russian Fronts were about to part, and in our heavy hearts we nursed the dread feeling that our work had been *all in vain.* . . . In the eyes of more than one Sister there were tell-tale tears. Our doctors and some of our Brothers who were riding could not accompany us; but two Brothers and Sandy, the liaison officer, were to follow us on horseback and see that we arrived safely at Yassy railway station.

The few orderlies who remained came with Smirnov to bid us safe journey; they had been so kind and helpful. What could one say at parting to a man like Smirnov? He looked dreadfully tired and ill. I took his hard, bony hand in both mine. 'Smirnov,' I said, 'God will reward you for your goodness and loyalty. If I return safely to my country, I shall always remember you with affection and gratitude.' He bowed, saluted, bowed again, and bade us farewell; his white, tired face retreated into the background. I was glad to think that his happy home was not far away and that his garden always produced such excellent crops.

Our Tatar drivers were likewise most faithful. Two of the older men had been chosen to drive the vans in which we four Sisters, Mamasha and Doctor Rakhil were to journey to Yassy. Difficulties beset us from the beginning: our luggage-van had gone on already with other vehicles of our *oboz*. Mamasha had told the orderly-in-charge to leave her bag with her rug behind, but, in the confusion, he must have forgotten, for we could not find it and Mamasha was badly needing extra warmth. We gave one last look at Ober Pertesti, and then set off along the narrow track which led towards the main road. It was bitterly cold and there were snow-drifts heaped on either side of the track. The main road was massed with soldiers and vehicles. We were thankful that our hooded vans hid us from view. At night we stopped in Botushany, where we succeeded in finding a hay-barn. Our three mounted escorts rode off to the *sklad*, where they hoped to tether their horses for the night.

That night not one of us slept; we were very cold and we were afraid. All around us were drunken, unruly men, drunken with freedom as well as with alcohol. Bands of them were passing through Botushany after dark; shouting, singing, swearing their way past our hiding-place – yes, hiding-place. It had come to that: we had to hide, because we were afraid of our *own* soldiers. As they passed, we would hold our breath and speak in whispers; a sharp tap from Mamasha now and then would remind us that even a whisper was too loud. And more than once, during that black, dreadful night, we heard a peasant-woman's shrill, desperate cry for help.

Soon after daybreak, one of the Brothers appeared and told us that our horses had been stolen. The *sklad* was shut and most of its equipment had been confiscated by the deserting soldiers. He suggested that we should start on foot and, if they found the horses, they would do their best to catch up with us. . . . So we had to walk; there was no alternative. Anna and I each took an arm of Mamasha; behind us came Doctor Rakhil, with Sofiya and Ekaterina. Slowly we made our way over the half-frozen, slippery roads. Vehicles of every description were trundling along, packed high with sacks and soldiers. Other soldiers, rough and ill-mannered, were pushing past us, jostling each other, intent only on making headway eastwards.

For the most part, they were rude and insolent; but even among those jeering, scoffing crowds, there were men whose simple, homely faces expressed dismay and disgust at the blustering behaviour of their fellows. . . .

In Bashkany, soldiers were everywhere and many of them were very hostile. They shouted at us and one actually caught hold of Doctor Rakhil's arm, but she poured out such a torrent of angry abuse that he let her go. 'Keep together,' we whispered, remembering our doctor's advice. 'Be sure to keep together!' We were lucky to fall in with other Red Cross units, all homeward bound, sorrow-stricken and despairing. Along the crowded wintry roads, where the trampling of feet had turned the drifting snow into blackened slush, there was nothing but chaos and confusion.

Something was pulling at the hem of my skirt; it had been caught by one of the hooks of my boot; so I released Mamasha's arm for a moment and bent down to free it. I managed it, but when I looked up, Mamasha and Anna had disappeared. I tried to force my way through to them, but I could cut no passage through that thick wall of uniformed men! I felt frightened, for I had lost my companions. In my fear, I began to shout 'Anna!' 'Anna!' An answering voice called 'Florence!' and to my indescribable relief I saw Doctor Rakhil edging back towards me. She seized my arm; I held on to her tightly; we were *together*; jostled backwards and forwards, but *together*! I could not speak, for my relief was so great. At last, I gasped: 'The others?' 'All together; they know I am with you.' I was overwhelmed with thankfulness.

We moved spasmodically with the masses. I tried to catch sight of the others, but I was not tall enough; the lumbering figures in front of me clogged my view. Suddenly the thought struck me: perhaps we should remain separated; perhaps I should never see Anna and Mamasha again! The possibility filled me with a sickening alarm. Spontaneously, almost involuntarily, I lifted my head, and, very loudly, shouted twice: 'Anna! Anna!' From a distance came the answering call: 'Florence!' She had heard and made reply. I was satisfied, but my shout had disturbed some of the soldiers and they began to insinuate spiteful things about me. Doctor Rakhil whispered: 'Don't shout again! We shall all meet on Yassy station.'

We reached Yassy railway station, but they were not there. We made our way laboriously through the crowds on the platform, but there was no sign of our Sisters. A train for Kiyev was standing in the station; there were soldiers even on the roof. We went to each window and peered into the crammed compartments; here and there we asked if anyone had seen some Red Cross Sisters. Perhaps they had been detained! I would wait for the next train. Doctor Rakhil said, 'You must come with me to Odessa. You can rest there for a day or two; it will be much easier for you to get to Kiyev from there. It is impossible for you to travel in a train like this.' She was right. I could not bear the thought of being alone among all those rough drunken deserters. Full of gratitude, I agreed.

The train to Odessa left at 9.30 p.m. It was 14th December. We got a corner seat; Doctor Rakhil put her arm round me. She was like a mother. We rested together, warming each other in body, mind and spirit.

At Kishinev the train stopped for some long while. As we jerked forward I realised that we had left Roumania behind. Our poor, plucky little ally!

We reached Odessa at 4 a.m. on 16th. It was too cold and dark to walk through the streets. We sat in one of the waiting-rooms, and dozed a little. When it was light enough, Doctor Rakhil took me to her home, or to the house which had once been her home, for Red commissaries were installed in it. One room had been left for Doctor Rakhil's husband. It was a wonderful relief to her to learn that he was alive and well – the fact that he was a doctor had probably saved his life, for the Red Guards were always ready to pick out those who could be of use to themselves and the Communist community; the hospitals, too, were always short-staffed.

Both the city and seaport of Odessa were under the yoke of Bolshevism. Red Guards were parading the streets and all the principal buildings were controlled by them, 'requisitioned', as they termed it, on behalf of the Proletarian Government.

When the Red commissaries heard that my companion was the doctor's wife, they gave her the key to his room. It contained very little: just a bed, a table, a chest-of-drawers and a couple of chairs. This was all that remained of her home and possessions! All the good furniture, the pictures, the carpets, had been 'requisitioned'. Her husband arrived, late from his day's work. He was a nice, quiet-looking man, but very tired and thin. Their happiness at seeing each other again was very real and touching. Naturally, I felt a little *de trop*, but when I suggested I should go to the city hospital and beg a corner for a night's rest, Doctor Rakhil would not hear of it. No, I must stay with them; I was their guest. Without more ado, they brought out a large sheet. The husband knocked a nail into a corner of the wall, then another nail into the opposite wall; the wife sewed a curtain-ring on to either end of the sheet, which was then hung up, making an excellent screen

and providing me with a triangular bedroom. Then the husband
went out and, after conferring amicably – as he put it – with a
Red commissary, returned with black bread, cheese, butter and
eggs. I had not seen butter for months; it was a great treat! We
sat on the bed and thoroughly enjoyed all the 'perquisites' so
graciously sent by the Red commissary.

Next morning, Doctor Rakhil and I went to the station to enquire about trains. We heard that there was one leaving Odessa
for Kiyev tomorrow, 18th December, at 9.30 p.m.; so it was arranged that I should stay a second night with my doctor friends.
On our way to and from the station, we met several friends of
Doctor Rakhil; each one of them seemed to have a sad personal
story to tell, and there were fearful tales of Bolshevist atrocities in
the city. One such story made a deep impression upon me. We
were told that many of the Front Line officers, escaping from their
deserting soldiers, had managed to reach Odessa, hoping to make
good their escape by sea; the Red Army had been expecting them
and were on the alert. By road and by train they had come; and
one by one they had been captured. In groups they had been tied
together, with heavy stones attached to their feet. Then they had
been taken out to sea and thrown overboard. It was said that in
some places their drowned bodies could be seen, still upright,
swaying backwards and forwards.

18th December

I am leaving Odessa tonight. There are fewer soldiers in this part
of the world, so I should find a seat. It will be difficult to express
my thanks to these kind hosts of mine. It seems strangely provi-
dential that this large-hearted, kindly woman should have come
into my life, as though predestined to be my friend and guardian.
Never shall I forget that feeling of infinite relief when I saw her so
bravely, forcefully, defying that seething mass of turbulent men
in order to look for me and protect me. When our head doctor
warned and advised us: 'Keep together!' I remember thinking that
I would be the last person to ignore his wise counsel; and yet it
was *I* who transgressed, *I* who broke away, unwillingly and
unwittingly, it is true; nevertheless, I had been the disobedient
one.

I felt acute despondency at the thought that I might never see
Annushka again, but Doctor Rakhil cheered me up by reminding

me that I should be able to contact all our Sisters through the reunion centres in Moscow.

26th December, 1917. Moscow
I arrived in Moscow yesterday and found my 'family' well and safe. I am terribly tired, so will write about my train experiences in a few days' time, when I have collected my thoughts.

28th December
I don't feel like dwelling on my seven-day journey from Odessa to Moscow; it was worse than any other journey I had experienced. Luckily, I had no luggage but a knapsack – everything else had been stolen or left behind.

Doctor Rakhil accompanied me to the station. It was very dark and we held tightly to each other, lest we should fall on the slippery, frozen ground. I tried to express my immense gratitude; she would hear none of it. 'Friendship makes life worth living,' she said. I had given her my home address and she knew that a warm welcome would be awaiting her and her husband, whenever they happened to be in England. We were on the platform by 8 p.m. but already most of the compartments were full. In one compartment I noticed some townspeople, a man and his wife, through the window. I begged them to keep a seat for me and I was fortunate enough to arrive in time to occupy it. Doctor Rakhil waited to see me seated and then disappeared. I had begged her not to wait. My heart was full of a strange emotion; I had lost Anna and now I had lost Doctor Rakhil. I felt lonely and forlorn.

The woman in my coupé was expecting a child and was far from well. Her husband was greatly concerned for her; he told me that they had wished to return to Kiyev some six weeks ago, but had been held up in Odessa by the Red Guards who, hearing that he had business connections with a ship-building firm in Odessa, would not allow him to leave the city until they had checked his affidavit concerning his home in Kiyev. The soldiers in our compartment were young and hilarious; they began to sing and swing their feet from side to side. One of them tried to dance where he was standing and succeeded in bringing half-a-dozen of them on to the floor – perilously near the sick woman. The husband was furious, but wisely said nothing. I received more than one kick and several pushes, but I, too, wisely said nothing.

We journeyed through Shmerinka, Vinnitsa, Kazatin, and finally arrived in Kiyev on Wednesday, 20th December, at 6.30 p.m. It was high time; the poor woman said that she feared that she was going to be sick. I was not surprised, because the atmosphere was nauseating. I tried to shield her from the soldiers while her husband held out a small bowl; fortunately the sick feeling passed, but when I turned to take my seat, I found it already occupied. The occupant offered me a seat on his lap. I, too, began to feel sick, and remained standing, pressing my aching head against the icy-cold window-pane. As we steamed into Kiyev, the soldiers made a dash for the door in the corridor; shouting, jostling, they piled themselves up, ready to jump out on to the platform. The rushing, jumping, lunging and plunging went on for several minutes; then things became quieter, the whirlwind had passed. We sat for a few minutes, enjoying the peace which now enveloped us and most thankful for the cold air which streamed towards us from the open doors.

I left Kiyev by the first available train to Moscow. That journey was infinitely worse than the former. I got a window seat, but could not move. The compartment was packed. Soldiers filled the train; there was neither standing nor sitting room. They must have come in their hundreds from the whole length of the south-western and southern Fronts; all intent on getting as far away from the enemy as possible. They must reach Moscow at any price. At each station, more soldiers tried to enter the train; they broke the central window near me and hauled themselves through, head first. There was a pile of them now on the floor, one on top of the other. The noise was dreadful and the smell almost unbearable.

I kept my seat for two days and nights without moving. I ate little and drank nothing, well-drilled in abstemious living after the spells of fasting at the Front. As time went on, the massed comrades in the compartments became more friendly. They would lift up a leg or an arm to give a comrade a breathing-space for a cramped limb. They already knew that I was an Englishwoman and seemed interested to hear where I had been working; some of them had come from the Fronts where our Red Cross unit had been encamped. We talked about many things and they tried to make things more comfortable for me; they even grew concerned about my immobility, and when at a small station we were told the train would have to wait a few minutes, they suggested that I should get out for a while. I was pulled out through the broken window by a comrade standing outside, and one and all promised me faithfully that they would keep my seat for me and haul me back when I returned. The comrade was waiting for me at the window. They had kept their word . . . I recalled Smirnov's words: 'At heart, they are all good and true.'

We had stopped at many stations; I remembered but a few of the names: Konotop, Khuta, Mikhailovskaya and Bryansk. We arrived at our destination on Monday, 25th December, at 12.30 p.m. I had returned like a vagrant, bereft of all that I had held dear. My Red Cross work was over; my wartime wanderings had ceased. There was an emptiness in heart and mind which was deeply distressing. Life seemed suddenly to have come to a full-stop. What the future held in store, it was impossible to predict; it all looked too dark and void. But in the remote background there was always, God be praised, my country – England! Like a beacon it shone through the darkness and beckoned me home.

PART FIVE

1918, The New Russia

January

I have already been in Moscow for several days and am able to take stock of my surroundings! I found the city in the throes of winter and famine; nevertheless, I was welcomed with open arms by my good friends and am staying with them as a member of the family, sharing their lot and partaking of their meagre rations. After due investigations, the Red commissioners agreed to give me a permit for my own rations. Two potatoes or one eighth of a pound of bread was the daily ration per head. We preferred the potatoes, for, washed and cooked, every bit of them could be eaten – that is when they were not bad! Whereas the bread inevitably contained sawdust and other 'foreign bodies', calculated to augment the weight. The market-places provided a convenient rendezvous for the surreptitious exchange of family heirlooms for foodstuffs. But no treasure could buy salt; it had ceased to exist.

Anna Ivanovna confided to me her fears for her relatives in Petrograd, where the Red Guards appeared particularly violent in their attitude towards educated people. The universities naturally suffered and many of the professors were not only deprived of their living, but of their private possessions and, not infrequently, their lives. The *Bolsheviki* seemed to find great satisfaction too in degrading all high-ranking officers. In a large hotel in Moscow, which now houses many Red Guards and Communist commissioners, an elderly general of the Imperial Army was forced to work the lift while his wife was given the post of washerwoman.

Thousands of people have fled the country. Thanks to dirty faces and hands, unkempt hair and soiled clothing, many a well-born person was able to cross the frontier and seek refuge in a neighbouring country. But woe betide those who were caught, for the

Bolsheviki were not slow in rounding up the 'runaways' and making them pay the penalty of the 'traitor's' death.

My friends have impressed on me the need to dress shabbily when in the street. It is sufficient to wear a white collar, or even to have white hands, to be recognised as a *bourgeois* and dealt with accordingly. A fur coat is instantly seized; should the owner show any resistance, he is liable to be arrested, or shot immediately. Among the many new laws which have been instituted by the Bolshevist régime is one which is known as *samosud,* or *samo-upravstvo,* which can be interpreted as 'self-judgment', whereby the Red Guards are entitled to take the law into their own hands and kill or torture as they deem it necessary. I saw an instance of this *samosud* only a day or two ago. I was walking towards Plushchika Street when, in a nearby house, rifle-shots were heard. A door in the wall suddenly opened and a *dvornik* [yard-porter] called to me hurriedly: *'Barishnya!* Come inside, quickly!' I went in and he closed the door. 'What is happening?' I asked. 'They are all a lot of thieves,' he answered. 'Some went into the house to steal; others wanted to do the same. They met, and began killing each other. Set a thief to catch a thief!' he added with a chuckle. When I left the yard, I saw two men, with guns, running off down the street; a third lay prostrate on the road near the house.

One morning, Asya came to my room. She said: 'Masha has gone!' (Masha, their only house-help, had been with them for more than ten years. She had been like a member of the family.) Her bed had not been slept in. Her chest-of-drawers and wardrobe had been emptied of her belongings. She had received her wages the previous day and Anna Ivanovna and given her an extra ten roubles. Anna Ivanovna and the girls were very upset. What could have impelled her to leave them? Then another discovery was made: Anna Ivanovna could not find her watch. Soon it was obvious that other valuables were missing: Anna Ivanovna's purse, some jewellery and a silver clock which had stood on the dining-room mantelpiece.

I lost no time in seeking out the two reunion centres of our Red Cross personnel, but, to my great disappointment, they no longer existed under the control of the *Zemstvo.* I am terribly anxious to have news of Anna – of all the Sisters. I could weep with despair when I remember what a trifling thing it was that brought about our separation.

I am glad to be with my friends again, but life is not really happy for anyone. Conditions have greatly deteriorated since I left Moscow on 29th November to return to my unit. For nights on end we never dare to undress; gangs of comrades scour the streets, invading private houses, smashing down doors and windows if admittance is denied them. Many families have paid with their lives for obstructing them.

One of the Usovs' many friends, who lived in the same street as the family of Asya's young officer, missing at Mogilev, told us that Red Guards had swooped down on the family during the night, arrested the parents, their daughter and younger son, and requisitioned the house and its belongings. Asya wept when she heard this bad news and asked more than once what could be done to assist them; she was ready, she declared, to go to the Red commissioners and beg them to be lenient with her friends. We were horrified when we heard this suggestion; Anna Ivanovna immediately showed her distress by exclaiming: 'I will not allow it; the Red Guards would immediately order your arrest.' We left it at that, but I could gather from Asya's absent-minded manner that she was intent on working out a scheme which would benefit the family of the dead man whom she had loved.

We also heard how a 12-year-old boy of good family had been decoyed to a secret rendezvous of the Red Guards, who told him that his father was suspected of counter-revolutionary propaganda. The boy was ordered to watch his father's movements, listen to his plans and divulge all that he knew to the Red Guards at their next meeting. Failing to comply with their orders, the boy would be imprisoned, his parents arrested and their possessions confiscated. But if he did give them the necessary information, they would see to it that he and his family remained unmolested. It was a pitiful story. The child did disclose the clandestine meeting-place of his father and his friends, the Red Guards pounced upon them during one of their secret sessions, killed two or three who resisted and then dragged the boy before his father, telling the latter that, thanks to his son's patriotism, their counter-revolutionary intrigue had been exposed.

Because a peasant-worker or a soldier-deserter is armed with a knife or gun, it is considered justifiable for them to stab or shoot whenever they think it expedient. To be killed without trial seems to be the order of the day; so every armed man in Russia nowadays can call himself 'judge', 'jury' and 'executioner'. . . . As a doctor friend told us: 'If only we could be freed from this eternal disorder and be sure of our *personal security*, we might be able to build up our lives anew, but in these barbarous conditions we cannot call our lives our own. We are unable to live; we just exist from day to day.' And another asserted: 'They call us free men: for my part, I am unable to enjoy any freedom in either word or deed; only my thoughts are my own. We are shackled, as it were, to the will of the arbitrary rulers of the Proletarian State. They have the power, so they make their will law.' 'Might is right,' they proclaim, and we must follow blindly wherever they will us to go. We are now more enslaved than ever before. And they call that freedom! God help us all if *that* is freedom!'

We are often hungry: we constantly wonder how we shall last out until midday tomorrow when the next quota is due. We received from Vladimir Nikolayevich's wife a tin of wheaten biscuits, made from the cereals which her husband had brought from his estate near Podolsk. We doled them out carefully and enjoyed them to the last crumb. Nadya, ever enterprising, now suggested that she should go to their country estate, find out what was happening to their crop of potatoes and try to persuade one of the peasants to bring a sack to Moscow. But Anna Ivanovna would not hear of it. The peasants had been disagreeable enough when they had last visited the *dacha*; now they would be worse. Besides, they would already have divided the crops among themselves.

For the past week, things have been quieter in our neighbourhood and we have been able to undress at night. But yesterday, during the afternoon, we heard and saw – from behind the curtains – several bands of hooligans pass, singing and shouting loudly. They came to a halt near our house; looked around; pointed at our house, then at others. Finally, they slouched off, singing their martial songs. Our hearts stood still with fear, thinking they might return last night; so we decided that it was wiser not to undress. . . .

We were sitting in our winter coats in front of the dying embers of a wood fire. Nadya suddenly said, '*Mamochka*, I am very hungry; as there is nothing to eat, I will make some tea to warm us.' Anna Ivanovna nodded and Nadya went into the kitchen. Scarcely had she left the room, when a loud knock came at the front door. We sat looking at each other in the dim light of the one candle.

Anna Ivanovna's breath came in short, hard gasps. Nadya appeared at the door, her face very white; she tiptoed across to us and sat down. The knock came a second time. We rose, moved silently towards the door and listened. There was no sound of voices – so there could not be *many* of them; that was a relief! We went nearer the front door, listened more intently. We heard someone breathing heavily. There came a third knock. Anna Ivanovna called out: '*Kto tam?* [Who is there?].' The answer came at once: 'Vasiliy.' 'Vasiliy,' we repeated in a whisper, 'which Vasiliy?' 'Vasiliy,' the voice called out again and something in the tone must have struck Anna Ivanovna as familiar, for she pushed back the bolt and opened the door.

A little figure, bowed down with a sack across his back, stumbled into the hall. 'Vasiliy!' we gasped. It was Vasiliy from Anna Ivanovna's *dacha*! Vasiliy, the little hairy gorilla, the misshapen ape-man! 'Potatoes,' he said briefly and plumped the sack on to the floor. We fell upon him in rapturous surprise and gratitude. We embraced him, kissed his hairy face and led him, still out of breath, to an armchair near the fire. Anna Ivanovna lighted a second candle. Nadya rushed into the kitchen to make the tea. Oh! the delightful surprise! Vasiliy of all people! And that great sack of potatoes – almost bigger than himself! How could we thank him?

, He had been on the road nearly three days, walking chiefly after dark. By day, there were those who would willingly have confiscated his potatoes. He wouldn't allow that; he had been determined to get them to Moscow. Once or twice he had been obliged to hide. He had been offered a seat in a cart, but didn't dare accept it, as he feared for his potatoes. Anna Ivanovna was looking at him with tears in her eyes. We were all half-laughing, half-crying. We had expected the *worst* when we had heard that knock. Had he eaten? Yes, he had eaten bread and cheese twice that day, but he was glad of the tea; he always liked hot tea. Where did he think of going for the night? He didn't know, but would find a corner where it was not too cold. Anna Ivanovna settled the question. 'You will stay here, Vasiliy. We'll make you warm and comfortable for the night and tomorrow you can leave at your leisure.'

We heard of the *dacha* and its staff. Ivan and his wife were still living in the house. There was plenty to eat. He would have brought potatoes before, but some of them wouldn't let him; said there would not be enough to go round. But he had made up his mind and had waited for an opportunity. Dasha, his wife, was well; she was expecting another child, but as she had no washing to do now, she didn't mind so much. His three small sons were tumbling about in the snow all day long; they were real little devils; he could do nothing with them.

Vasiliy left us next morning. He felt sure he would be able to get a lift here and there. Anna Ivanovna packed a couple of sheets and a blanket for Dasha, but Vasiliy refused to take them; said that it might arouse suspicion and, in any case, there had been plenty in Anna Ivanovna's *dacha* and he had been given his share! He promised to come again with another sack, but couldn't say when; it depended on the potatoes; if they gave out, then there would be nothing to bring! He told us that Ivan and his wife were looking after the house, because they considered it their own, but two of the other men had said that they would welcome Anna Ivanovna back; they had never approved of the way some men had seized other people's property. . . . It was comforting to know that there were still loyal hearts and true among those simple country retainers. Vasiliy's unexpected visit did much to revive our spirits; it had come at a moment when life had seemed very dark and dreary. The potatoes, too, would be a most welcome extra and last for several weeks.

We had another unexpected visitor a few days later. A distant cousin of her husband came to call on Anna Ivanovna. He was a funny-looking little man, with long beard and whiskers, from Tomsk in Siberia, where he had lived for the last 20 years. I was interested in Siberia, for if I wished to return to England, that route would be the only one open to me. So I seized the opportunity to ask him many questions. He was not over-enthusiastic about the country. The winters were long and very cold, but he never found them boring, for he was a great reader and liked the long, quiet evenings with his books. I noticed at once that he had a rather unusual accent and very awkward manners and I summed him up, to myself, as one who had lived in the background all his days, undisturbed by the great upheavals. 'Smug little man,' I thought. 'What a useless life!'

He had brought Anna Ivanovna a small sack of rice, some sugar and a tin of salt, as he was passing through Moscow on his way to the Ukraine. When he took leave of us, Anna Ivanovna and the girls kissed him most affectionately. When we were alone, Anna Ivanovna said: 'He is a very brave man; Pasha was always so proud of him.' He had been a schoolmaster: history and literature were his two main subjects. In the Russo-Japanese War of 1904–5 he volunteered for active service. Twice he had been badly wounded; once so severely that his body had been laid aside for burial! Three times he had been decorated for valour and awarded the St George's Cross for the rescue of three officers whom he had carried, one by one, to safety under a terrific barrage of Japanese guns. He had refused a commission. When the war was over he had returned to his school. He had never married; preferred his books and a quiet life, and had already published two books on literature. . . .

That was my 'smug little man' who had led a 'useless life'! I felt humbled and ashamed. The courage of the little ape-man Vasiliy should have been enough to teach me never to judge from outward appearances. I remembered the Russian saying: *'Dusha drugovo dremuchy les* [The soul of another is like unto a very dark forest]'.

The food rations are, naturally, quite inadequate; many people have sought work with, or sanctioned by, the *Bolsheviki*, in order to supplement their meagre diet. Gradually, as foodstuffs become more and more scarce, there is no doubt that a large percentage of the Muscovite population is half-starved. Some restaurants are still open, but they can supply food only at a price. If one is hungry – as one always is – one does not enquire too closely into the kind, or quality, of the meat. Horse flesh provides the main meat supply; it can be cooked and served in a variety of ways in order to disguise both origin and taste. Twice I have eaten horse flesh with relish: the first time, it had no specific taste, rather like a well-spiced mince; the second time, there was no mistaking it; it was a steak, coarse and stringy with a slightly sweet flavour. At the first mouthful I knew what I was eating; but, as hunger is the best sauce, I had no qualms in demolishing every scrap. Horse flesh has, however, now become a real delicacy and can be compared favourably with the flesh of cats, dogs and rodents.

There is no uncertainty about the rations supplied to the Red

Guards, commissaries, members of the several soviets, or councils; they are entitled to 'first service'; what is left over can be divided among the masses – those same masses whom Lenin and Trotsky promised to take under their protective wing. I was walking the other morning on one of the side-streets when I happened to see the lean horse of a *droschki* fall dead. The driver pulled the harness clear and left it where it had fallen. Some time later I returned by the same street. The carcass of the horse was still there, but devoid of most of its flesh. Some of the starving had seized the opportunity to cut away all the meat they could. It seems incongruous that an animal, dying of starvation, can yet provide food for starving humans!

Perhaps Lenin realises that poverty and starvation provide a convenient medium with which to enforce his will on the masses. There are many upright men who, stifling their personal feelings, openly admit that they will support the Lenin Government for the sake of their wives and children. Others continue to resist nobly until starvation, with all its accompanying ills, stare their families in the face, and then they too are obliged to give way. The Bolshevist, or Communist, organisations which have come into existence are legion. Some of them are known as soviets, or councils; of these, there are at least a dozen different ones, including the Council of People's Commissars, Security Council, Council of the Union, Supreme Council, etc. Nearly every day new tribunals, committees and cabinets spring into being; they play an important role, especially in the provincial towns and districts. The *Komissar* (head) of each of these organisations is invariably drawn from the criminal elements which abound in all parts and are well-known to the Communist leaders; for the prisons in Russia and Siberia have opened their doors, and anarchists, nihilists, criminals of every kind, have made good their escape into the freedom of the new Free Russia. The majority of them being penniless, they waste no time in instituting new laws relating to taxation; their victims belong mainly to the better-class families, but these, already drained of their possessions, are unable to meet the demands and consequently suffer arrest, imprisonment and often death.

But not all the prisoners freed from gaol after October 1917 were thieves, assassins, anarchists. There were many political prisoners, serving life sentences in the solitary wastes of Siberia, whose only crime was that their views differed from those of the Tsarist Government. The majority of these were accused of contravening the established laws, or of endeavouring to overthrow the Tsarist régime. Sentence was passed on them for treason and, in most cases, their lands and goods were forfeited.

Among these political prisoners were men of great culture and talent; they will be of little use to the *Bolsheviki*, for few of them will condone violence. And the fact that they are highly educated will cause them to be denounced as 'intelligentsia' or 'bourgeoisie'. It is an illogical situation: a political prisoner condemned as a revolutionary during the Imperial régime is denounced as a counter-revolutionary by Lenin's Revolutionary Party. I can see little reason in thus differentiating 'revolutionaries'; after all, they both wish to overthrow the 'established authority'.

We heard one day that Prince Piotr Alexeyevich Kropotkin had arrived in Moscow, having been absent for many years, due to the fact that he had been an acknowledged revolutionary. He belonged to an old Muscovite family and, while still in his early thirties, had been imprisoned in the fortress of St Peter and St Paul in St Petersburg, but had escaped abroad and had lived in many countries, England included. A friend offered to take me to a meeting at which the Prince – now 76 years old – was speaking. He made a great impression on me. He was bald, but had a fine head and a long, voluminous white beard. His voice was not strong and I could catch only a word of his speech now and then. But I heard him say he was glad to be back in his native city and hoped to spend the rest of his life there. Despite his title and his great learning, I have an idea that the *Bolsheviki* are quite pleased to have him back. They must be making an exception in his case!

The country landlords are faring even worse than the wealthy city families. Since last autumn the peasants have been in rebellion and have expropriated large plots of land. For the rural masses it is a case of 'first come, first served', in their headlong scramble to seize any land they can lay their hands on. They do not consider that they are stealing, their Communist leaders have times without number impressed upon them that the land is their rightful property. So they remind each other: 'We are acquiring what is *ours*, but has been stolen from us.' Thus enormous estates have been pounced upon and parcelled out among the illiterate peasantry. This system of commandeering has reached such a pitch that any plot of land ploughed and tilled by a peasant can be regarded by him as his own property.

The large ancestral homes are being burnt, or made unfit for human habitation. The imported land-machinery, valued in these days at enormous sums, is being broken up, because the peasantry, accustomed to their own primitive implements, cannot work it. If they but knew the help those machines could offer them in their toil! But how are they in their blind ignorance to know? What their blunt minds do realise is that this strange machinery belongs to the 'bourgeoisie' and therefore there is only one way to deal with it – to destroy!

In the beautiful woodlands thousands of trees are being felled and left to decay. It is as though the clarion call 'Destroy!' has been heard throughout the new republic. The cattle – pedigree herds included – are being distributed; many are slaughtered for food. In the old days before the war, many peasants were not interested in meat; more than one had told me that he had never eaten meat in his life. So they have come a long way! The thought of a peasant-hut with a large joint of beef on the table seems inconsistent.

No word has been heard of Masha. There is little doubt that she left us of her own accord to join the Communist populace. Domestic servants have ceased to exist in Russia; it is now the mistress's turn to wait upon the will of her servants.

The Bolshevist régime has now imposed further arbitrary laws. All able-bodied men and women must share the responsibilities of the State and participate in the work. So the Red Guards descend upon the bourgeoisie, call them out into the streets and allot to each his task. The better educated the person, the more degrading the task. Women and girls of cultured families are given brooms and made to sweep the streets, sell newspapers, clean out public lavatories; their men-folk are ordered to cart away rubble, act as porters, and run errands for their Bolshevist masters. No protest is recognised; to oppose the Red Guards is to antagonise them and, in due course, be denounced as counter-revolutionary.

Now the *Bolsheviki* have devised another plan. 'No work, no food!' they decree. Women of gentle birth, even the elderly, if able-bodied, are ordered to go to work in this or that factory or mill, and where transport is not available, they are expected to walk there and back; otherwise no food ration will be forthcoming. I know what this will mean to my Russian family. Even Anna Ivanovna will not be exempt. We talk it over continually and they, seeing that life in Moscow is daily becoming more and more difficult, beg me to make arrangements to go home. 'You must go,' they urge, 'while the going is good.' They have heard that a foreigner is soon to become *persona non grata* to the Lenin Government; in Petrograd, some foreigners have already been imprisoned.

Religion is being savagely suppressed. Monasteries and convents are ransacked and destroyed; the monks and nuns are mercilessly treated and think themselves lucky if they escape with their lives. Churches and all religious institutions are being desecrated and despoiled of their treasures.

These details have been given us by our friends, in particular by Vladimir Nikolayevich, who, as a doctor, can move about the city at will. I have always been interested in Moscow's beautiful churches; there were no fewer than 40 times 40 it was said! Before the war, I attended many services, and vividly remember the intensity of religious fervour, the marvellous icons and the glorious voices of the invisible choir. Now, I was told, all these had disappeared; it seemed incredible, so I went one morning to see for myself. It is true. They are derelict; their beauty despoiled. They have suffered violently at the ruthless hands of iconoclasts.

Sacred images had been pulled down, stamped upon and broken; age-old icons mutilated and slashed; the altars and walls daubed with coloured paint. Rusty tins and soiled clothing were thrown here and there. One wonders how these vandals dared to play such havoc, for are they not the same who, only a year ago, had been kneeling and devoutly crossing themselves as the name of God the Father passed their lips? Now God has ceased to exist for them; they have driven Him out of their hearts. It seems incredible that Lenin and Trotsky have in so short a time stamped out all that the Holy Orthodox faith had inculcated in the Russian soul through almost ten centuries. In another church, exquisitely moulded and decorated in the Byzantine style, the small side chapels had been converted into stables; while others, similarly carpeted with straw, had been used as night-clubs, where the Red Guards could play cards and take their girlfriends.

I have a printed leaflet which has been secretly distributed among the followers of the Greek Orthodox faith. It is addressed to the *Pravoslavnie* in Moscow. It points out that the Orthodox Church is enduring terrible persecution at the hands of the enemies of Christ, and urges all Russians who profess the Orthodox faith to rise in defence of their Church and its possessions. It announces that it is about to organise a *Krestnui Khod* [procession with cross and banners] from all churches to march to the Red Square, and calls on all members to join the procession as witnesses to their faith and to their devotion for their Mother Church.

Only recently my friends were asking: 'Will the Orthodox Church break under the heavy strain laid upon her by her godless Marxian oppressors?' 'No!' they decided. 'She might bend, but break – never!' Perhaps from the present cruel persecution, she will emerge strengthened, purified. Meanwhile, her sufferings are legion. All church services have been abolished. There is no marriage ceremony, no baptism, not even a Christian burial for the dead. The Church has already been forced to separate from the State and the State is now compelling the people to separate themselves from God. The younger generation are not slow to conform, but among the aged there are those who would rather renounce all they hold most dear than renounce their belief in God. Strong, they say, is the power of evil to corrupt, but stronger still is the power of faith, so deeply-rooted in the hearts of the people who love God.

A new law is about to be established by Government decree. It relates to the status of women in Bolshevist Russia. It might have been adopted from some ancient code of primitive savages!

This new law decrees that all young women are to be considered the property of the State, and, if unmarried at the age of eighteen, must register at a special Bureau of Surveillance with a view to acquiring a husband! They are then told to choose a man as a legal husband and their union will receive State approbation. All children born to them will automatically become the property of the State. In the majority of cases, the children will be taken from their mothers in infancy and reared in special institutions; each child will be given a name and number which will ensure its position in the Free State and its right to privileges accorded by the Proletarian Government. Young men, too, are allowed to choose a wife from the girls registered at the Bureau. So Free Russia is to legalise free love 'in the interests of the State'.

Nadya told me that in the market-place she had seen more than one man offering his war decorations in exchange for food. They must indeed be hungry to part with such precious possessions.

All the surgical staff of our 1st *Letuchka* have received two medals: the 4th and 3rd degrees of the Russian Order of St George. At one time a small pension was paid to the recipients of these medals, but since the advent of the Bolshevist régime all pensions connected with war services have been abolished. Alas for the young widows who depended on the income to bring up their fatherless children! Our head doctor once said that we were to be presented with the Order of St Anna at the close of the war. Neither he nor we had reckoned with the collapse of the Empire and of all Imperial institutions. I prize my medals very much and keep them well out of sight, for a recent decree has pronounced all war decorations 'degrading and void'. All ex-officers of the Imperial Russian Army have been ordered to do away with war-time insignia. There have been stories of officers who have refused to remove their epaulettes, at the risk of either having them torn off, or a bullet through their hearts. Knowing the proud patriotism of these loyal men, I can well believe that they would prefer the bullet to the dishonour.

Tsarist money is, likewise, no longer of any value. When I wished to change some banknotes, I was told they were not worth the paper they were printed on. That was a blow! I resolved to keep them as souvenirs. The banks were broken into and taken over by Lenin's supporters in November 1917. I applied to the Volkov Bank for permission to take out the few cherished items I had deposited in its strongroom. That too was out of the question; for the contents of the strongroom had been confiscated by the *Bolsheviki*. So I kept the two keys, stamped with the number of my box; they too would add to my collection of souvenirs.

In 1914, I had transfered £200 from my bank in England to the Government Savings Bank in Moscow. Anna Ivanovna had said: 'It will be quite safe. The bank can only collapse if the Imperial Government collapses.' Now my bank-book too was just another souvenir!

On the horse-trams one can pay with a small silver coin of the Imperial currency; otherwise postage stamps, printed – for lack of suitable paper – on German banknotes, are usually accepted. To pay for my ticket to Vladivostok, I have sold my second camera, bought in the Crimea in 1916. I had left it in Moscow because the one I had at the Front, although old, was still quite serviceable. My new camera was a very good one, so it was with dismay that I learnt it would fetch only half what I had paid for it; but, as Bolshevist money is essential to me, I was forced to comply.

I sought out the relevant authorities, and told them I wished to return to England via Siberia and the United States. They told me not to expect any train comforts nowadays; it was their turn now to travel in the first and second classes. Heatedly I told them that, if they would not let me travel by train, I would go *on foot*! It was sheer idiocy on my part, of course. But I felt sure that the vital thing was to show them that one was not afraid of them. They knew that I was an Englishwoman and had been a Red Cross nurse with the Imperial Russian Army: whether that added to, or detracted from, my prestige it was difficult to say. Then, at last, they declared that no more passenger-trains were running on the Trans-Siberian railway; only an occasional goods-train. *'Ochen khorosho!'* I answered. 'I will take a ticket for the next goods-train.'

The Germans must have experienced enormous satisfaction at the civil war which is ravaging Russia. They knew that sooner or later Lenin and Trotsky would be obliged to accept their peace terms. In December 1917, the *Bolsheviki* persuaded Germany to sign a general armistice. But disputes arose relating to the Ukraine and the armistice was annulled; so German troops have resumed their invasion of Russian territory. In one or two sections, we are told, the *Bolsheviki* have put up a stand, but they are far too disorganised to meet with any success. When, however, they saw that the Germans were sweeping rapidly eastwards towards Petrograd, they capitulated.

The peace treaty of Brest-Litovsk has been signed by the Bolshevist leaders and the German high command on 19th February and the war has at last come to an end. Lenin tried to make good his case by assuring his compatriots that Germany had been fighting on behalf of democracy in order to overthrow what he termed Anglo-Franco-American imperialism. But the treaty which brought the war officially to an end is not being recognised by patriotic Russians, and countless Russians are horrified to hear about it. There is, of course, overpowering relief that soldiers' lives are no longer in danger; on the other hand, peace has been bought at a heavy price, namely dishonour to their country and disloyalty to their allies.

'It is the darkest defeat of all,' said Vladimir Nikolayevich. 'We have descended to the lowest depths; now we shall be forced to grovel at the feet of our worst enemy.' Anna Ivanovna was greatly moved: 'Have we not already suffered sufficiently at the hands of these tyrants?' Asya, with clasped hands and tears in her eyes, asked, 'What is happening to Russia? And what is going to happen?' Nadya, with her sweet, cheerful nature, sought to comfort them, but words were of little avail. The distress is general, but it is dangerous to voice one's feelings in public, so a stubborn silence has settled down on the greater part of the Muscovite 'bourgeoisie'. Many of them regard the treaty as a death-blow to their hopes for their country and despite the bitterness of life under the despotic Proletarian Government, they dread the prospect of being obliged to welcome the German military chiefs as 'liberators'.

This afternoon, Vladimir Nikolayevich brought an old friend of his – an ex-general of the Imperial Army. General Y, heavily wounded in the summer of 1916 and forced to leave active service, was now acting as *shveitzar*, or concierge, in a large house occupied by Red commissioners. He had accepted his fate as only an old soldier can, but he cherished every memory of his military life and especially of his soldiers. He called them 'my men', and said that they were heroes. He recalled the tragic days of 1915 when, unable to use their rifles for lack of ammunition, they had been told to take sticks with them into the trenches, and the Germans had spread the report that the Russians were fighting with cudgels. He continued: 'They were tattered and torn, had bad food, no real rest and lived like dogs; and yet they were true to the core and ready to lay down their lives whenever necessary.' Last autumn, in Petrograd, he had met a very highly respected general, who had told him that it would soon be imperative to leave the capital – meaning that the enemy was fast approaching. General

Y told him to his face that he ought to be ashamed of himself, turned his back on him and walked away.

Despite the appropriation of the land by the Russian peasantry, neither famine nor misery can be stamped out. The unscrupulous members on the land tribunals are so intent on feathering their own nests that they have completely disregarded the plight of the peasants. Foreigners who have, even in a limited way, come into contact with the Russian peasant, could not but be impressed by his stoical indifference to pleasure or pain, his childish simplicity and superstition where religious matters were concerned and his implicit faith in the proprietors for whom he worked. How deadly then must be the influence of the fell epidemic of Bolshevism. Swept off their feet by the wild, impassioned speeches of their comrades, the peasants have been dragged forward by the wave of anarchy which was enveloping the countryside. But reaction is inevitable and in its train has come bitter remorse and fierce enmity against those who have lured them on to bloodshed and disaster. In many parts the peasants have rebelled against the new order and peasant risings are constantly reported from this or that district. There is no doubt that numerous peasant communities regret the passing of the old régime, which gave them – despite their poverty – both peace and security.

But the Red Guards are ever on the alert to note disaffection among the rank and file of their adherents. As an example of the thoroughness shown by the Red police tribunals, it is said that one of their first acts was to ransack the archives of the Tsarist secret police and burn their contents wholesale, so that not a vestige remained of the names of men who had been sentenced under the Tsarist criminal law. But the new archives are slowly but surely accumulating records of persons suspected of counter-revolutionary propaganda.

Recently [mid-February] there was heard again, more vehemently than before, the call for allied intervention. Word had, in some mysterious way, got round that an English Red Cross nurse living in Moscow was about to return to England. I became aware that this plan of mine was known when I received, one morning, two letters from ex-officers of the Imperial Army, begging me to use my influence with the British military authorities and the consular officers of the Entente to enable them to enlist with the allied armies, as they were eager to continue the war at any price.

That was the beginning of a considerable correspondence with persons unknown. Alas! how little I can do for them! How can I explain to them that I am too insignificant to be of any help! The name of England had conjured up for them a faint glimmer of hope. Their pleading has only enhanced the knowledge of my own helplessness and caused me considerable sorrow and regret. . . .

In my heart I am afraid that England has neither the wish nor the intention of intervening. It seems to me that my country has never shown herself anxious to study the real Russia. The 'Land of the Great White Tsars' has been for us a legendary, fantastic land. Few writers have even endeavoured to pull aside the veil which hides the fascinating customs of Russian everyday life. There was once, I remember, an Englishman who stated that the only distinction between the classes was in the mode of wearing the *rubashka* [shirt]: the *intelligentsia* tucked the shirt inside the trousers, while the *ne-intelligentsia* wore it outside, strapped round the waist with a belt.

On the other hand the Englishman, although somewhat of an enigma to the Russian, is – in general – admired and respected. Even among illiterate soldiers, my nationality has never proved a stumbling-block; on the contrary, the word *Anglichanka* [English-woman] has called forth a host of small acts of courtesy; and I have always been so glad and proud to be English.

Letters and messages have recently been brought to me by friends; I seldom know the people who send them. One such letter touched me deeply. I quote from it: 'Each day brings fresh horrors; but we are hardened and pay little attention to sufferings. . . . Such misery as ours no nation has endured. . . . Pray for us and for our Russia, and do not let bitter English tongues call us all scoundrels.' And another: 'Nothing can astonish or frighten us now, for we have experienced every form of astonishment and fear; we have passed through all.'

I have taken up my diary again. The word 'diary' conjures up the picture of a neat booklet, in which daily events are recorded in small clear handwriting. I am afraid that I do not conform to this customary rule. My diary consists of a conglomeration of scraps of odd paper, any paper which comes to hand. I am going to have trouble in sorting out these fragments, all hastily scribbled notes *in pencil*; on some, no dates have been noted, no pages numbered and often only the key-word can give a clue to the

episode I wished to remember. I am writing this in my bedroom
at my Russian 'mother's' house in Moscow. My mind is troubled,
for in a day or two I shall have to say good-bye and start my
homeward journey.

Now, for me, the war is over and my Red Cross work finished. I
cannot express the dreadful emptiness which has come into my
life. Anna Ivanovna found me weeping one day; I could not tell
her why, because I myself did not know. She said it was 'reaction'.
I did not contradict her, but I knew it was something much
deeper than that. As I looked through those fragmentary notes of
mine, I relived all the tragic scenes again and asked myself:
'Was it *I* – really *I* – who saw that? Was it *I* – really *I* – who did
that?' From where had the strength come to endure those ghastly
moments? I shivered at the memories they brought back. I
recalled the desolate battlefields and saw the soldiers lying amid
the twisted wires and shell cavities. Will they be remembered?
But who could remember all those many thousands and thousands?

I have heard nothing of Anna, or my other Red Cross Sisters.
It grieves me deeply, for once I have left Russia there will never
be the slightest hope of contacting her again. Already all postal
services, telegraph and telephone transmissions have come to a
standstill. I did, however, find Alexander Ivanovich Ugrimov at
home when I called the second time. It was just by chance that he
and his wife happened to be in Moscow, having come from some
country district for a few hours only. He had ceased to wear
uniform; I, too, had discarded mine. It was a sad meeting. I
recalled the day when he had stood among us – his newly-formed
Red Cross Surgical *Otryad* – on Alexandrovski station, about to
start for Galicia. How active and energetic he had been then!
And how high our spirits! That was only three years ago. Now I
could scarcely recognise him. His face was pale and lined, his
eyes sunken. Suffering was stamped on his face. It was unmistakable; I had seen it so often before – on the faces of all patriots,
in mourning for their dying country.

I wondered if he found much difference in me; I knew that I
was much thinner. He had no news from any of the other Sisters,
except that they had safely reached Kiyev.

There was little we could say to each other; he just pressed my
hand at parting and wished me 'God Speed!' I wanted to say

something to let him know that we had loved and respected him as our leader, our plenipotentiary; but I could not find the words. His wife came in for a few minutes; she put her arm round him and I saw how he leaned towards her.

I have become acquainted with two American ladies working in Moscow with a Voluntary Aid Organisation. I introduced them to Anna Ivanovna and the girls and was overjoyed to hear that they would watch over my friends and do all they could to make their life more comfortable. I gave Miss Dunham my home address and she promised to let me have news of them now and then; now I shall not feel the parting quite so much.

For some days past I have been prepared for my journey. I have contacted the British authorities and been told that my papers are all in order. I dread the moment of farewell, for I am heartbroken at parting from my beloved 'family'; I cannot bear to leave them in such terrible circumstances. But they themselves wish me to go – not to miss the opportunity, for there might not be another – and life is daily growing more difficult and food more scarce. Many kind people came to wish me a safe journey! I had not realised that I had so many friends. Anna Ivanovna and the girls have had a notice from the employment commissaries, who allot work to the 'bourgeoisie', informing them that their names are on the 'Workers' List' and that work will, in due course, be found for them. The notice bears the significant words: 'He who does not work, does not eat.'

We have heard that Lenin has transferred the title of capital from Petrograd to Moscow: so the Bolshevist Government will make its headquarters here. One is afraid that this will imply more drastic laws being clamped down on Muscovite citizens. Foreigners are already being looked upon with suspicion.

The day of departure came . . . then the hour . . . then the minute! I was saying good-bye to those whom I truly loved; to those who had protected me, given me home, comforts, affection. I might never see them again. I was saying good-bye to my life in Russia. I felt numb and cold. My heart prompted me to say so much, but my lips could not express it in words. It was over! I had left my Russian 'family'. My homeward journey had begun.

It is a cold night in early March and we are tossing and jerking our way through the darkness in a wheezing, creaking train bound for Vladivostok. It is a goods-train, just as the railway commissioners had said, for passenger-trains are no longer allowed to use the Trans-Siberian railway. It is possible, someone whispered, that this is the *last* goods-train to run! So we must consider ourselves lucky!

I was glad to note that several Englishmen were among my travelling companions, a few with their wives and children. We are, in fact, a large band of foreigners – drawn together by a common desire to escape from a country where political persecution and class warfare have made life impossible. A 4th class carriage has been granted to us. I have had experience of 4th class carriages but such a one as this I have never seen before; I would have rated it as 5th class! It is composed of six wooden trucks, under the same roof, with a corridor running the length of the carriage and giving access to each doorless compartment. I was not surprised to hear that such carriages had been in constant use in the east-bound trains, carrying convicts and exiles to the penal colonies of Siberia.

Each compartment has sleeping places for nine persons. Tiers of wooden planks provide the sleeping accommodation: by day, these planks form a separating wall; by night, pulled out, they leave open to view the full length of the carriage. In a second 4th class carriage, tacked on to ours, another contingent of foreigners is travelling. Our English party manage to keep together and, thanks to the menfolk, we Englishwomen enjoy an extra amount of rest, for the men take it in turns to attend to the wood supplies and stoke the two stoves, one at either end of the corridor; they provide our only means of warming the compartments and heating the food. The men, in relays, keep watch over our carriage to prevent the entrance of undesirable intruders. We knew, of course, that prisons and concentration camps had opened their doors and that criminals of every description were at large; in fact the whole of Siberia had by now come under the sway of Lenin's Proletarian Government. We were quite prepared to meet unfriendly gangs of Siberian *Bolsheviki*, but there were small Union Jacks pinned on the window-frames, and documents, signed by British officials as well as the Red commissioners, were pasted on the panes, proclaiming that the occupants had received special dispensation from the powers that be, and were to be treated with respect.

I have read much about Siberia, the semi-discovered Russian territory which stretches from the Ural Mountains to the Pacific. I have read about the tundra, that frozen desert bordering the Arctic, still inhabited by a strange tribe known as *Samoyed* [self-eater], who depended chiefly on the reindeer for existence. The tundra extended inland to the *taiga*, a belt of age-old coniferous forests. Farther south there came the steppes, the vast treeless plains, covered with thick, unwieldy grass, regarded as useless to man and beast.

The Russians will tell you that the Siberian climate is eight months of winter and four of summer. Those eight long, dreary months of ice. and snow are followed by four months of unbelievably beautiful summer weather, when Nature decks the fields and hills with a lavish display of flower and foliage . . . I could scarcely believe my eyes when I was shown some pictures of Siberian flora. The simple moon-daisy of our English hayfields grows in Siberia to a height of four and even five feet, while many cottage flowers can reach the stature of a man. Even corn, sown after the late thaws in early May, can give rich crops during the hot days of August.

There is an old Siberian saying: 'Tickle the earth, it will respond with a smile.' So the cruel winter is transformed into a fairyland of colour and sunshine. But we are still in early March and a journey of more than twenty days through ice and snow is ahead.

As the days pass, our small party has become very friendly. My neighbour is a young Russian girl married to an Englishman, Mr Robins, one of our company. She is a very sweet-faced young woman, with large dark eyes, in which at times one can read deep sorrow. Her baby girl has not yet been christened, but the parents have already agreed on the names, one of which is to be Victoria.

It is exceedingly cold and the grime and dust have become so incredible that we have nicknamed our carriage the 'coal-scuttle'. Water, too, is scarce; sometimes even hand-washing is a forbidden luxury. When our train stops for a few minutes, there is a frantic rush for the *kipyatok* [boiling water], which the majority of stations are still supplying. Now and then we can see traces of the tidal-wave of violence which has swept over Russia: a skeleton town; lines of broken walls which were once homesteads; factories burnt to the ground; a ruined church, its cupolas blasted, its gilded cross hanging downwards. Over all this débris, winter has spread its white mantle of snow, hiding many deep wounds.

The cold has become intolerable. By day we do not mind it so much, but at night we huddle ourselves up in all our warmest garments, and still shiver as though with ague. Mrs Robins put the baby's milk-bottle under her pillow one night; in the morning, she found the milk frozen hard – a solid block of ice! Our wooden berths have been given the names of frigid, temperate and torrid zones, for the heat – such as it is – collects under the roof and gives the sleepers on the uppermost tier – the torrid zone – quite a warm night; so warm, in fact, that on one occasion a sleeper was prompted to slip off his high perch and find cooler accommodation on the ground floor! On the big station of Vyatka a thermometer registered 38° below zero (Réaumur). And we are still in Russia: what might we expect in Siberia?

At first, we expected to take the more southerly route through Tula, Pensa, Samara, Ufa and Chelyabinsk; but for some un-known reason we have been sent in the opposite direction, and find ourselves on the more northerly and longer route – nearly 600 versts longer – via Vologda. So, from Moscow, we steamed due north through Vladimir and Yaroslav to Vologda; there, we turned sharply eastwards to Vyatka, Vereshchagin, Perm, Ekaterinburg and Tyumen; we are already in Siberia!

Near Perm, the beautiful Ural Mountains came into view, the natural boundary between Europe and Asia. They are a rich source of mineral wealth for Russia. Apart from the usual minerals, gold, silver and platinum are mined, while many precious stones abound which are valued for their beauty, colour and variety. Before the war, a necklace of pale pink-mauve beads was given to me, made from a semi-precious stone found in the Urals.

From Perm, we moved slowly on to Ekaterinburg, a quaint little town, founded, I was told, by Peter the Great in 1723 and named after his wife. Then we turned southwards, passing Tyumen and reaching Omsk, where we joined the branch-line of the Trans-Siberian railway from Chelyabinsk. The Trans-Siberian railway was a dream of the Tsar as far back as 1891; it was begun in 1892, and, not surprisingly, seeing that it covered more than 8,000 versts, took thirteen years – until 1905 – to complete. The cost was terrific; someone told me that it exceeded £85,000,000. But it must have been well worth it, in aiding the development of

Siberia as well as stimulating industry and commerce. It provides transport for thousands of emigrants who seek the new Russia in hope of finding freedom from the despotism in the old. This magnificent railway runs like a great artery across the whole length of Siberia from the Urals to Vladivostok, where Nicholas II himself laid the foundation-stone in 1892.

As we steam through the wide, empty wastes of the Siberian steppes, I sometimes stand on the small gangway outside our carriage and, well-wrapped with muffler around head and shoulders, survey the passing landscape. It is bleak enough in all truth; the vast plain thickly covered with snow – miles and miles of it, no trees to break the limitless horizon.

Once over the border, we knew we would be at the mercy of the Siberian Red Guards. As we drew into Omsk station, they made a rush towards our carriage, but their way was barred by some of our menfolk. A voluble altercation ensued. Finally, the Red Guards were permitted to enter; astonished to find women and children instead of the Russian ex-officers they were after, they were not only crestfallen but piqued in the extreme. Then they fixed on the luggage, and ordered it to be transferred forthwith to the luggage-van. Our men explained and documents were produced. Why had not excess been paid on so much luggage? Again explanations; again documents. Then the luggage must be examined and all fire-arms confiscated. Boxes, bags, cases and wrappers were opened; nothing suspicious was found.

The Red Guards withdrew, conscious of having played a losing game. It was, however, depressing to find that our Union Jacks and documents had been ignored as of no account. We came to the conclusion that these Siberian 'warriors' had never heard of a Union Jack and, unable to read, had not understood the documents! So, they were looking for army officers! It was quite possible that officers were endeavouring to escape, they might even be masquerading as foreigners in another carriage. I remembered the savage cruelty meted out to the men of the Imperial Army who had sought refuge in Odessa and the Crimea.

All we could see of Omsk, since we dared not leave our carriage, was a collection of small, wooden houses and the roads adjoining the station, thick with slush, churned constantly by the coming and going of booted feet. As usual on Siberian railway-stations, there were numbers of people milling up and down the platforms, a rare collection of nationalities, mainly Mongolian types; and among the diversity of face and figure a uniformed Austrian and German would stand out in striking relief. They were prisoners, but Siberia for them was an open prison and they could walk about at will.

From Omsk, we have continued east towards Irkutsk. On average, our train is making 15 versts an hour; sometimes it slows down and resumes a languid pace. Now and then, it decides to have a breathing-space: the engine stops. Then we look at each other and laugh, remembering one of our Englishmen who had warned us to expect from our engine only two speeds: dead slow, and stop! Occasionally, during these halts, we get out and take a little exercise. Once we borrowed a ball from one of the children, and indulged in a game of rounders!

Although food is so scarce in Russia, in Siberia we have it brought to us! At every small station, villagers meet the train with tempting morsels, home-made and home-cooked. One great favourite with us is snipe, roasted to a turn, its long pointed beak vouching for its authenticity. We also buy *pryaniki*, hardish biscuits flavoured with ginger, which delight the children. Sometimes, eggs are available and cheese.

It is entertaining to see these Siberian peasants: the children look very robust, enveloped – like the grown-ups – in well-padded coats, tied round the waist; their feet in *valenki*, those thick felt boots which are so excellent for walking in the snow; and round their heads fur-lined hoods, not unlike the Caucasian *bashlyk*, worn in winter by the Russian soldiers.

As we gradually make our way across this mighty land of Siberia so, gradually, do my overwrought feelings find solace. The unusual train, the proximity of compatriots, the familiar mother tongue, the discomforts we are sharing; all these help. And strange though it may sound – Siberia is for me the greatest tonic of all. I begin to love this immense spacious land, with its wealth of weird and rare lineaments. I know that its very name conjures up torment for thousands of Russians but, I tell myself, that misery comes from the harassed people, not from the land; these wide, changeless spaces can bring only comfort and peace.

At first I fretted over the dear ones left behind in Russia to suffer, perhaps to starve. I felt like a coward, because I had forsaken them in their distress. Then, as the days pass, those thoughts become less troublesome; perhaps in England I shall find some means of contacting them and helping them. Perhaps one day I shall write a book about my experiences and perpetuate their memory. Sister Anna – Annushka of the impish face and laughing eyes – she will be there with her brave heart, in the thick of bombs and bullets and bayonets. Nothing could make her quail – only, perhaps, the bitter thought that it had been *all in vain*: It was she who had said that we must pray, pray hard; that great, unbelievable things can be wrought by prayer. It will be, I know, a life-long grief for me that I shall never see her again.

Ásya too, my Russian 'sister', must occupy a prominent place in my book. It will be difficult to do full justice to her; there are such great depths of feeling in her slight, delicate form, and her great love for her country can only be equalled by the great sadness which is weighing down her heart because of her country's downfall. . . .

I will always remember Doctor Rakhil, the generous woman who, at the moment of my deep distress, rescued me, sheltered and fed me in Odessa.

So it has come to pass that Siberia herself, the soothing saunter of our lazy locomotive and the slowly passing days and nights spent in the wide, open spaces, far from human habitations, have reacted upon me as a wholesome, bracing stimulus. There is an openness, a wideness, an emptiness about these immense stretches of flat land which make an instant appeal. I came immediately under their gentle influence. I can sense the marvellous undercurrent of peace which pervades earth and sky.

We are now leaving the steppes behind. To our right is rich agricultural land, and, in the background, the Altai Mountains, which belong partly to Russia and partly to Mongolia. We strain our eyes to catch a glimpse of Mount Byeloukha, the giant of the range. But we can distinguish nothing; the white snow hides even the horizon from sight. We steam slowly through wide stretches of forest, fir and silver birch. I am glad to see the silver birch – my favourite tree – which, even in winter, is conspicuous among the snow-bedecked firs and pines by reason of its white mottled trunk and the graceful line of its branches.

Now and then we pass small, wooden huts; they are the homes of settlers! As a child, I saw a picture of a settler's hut in Siberia,

surrounded by fir-trees, under which two big bears were strolling.
And there are the huts now, before my very eyes! They are just as
I knew that they would be, but there are no men or bears to be
seen! There is something about the thought of the recluses who
occupy them which arouses my envy.

At Novo Nikolayevski we heard that our train might have
difficulty in reaching Irkutsk; sabotage was reported on the line.
At the small station of Taiga our carriage was besieged by a crowd
of peasant-women, anxious to sell their wares. Perhaps they had
heard that no more passenger-trains would be running, so they
could no longer rely on the travellers of the 'soft compartments';
in any case, they were intent on giving the 'hard class' passengers
full value for their money. They bartered and bargained; they
babbled and gabbled in their curious eastern vernacular. One of
our company remarked: 'How true is the old Russian adage:
"Odna baba – baba; dvye babi – bazar! [One country-woman is
one country-woman; two country-women are a bazaar!].'' '

Between Krasnoyarsk and Kansk the distant range of the
Sayansk Mountains, bordering northern Mongolia, came into sight.
To our right were the famous Kuznetsk coalfields, some 4,000 to
5,000 square miles in extent, but not yet fully exploited. Coal is,
naturally, not in great demand in Siberia, where manufacture is
on a very small scale and the main fuel is, of course, wood. One
of our Englishmen declared that Siberia could be one of the richest
lands in the world if all her resources were exploited.

The forebodings about sabotage have proved groundless. We
arrived in Irkutsk. I must confess that most of us were disappointed at the town's appearance. It looked a mere conglomeration
of wooden houses. But cupolas and domes indicated the presence
of several churches. We saw many ruined buildings, not a few of
which had been burnt. So Irkutsk, too, had suffered. Later,
we learned that the Siberian *Bolsheviki* closely resembled their
counterparts in European Russia, and that class war had descended even upon this remote Siberian town, devastated a large
part of it and killed off many inhabitants who had been loyal to
the 'old régime'.

We were able to leave our carriage but not before a gruelling
investigation by the Red Guards who, as ever, were peering into
every corner, intent on discovering the hiding-place of any suspect.
On the station walls large placards proclaimed that any ex-

officer found in Irkutsk would be arrested, charged with attempting to flee the country, and shot. Loud shouting and arguing were heard from the platform. Alas! Some men were being marched off, under armed escort, towards a carriage farther up the line which served as the *arestantski vagon* [prison-van].

We have left Irkutsk and are making our way towards Lake Baikal, the largest lake in Asia. Our train will follow the line which skirts the southern shore. In normal times ice-breakers are at the station on the south-west of the lake to assist the ferry-boats to carry the train across, but now crossing the lake is out of the question. Slowly our train rounds the southern end and there below us we can see the two ice-breakers! Their ice-breaking activities are clearly over for this winter. They are prisoners themselves; embedded in the ice like phantom ships. Enormous icicles, like giant stalactites, decorate their funnels and decks. They are lovely to look at, for they scintillate in the sunlight as though they were made of clear crystal.

The section of the railway which rounds the lake must have caused the Russian engineers many a headache, for the mountains dip steeply to the water's edge. So we are not surprised to find that, in traversing those 65-odd versts, we are obliged to creep through nearly 40 tunnels.

Emerging from the tunnels, we steamed out into the territory known as Trans-Baikalia, still in the heart of the mountains, all densely covered with magnificent trees. I kept my eyes fixed as long as possible on that marvellous expanse of frozen lake, the 'Holy Sea of Siberia', as it is known to the Russians. It is some 420 miles long and 90 miles wide, and the immensity of it seems almost beyond belief. The tribes which live in its vicinity are chiefly Mongols, although Tatars are to be found in many regions of South Siberia. Sometimes we catch sight of a couple of corpulent figures, probably members of the Buriat tribe, in their thickly padded winter attire. They look so huge and ponderous that one wonders where the human body begins and ends within such an exaggerated bulk. Twice I spied some quaint-looking structures, half-tent, half-wigwam; these would be the primitive dwellings of the Buriats, or some other Mongol tribe. I think such a dwelling is called a *yurta* in Russian. In Trans-Baikalia, as in most regions of Eastern Siberia, mineral wealth is known to exist in vast quantities, but very little has been done to survey it.

At a small wayside station in Trans-Baikalia, an elderly Russian guard journeyed with us for a short distance. Naturally, we plied him with questions. He was deeply disturbed by the advent of Bolshevism in Siberia; he said that the districts around were overrun by gangs of hooligans, most of whom were criminals. They stole and pillaged as their fancy led them and the villagers were never safe. He had had many belongings stolen and when he had remonstrated with the thieves, they had called him a *bourjouie* and advised him to hold his tongue. 'We older men who have served faithfully all our days, are now ousted from our posts,' he said sadly. 'What will become of us, we can't tell. And what will become of Siberia, of Russia? Our only hope is that foreign friends will come to our aid.' So here, too, in this remote eastern corner of the Russian Asiatic territory, the cry for help was heard!

The Trans-Baikalian forests are extraordinarily beautiful. There seems no end to them. They are no ordinary firs and pines; they have been left to fend for themselves, and they have grown up so high and straight that from our low seats in the train we cannot hope to see their crowns, but only the great girth of the massive trunks. Trees have always fascinated me and these Siberian giants seem to possess some secret power, for they belong to a mysteriously isolated world.

One can sense that, in the deep shadows, there are concealed wild creatures, large and small: wolf and brown bear; sable and ermine. But whatever life they shelter, those inscrutable trees divulge no secrets and not once have I discerned either bird or beast.

But one evening I was rewarded for my tireless observation. The sun was setting behind us and the western sky was a sea of scarlet. Blood-red shafts of light played among the trees. As we rounded a curve, the full glory of the scarlet sunset suddenly caught the trees – the forest was on fire! Each trunk was a flaming torch! Then the brilliance faded and gave place to twilight.

Siberia has often been called a vast penal colony; certainly, during the Tsarist régime, thousands of Russians – criminals, anarchists, nihilists and political prisoners – were yearly deported, condemned to hard labour in the salt and coal mines. The majority of political prisoners were cultured and intellectual men; so they were merely exiled and warned never to return to their mother country. These exiles made excellent pioneers; they acquired plots of land and were able to depend on the fertile soil for a living. Many a present-day Sibiryak, renowned for his skill as writer, poet or musician, can claim descent from a political prisoner exiled to Siberia by a ruthless Government.

At Chita we stopped for some little time. Chita appeared to be a brisk, enterprising little town, deriving its prosperity perhaps from the railway which ran straight through Manchuria to Vladivostok, converting it into an important junction. We were informed that because the Manchurian frontier had been closed we were obliged to resort to another line, which followed the course of the Amur River skirting northern Manchuria and dividing that Chinese province from Siberian territory.

Here on the station was a mass of mixed races; the aborigines, probably Kalmuks or Buriats, were instantly recognisable by their extraordinarily long, coat-like garments and their weather-beaten, lined faces. And here too the Red Guards zealously scrutinised our Englishmen.

Northwards we steamed, the River Amur our guide. I was amazed to note on my map the perfection of the curve it traced round the northern territory of Manchuria. Before we had completed the 'curve', the Yablonoi Mountains came into view on our left; I knew that *yabloko* was the Russian word for 'apple'; so these were the Apple-tree Mountains!

On the Amur's frozen surface a few sleighs were visible and here and there a hardy soul was fishing through a hole cut into the thick ice. Navigation is by ship, during the short summer; by sleigh during the long winter months.

At one point we caught sight of some Chinese coolies sifting soil on the stony slopes of a hill, near which were gold-mines. A little farther on, our attention was drawn to a group of wooden huts in a forest clearing; these, we were told, were the homes of political prisoners. We saw few signs elsewhere of prison encampments; no doubt, for obvious reasons, they had been established at a safe distance from the railway.

As we crossed the Amur, by the magnificent seventeen-span bridge, we saw a few barges and small ships at anchor waiting for the thaw which would be due in about six weeks' time. The ubiquitous Chinaman was, of course, there, fishing through his hole in the ice.

We have reached the Maritime Province and halted at Khabarovsk. What a station! Such a dirty, disorderly place and so many dirty and dishevelled people. Chinamen are in the majority; Mongolians, Koreans, Cossacks, Russian soldiers, Siberian peasants and tribesmen: all rubbing shoulders with each other.

We thought it best not to descend from our carriage, for mud was thick on the platform – in some parts, ankle-deep – and the smell was disagreeable in the extreme. But we did not escape the notice of the Red Guards, who considered it necessary to pay us a long and tiring visit. Some poverty-stricken Chinamen had also spied our carriage and, together with several pariah dogs, prowled around beneath the windows, ready to pounce upon any edible odds and ends which came their way. . . .

We are glad to leave Khabarovsk and start the last lap of our journey. We are steaming due south through the Maritime Province towards the great Russian seaport of Vladivostok. So far, we have been remarkably lucky; we have escaped every kind of danger. More than once we have seen objectionable individuals walking near our railroad. They belong, we know, to the bands of criminals who, freed from imprisonment, are roaming the eastern districts of Siberia, and attacking villagers or any innocent people who cross their path. They made no attempt to board our train; perhaps the faces of our menfolk indicated that an assault on our persons would not be all plain-sailing.

We know that Vladivostok is in the hands of the *Bolsheviki*. What will be their attitude towards foreigners? Is civil war still raging in the streets? Will a British consul be available? What will happen if we cannot find a ship? Will Japan grant us asylum? A thousand doubts assail our minds.

We are in Vladivostok! We arrived early this morning. It is 2nd April 1918, and exactly 27 days since we boarded our goods-train in Moscow. It is wonderful that we are really here – at last! But what makes it all the more wonderful is that when we steamed slowly into the station, Vladivostok's magnificent harbour was spread before our eyes. In that harbour four large cruisers were anchored, and one of them was flying the UNION JACK! Oh! The joy! The relief! The comfort! The security! Who will ever know all that this glorious flag symbolised for us travel-stained, weary refugees? It was as though we had heard a dear, familiar voice bidding us 'Welcome home!' As I write these words I can feel my heart palpitating with emotion; it holds a depth of gratitude which can never be expressed. That one glimpse of the Union Jack dispelled all our fears, quietened all our doubts, answered all our questions. It was a truly wonderful 'home-coming' and one which we had least expected. The Union Jack was our talisman, our guarantee, our surety!

Things sorted themselves out very quickly. The town was overcrowded; no rooms were available. It was finally arranged – but not before the British consulate in Vladivostok had intervened on our behalf – that our carriage should be shunted on to a siding and that we should remain in our 4th class truck until arrangements had been made for our departure by sea. That our siding turned out to be a coal-siding made little difference to us; after all, for our old 'coal-scuttle' and its hard shelves, a coal-siding seemed to be the most appropriate place.

Despite the fact that Vladivostok was overflowing with men of many nations, one seldom heard of any grave disorders. Not far from our British cruiser HMS *Suffolk* lay an American cruiser, the Stars and Stripes hoisted aloft. A little farther away, two Japanese men-of-war were anchored; one of them, it was said, captured in the Russo-Japanese War of 1904–5. So to these watch-dogs of the three allied nations, we – and all foreign elements in the town – owed safety and a quiet night's sleep.

We viewed these warships with the greatest pride; they looked so formidable, so invincible, with their guns levelled towards the town. One of our naval officers told us: 'The *Bolsheviki* must mind their p's and q's, for in five minutes we can be out of the bay and, in another five minutes, Vladivostok can be blown into the air!' The crews of both the British and American cruisers showed us endless hospitality; they imagined that we were all half-starved! Certainly, it was a great luxury for us all to taste white bread again, and plum-cake and strawberry jam!

The Russian name Vladivostok signifies 'Power of the East'; and, indeed, as a fortified naval and commercial seaport, it can wield much authority in and around the numerous islands and seas bordering the Pacific Ocean. As the terminus of the Trans-Siberian railway which runs direct to Moscow, it offers a strategic link with Europe and the Far East; Tsar Nicholas II was aware of this fact when he made the great decision to create 'an outlet to the Pacific'; even as his illustrious ancestor, Peter the Great, dreaming of a new capital city for Russia, determined to 'cut a window into Europe' on the shores of the River Neva and the Gulf of Finland.

I called at the British consulate and spoke to the consul, who was kindness itself. He gave me the good news that my elder brother had sent me £20. This seemed like a small fortune and I was intensely grateful for my brother's thoughtfulness. The days passed quickly; there was always something interesting to see, for a more cosmopolitan, polyglot town than this eastern seaport would be difficult to find. One afternoon, walking along the main street, known as Svetlandskaya Ulitsa, we counted twelve different nationalities: British, American, French, Belgian, Italian, Roumanian, Russian, Japanese, Chinese, Mongolian, Tatar and Hindu.

We have heard that 350 Belgian soldiers have recently arrived; they were fighting with the Russians but, after the *Bolsheviki* signed the Treaty of Brest-Litovsk, they found it necessary to leave. Among the Italian soldiers are many who, having been born on Austrian territory, were drafted into the Austrian Army; but being loyal to Italy lost no time in surrendering to the Russians; now their one aim is to return to Italy, and enter the Italian Army. So we are not the only foreigners waiting impatiently for transport.

News was brought one day of the shooting of three Japanese merchants by Red Guards; Japan immediately sent an armed force to the town. Their presence aroused consternation. Within minutes, a contingent of British sailors was landed and patrolling the streets round the British consulate. They swung with easy, unvarying gait up and down the streets, exciting enormous curiosity and admiration from the crowd.

The expected rioting did not take place. Japan withdrew her armed men, but her patrols remained. While walking over the neighbouring hills, we often met a Japanese sailor, gun slung over shoulder, scrutinising the surrounding landscape.

We enjoyed those strolls on the hills; there were so many new items of interest to discover. And the views were superb. The main section of Vladivostok lay directly below us, while the outlying districts straggled away at random to right and left. One could stand and study the great harbour for hours, smooth and shining as a mirror, and stretching away – a full four miles in length – towards the distant range of hills which sloped down gradually into the waters of the Bay of Peter the Great. This remarkable harbour, known as the Golden Horn, is guarded on its approach by several islands, which give it the appearance of a land-locked haven, thus greatly enhancing its strategic value as a naval base. It is, naturally, frozen over in mid-winter, but ice-breakers keep a more or less permanent channel clear for navigation. The only sign of winter still visible to us was the snow which covered the high ground on the islands and on the long ranges of distant hills.

Although all was fairly quiet in the town, rumours are afoot that trouble is brewing for the *Bolsheviki*. General Semenov, of the Trans-Baikalian Cossacks, is said to have raised a large army, consisting of Cossacks, Mongols and ex-officers of the Imperial Army, and to be about to seize Vladivostok, put the *Bolsheviki* to flight and establish command over Eastern Siberia. These rumours must have caused concern among Bolshevist elements in the town, for many Red Guards are said to have left their posts; whether obeying orders or their own free will, it is impossible to say.

Now and then, at night, rifle-shots can be heard, but daylight brings the usual calm. We do not worry overmuch. Had any fighting broken out in the town we know that our resolute country-men on HMS *Suffolk* would have come to the rescue. They are keeping watch over us and we have been told that a couple of armed British sailors have been seen at night on the station-bridge, looking intently up the line to make sure that the 4th class carriage and its occupants are at peace and free from annoyance.

As time goes by, we have been unable to help feeling anxious about our departure. 'It might be tomorrow, or it might be in a month's time!' has been the answer to our eager enquiries. But today we were told by our consul that President Wilson has instructed an American transport coming north from the Philippine Islands to call at Vladivostok, pick up all the refugees and carry them to San Francisco. So we are not forgotten!

Although our sleeping-quarters are overcrowded and un-comfortable, we are living quite well as regards food. Compared with the scanty rations in European Russia, food in Vladivostok is good and varied. In the Chinese market, bread is plentiful and even the forgotten luxury – butter – can be obtained at 10 shillings a pound. Rather than visit this market, where dogs and flies ravage the fruit and vegetables spread around the fish and meat counters, we prefer the general store, which belongs to a clean, fine-faced old Chinaman. He can supply us not only with whole-some food, but with the latest news. He is a grand raconteur and his fantastic English provokes many a laugh. He told us that he always welcomed Britishers and that his greatest wish is to see Vladivostok a real international town.

This morning we saw a large ship come gliding into harbour. Hopes rose high! Our Englishmen went to inspect it more closely. They returned with the news that it was a Chinese hospital ship, flying the yellow flag of fever, which had called to collect the many sick coolies. Only then did we realise that numbers of Chinese coolies in Vladivostok had fallen victims to an epidemic of smallpox and typhoid.

To while away the hours, we sometimes hire a sampan and go for a row in the harbour. It is a soothing pastime; the motionless, serene water contrasts sharply with the confused, clattering racket on the mainland. We noted fortifications on one island; we won-dered when they would be used, and by *whom*! Naturally, we base our hopes on the Cossack leader. More and more refugees are arriving in Vladivostok, Russians among them. Once they reach Vladivostok, they stand a very good chance of escaping from Siberia. The United States will soon be full of foreign *émigrés*; but in that large, hospitable land, a temporary lodging will be sure to be found for them.

This morning, we were approached by two Chinese coolies. Instead of holding out begging hands for a kopek, they produced a box containing a few oddments for sale. An unusual souvenir drew our attention; it was a pigtail, cut off the head of one of the men in the hope that an English lady would buy it as a mascot! We looked at the tail of dirty black hair and declined the offer. Despite my interest in souvenirs, I decided that this one was definitely not suitable for my collection!

I often long to be back with my 'family' in Moscow, to share their joys and their sorrows. The empty, aimless existence in our coal-siding is far from inspiring; and England, my family and my home are so far away. Shall I ever reach them? . . . Sometimes we discuss Siberia and its immense possibilities. One member of our party said that he would like to explore the gold-bearing rocks on the Lena River; another preferred the silver mines of Eastern Siberia. For my part, I should like to be a settler in a *taiga* forest, but near enough to the tundra to be able to dig up fossil remains of prehistoric animals, perhaps even a mammoth, similar to the wonderful specimen which I saw in the St Petersburg museum before the war and which, in a marvellous state of preservation, was found embedded in the Arctic ice of Siberia.

We are all greatly impressed by what we have seen of Siberia, that great white land of amazing contrasts. I know that I shall never forget it, or the strange fascination which it has wielded over me. It is the land of cruel, icy winters and fierce, flaming summers; a land which has never known the loveliness of spring-time, or the colourful beauty of an autumn day. I shall remember it for its measureless horizons; enormous, open plains; gigantic, inaccessible mountains; massive, from-time-immemorial forests; deep, wide lakes; immensely long rivers; wild wastes of perpetual ice and snow; and, everywhere, its soil teeming with limitless, hidden treasures of every variety.

The third week of our stay in the coal-siding has come and gone; the fourth has already begun. Life is becoming more tedious, more disquieting. Twice our hopes have been frustrated. But this morning, the word went round: 'A large vessel is coming into port!'

In a fraction of a second, we were all out in the open air. There was no mistake – the transport had arrived! We stood and watched it with rapturous delight. It looked like a floating palace! In the far distance, one could hear music and singing; some bars of 'God Save the King' came distinctly to our ears. Our sailors on the British cruiser were finishing their morning prayers. Then followed a few hours of intense bustle. Our goods were quickly packed. We gave one last grateful look at our 4th class carriage.

On the wharf, the American soldiers were displaying their outstanding ability for organisation; not a single loiterer or curious sightseer was allowed to approach the boarding parties or their luggage. A wave of the baton by one of these finely-built men was more than sufficient to keep the worst offender at bay. Our luggage was taken on board; it must have been the very first time that the belongings of a foreigner had left Russian soil without the dreaded formalities of a Russian custom house! The ship's doctor asked a few questions, felt our pulses and pronounced us healthy enough to undertake a long voyage. Then we were transferred by steam-launch to the transport *Sheridan*.

By a strange working of fate, one of the first persons I have seen on board is Yasha Bachkarova, erstwhile leader of the Women's Death Battalion. She has eluded the spy-net of the Red Guards and is making good her escape to the United States.

It is blissful to sleep in a delightfully clean cabin, with white curtains, white sheets and white towels. We, who have for so long experienced 'hard shelf' service, can appreciate to the full the restfulness of a spring mattress!

Now only a day later our transport has slipped anchor, wheeled about and is heading leisurely for the harbour outlet to the bay. On the British and American cruisers the sailors were standing at the salute; we heard their bands playing; we saw their signal-flags sending forth messages of good will; their cheers rent the air. A similar 'welcome and farewell' came from the Japanese men-of-war. It was a stirring moment, one of great emotion for us Britishers, as well as for the massed company of foreign refugees that throng the deck. Slowly our transport drew away from our friendly allies; more and more faintly their 'God speeds' reached our ears. . . . We are leaving the Golden Horn of Asia for the Golden Gate of America. The voyage may take three weeks, for our passage lies through the northern Pacific, and German U-boats are still active round the Hawaiian Islands and the South Pacific. Now we have passed through the harbour and are rounding the last island into the Bay of Peter the Great. The wide Sea of Japan is before us; beyond lies the boundless expanse of the Pacific Ocean.

I stood on deck and watched Russia slowly recede. Soon all that was visible was a range of pale-grey mountains on the horizon. Then a thick, blue curtain of mist fell and hid from my sight the land which I had loved so truly and which I had served so gladly. As I pondered on all that had happened, in that great suffering Russia, my heart contracted with pain, and I felt that I could weep . . . and weep. . . . I prayed that those bitter-sweet wartime experiences of mine had not been in vain. And, because sorrow and suffering teach great truths, I prayed too that I had learnt from them never to grumble; to be compassionate and merciful; and to recognise always, and try to alleviate, the sorrow in another human heart.

For days I lay in my cabin with intolerable 'sea-sickness', a fair enough name for the grievous heartache which overwhelmed me; heartache for a surpassingly beautiful land which had been laid waste, for a mighty Empire which had been brought low – by its own sons.

INDEX

Adamchuki, 106
Alexander III, Tsar, 261
Alexander Alexandrovich
(Transport Head), 193, 276
Alexander Andreyevich (Staff
Officer), 280, 281, 286, 316
Alexander Ivanovich *see* Ugrimov
Alexander Mikhaylovich
(Surgeon), 38–40, 44, 45, 47–8,
49, 55, 57, 66, 74, 87–8, 95,
97, 100, 103, 119–20, 129, 130,
198, 205, 209
Alexander Palace, Tsarskoe Selo,
272
Alexander Sergeyevich (Staff
Officer), 280
Alexander Vasiliyevich (Officer
in Mariupolski Regiment), 115,
117
Alexandra Feodorovna, Empress,
20, 92, 107, 231, 233, 237, 246,
248, 271, 349
Alexeyev, General, 298
Alexis (Alexei), Grand Duke, 20,
216, 231, 246, 256
Altai Mountains, 397
Alupka, Crimea, 243, 244
Amur River, 401
Anastasia, Grand Duchess, 20
Anna, Sister (Annushka), 39, 42,
44, 47, 53, 65, 75, 83, 87, 88,
97, 125, 185, 213, 215, 247,
275, 288, 294, 295, 296, 298,
306, 309, 316, 390, 397; her
distress at German advance
across San River, 70–1;

awarded St George silver
medal, 93; Florence's admiration
for, 95; death of peasant child
and, 98–9; her feelings of
compassion, 101–2; during
bombardment of Skidel, 127–9;
travels back to unit from
Moscow with Florence, 159–60;
at Volochisk, 175–6; comforts
Florence after death of father,
248; unhappy at Tsar's
abdication, 256–7; departure
from Roumania of, 363, 364,
366
Austria-Hungary, Austrians, 176,
179, 186, 215; War declared,
19; retreat in Poland and
Galicia of (1914), 27; in
Gorlitse, 32; prisoners-of-war,
61, 204, 285, 297; and
internment camp, 114;
Podolskaya Government in,
168–9; Russian opinion of
soldiers of, 173; treatment of
Jews by, 180; Russian 9th
Army offensive against, 188–91,
194; construction of trenches
of, 192, 193, 199, 205–6, 221;
Chernovits surrenders to
Russians, 199, 200; refugees,
201–2; Kolomea recaptured by
Russians, 203–4; wounded,
204–5, 219–20; German
reinforcements for, 213; and
fall of Dubenko, 213; fall of
Monasterzhiska and Stanislav,

OTHER COOPER SQUARE PRESS TITLES OF INTEREST

MARGARET SANGER
An Autobiography
Margaret Sanger
New introduction by Kathryn Cullen-DuPont
516 pp., 1 b/w photo
0-8154-1015-8
$17.95

LETTERS TO HIS FAMILY
An Autobiography
Piotr Ilyich Tchaikovsky
Translated by Galina von Meck
612 pp.
0-8154-1087-5
$22.95

TOLSTOY
Tales of Courage and Conflict
Count Leo Tolstoy
Edited by Charles Neider
576 pp.
0-8154-1010-7
$19.95

T. E. LAWRENCE
A Biography
Michael Yardley
308 pp., 71 b/w photos, 5 maps
0-8154-1054-9
$17.95

HISTORY OF THE CONQUEST OF MEXICO & HISTORY
OF THE CONQUEST OF PERU
William H. Prescott
1328 pp., 2 maps
0-8154-1004-2
$32.00

ROE V. WADE
The Untold Story of the Landmark Supreme
Court Decision that Made Abortion Legal
Updated Edition
Marian Faux
404 pp., 15 b/w photos
0-8154-1093-X
$19.95

Available at bookstores; or call 1-800-462-6420

Cooper Square Press

150 Fifth Avenue
Suite 911
New York, NY 10011